D0084247

Just The

facts101
Textbook Key Facts

Textbook Outlines, Highlights, and Practice Quizzes

Chemsistry

by Raymond Chang, Kenneth Goldsby, 11th Edition

All "Just the Facts101" Material Written or Prepared by Cram101 Publishing

Title Page

"Just the Facts101" is a Cram101 publication and tool designed to give you all the facts from your textbooks. Visit Cram101.com for the full practice test for each of your chapters for virtually any of your textbooks.

Cram101 has built custom study tools specific to your textbook. We provide all of the factual testable information and unlike traditional study guides, we will never send you back to your textbook for more information.

YOU WILL NEVER HAVE TO HIGHLIGHT A BOOK AGAIN!

Cram101 StudyGuides

All of the information in this StudyGuide is written specifically for your textbook. We include the key terms, places, people, and concepts... the information you can expect on your next exam!

Want to take a practice test?

Throughout each chapter of this StudyGuide you will find links to cram101.com where you can select specific chapters to take a complete test on, or you can subscribe and get practice tests for up to 12 of your textbooks, along with other exclusive cram101.com tools like problem solving labs and reference libraries.

Cram101.com

Only cram101.com gives you the outlines, highlights, and PRACTICE TESTS specific to your textbook. Cram101.com is an online application where you'll discover study tools designed to make the most of your limited study time.

By purchasing this book, you get 50% off the normal subscription free!. Just enter the promotional code **'DK73DW20267'** on the Cram101.com registration screen.

www.Cram101.com

Learning System

facts101

Chemsistry
Raymond Chang, Kenneth Goldsby, 11th

CONTENTS

Chapter 1. Chemistry: The Study of Change

CHAPTER OUTLINE: KEY TERMS, PEOPLE, PLACES, CONCEPTS

	Angular momentum
	Momentum
	Quantum
	Quantum number
	Alkane
	Newton
	Scientific method
	Big Bang
	Helium
	Homogeneous
	Mixture
	Alkene
	Combustion
	Density
	Hydrogen
	Mass
	Molecule
	Burette
	Macromolecule

Chapter 1. Chemistry: The Study of Change

	Litre
	Celsius
	Scientific notation
	Dimensional analysis
	Aniline
	Iridium

Angular momentum	In physics, angular momentum, moment of momentum, or rotational momentum is a vector quantity that can be used to describe the overall state of a physical system. The angular momentum L of a particle with respect to some point of origin is $\mathbf{L} = \mathbf{r} \times \mathbf{p} = \mathbf{r} \times m\mathbf{v}$,

where r is the particle's position from the origin, p = mv is its linear momentum, and × denotes the cross product.

The angular momentum of a system of particles (e.g. a rigid body) is the sum of angular momenta of the individual particles. |
| Momentum | In classical mechanics, linear momentum or translational momentum is the product of the mass and velocity of an object: $\mathbf{P} \equiv m\mathbf{v}$.

Like velocity, linear momentum is a vector quantity, possessing a direction as well as a magnitude. Linear momentum is also a conserved quantity, meaning that if a closed system is not affected by external forces, its total linear momentum cannot change. |
| Quantum | In physics, a quantum is the minimum amount of any physical entity involved in an interaction. |

Behind this, one finds the fundamental notion that a physical property may be 'quantized,' referred to as 'the hypothesis of quantization'. This means that the magnitude can take on only certain discrete values.

Quantum number	Quantum numbers describe values of conserved quantities in the dynamics of the quantum system. Perhaps the most peculiar aspect of quantum mechanics is the quantization of observable quantities, since quantum numbers are discrete sets of integers or half-integers. This is distinguished from classical mechanics where the values can range continuously.
Alkane	Alkanes (also known as paraffins or saturated hydrocarbons) are chemical compounds that consist only of hydrogen and carbon atoms and are bonded exclusively by single bonds (i.e., they are saturated compounds) without any cycles . Alkanes belong to a homologous series of organic compounds in which the members differ by a constant relative molecular mass of 14. They have 2 main commercial sources, crude oil and natural gas.
	Each carbon atom has 4 bonds (either C-H or C-C bonds), and each hydrogen atom is joined to a carbon atom (H-C bonds).
Newton	The newton (symbol: N) is the SI derived unit of force. It is named after Isaac Newton in recognition of his work on classical mechanics, specifically Newton's second law of motion.
	The newton is the SI unit for force; it is equal to the amount of net force required to accelerate a mass of one kilogram at a rate of one metre per second squared.
Scientific method	Scientific method refers to a body of techniques for investigating phenomena, acquiring new knowledge, or correcting and integrating previous knowledge. To be termed scientific, a method of inquiry must be based on empirical and measurable evidence subject to specific principles of reasoning. The Oxford English Dictionary says that scientific method is: 'a method or procedure that has characterized natural science since the 17th century, consisting in systematic observation, measurement, and experiment, and the formulation, testing, and modification of hypotheses.'
	The chief characteristic which distinguishes a scientific method of inquiry from other methods of acquiring knowledge is that scientists seek to let reality speak for itself, supporting a theory when a theory's predictions are confirmed and challenging a theory when its predictions prove false.
Big Bang	The Big Bang theory is the prevailing cosmological model that explains the early development of the Universe. According to the Big Bang theory, the Universe was once in an extremely hot and dense state which expanded rapidly.

Chapter 1. Chemistry: The Study of Change

Helium	Helium is the chemical element with atomic number 2 and an atomic weight of 4.002602, which is represented by the symbol He. It is a colorless, odorless, tasteless, non-toxic, inert, monatomic gas that heads the noble gas group in the periodic table. Its boiling and melting points are the lowest among the elements and it exists only as a gas except in extreme conditions.
Homogeneous	A substance that is uniform in composition is a definition of homogeneous. This is in contrast to a substance that is heterogeneous. The definition of homogeneous strongly depends on the context used.
Mixture	In chemistry, a mixture is a material system made up by two or more different substances which are mixed but are not combined chemically. Mixture refers to the physical combination of two or more substances the identities of which are retained and are mixed in the form of alloys, solutions, suspensions, and colloids. Mixtures are the product of a mechanical blending or mixing of chemical substances like elements and compounds, without chemical bonding or other chemical change, so that each ingredient substance retains its own chemical properties and makeup.
Alkene	In organic chemistry, an alkene, olefin, or olefine is an unsaturated chemical compound containing at least one carbon-to-carbon double bond. The simplest acyclic alkenes, with only one double bond and no other functional groups, form an homologous series of hydrocarbons with the general formula C_nH_{2n}. The simplest alkene is ethylene (C_2H_4), which has the International Union of Pure and Applied Chemistry (IUPAC) name ethene.
Combustion	Combustion or burning is the sequence of exothermic chemical reactions between a fuel and an oxidant accompanied by the production of heat and conversion of chemical species. The release of heat can result in the production of light in the form of either glowing or a flame. Fuels of interest often include organic compounds (especially hydrocarbons) in the gas, liquid or solid phase.
Density	The mass density is defined as its mass per unit volume. The symbol most often used for density is ρ. In some cases (for instance, in the United States oil and gas industry), density is also defined as its weight per unit volume; although, this quantity is more properly called specific weight.
Hydrogen	

Hydrogen is the chemical element with atomic number 1. It is represented by the symbol H. With an average atomic weight of 1.00794 u (1.007825 u for hydrogen-1), hydrogen is the lightest element and its monatomic form (H_1) is the most abundant chemical substance, constituting roughly 75% of the Universe's baryonic mass. Non-remnant stars are mainly composed of hydrogen in its plasma state.

At standard temperature and pressure, hydrogen is a colorless, odorless, tasteless, non-toxic, nonmetallic, highly combustible diatomic gas with the molecular formula H_2.

Mass

The mass recorded by a mass spectrometer can refer to different physical quantities depending on the characteristics of the instrument and the manner in which the mass spectrum is displayed.

The accurate mass (more appropriately, the measured accurate mass) is an experimentally determined mass that allows the elemental composition to be determined. For molecules with mass below 200 u, a 5 ppm accuracy is sufficient to uniquely determine the elemental composition.

Molecule

A molecule is an electrically neutral group of two or more atoms held together by covalent chemical bonds. Molecules are distinguished from ions by their lack of electrical charge. However, in quantum physics, organic chemistry, and biochemistry, the term molecule is often used less strictly, also being applied to polyatomic ions.

Burette

A burette is a vertical cylindrical piece of laboratory glassware with a volumetric graduation on its full length and a precision tap, or stopcock, on the bottom. It is used to dispense known amounts of a liquid reagent in experiments for which such precision is necessary, such as a titration experiment. Burettes are extremely accurate - a 50 cm^3 burette has a tolerance of 0.1 cm^3 (class B) or 0.06 cm^3 (class A).

Macromolecule

A macromolecule is a very large molecule commonly created by polymerization of smaller subunits. In biochemistry, the term is applied to the four conventional biopolymers (nucleic acids, proteins, carbohydrates, and lipids), as well as non-polymeric molecules with large molecular mass such as macrocycles. The individual constituent molecules of macromolecules are called monomers (mono=single, meros=part).

Litre

The litre is a unit of volume equal to 1 cubic decimetre (dm^3), to 1,000 cubic centimetres (cm^3), and to 1/1,000 cubic metre. The unit has two official symbols: the Latin letter L in lower and upper case (l and L). If the lower case L is used it is sometimes written as a cursive l, although this usage has no official approval by any international bureau.

Chapter 1. Chemistry: The Study of Change

Celsius	Celsius is a scale and unit of measurement for temperature. It is named after the Swedish astronomer Anders Celsius who developed a similar temperature scale two years before his death. The degree Celsius can refer to a specific temperature on the Celsius scale as well as a unit to indicate a temperature interval, a difference between two temperatures or an uncertainty.
Scientific notation	Scientific notation is a way of writing numbers that are too large or too small to be conveniently written in standard decimal notation. Scientific notation has a number of useful properties and is commonly used in calculators and by scientists, mathematicians and engineers. In scientific notation all numbers are written in the form of $a \times 10^{b}$ (a times ten raised to the power of b), where the exponent b is an integer, and the coefficient a is any real number , called the significand or mantissa.
Dimensional analysis	In physics and all science, dimensional analysis is a tool to find or check relations among physical quantities by using their dimensions. The dimension of a physical quantity is the combination of the basic physical dimensions (usually mass, length, time, electric charge, and temperature) which describe it; for example, speed has the dimension length per unit time, and may be measured in meters per second, miles per hour, or other units. Dimensional analysis is based on the fact that a physical law must be independent of the units used to measure the physical variables.
Aniline	Aniline, phenylamine or aminobenzene is an organic compound with the formula $C_6H_5NH_2$. Consisting of a phenyl group attached to an amino group, aniline is the prototypical aromatic amine. Being a precursor to many industrial chemicals, its main use is in the manufacture of precursors to polyurethane.
Iridium	Iridium is the chemical element with atomic number 77, and is represented by the symbol Ir. A very hard, brittle, silvery-white transition metal of the platinum family, iridium is the second-densest element (after osmium) and is the most corrosion-resistant metal, even at temperatures as high as 2000 °C. Although only certain molten salts and halogens are corrosive to solid iridium, finely divided iridium dust is much more reactive and can be flammable. Iridium was discovered in 1803 among insoluble impurities in natural platinum.

1. In classical mechanics, linear _____ or translational _____ is the product of the mass and velocity of an object: $\mathbf{P} \equiv m\mathbf{v}$.

    Like velocity, linear _____ is a vector quantity, possessing a direction as well as a magnitude. Linear _____ is also a conserved quantity, meaning that if a closed system is not affected by external forces, its total linear _____ cannot change.

    a. Neutron magnetic moment
    b. Noise-equivalent flux density
    c. Noise-equivalent target
    d. Momentum

2. In physics, _____, moment of momentum, or rotational momentum is a vector quantity that can be used to describe the overall state of a physical system. The _____ L of a particle with respect to some point of origin is

    $$\mathbf{L} = \mathbf{r} \times \mathbf{p} = \mathbf{r} \times m\mathbf{v},$$

    where r is the particle's position from the origin, p = mv is its linear momentum, and × denotes the cross product.

    The _____ of a system of particles (e.g. a rigid body) is the sum of angular momenta of the individual particles.

    a. Angular velocity
    b. Angular momentum
    c. Areal velocity
    d. Attenuation coefficient

3. In physics, a _____ is the minimum amount of any physical entity involved in an interaction. Behind this, one finds the fundamental notion that a physical property may be 'quantized,' referred to as 'the hypothesis of quantization'. This means that the magnitude can take on only certain discrete values.

    a. Quantum 1/f noise
    b. Quantum Aspects of Life
    c. Quantum
    d. Quantum capacitance

4. _____s describe values of conserved quantities in the dynamics of the quantum system. Perhaps the most peculiar aspect of quantum mechanics is the quantization of observable quantities, since _____s are discrete sets of integers or half-integers. This is distinguished from classical mechanics where the values can range continuously.

    a. Quantum potential
    b. Quantum number
    c. Quark
    d. Quasiparticle

5. . _____s (also known as paraffins or saturated hydrocarbons) are chemical compounds that consist only of hydrogen and carbon atoms and are bonded exclusively by single bonds (i.e., they are saturated compounds) without any cycles .

_____s belong to a homologous series of organic compounds in which the members differ by a constant relative molecular mass of 14. They have 2 main commercial sources, crude oil and natural gas.

Each carbon atom has 4 bonds (either C-H or C-C bonds), and each hydrogen atom is joined to a carbon atom (H-C bonds).

a. Alkane
b. Aminoketone
c. Ethylenediamine pyrocatechol
d. Explosophore

1. d
2. b
3. c
4. b
5. a

You can take the complete Chapter Practice Test

for Chapter 1. Chemistry: The Study of Change
on all key terms, persons, places, and concepts.

Online 99 Cents

http://www.epub14.1.20267.1.cram101.com/

Use www.Cram101.com for all your study needs

including Cram101's online interactive problem solving labs in

chemistry, statistics, mathematics, and more.

Chapter 2. Atoms, Molecules, and Ions

CHAPTER OUTLINE: KEY TERMS, PEOPLE, PLACES, CONCEPTS

_____ Oxidation number

_____ Halogen

_____ PLATO

_____ Atomic theory

_____ Atom

_____ Conservation of mass

_____ Mass

_____ Partial pressure

_____ Anode

_____ Cathode

_____ Cathode ray

_____ Electron

_____ Radiation

_____ Thomson

_____ Zinc

_____ Zinc sulfide

_____ Sulfide

_____ Alpha particle

_____ Becquerel

Beryllium

Beryllium hydride

Curie

GAMMA

Hydride

Analytical chemistry

Atomic nucleus

Proton

Rutherford

Scattering

Neutron

Atomic number

Deuterium

Hydrogen

Isotope

Mass number

Nucleon

Subatomic particle

Tritium

CHAPTER OUTLINE: KEY TERMS, PEOPLE, PLACES, CONCEPTS

|_____| Molecule

|_____| Uranium

|_____| Fission products

|_____| Group

|_____| Metalloid

|_____| Nonmetal

|_____| Alkaline earth metal

|_____| Diatomic molecule

|_____| Hydrocarbon

|_____| Iodine

|_____| Ionic compound

|_____| Monatomic ion

|_____| Ball-and-stick model

|_____| Carbon

|_____| Chemical formula

|_____| Graphite

|_____| Molecular model

|_____| Oxygen

|_____| Ozone

_____ | Empirical formula _____

_____ | Space-filling model _____

_____ | Structural formula _____

_____ | Sodium _____

_____ | Sodium carbonate _____

_____ | Ammonium _____

_____ | Binary compound _____

_____ | Inorganic compound _____

_____ | Organic compound _____

_____ | Atomic mass _____

_____ | Ternary compound _____

_____ | Isomer _____

_____ | Transition metal _____

_____ | Corrosion _____

_____ | Oxoacid _____

_____ | Hypochlorous acid _____

_____ | Perchloric acid _____

_____ | Anhydrous _____

_____ | Alkane _____

CHAPTER OUTLINE: KEY TERMS, PEOPLE, PLACES, CONCEPTS

	Dry ice
	Functional group
	Nitroglycerin
	Ionization

CHAPTER HIGHLIGHTS & NOTES: KEY TERMS, PEOPLE, PLACES, CONCEPTS

| Oxidation number | In coordination chemistry, the oxidation number of a central atom in a coordination compound is the charge that it would have if all the ligands were removed along with the electron pairs that were shared with the central atom.

The oxidation number is used in the nomenclature of inorganic compounds. It is represented by a Roman numeral. |
| --- | --- |
| Halogen | The halogens or halogen elements are a series of nonmetal elements from Group 17 IUPAC Style (formerly: VII, VIIA) of the periodic table, comprising fluorine (F), chlorine (Cl), bromine (Br), iodine (I), and astatine (At). The artificially created element 117, provisionally referred to by the systematic name ununseptium, may also be a halogen.

The group of halogens is the only periodic table group which contains elements in all three familiar states of matter at standard temperature and pressure. |
| PLATO | PLATO (Package for Linear-combination of ATomic Orbitals) is a suite of programs for electronic structure calculations originally designed and written by Andrew Horsfield and Steven Kenny, but now with contributions from others. It receives its name from the choice of basis set (numeric atomic orbitals) used to expand the electronic wavefunctions.

PLATO is a code, written in C, for the efficient modelling of materials. |

Chapter 2. Atoms, Molecules, and Ions

Atomic theory	In chemistry and physics, atomic theory is a theory of the nature of matter, which states that matter is composed of discrete units called atoms, as opposed to the obsolete notion that matter could be divided into any arbitrarily small quantity. It began as a philosophical concept in ancient Greece (Democritus) and India and entered the scientific mainstream in the early 19th century when discoveries in the field of chemistry showed that matter did indeed behave as if it were made up of particles. The word 'atom' was applied to the basic particle that constituted a chemical element, because the chemists of the era believed that these were the fundamental particles of matter.
Atom	The atom is a basic unit of matter that consists of a dense central nucleus surrounded by a cloud of negatively charged electrons. The atomic nucleus contains a mix of positively charged protons and electrically neutral neutrons (except in the case of hydrogen-1, which is the only stable nuclide with no neutrons). The electrons of an atom are bound to the nucleus by the electromagnetic force.
Conservation of mass	The law of conservation of mass, states that the mass of an isolated system (closed to all matter and energy) will remain constant over time. This principle is equivalent to the conservation of energy, in the sense when energy or mass is enclosed in a system and none is allowed in or out, its quantity cannot otherwise change (hence, its quantity is 'conserved'). The mass of an isolated system cannot be changed as a result of processes acting inside the system.
Mass	The mass recorded by a mass spectrometer can refer to different physical quantities depending on the characteristics of the instrument and the manner in which the mass spectrum is displayed. The accurate mass (more appropriately, the measured accurate mass) is an experimentally determined mass that allows the elemental composition to be determined. For molecules with mass below 200 u, a 5 ppm accuracy is sufficient to uniquely determine the elemental composition.
Partial pressure	In a mixture of ideal gases, each gas has a partial pressure which is the pressure which the gas would have if it alone occupied the volume. The total pressure of a gas mixture is the sum of the partial pressures of each individual gas in the mixture. In chemistry, the partial pressure of a gas in a mixture of gases is defined as above.
Anode	An anode is an electrode through which electric current flows into a polarized electrical device. The direction of electric current is, by convention, opposite to the direction of electron flow.

Cathode	A cathode is an electrode through which electric current flows out of a polarized electrical device. The direction of electric current is, by convention, opposite to the direction of electron flow. Therefore the electrons flow into the polarized electrical device and out of, for example, the connected electrical circuit.
Cathode ray	Cathode rays (also called an electron beam or e-beam) are streams of electrons observed in vacuum tubes. If an evacuated glass tube is equipped with two electrodes and a voltage is applied, the glass opposite of the negative electrode is observed to glow, due to electrons emitted from and travelling perpendicular to the cathode (the electrode connected to the negative terminal of the voltage supply). They were first observed in 1869 by German physicist Johann Hittorf, and were named in 1876 by Eugen Goldstein kathodenstrahlen, or cathode rays.
Electron	The electron is a subatomic particle with a negative elementary electric charge. It has no known components or substructure; in other words, it is generally thought to be an elementary particle. An electron has a mass that is approximately 1/1836 that of the proton.
Radiation	In physics, radiation is a process in which energetic particles or energetic waves travel through a medium or space. Two types of radiation are commonly differentiated in the way they interact with normal chemical matter: ionizing and non-ionizing radiation. The word radiation is often colloquially used in reference to ionizing radiation but the term radiation may correctly also refer to non-ionizing radiation.
Thomson	The thomson (symbol: Th) is a unit that has appeared infrequently in scientific literature relating to the field of mass spectrometry as a unit of mass-to-charge ratio. The unit was proposed by Cooks and Rockwood naming it in honour of J. J. Thomson who measured the mass-to-charge ratio of electrons and ions. $$1 \text{ Th} = 1 \frac{\text{u}}{e} = 1 \frac{\text{Da}}{e} = 1.036426 \times 10^{-8} \, kg \, C^{-1}$$ where u represents the unified atomic mass unit, Da represents the unit dalton, and e represents the elementary charge which is the electric charge unit in the atomic unit system.
Zinc	Zinc, is a metallic chemical element; it has the symbol Zn and atomic number 30. It is the first element in group 12 of the periodic table. Zinc is, in some respects, chemically similar to magnesium, because its ion is of similar size and its only common oxidation state is +2. Zinc is the 24th most abundant element in the Earth's crust and has five stable isotopes. The most common zinc ore is sphalerite (zinc blende), a zinc sulfide mineral.

Chapter 2. Atoms, Molecules, and Ions

Zinc sulfide	Zinc sulfide is a inorganic compound with the formula ZnS. It is the main form of zinc in nature, where it mainly occurs as the mineral sphalerite. Although the mineral is black owing to impurities, the pure material is white and is in fact used widely as a pigment. In its dense synthetic form, zinc sulfide can be transparent and is used as a window for visible and infrared optics.
Sulfide	A sulfide is an anion of sulfur in its lowest oxidation state of 2-. Sulfide is also a slightly archaic term for thioethers, a common type of organosulfur compound that are well known for their bad odors.
	The dianion S^{2-} exists only in strongly alkaline aqueous solutions.
Alpha particle	Alpha particles consist of two protons and two neutrons bound together into a particle identical to a helium nucleus, which is classically produced in the process of alpha decay, but may be produced also in other ways and given the same name. The alpha particle can be written as He^{2+}, $42He^{2+}$ or $42He$ (as it is possible that the ion gains electrons from the environment; also, electrons are not important in nuclear chemistry).
	The nomenclature is not well defined, and thus not all high-velocity helium nuclei are considered by all authors as alpha particles.
Becquerel	The becquerel is the SI-derived unit of radioactivity. One Bq is defined as the activity of a quantity of radioactive material in which one nucleus decays per second. The Bq unit is therefore equivalent to an inverse second, s^{-1}.
Beryllium	Beryllium is the chemical element with the symbol Be and atomic number 4. Because any beryllium synthesized in stars is short-lived, it is a relatively rare element in both the universe and in the crust of the Earth. It is a divalent element which occurs naturally only in combination with other elements in minerals. Notable gemstones which contain beryllium include beryl (aquamarine, emerald) and chrysoberyl.
Beryllium hydride	Beryllium hydride, BeH_2, is a chemical compound of beryllium and hydrogen commonly used in rocket fuel. Unlike the ionically bonded hydrides of the heavier Group 2 elements, beryllium hydride is covalently bonded.
	BeH_2 was first synthesised in 1951 by reacting dimethylberyllium, $Be(CH_3)_2$, with lithium aluminium hydride, $LiAlH_4$.
Curie	The curie is a non-SI unit of radioactivity. It is defined as 1 Ci = 3.7×10^{10} decays per second.

Its continued use is discouraged.

One Curie is roughly the activity of 1 gram of the radium isotope ^{226}Ra, a substance studied by the Curies.

GAMMA

GAMMA experiment is a study of: a) Primary cosmic ray energy spectra and elemental composition (abundances of the elements) at energies 10^{15}-10^{18}eV (so called knee energy region) ; b) Galactic diffuse gamma-ray intensity at energies 10^{14}-10^{15}eV ; c) Extensive Air Showers (EAS) at the mountain level by the ground-based EAS array and underground muon scintillation counters; d) Hard jets production at energies ~10^{16}eV by the muon multi-core shower events.

GAMMA experiment is deployed on the South side of Mount Aragats in Armenia (Cosmic-ray observatory). The facility consists of a ground-based extensive air shower (EAS) array of 33 surface detection stations and 150 underground muon detectors.

Hydride

In chemistry, a hydride is the anion of hydrogen, H⁻, or, more commonly, a compound in which one or more hydrogen centres have nucleophilic, reducing, or basic properties. In compounds that are regarded as hydrides, hydrogen is bonded to a more electropositive element or group. Compounds containing metal or metalloid bonds to hydrogen are often referred to as hydrides, even though these hydrogen centres can have a protic character.

Analytical chemistry

Analytical chemistry is the study of the separation, identification, and quantification of the chemical components of natural and artificial materials. Qualitative analysis gives an indication of the identity of the chemical species in the sample and quantitative analysis determines the amount of one or more of these components. The separation of components is often performed prior to analysis.

Atomic nucleus

The nucleus is the very dense region consisting of protons and neutrons at the center of an atom. It was discovered in 1911, as a result of Ernest Rutherford's interpretation of the famous 1909 Rutherford experiment performed by Hans Geiger and Ernest Marsden, under the direction of Rutherford. The proton-neutron model of nucleus was proposed by Dmitry Ivanenko in 1932. Almost all of the mass of an atom is located in the nucleus, with a very small contribution from the orbiting electrons.

The diameter of the nucleus is in the range of 1.75 fm (femtometre) (1.75×10^{-15} m) for hydrogen (the diameter of a single proton) to about 15 fm for the heaviest atoms, such as uranium. These dimensions are much smaller than the diameter of the atom itself (nucleus + electronic cloud), by a factor of about 23,000 (uranium) to about 145,000 (hydrogen).

Chapter 2. Atoms, Molecules, and Ions

Proton	The proton is a subatomic particle with the symbol p or p+and a positive electric charge of 1 elementary charge. One or more protons are present in the nucleus of each atom, along with neutrons. The number of protons in each atom is its atomic number.
Rutherford	The rutherford (symbol rd) is an obsolete unit of radioactivity, defined as the activity of a quantity of radioactive material in which one million nuclei decay per second. It is therefore equivalent to one megabecquerel. It was named after Ernest Rutherford.
Scattering	Scattering is a general physical process where some forms of radiation, such as light, sound, or moving particles, are forced to deviate from a straight trajectory by one or more localized non-uniformities in the medium through which they pass. In conventional use, this also includes deviation of reflected radiation from the angle predicted by the law of reflection. Reflections that undergo scattering are often called diffuse reflections and unscattered reflections are called specular (mirror-like) reflections
	The types of non-uniformities which can cause scattering, sometimes known as scatterers or scattering centers, are too numerous to list, but a small sample includes particles, bubbles, droplets, density fluctuations in fluids, crystallites in polycrystalline solids, defects in monocrystalline solids, surface roughness, cells in organisms, and textile fibers in clothing.
Neutron	The neutron is a subatomic hadron particle which has the symbol n or n0, no net electric charge and a mass slightly larger than that of a proton. With the exception of hydrogen, nuclei of atoms consist of protons and neutrons, which are therefore collectively referred to as nucleons. The number of protons in a nucleus is the atomic number and defines the type of element the atom forms.
Atomic number	In chemistry and physics, the atomic number is the number of protons found in the nucleus of an atom and therefore identical to the charge number of the nucleus. It is conventionally represented by the symbol Z. The atomic number uniquely identifies a chemical element. In an atom of neutral charge, the atomic number is also equal to the number of electrons.
Deuterium	Deuterium, is one of two stable isotopes of hydrogen. It has a natural abundance in Earth's oceans of about one atom in 6,420 of hydrogen (~156.25 ppm on an atom basis). Deuterium accounts for approximately 0.0156% of all naturally occurring hydrogen in Earth's oceans, while the most common isotope (hydrogen-1 or protium) accounts for more than 99.98%.
Hydrogen	Hydrogen is the chemical element with atomic number 1. It is represented by the symbol H. With an average atomic weight of 1.00794 u (1.007

825 u for hydrogen-1), hydrogen is the lightest element and its monatomic form (H_1) is the most abundant chemical substance, constituting roughly 75% of the Universe's baryonic mass. Non-remnant stars are mainly composed of hydrogen in its plasma state.

At standard temperature and pressure, hydrogen is a colorless, odorless, tasteless, non-toxic, nonmetallic, highly combustible diatomic gas with the molecular formula H_2.

Isotope	Isotopes are variants of a particular chemical element. While all isotopes of a given element share the same number of protons, each isotope differs from the others in its number of neutrons. The term isotope is formed from the Greek roots isos and topos .
Mass number	The mass number also called atomic mass number, is the total number of protons and neutrons (together known as nucleons) in an atomic nucleus. Because protons and neutrons both are baryons, the mass number A is identical with the baryon number B as of the nucleus as of the whole atom or ion. The mass number is different for each different isotope of a chemical element.
Nucleon	In chemistry and physics, a nucleon is one of the particles that makes up the atomic nucleus. Each atomic nucleus consists of one or more nucleons, and each atom in turn consists of a cluster of nucleons surrounded by one or more electrons. There are two kinds of nucleon: the neutron and the proton.
Subatomic particle	In physics or chemistry, subatomic particles are the particles, which are smaller than an atom. There are two types of subatomic particles: elementary particles, which are not made of other particles, and composite particles. Particle physics and nuclear physics study these particles and how they interact.
Tritium	Tritium is a radioactive isotope of hydrogen. The nucleus of tritium contains one proton and two neutrons, whereas the nucleus of protium (by far the most abundant hydrogen isotope) contains one proton and no neutrons. Naturally occurring tritium is extremely rare on Earth, where trace amounts are formed by the interaction of the atmosphere with cosmic rays.
Molecule	A molecule is an electrically neutral group of two or more atoms held together by covalent chemical bonds. Molecules are distinguished from ions by their lack of electrical charge. However, in quantum physics, organic chemistry, and biochemistry, the term molecule is often used less strictly, also being applied to polyatomic ions.
Uranium	Uranium is a silvery-white metallic chemical element in the actinide series of the periodic table, with atomic number 92. It is assigned the chemical symbol U.

Chapter 2. Atoms, Molecules, and Ions

A uranium atom has 92 protons and 92 electrons, of which 6 are valence electrons. The uranium nucleus binds between 141 and 146 neutrons, establishing six isotopes (^{233}U through ^{238}U), the most common of which are uranium-238 (146 neutrons) and uranium-235 (143 neutrons). All isotopes are unstable and uranium is weakly radioactive.

Fission products	On this page, a discussion of each of the main elements in the fission product mixture from the nuclear fission of an actinide such as uranium or plutonium is set out by element. Krypton 83-86 Krypton-85 is formed by the fission process with a fission yield of about 0.3%. Only 20% of the fission products of mass 85 become ^{85}Kr itself; the rest passes through a short-lived nuclear isomer and then to stable ^{85}Rb.
Group	In chemistry, a group (also known as a family) is a vertical column in the periodic table of the chemical elements. There are 18 groups in the standard periodic table, including the d-block elements, but excluding the f-block elements. The explanation of the pattern of the table is that the elements in a group have similar physical or chemical characteristic of the outermost electron shells of their atoms (i.e. the same core charge), as most chemical properties are dominated by the orbital location of the outermost electron.
Metalloid	A metalloid is a chemical element with properties that are in-between or a mixture of those of metals and nonmetals, and which is considered to be difficult to classify unambiguously as either a metal or a nonmetal. There is no standard definition of a metalloid nor is there agreement as to which elements are appropriately classified as such. Despite this lack of specificity the term continues to be used in the chemistry literature.
Nonmetal	Nonmetal, is a term used in chemistry when classifying the chemical elements. On the basis of their general physical and chemical properties, every element in the periodic table can be termed either a metal or a nonmetal. (A few elements with intermediate properties are referred to as metalloids).
Alkaline earth metal	The alkaline earth metals are a group of chemical elements in the periodic table with very similar properties: they are all shiny, silvery-white, somewhat reactive metals at standard temperature and pressure and readily lose their two outermost electrons to form cations with charge +2. In the modern IUPAC nomenclature, the alkaline earth metals comprise the group 2 elements.

The alkaline earth metals are beryllium (Be), magnesium (Mg), calcium (Ca), strontium (Sr), barium (Ba), and radium (Ra). This group lies in the s-block of the periodic table as all alkaline earth metals have their outermost electron in an s-orbital.

Diatomic molecule	Diatomic molecules are molecules composed only of two atoms, of either the same or different chemical elements. The prefix di- is of Greek origin, meaning 2. Common diatomic molecules are hydrogen (H_2), nitrogen (N_2), oxygen (O_2), and carbon monoxide (CO). Seven elements exist as homonuclear diatomic molecules at room temperature: H_2, N_2, O_2, F_2, Cl_2, Br_2, and I_2.
Hydrocarbon	In organic chemistry, a hydrocarbon is an organic compound consisting entirely of hydrogen and carbon. Hydrocarbons from which one hydrogen atom has been removed are functional groups, called hydrocarbyls. Aromatic hydrocarbons (arenes), alkanes, alkenes, cycloalkanes and alkyne-based compounds are different types of hydrocarbons.
Iodine	Iodine is a chemical element with the symbol I and atomic number 53./ syllable break' style='border-bottom:1px dotted'>.?da?n-o-dyne, 'a?.?d?n-o-d?n, or 'a?.?di?n-o-deen in both American and British English. The name is from Greek ?οειδ?ς ioeides, meaning violet or purple, due to the color of elemental iodine vapor.

Iodine and its compounds are primarily used in nutrition, and industrially in the production of acetic acid and certain polymers. |
| Ionic compound | In chemistry, an ionic compound is a chemical compound in which ions are held together in a lattice structure by ionic bonds. Usually, the positively charged portion consists of metal cations and the negatively charged portion is an anion or polyatomic ion. Ions in ionic compounds are held together by the electrostatic forces between oppositely charged bodies. |
| Monatomic ion | A monatomic ion is an ion consisting of one or more atoms of a single element (unlike a polyatomic ion, which consists of more than one element in one ion). For example calcium carbonate consists of the monatomic ion Ca^{2+} and the polyatomic ion CO_3^{2-}.

A type I binary ionic compound contains a metal (cation) that forms only one type of ion. |
| Ball-and-stick model | In chemistry, the ball-and-stick model is a molecular model of a chemical substance which is to display both the three-dimensional position of the atoms and the bonds between them. The atoms are typically represented by spheres, connected by rods which represent the bonds. Double and triple bonds are usually represented by two or three curved rods, respectively. |

Chapter 2. Atoms, Molecules, and Ions

Carbon	Carbon is the chemical element with symbol C and atomic number 6. As a member of group 14 on the periodic table, it is nonmetallic and tetravalent--making four electrons available to form covalent chemical bonds. There are three naturally occurring isotopes, with ^{12}C and ^{13}C being stable, while ^{14}C is radioactive, decaying with a half-life of about 5,730 years. Carbon is one of the few elements known since antiquity.
Chemical formula	A chemical formula is a way of expressing information about the atoms that constitute a particular chemical compound. The chemical formula identifies each constituent element by its chemical symbol and indicates the number of atoms of each element found in each discrete molecule of that compound. If a molecule contains more than one atom of a particular element, this quantity is indicated using a subscript after the chemical symbol (although 18th-century books often used superscripts) and also can be combined by more chemical elements.
Graphite	The mineral graphite is an allotrope of carbon. It was named by Abraham Gottlob Werner in 1789 from the Ancient Greek γρ?φω (grapho), 'to draw/write', for its use in pencils, where it is commonly called lead (not to be confused with the metallic element lead). Unlike diamond (another carbon allotrope), graphite is an electrical conductor, a semimetal.
Molecular model	(Some of these have interesting and/or beautiful images)•Barlow, W. (1883). 'Probable Nature of the Internal Symmetry of Crystals'. Nature 29 (738): 186-8. Bibcode 1883Natur..29..186B. doi:10.1038/029186a0. •Barlow, W.; Pope, W.J. (1906). 'A development of the atomic theory which correlates chemical and crystalline structure and leads to a demonstration of the nature of valency'. J. Chem. Soc. 89: 1675-1744. •Dalton's paper on atoms and chemical compounds.•history of molecular models Paper presented at the Euroscience Open Forum (ESOF), Stockholm on August 25, 2004 W. Gerhard Pohl, Austrian Chemical Society.
Oxygen	Oxygen is the element with atomic number 8 and represented by the symbol O. Its name derives from the Greek roots ?ξ?ς (oxys) ('acid', literally 'sharp', referring to the sour taste of acids) and -γεν?ς (-genes) ('producer', literally 'begetter'), because at the time of naming, it was mistakenly thought that all acids required oxygen in their composition. At standard temperature and pressure, two atoms of the element bind to form dioxygen, a very pale blue, odorless, tasteless diatomic gas with the formula O_2.

Ozone	Ozone or trioxygen, is a triatomic molecule, consisting of three oxygen atoms. It is an allotrope of oxygen that is much less stable than the diatomic allotrope (O_2), breaking down with a half life of about half an hour in the lower atmosphere, to normal dioxygen. Ozone is formed from dioxygen by the action of ultraviolet light and also atmospheric electrical discharges, and is present in low concentrations throughout the Earth's atmosphere.
Empirical formula	In chemistry, the empirical formula of a chemical compound is the simplest positive integer ratio of atoms of each element present in a compound. An empirical formula makes no reference to isomerism, structure, or absolute number of atoms. The empirical formula is used as standard for most ionic compounds, such as $CaCl_2$, and for macromolecules, such as SiO_2.
Space-filling model	In chemistry, a space-filling model, is a type of three-dimensional molecular model where the atoms are represented by spheres whose radii are proportional to the radii of the atoms and whose center-to-center distances are proportional to the distances between the atomic nuclei, all in the same scale. Atoms of different chemical elements are usually represented by spheres of different colors. Calotte models are distinguished from other 3D representations, such as the ball-and-stick and skeletal models, by the use of 'full size' balls for the atoms.
Structural formula	The structural formula of a chemical compound is a graphical representation of the molecular structure, showing how the atoms are arranged. The chemical bonding within the molecule is also shown, either explicitly or implicitly. Also several other formats are used, as in chemical databases, such as SMILES, InChI and CML. Unlike chemical formulas or chemical names, structural formulas provide a representation of the molecular structure.
Sodium	Sodium is a chemical element with the symbol Na and atomic number 11. It is a soft, silvery-white, highly reactive metal and is a member of the alkali metals; its only stable isotope is ^{23}Na. The free metal does not occur in nature, but instead must be prepared from its compounds; it was first isolated by Humphry Davy in 1807 by the electrolysis of sodium hydroxide. Sodium is the sixth most abundant element in the Earth's crust, and exists in numerous minerals such as feldspars, sodalite and rock salt.
Sodium carbonate	Sodium carbonate Na_2CO_3 is a sodium salt of carbonic acid. It most commonly occurs as a crystalline heptahydrate, which readily effloresces to form a white powder, the monohydrate. Sodium carbonate is domestically well known for its everyday use as a water softener.

Chapter 2. Atoms, Molecules, and Ions

Ammonium	The ammonium cation is a positively charged polyatomic cation with the chemical formula NH_4^+. It is formed by the protonation of ammonia (NH_3). Ammonium is also a general name for positively charged or protonated substituted amines and quaternary ammonium cations (NR_4^+), where one or more hydrogen atoms are replaced by organic radical groups (indicated by R).
Binary compound	A binary compound is a chemical compound that contains exactly two different elements. Examples of binary ionic compounds include calcium chloride ($CaCl_2$), sodium fluoride (NaF), and magnesium oxide (MgO), whilst examples of binary covalent compounds include water (H_2O), carbon monoxide (CO), and sulfur hexafluoride (SF_6). In the group of binary compounds of hydrogen a binary acid will include a hydrogen atom attached to another atom that will typically be in the 17th group of the periodic Table.
Inorganic compound	Inorganic compounds are of inanimate, not biological origin. Inorganic compounds lack carbon and hydrogen atoms and are synthesized by the agency of geological systems. In contrast, the synthesis of organic compounds in biological systems incorporates carbohydrates into the molecular structure.
Organic compound	An organic compound is any member of a large class of gaseous, liquid, or solid chemical compounds whose molecules contain carbon. For historical reasons discussed below, a few types of carbon-containing compounds such as carbides, carbonates, simple oxides of carbon, and cyanides, as well as the allotropes of carbon such as diamond and graphite, are considered inorganic. The distinction between 'organic' and 'inorganic' carbon compounds, while 'useful in organizing the vast subject of chemistry... is somewhat arbitrary'.
Atomic mass	The atomic mass is the mass of a specific isotope, most often expressed in unified atomic mass units. The atomic mass is the total mass of protons, neutrons and electrons in a single atom. The atomic mass is sometimes incorrectly used as a synonym of relative atomic mass, average atomic mass and atomic weight; these differ subtly from the atomic mass.
Ternary compound	In chemistry, a ternary compound is a compound containing three different elements. An example of this is sodium phosphate, Na_3PO_4. The sodium ion has a charge of 1+ and the phosphate ion has a charge of 3-.
Isomer	In chemistry, isomers are compounds with the same molecular formula but different structural formulas. Isomers do not necessarily share similar properties, unless they also have the same functional groups. There are many different classes of isomers, like stereoisomers, enantiomers, geometrical isomers, etc.

Chapter 2. Atoms, Molecules, and Ions

Transition metal	In chemistry, the term transition metal has two possible meanings:•The IUPAC definition states that a transition metal is 'an element whose atom has an incomplete d sub-shell, or which can give rise to cations with an incomplete d sub-shell'.•Most scientists describe a 'transition metal' as any element in the d-block of the periodic table, which includes groups 3 to 12 on the periodic table. All elements in the d-block are metals. In actual practice, the f-block is also included in the form of the lanthanide and actinide series. Jensen has reviewed the history of the terms transition element and d-block.
Corrosion	Corrosion is the gradual destruction of material, usually metals, by chemical reaction with its environment. In the most common use of the word, this means electro-chemical oxidation of metals in reaction with an oxidant such as oxygen. Rusting, the formation of iron oxides, is a well-known example of electrochemical corrosion.
Oxoacid	An oxoacid is an acid that contains oxygen. To be more specific, it is an acid that:•contains oxygen•contains at least one other element•has at least one hydrogen atom bound to oxygen•forms an ion by the loss of one or more protons. The name oxyacid is sometimes used, although this is not recommended. Description Generally, oxoacids are simply polyatomic ions with a positively polarized hydrogen, which can be split off as a cation(ion).
Hypochlorous acid	Hypochlorous acid is a weak acid with the chemical formula $HClO$. It forms when chlorine dissolves in water. It cannot be isolated in pure form due to rapid equilibration with its precursor. $HClO$ is an oxidizer, and as its sodium salt sodium hypochlorite, ($NaClO$), or its calcium salt calcium hypochlorite, ($Ca(ClO)_2$) is used as a bleach, a deodorant, and a disinfectant.
Perchloric acid	Perchloric acid is the inorganic compound with the formula $HClO_4$. Usually found as an aqueous solution, this colorless compound is a stronger acid than sulfuric and nitric acids. It is a powerful oxidizer, but its aqueous solutions up to appr. 70% are generally safe, only showing strong acid features and no oxidizing properties.
Anhydrous	As a general term, a substance is said to be anhydrous if it contains no water. The way of achieving the anhydrous form differs from one substance to another. That is to say, anhydrous matter is prepared or used as a form with no water, and specifically the form of a chemical without water of crystallization.
Alkane	Alkanes (also known as paraffins or saturated hydrocarbons) are chemical compounds that consist only of hydrogen and carbon atoms and are bonded exclusively by single bonds (i.e., they are saturated compounds) without any cycles .

Alkanes belong to a homologous series of organic compounds in which the members differ by a constant relative molecular mass of 14. They have 2 main commercial sources, crude oil and natural gas.

Each carbon atom has 4 bonds (either C-H or C-C bonds), and each hydrogen atom is joined to a carbon atom (H-C bonds).

Dry ice	Dry ice, is the solid form of carbon dioxide. It is used primarily as a cooling agent. Its advantages include lower temperature than that of water ice and not leaving any residue (other than incidental frost from moisture in the atmosphere).
Functional group	In organic chemistry, functional groups are lexicon specific groups of atoms or bonds within molecules that are responsible for the characteristic chemical reactions of those molecules. The same functional group will undergo the same or similar chemical reaction(s) regardless of the size of the molecule it is a part of. However, its relative reactivity can be modified by nearby functional groups.
Nitroglycerin	Nitroglycerin also known as nitroglycerine, trinitroglycerin, trinitroglycerine, 1,2,3-trinitroxypropane and glyceryl trinitrate, is a heavy, colorless, oily, explosive liquid produced by nitrating glycerol. Chemically, the substance is an organic nitrate compound rather than a nitro compound, but the traditional name is often retained. Since the 1860s, nitroglycerin has been used as an active ingredient in the manufacture of explosives, mostly dynamite, and as such it is employed in the construction, demolition, and mining industries.
Ionization	Ionization is the process of converting an atom or molecule into an ion by adding or removing charged particles such as electrons or ions. In the case of ionisation of a gas, ion-pairs are created consisting of a free electron and a +ve ion.

The process of ionization works slightly differently depending on whether an ion with a positive or a negative electric charge is being produced. |

Chapter 2. Atoms, Molecules, and Ions

1. _____s consist of two protons and two neutrons bound together into a particle identical to a helium nucleus, which is classically produced in the process of alpha decay, but may be produced also in other ways and given the same name. The _____ can be written as He^{2+}, $^{4}_{2}He^{2+}$ or $^{4}_{2}He$ (as it is possible that the ion gains electrons from the environment; also, electrons are not important in nuclear chemistry).

   The nomenclature is not well defined, and thus not all high-velocity helium nuclei are considered by all authors as _____s.

   a. Anechoic chamber
   b. Electromagnetic radiation
   c. Epcard
   d. Alpha particle

2. _____, is one of two stable isotopes of hydrogen. It has a natural abundance in Earth's oceans of about one atom in 6,420 of hydrogen (~156.25 ppm on an atom basis). _____ accounts for approximately 0.0156% of all naturally occurring hydrogen in Earth's oceans, while the most common isotope (hydrogen-1 or protium) accounts for more than 99.98%.

   a. Deuterium
   b. Gadolinium
   c. Lead-bismuth eutectic
   d. Lithium hydride

3. The _____ is a subatomic particle with a negative elementary electric charge. It has no known components or substructure; in other words, it is generally thought to be an elementary particle. An _____ has a mass that is approximately 1/1836 that of the proton.

   a. Electron hole
   b. Electron
   c. Charge conservation
   d. Charged particle

4. The _____ is the SI-derived unit of radioactivity. One Bq is defined as the activity of a quantity of radioactive material in which one nucleus decays per second. The Bq unit is therefore equivalent to an inverse second, s^{-1}.

   a. Counts per minute
   b. Curie
   c. Becquerel
   d. Radiation flux

5. . In coordination chemistry, the _____ of a central atom in a coordination compound is the charge that it would have if all the ligands were removed along with the electron pairs that were shared with the central atom.

   The _____ is used in the nomenclature of inorganic compounds. It is represented by a Roman numeral.

a. Aalto Vase
b. Ajax
c. Oxidation number
d. Electric Youth

ANSWER KEY
Chapter 2. Atoms, Molecules, and Ions

1. d
2. a
3. b
4. c
5. c

You can take the complete Chapter Practice Test

for Chapter 2. Atoms, Molecules, and Ions
on all key terms, persons, places, and concepts.

Online 99 Cents

http://www.epub14.1.20267.2.cram101.com/

Use www.Cram101.com for all your study needs

including Cram101's online interactive problem solving labs in

chemistry, statistics, mathematics, and more.

Chapter 3. Mass Relationships in Chemical Reactions

CHAPTER OUTLINE: KEY TERMS, PEOPLE, PLACES, CONCEPTS

_____ | Atomic mass

_____ | Atomic mass unit

_____ | Graphite

_____ | Mass

_____ | Mole

_____ | Avogadro

_____ | Molar mass

_____ | Molecular mass

_____ | Mass formula

_____ | Neon

_____ | Spectrometer

_____ | Lewis structure

_____ | Chemical formula

_____ | Empirical formula

_____ | Ethanol

_____ | Chemical equation

_____ | Chemical reaction

_____ | Stoichiometry

_____ | Limiting reagent

Chapter 3. Mass Relationships in Chemical Reactions

_____ | Reagent

_____ | Yield

_____ | Amino acid

_____ | Fertilizer

_____ | Phosphate

_____ | Urea

CHAPTER HIGHLIGHTS & NOTES: KEY TERMS, PEOPLE, PLACES, CONCEPTS

Atomic mass	The atomic mass is the mass of a specific isotope, most often expressed in unified atomic mass units. The atomic mass is the total mass of protons, neutrons and electrons in a single atom.
	The atomic mass is sometimes incorrectly used as a synonym of relative atomic mass, average atomic mass and atomic weight; these differ subtly from the atomic mass.
Atomic mass unit	The unified atomic mass unit or dalton (symbol: Da) is a unit that is used for indicating mass on an atomic or molecular scale. It is defined as one twelfth of the rest mass of an unbound neutral atom of carbon-12 in its nuclear and electronic ground state, and has a value of 1.660538921(73) $\times 10^{-27}$ kg. One dalton is approximately equal to the mass of one proton or one neutron; an equivalence of saying 1 g mol^{-1} .
Graphite	The mineral graphite is an allotrope of carbon. It was named by Abraham Gottlob Werner in 1789 from the Ancient Greek γρ?φω (grapho), 'to draw/write', for its use in pencils, where it is commonly called lead (not to be confused with the metallic element lead). Unlike diamond (another carbon allotrope), graphite is an electrical conductor, a semimetal.

Mass	The mass recorded by a mass spectrometer can refer to different physical quantities depending on the characteristics of the instrument and the manner in which the mass spectrum is displayed.

The accurate mass (more appropriately, the measured accurate mass) is an experimentally determined mass that allows the elemental composition to be determined. For molecules with mass below 200 u, a 5 ppm accuracy is sufficient to uniquely determine the elemental composition. |
| Mole | The mole is a unit of measurement for the amount of substance or chemical amount. It is one of the base units in the International System of Units, and has the unit symbol mol.

The name mole is an 1897 translation of the German unit Mol, coined by the chemist Wilhelm Ostwald in 1893, although the related concept of equivalent mass had been in use at least a century earlier. |
Avogadro	Avogadro (software) is a molecular editor designed for cross-platform use in computational chemistry, molecular modeling, bioinformatics, materials science, and related areas. It is extensible through a plugin architecture. •Molecular builder/editor for Windows, Linux, and Mac OS X.•All source code is available under the GNU GPL.•Translations into Chinese, French, German, Italian, Russian, and Spanish.•Supports multi-threaded rendering and computation.•Plugin architecture for developers, including rendering, interactive tools, commands, and Python scripts.•OpenBabel import of files, input generation for multiple computational chemistry packages, crystallography, and biomolecules..
Molar mass	Molar mass, symbol M, is a physical property of a given substance (chemical element or chemical compound), namely its mass per amount of substance. The base SI unit for mass is the kilogram and that for amount of substance is the mole. Thus, the derived unit for molar mass is kg/mol.
Molecular mass	The molecular mass of a substance is the mass of one molecule of that substance, in unified atomic mass unit(s) u (equal to 1/12 the mass of one atom of the isotope carbon-12). This is numerically equivalent to the relative molecular mass of a molecule, frequently referred to by the term molecular weight, which is the ratio of the mass of that molecule to 1/12 of the mass of carbon-12 and is a dimensionless number. Thus, it is incorrect to express relative molecular mass in daltons (Da).
Mass formula	A mass formula is an equation or set of equations in physics which attempts to predict the mass or mass ratios of the subatomic particles.

An important step in high energy physics was the discovery of the Gell-Mann-Okubo mass formula predicting relationships between masses of the members of SU(3) multiplets. HI The development of an accurate mass formula is one of several fundamental aspects to developing a working theory of everything, which can overcome the incompatibilities between current classical and quantum physics theories.

Neon

Neon is the chemical element that has the symbol Ne and an atomic number of 10. Although a very common element in the universe, it is rare on Earth. A colorless, inert noble gas under standard conditions, neon gives a distinct reddish-orange glow when used in either low-voltage neon glow lamps or in high-voltage discharge tubes or neon advertising signs. It is commercially extracted from air, in which it is found in trace amounts.

Spectrometer

A spectrometer is an instrument used to measure properties of light over a specific portion of the electromagnetic spectrum, typically used in spectroscopic analysis to identify materials. The variable measured is most often the light's intensity but could also, for instance, be the polarization state. The independent variable is usually the wavelength of the light or a unit directly proportional to the photon energy, such as wavenumber or electron volts, which has a reciprocal relationship to wavelength.

Lewis structure

Lewis structures (also known as Lewis dot diagrams, electron dot diagrams, and electron dot structures) are diagrams that show the bonding between atoms of a molecule and the lone pairs of electrons that may exist in the molecule.

Chemical formula

A chemical formula is a way of expressing information about the atoms that constitute a particular chemical compound.

The chemical formula identifies each constituent element by its chemical symbol and indicates the number of atoms of each element found in each discrete molecule of that compound. If a molecule contains more than one atom of a particular element, this quantity is indicated using a subscript after the chemical symbol (although 18th-century books often used superscripts) and also can be combined by more chemical elements.

Empirical formula

In chemistry, the empirical formula of a chemical compound is the simplest positive integer ratio of atoms of each element present in a compound. An empirical formula makes no reference to isomerism, structure, or absolute number of atoms. The empirical formula is used as standard for most ionic compounds, such as $CaCl_2$, and for macromolecules, such as SiO_2.

Ethanol

Ethanol, pure alcohol, grain alcohol, or drinking alcohol, is a volatile, flammable, colorless liquid.

It is a psychoactive drug and one of the oldest recreational drugs. Best known as the type of alcohol found in alcoholic beverages, it is also used in thermometers, as a solvent, and as a fuel.

Chemical equation	A chemical equation is the symbolic representation of a chemical reaction where the reactant entities are given on the left hand side and the product entities on the right hand side. The coefficients next to the symbols and formulae of entities are the absolute values of the stoichiometric numbers. The first chemical equation was diagrammed by Jean Beguin in 1615.
Chemical reaction	A chemical reaction is a process that leads to the transformation of one set of chemical substances to another. Chemical reactions can be either spontaneous, requiring no input of energy, or non-spontaneous, typically following the input of some type of energy, such as heat, light or electricity. Classically, chemical reactions encompass changes that strictly involve the motion of electrons in the forming and breaking of chemical bonds, although the general concept of a chemical reaction, in particular the notion of a chemical equation, is applicable to transformations of elementary particles (such as illustrated by Feynman diagrams), as well as nuclear reactions.
Stoichiometry	Stoichiometry is a branch of chemistry that deals with the relative quantities of reactants and products in chemical reactions. In a balanced chemical reaction, the relations among quantities of reactants and products typically form a ratio of whole numbers. For example, in a reaction that forms ammonia (NH_3), exactly one molecule of nitrogen (N_2) reacts with three molecules of hydrogen (H_2) to produce two molecules of NH_3:$N_2 + 3 H_2 \rightarrow 2 NH_3$ Stoichiometry can be used to find quantities such as the amount of products (in mass, moles, volume, etc).
Limiting reagent	In a chemical reaction, the limiting reagent, is the substance which is totally consumed when the chemical reaction is complete. The amount of product formed is limited by this reagent since the reaction cannot proceed further without it. The other reagents may be present in excess of the quantities required to react with the limiting reagent.
Reagent	A reagent is a 'substance or compound that is added to a system in order to bring about a chemical reaction, or added to see if a reaction occurs.' Although the terms reactant and reagent are often used interchangeably, a reactant is less specifically a 'substance that is consumed in the course of a chemical reaction'. Solvents and catalysts, although they are involved in the reaction, are usually not referred to as reactants. In organic chemistry, reagents are compounds or mixtures, usually composed of inorganic or small organic molecules, that are used to affect a transformation on an organic substrate.

Chapter 3. Mass Relationships in Chemical Reactions

Yield	In chemistry, yield, also referred to as and reaction yield, is the amount of product obtained in a chemical reaction. The absolute yield can be given as the weight in grams or in moles (molar yield). The fractional yield, relative yield, or percentage yield, which serve to measure the effectiveness of a synthetic procedure, is calculated by dividing the amount of the obtained product by the theoretical yield (the unit of measure for both must be the same): $$\text{fractional yield} = \frac{\text{actual yield}}{\text{theoretical yield}}$$ One or more reactants in a chemical reaction are often used in excess.
Amino acid	Amino acids are molecules containing an amine group, a carboxylic acid group, and a side-chain that is specific to each amino acid. The key elements of an amino acid are carbon, hydrogen, oxygen, and nitrogen. They are particularly important in biochemistry, where the term usually refers to alpha-amino acids.
Fertilizer	Fertilizer is any organic or inorganic material of natural or synthetic origin (other than liming materials) that is added to a soil to supply one or more plant nutrients essential to the growth of plants. A recent assessment found that about 40 to 60% of crop yields are attributable to commercial fertilizer use. They are essential for high-yield harvest: European fertilizer market is expected to grow to €15.3 billion by 2018.
Phosphate	A phosphate, an inorganic chemical, is a salt of phosphoric acid. In organic chemistry, a phosphate, or organophosphate, is an ester of phosphoric acid. Organic phosphates are important in biochemistry and biogeochemistry or ecology.
Urea	Urea is an organic compound with the chemical formula $CO(NH_2)_2$. The molecule has two --NH_2 groups joined by a carbonyl (C=O) functional group. Urea serves an important role in the metabolism of nitrogen-containing compounds by animals and is the main nitrogen-containing substance in the urine of mammals.

1. The unified _____ or dalton (symbol: Da) is a unit that is used for indicating mass on an atomic or molecular scale. It is defined as one twelfth of the rest mass of an unbound neutral atom of carbon-12 in its nuclear and electronic ground state, and has a value of $1.660538921(73)\times10^{-27}$ kg. One dalton is approximately equal to the mass of one proton or one neutron; an equivalence of saying 1 g mol^{-1} .

    a. Atomic mass unit
    b. Environmental radioactivity
    c. Oddo-Harkins rule
    d. Aalto Vase

2. The mass recorded by a _____spectrometer can refer to different physical quantities depending on the characteristics of the instrument and the manner in which the _____spectrum is displayed.

The accurate _____(more appropriately, the measured accurate mass) is an experimentally determined mass that allows the elemental composition to be determined. For molecules with mass below 200 u, a 5 ppm accuracy is sufficient to uniquely determine the elemental composition.

    a. Mass chromatogram
    b. Mass spectrometry imaging
    c. Mass spectrum
    d. Mass

3. _____ is a branch of chemistry that deals with the relative quantities of reactants and products in chemical reactions. In a balanced chemical reaction, the relations among quantities of reactants and products typically form a ratio of whole numbers. For example, in a reaction that forms ammonia (NH_3), exactly one molecule of nitrogen (N_2) reacts with three molecules of hydrogen (H_2) to produce two molecules of NH_3:$N_2 + 3 H_2 \rightarrow 2 NH_3$

_____ can be used to find quantities such as the amount of products (in mass, moles, volume, etc).

    a. Chemical equation
    b. Conversion
    c. Stoichiometry
    d. Limiting reagent

4. _____ is an organic compound with the chemical formula $CO(NH_2)_2$. The molecule has two --NH_2 groups joined by a carbonyl (C=O) functional group.

_____ serves an important role in the metabolism of nitrogen-containing compounds by animals and is the main nitrogen-containing substance in the urine of mammals.

    a. Aalto Vase
    b. River continuum concept
    c. Scale relativity
    d. Urea

5. The _____ is the mass of a specific isotope, most often expressed in unified _____ units. The _____ is the total mass of protons, neutrons and electrons in a single atom.

   The _____ is sometimes incorrectly used as a synonym of relative _____, average _____ and atomic weight; these differ subtly from the _____.

   a. 1,2-Dioxetanedione
   b. 1,8-Diaminonaphthalene
   c. Atomic mass
   d. Prout's hypothesis

1. a
2. d
3. c
4. d
5. c

You can take the complete Chapter Practice Test

for Chapter 3. Mass Relationships in Chemical Reactions
on all key terms, persons, places, and concepts.

Online 99 Cents

http://www.epub14.1.20267.3.cram101.com/

Use www.Cram101.com for all your study needs

including Cram101's online interactive problem solving labs in

chemistry, statistics, mathematics, and more.

Chapter 4. Reactions in Aqueous Solutions

CHAPTER OUTLINE: KEY TERMS, PEOPLE, PLACES, CONCEPTS

- Aqueous solution
- Electrolyte
- Solution
- Solvent
- Iodine
- Strong electrolyte
- Acetic acid
- Chemical equilibrium
- Reversible reaction
- Halide
- Solubility
- Spectator ion
- Boiler
- Hard water
- Litmus
- Diprotic acid
- Hydrochloric acid
- Hydrogen
- Hydrogen ion

	Hydronium
	Monomer
	Phosphoric acid
	Sulfur
	Sulfur trioxide
	Proton
	Trioxide
	Amino acid
	Ammonium
	Chemical reaction
	Half-reaction
	Magnesium oxide
	Reduction potential
	Combustion
	Oxide
	Potential
	Oxidizing agent
	Reducing agent
	Oxidation number

Chapter 4. Reactions in Aqueous Solutions

CHAPTER OUTLINE: KEY TERMS, PEOPLE, PLACES, CONCEPTS

Fluorine

Combination

Combination reaction

Methane

Oxygen

Isomer

Mercury oxide

Sodium

Activity

Halogen

Bromine

Disproportionation

Lewis structure

Breathalyzer

Concentration

Molar concentration

Stock solution

Acid-base titration

Gravimetric analysis

_____ Silver chloride

_____ Chloride

_____ Stoichiometry

_____ Titration

_____ Standard solution

_____ Burette

_____ Equivalence point

_____ Phenolphthalein

_____ Sodium hydroxide

_____ Hydroxide

_____ Point

_____ Oxidation state

_____ Permanganate

_____ Redox

_____ Redox titration

_____ Arsenic

_____ Neutron

_____ Neutron activation

_____ Neutron activation analysis

CHAPTER OUTLINE: KEY TERMS, PEOPLE, PLACES, CONCEPTS

| Activation |

CHAPTER HIGHLIGHTS & NOTES: KEY TERMS, PEOPLE, PLACES, CONCEPTS

Aqueous solution	An aqueous solution is a solution in which the solvent is water. It is usually shown in chemical equations by appending (aq) to the relevant formula, such as NaCl (aq). The word aqueous means pertaining to, related to, similar to, or dissolved in water.
Electrolyte	An electrolyte is any substance containing free ions that make the substance electrically conductive. The most typical electrolyte is an ionic solution, but molten electrolytes and solid electrolytes are also possible. Commonly, electrolytes are solutions of acids, bases or salts.
Solution	In chemistry, a solution is a homogeneous mixture composed of only one phase. In such a mixture, a solute is a substance dissolved in another substance, known as a solvent. The solvent does the dissolving.
Solvent	A solvent is a liquid, solid, or gas that dissolves another solid, liquid, or gaseous solute, resulting in a solution that is soluble in a certain volume of solvent at a specified temperature. Common uses for organic solvents are in dry cleaning (e.g., tetrachloroethylene), as paint thinners (e.g., toluene, turpentine), as nail polish removers and glue solvents (acetone, methyl acetate, ethyl acetate), in spot removers (e.g., hexane, petrol ether), in detergents (citrus terpenes), in perfumes (ethanol), nail polish and in chemical synthesis. The use of inorganic solvents (other than water) is typically limited to research chemistry and some technological processes.
Iodine	Iodine is a chemical element with the symbol I and atomic number 53./ syllable break' style='border-bottom:1px dotted'>.?da?n-o-dyne, 'a?.?d?n-o-d?n, or 'a?.?di?n-o-deen in both American and British English. The name is from Greek ?οειδ?ς ioeides, meaning violet or purple, due to the color of elemental iodine vapor.

Chapter 4. Reactions in Aqueous Solutions

Strong electrolyte	A strong electrolyte is a solute that completely, or almost completely, ionizes or dissociates in a solution. These ions are good conductors of electric current in the solution. Originally, a 'strong electrolyte' was defined as a chemical that, when in aqueous solution, is a good conductor of electricity.
Acetic acid	Acetic acid ?'si?t?k is an organic compound with the chemical formula CH_3CO_2H (also written as CH_3COOH). It is a colourless liquid that when undiluted is also called glacial acetic acid. Acetic acid is the main component of vinegar (apart from water), and has a distinctive sour taste and pungent smell.
Chemical equilibrium	In a chemical reaction, chemical equilibrium is the state in which both reactants and products are present at concentrations which have no further tendency to change with time. Usually, this state results when the forward reaction proceeds at the same rate as the reverse reaction. The reaction rates of the forward and reverse reactions are generally not zero but, being equal, there are no net changes in the concentrations of the reactant and product.
Reversible reaction	A reversible reaction is a chemical reaction that results in an equilibrium mixture of reactants and products. For a reaction involving two reactants and two products this can be expressed symbolically as $aA + bB \rightleftharpoons cC + dD$ A and B can react to form C and D or, in the reverse reaction, C and D can react to form A and B. This is distinct from reversible process in thermodynamics. The concentrations of reactants and products in an equilibrium mixture are determined by the analytical concentrations of the reagents (A and B or C and D) and the equilibrium constant, K. The magnitude of the equilibrium constant depends on the Gibbs free energy change for the reaction.
Halide	A halide is a binary compound, of which one part is a halogen atom and the other part is an element or radical that is less electronegative than the halogen, to make a fluoride, chloride, bromide, iodide, or astatide compound. Many salts are halides. All Group 1 metals form halides which are white solids at room temperature.
Solubility	Solubility is the property of a solid, liquid, or gaseous chemical substance called solute to dissolve in a solid, liquid, or gaseous solvent to form a homogeneous solution of the solute in the solvent. The solubility of a substance fundamentally depends on the used solvent as well as on temperature and pressure.

Spectator ion	A spectator ion is an ion that exists as a reactant and a product in a chemical equation. Spectator ions can be observed in the reaction of aqueous solutions of sodium chloride and copper(II) sulfate but does not affect the equilibrium: The Na^+ and SO_4^{2-} ions are spectator ions since they remain unchanged on both sides of the equation. They simply 'watch' the other ions react, hence the name.
Boiler	A boiler is a closed vessel in which water or other fluid is heated. The heated or vaporized fluid exits the boiler for use in various processes or heating applications, including boiler-based power generation, cooking, and sanitation. Materials The pressure vessel in a boiler is usually made of steel , or historically of wrought iron.
Hard water	Hard water is water that has high mineral content (in contrast with 'soft water'). Hard water is generally not harmful to one's health, but can pose serious problems in industrial settings, where water hardness is monitored to avoid costly breakdowns in boilers, cooling towers, and other equipment that handles water. In domestic settings, hard water is often indicated by a lack of suds formation when soap is agitated in water.
Litmus	Litmus is a water-soluble mixture of different dyes extracted from lichens, especially Roccella tinctoria. It is often absorbed onto filter paper to produce one of the oldest forms of pH indicator, used to test materials for acidity. Blue litmus paper turns red under acidic conditions and red litmus paper turns blue under basic (i.e. alkaline) conditions, with the color change occurring over the pH range 4.5-8.3 at 25 °C. Neutral litmus paper is purple.
Diprotic acid	A diprotic acid is an acid such as H_2SO_4 (sulfuric acid) that contains within its molecular structure two hydrogen atoms per molecule capable of dissociating (i.e. ionizable) in water. The complete dissociation of diprotic acids is of the same form as sulfuric acid:$H_2SO_4 \rightarrow H^+(aq) + HSO_4^-(aq)$ K_a = 1 × $10^3$$HSO_4^- \rightarrow H^+(aq) + SO_4^{2-}(aq)$ K_a = 1 × 10^{-2} The dissociation does not happen all at once due to the two stages of dissociation having different K_a values. The first dissociation will, in the case of sulfuric acid, occur completely, but the second one will not.
Hydrochloric acid	Hydrochloric acid is a clear, colourless solution of hydrogen chloride (HCl) in water. It is a highly corrosive, strong mineral acid with many industrial uses. Hydrochloric acid is found naturally in gastric acid.
Hydrogen	Hydrogen is the chemical element with atomic number 1. It is represented by the symbol H.

With an average atomic weight of 1.00794 u (1.007825 u for hydrogen-1), hydrogen is the lightest element and its monatomic form (H_1) is the most abundant chemical substance, constituting roughly 75% of the Universe's baryonic mass. Non-remnant stars are mainly composed of hydrogen in its plasma state.

At standard temperature and pressure, hydrogen is a colorless, odorless, tasteless, non-toxic, nonmetallic, highly combustible diatomic gas with the molecular formula H_2.

Hydrogen ion

Hydrogen ion is recommended by IUPAC as a general term for all ions of hydrogen and its isotopes. Depending on the charge of the ion, two different classes can be distinguished: positively charged ions and negatively charged ions.

Under aqueous conditions found in biochemistry, hydrogen ions exist as the hydrated form hydronium, H_3O^+, but these are often still referred to as 'hydrogen ions' or even 'protons' by biochemists.

Hydronium

In chemistry, a hydronium ion is the cation H_3O^+, a type of oxonium ion produced by protonation of water. This cation is often used to represent the nature of the proton in aqueous solution, where the proton is highly solvated (bound to a solvent). The reality is far more complicated, and a proton is bound to several molecules of water, such that other descriptions such as $H_5O_2^+$, $H_7O_3^+$ and $H_9O_4^+$ are increasingly accurate descriptions of the environment of a proton in water.

Monomer

A monomer is a molecule that may bind chemically to other molecules to form a polymer. The term 'monomeric protein' may also be used to describe one of the proteins making up a multiprotein complex. The most common natural monomer is glucose, which is linked by glycosidic bonds into polymers such as cellulose and starch, and is over 77% of the mass of all plant matter.

Phosphoric acid

Phosphoric acid, is a mineral (inorganic) acid having the chemical formula H_3PO_4.
Orthophosphoric acid molecules can combine with themselves to form a variety of compounds which are also referred to as phosphoric acids, but in a more general way. The term phosphoric acid can also refer to a chemical or reagent consisting of phosphoric acids, usually orthophosphoric acid.

Sulfur

Sulfur or sulphur is the chemical element with atomic number 16. In the periodic table it is represented by the symbol S. It is an abundant, multivalent non-metal. Under normal conditions, sulfur atoms form cyclic octatomic molecules with chemical formula S_8. Elemental sulfur is a bright yellow crystalline solid when at room temperature.

Sulfur trioxide	Sulfur trioxide is the chemical compound with the formula SO_3. In the gaseous form, this species is a significant pollutant, being the primary agent in acid rain. It is prepared on massive scales as a precursor to sulfuric acid.
Proton	The proton is a subatomic particle with the symbol p or p+and a positive electric charge of 1 elementary charge. One or more protons are present in the nucleus of each atom, along with neutrons. The number of protons in each atom is its atomic number.
Trioxide	A trioxide is a compound with three oxygen atoms. For metals with the M_2O_3 formula there are several common structures. Al_2O_3, Cr_2O_3, Fe_2O_3, and V_2O_3 adopt the corundum structure.
Amino acid	Amino acids are molecules containing an amine group, a carboxylic acid group, and a side-chain that is specific to each amino acid. The key elements of an amino acid are carbon, hydrogen, oxygen, and nitrogen. They are particularly important in biochemistry, where the term usually refers to alpha-amino acids.
Ammonium	The ammonium cation is a positively charged polyatomic cation with the chemical formula NH_4^+. It is formed by the protonation of ammonia (NH_3). Ammonium is also a general name for positively charged or protonated substituted amines and quaternary ammonium cations (NR_4^+), where one or more hydrogen atoms are replaced by organic radical groups (indicated by R).
Chemical reaction	A chemical reaction is a process that leads to the transformation of one set of chemical substances to another. Chemical reactions can be either spontaneous, requiring no input of energy, or non-spontaneous, typically following the input of some type of energy, such as heat, light or electricity. Classically, chemical reactions encompass changes that strictly involve the motion of electrons in the forming and breaking of chemical bonds, although the general concept of a chemical reaction, in particular the notion of a chemical equation, is applicable to transformations of elementary particles (such as illustrated by Feynman diagrams), as well as nuclear reactions.
Half-reaction	A half-reaction is either the oxidation or reduction reaction component of a redox reaction. A half reaction is obtained by considering the change in oxidation states of individual substances involved in the redox reaction.
	Consider the reaction below:$Cl_2 + 2Fe^{2+} \rightarrow 2Cl^- + 2Fe^{3+}$
	The two elements involved, iron and chlorine, each change oxidation state; iron from 2+ to 3+, chlorine from 0 to 1−. There are then effectively two half-reactions occurring.
Magnesium oxide	Magnesium oxide or magnesia, is a white hygroscopic solid mineral that occurs naturally as periclase and is a source of magnesium .

It has an empirical formula of MgO and consists of a lattice of Mg^{2+} ions and O^{2-} ions held together by ionic bonds. Magnesium hydroxide forms in the presence of water ($MgO + H_2O \rightarrow Mg(OH)_2$), but it can be reversed by heating it to separate moisture.

Reduction potential	Reduction potential (also known as redox potential, oxidation / reduction potential is a measure of the tendency of a chemical species to acquire electrons and thereby be reduced. Reduction potential is measured in volts (V), or millivolts (mV). Each species has its own intrinsic reduction potential; the more positive the potential, the greater the species' affinity for electrons and tendency to be reduced.
Combustion	Combustion or burning is the sequence of exothermic chemical reactions between a fuel and an oxidant accompanied by the production of heat and conversion of chemical species. The release of heat can result in the production of light in the form of either glowing or a flame. Fuels of interest often include organic compounds (especially hydrocarbons) in the gas, liquid or solid phase.
Oxide	An oxide is a chemical compound that contains at least one oxygen atom and one other element in its chemical formula. Metal oxides typically contain an anion of oxygen in the oxidation state of −2. Most of the Earth's crust consists of solid oxides, the result of elements being oxidized by the oxygen in air or in water . Hydrocarbon combustion affords the two principal carbon oxides: carbon monoxide and carbon dioxide.
Potential	•In linguistics, the potential mood•The mathematical study of potentials is known as potential theory; it is the study of harmonic functions on manifolds. This mathematical formulation arises from the fact that, in physics, the scalar potential is irrotational, and thus has a vanishing Laplacian -- the very definition of a harmonic function.•In physics, a potential may refer to the scalar potential or to the vector potential. In either case, it is a field defined in space, from which many important physical properties may be derived.
Oxidizing agent	An oxidizing agent can be defined as a substance that removes electrons from another reactant in a redox chemical reaction. The oxidizing agent is 'reduced' by taking electrons onto itself and the reactant is 'oxidized' by having its electrons taken away. Oxygen is the prime example of an oxidizing agent, but it is only one among many.
Reducing agent	A reducing agent is the element or compound in a reduction-oxidation (redox) reaction that donates an electron to another species; however, since the reducer loses an electron we say it is 'oxidized'. This means that there must be an 'oxidizer'; because if any chemical is an electron donor (reducer), another must be an electron recipient (oxidizer). Thus reducers are 'oxidized' and oxidizers are 'reduced'.

Oxidation number	In coordination chemistry, the oxidation number of a central atom in a coordination compound is the charge that it would have if all the ligands were removed along with the electron pairs that were shared with the central atom. The oxidation number is used in the nomenclature of inorganic compounds. It is represented by a Roman numeral.
Fluorine	Fluorine is the chemical element with atomic number 9, represented by the symbol F. It is the lightest element of the halogen column of the periodic table and has a single stable isotope, fluorine-19. At standard pressure and temperature, fluorine is a pale yellow gas composed of diatomic molecules, F_2. In stars, fluorine is rare compared to other light elements. In Earth's crust, fluorine is more common, being the thirteenth most abundant element.
Combination	In mathematics a combination is a way of selecting several things out of a larger group, where (unlike permutations) order does not matter. In smaller cases it is possible to count the number of combinations. For example given three fruit, say an apple, orange and pear, there are three combinations of two that can be drawn from this set: an apple and a pear; an apple and an orange; or a pear and an orange.
Combination reaction	In a combination reaction the atoms and/or molecules do what the name implies: they combine to form the product. Combination reactions are usually exothermic. For example barium metal and fluorine gas will combine in a highly exothermic reaction to form the salt barium fluoride: Another example is given by magnesium oxide combining with carbon dioxide: Often, reaction can fall into more than one category.
Methane	Methane is a chemical compound with the chemical formula CH4. It is the simplest alkane, the main component of natural gas, and probably the most abundant organic compound on earth. The relative abundance of methane makes it an attractive fuel. However, because it is a gas at normal conditions, methane is difficult to transport from its source.
Oxygen	Oxygen is the element with atomic number 8 and represented by the symbol O. Its name derives from the Greek roots ?ξ?ς (oxys) ('acid', literally 'sharp', referring to the sour taste of acids) and -γεν?ς (-genes) ('producer', literally 'begetter'), because at the time of naming, it was mistakenly thought that all acids required oxygen in their composition.

	At standard temperature and pressure, two atoms of the element bind to form dioxygen, a very pale blue, odorless, tasteless diatomic gas with the formula O_2.

Oxygen is a member of the chalcogen group on the periodic table and is a highly reactive nonmetallic element that readily forms compounds (notably oxides) with almost all other elements. |
Isomer	In chemistry, isomers are compounds with the same molecular formula but different structural formulas. Isomers do not necessarily share similar properties, unless they also have the same functional groups. There are many different classes of isomers, like stereoisomers, enantiomers, geometrical isomers, etc.
Mercury oxide	Mercury oxide, has a formula of HgO. It has a red or orange color. Mercury(II) oxide is a solid at room temperature and pressure. The mineral form montroydite is very rarely found.
Sodium	Sodium is a chemical element with the symbol Na and atomic number 11. It is a soft, silvery-white, highly reactive metal and is a member of the alkali metals; its only stable isotope is ^{23}Na. The free metal does not occur in nature, but instead must be prepared from its compounds; it was first isolated by Humphry Davy in 1807 by the electrolysis of sodium hydroxide. Sodium is the sixth most abundant element in the Earth's crust, and exists in numerous minerals such as feldspars, sodalite and rock salt.
Activity	In chemical thermodynamics, activity (symbol a) is a measure of the 'effective concentration' of a species in a mixture, meaning that the species' chemical potential depends on the activity of a real solution in the same way that it would depend on concentration for an ideal solution.

By convention, activity is treated as a dimensionless quantity, although its actual value depends on customary choices of standard state for the species. The activity of pure substances in condensed phases (solid or liquids) is normally taken as unity (the number 1). |
| Halogen | The halogens or halogen elements are a series of nonmetal elements from Group 17 IUPAC Style (formerly: VII, VIIA) of the periodic table, comprising fluorine (F), chlorine (Cl), bromine (Br), iodine (I), and astatine (At). The artificially created element 117, provisionally referred to by the systematic name ununseptium, may also be a halogen.

The group of halogens is the only periodic table group which contains elements in all three familiar states of matter at standard temperature and pressure. |
| Bromine | |

Bromine ('bro?mi?n-meen or 'bro?m?n-min; from Greek: βρ?μος, brómos, meaning 'stench (of he-goats)') is a chemical element with the symbol Br, an atomic number of 35, and an atomic mass of 79.904. It is in the halogen element group. The element was isolated independently by two chemists, Carl Jacob Löwig and Antoine Jerome Balard, in 1825-1826. Elemental bromine is a fuming red-brown liquid at room temperature, corrosive and toxic, with properties between those of chlorine and iodine. Free bromine does not occur in nature, but occurs as colorless soluble crystalline mineral halide salts, analogous to table salt.

Disproportionation	Disproportionation, is a specific type of redox reaction in which a species is simultaneously reduced and oxidized to form two different products.

For example: the UV photolysis of mercury(I) chloride $Hg_2Cl_2 \rightarrow Hg + HgCl_2$ is a disproportionation. Mercury (I) is a diatomic dication Hg_2^{2+}.

Lewis structure

Lewis structures (also known as Lewis dot diagrams, electron dot diagrams, and electron dot structures) are diagrams that show the bonding between atoms of a molecule and the lone pairs of electrons that may exist in the molecule.

Breathalyzer

A breathalyzer is a device for estimating blood alcohol content (BAC) from a breath sample. Breathalyzer is the brand name of a series of models made by one manufacturer of breath alcohol testing instruments (originally Smith and Wesson, later sold to National Draeger), and is a registered trademark for such instruments. In Canada, a preliminary non-evidentiary screening device can be approved by Parliament as an approved screening device, and an evidentiary breath instrument can be similarly designated as an approved instrument.

Concentration

In chemistry, concentration is defined as the abundance of a constituent divided by the total volume of a mixture. Furthermore, in chemistry, four types of mathematical description can be distinguished: mass concentration, molar concentration, number concentration, and volume concentration. The term concentration can be applied to any kind of chemical mixture, but most frequently it refers to solutes in solutions.

Molar concentration

In chemistry, the molar concentration, c_i is defined as the amount of a constituent n_i divided by the volume of the mixture V :

$$c_i = \frac{n_i}{V}$$

It is also called molarity, amount-of-substance concentration, amount concentration, substance concentration, or simply concentration. The volume V in the definition $c_i = n_i/V$ refers to the volume of the solution, not the volume of the solvent.

Chapter 4. Reactions in Aqueous Solutions

Stock solution	A Stock Solution is a concentrated solution that will be diluted to some lower concentrated for actual use. Stock solutions are used to save preparation time, conserve materials, reduce storage space, and improve the accuracy with which working lower concentration solutions are prepared. In chemistry, a stock solution is a large volume of a common reagent, such as hydrochloric acid or sodium hydroxide, at a standardized concentration.
Acid-base titration	An acid-base titration is the determination of the concentration of an acid or base by exactly neutralizing the acid/base with an acid or base of known concentration. This allows for quantitative analysis of the concentration of an unknown acid or base solution. It makes use of the neutralization reaction that occurs between acids and bases and the knowledge of how acids and bases will react if their formulas are known.
Gravimetric analysis	Gravimetric analysis describes a set of methods in analytical chemistry for the quantitative determination of an analyte based on the mass of a solid. A simple example is the measurement of solids suspended in a water sample: A known volume of water is filtered, and the collected solids are weighed. In most cases, the analyte must first be converted to a solid by precipitation with an appropriate reagent.
Silver chloride	Silver chloride is a chemical compound with the chemical formula AgCl. This white crystalline solid is well known for its low solubility in water (this behavior being reminiscent of the chlorides of Tl^+ and Pb^{2+}). Upon illumination or heating, silver chloride converts to silver (and chlorine), which is signalled by greyish or purplish coloration to some samples.
Chloride	The chloride ion is formed when the element chlorine, a halogen, gains an electron to form an anion (negatively-charged ion) Cl^-. The salts of hydrochloric acid contain chloride ions and can also be called chlorides. The chloride ion, and its salts such as sodium chloride, are very soluble in water.
Stoichiometry	Stoichiometry is a branch of chemistry that deals with the relative quantities of reactants and products in chemical reactions. In a balanced chemical reaction, the relations among quantities of reactants and products typically form a ratio of whole numbers. For example, in a reaction that forms ammonia (NH_3), exactly one molecule of nitrogen (N_2) reacts with three molecules of hydrogen (H_2) to produce two molecules of NH_3: $N_2 + 3 H_2 \rightarrow 2 NH_3$ Stoichiometry can be used to find quantities such as the amount of products (in mass, moles, volume, etc).

Chapter 4. Reactions in Aqueous Solutions

CHAPTER HIGHLIGHTS & NOTES: KEY TERMS, PEOPLE, PLACES, CONCEPTS

Titration	Titration, is a common laboratory method of quantitative chemical analysis that is used to determine the unknown concentration of an identified analyte. Because volume measurements play a key role in titration, it is also known as volumetric analysis. A reagent, called the titrant or titrator is prepared as a standard solution.
Standard solution	In analytical chemistry, a standard solution is a solution containing a precisely known concentration of an element or a substance i.e., a known weight of solute is dissolved to make a specific volume. It is prepared using a standard Rsubstance, such as a primary standard. Standard solutions are used to determine the concentrations of other substances, such Das solutions in titrations.
Burette	A burette is a vertical cylindrical piece of laboratory glassware with a volumetric graduation on its full length and a precision tap, or stopcock, on the bottom. It is used to dispense known amounts of a liquid reagent in experiments for which such precision is necessary, such as a titration experiment. Burettes are extremely accurate - a 50 cm^3 burette has a tolerance of 0.1 cm^3 (class B) or 0.06 cm^3 (class A).
Equivalence point	The equivalence point, of a chemical reaction is when a titrant is added and is stoichiometrically equal to the amount of moles of substance (known as analyte) present in the sample: the smallest amount of titrant that is sufficient to fully neutralize or react with the analyte. In some cases there are multiple equivalence points which are multiples of the first equivalent point, such as in the titration of a diprotic acid. A graph of the titration curve exhibits an inflection point at the equivalence point--where the graph is steepest.
Phenolphthalein	Phenolphthalein is a chemical compound with the formula $C_{20}H_{14}O_4$ and is often written as 'HIn' or 'phph' in shorthand notation. Often used in titrations, it turns colorless in acidic solutions and pink in basic solutions. If the concentration of indicator is particularly strong, it can appear purple.
Sodium hydroxide	Sodium hydroxide also known as lye and caustic soda, is a caustic metallic base. It is used in many industries, mostly as a strong chemical base in the manufacture of pulp and paper, textiles, drinking water, soaps and detergents and as a drain cleaner. Worldwide production in 2004 was approximately 60 million tonnes, while demand was 51 million tonnes.
Hydroxide	Hydroxide is a diatomic anion with chemical formula OH$^-$. It consists of an oxygen and a hydrogen atom held together by a covalent bond, and carrying a negative electric charge. It is an important but usually minor constituent of water.
Point	Points, sometimes also called a 'discount point', are a form of pre-paid interest.

Chapter 4. Reactions in Aqueous Solutions

	One point equals one percent of the loan amount. By charging a borrower points, a lender effectively increases the yield on the loan above the amount of the stated interest rate.
Oxidation state	In chemistry, the oxidation state is an indicator of the degree of oxidation of an atom in a chemical compound. The formal oxidation state is the hypothetical charge that an atom would have if all bonds to atoms of different elements were 100% ionic. Oxidation states are typically represented by integers, which can be positive, negative, or zero.
Permanganate	A permanganate is the general name for a chemical compound containing the manganate(VII) ion, (MnO_4^-). Because manganese is in the +7 oxidation state, the permanganate(VII) ion is a strong oxidizing agent. The ion has tetrahedral geometry.
Redox	Redox reactions include all chemical reactions in which atoms have their oxidation state changed. This can be either a simple redox process, such as the oxidation of carbon to yield carbon dioxide (CO_2) or the reduction of carbon by hydrogen to yield methane (CH_4), or a complex process such as the oxidation of glucose $(C_6H_{12}O_6)$ in the human body through a series of complex electron transfer processes. Redox reactions, or oxidation-reduction reactions, have a number of similarities to acid-base reactions.
Redox titration	Redox titration is a type of titration based on a redox reaction between the analyte and titrant. Redox titration may involve the use of a redox indicator and/or a potentiometer. Example An example of a redox titration is treating a solution of iodine with a reducing agent and using starch as indicator.
Arsenic	Arsenic is a chemical element with the symbol As, atomic number 33 and relative atomic mass 74.92. Arsenic occurs in many minerals, usually in conjunction with sulfur and metals, and also as a pure elemental crystal. It was first documented by Albertus Magnus in 1250. Arsenic is a metalloid. It can exist in various allotropes, although only the grey form has important use in industry.
Neutron	The neutron is a subatomic hadron particle which has the symbol n or n0, no net electric charge and a mass slightly larger than that of a proton. With the exception of hydrogen, nuclei of atoms consist of protons and neutrons, which are therefore collectively referred to as nucleons.

Neutron activation	Neutron activation is the process in which neutron radiation induces radioactivity in materials, and occurs when atomic nuclei capture free neutrons, becoming heavier and entering excited states. The excited nucleus often decays immediately by emitting particles such as neutrons, protons, or alpha particles. The neutron capture, even after any intermediate decay, often results in the formation of an unstable activation product.
Neutron activation analysis	In chemistry, neutron activation analysis is a nuclear process used for determining the concentrations of elements in a vast amount of materials. NAA allows discrete sampling of elements as it disregards the chemical form of a sample, and focuses solely on its nucleus. The method is based on neutron activation and therefore requires a source of neutrons.
Activation	Activation in (bio-)chemical sciences generally refers to the process whereby something is prepared or excited for a subsequent reaction. In chemistry, activation of molecules is where the molecules enter a state that avails for a chemical reaction to occur. The phrase energy of activation refers to the energy the reactants must acquire before they can successfully react with each other to produce the products, that is, to reach the transition state.

1. A _____ is a device for estimating blood alcohol content (BAC) from a breath sample. _____ is the brand name of a series of models made by one manufacturer of breath alcohol testing instruments (originally Smith and Wesson, later sold to National Draeger), and is a registered trademark for such instruments. In Canada, a preliminary non-evidentiary screening device can be approved by Parliament as an approved screening device, and an evidentiary breath instrument can be similarly designated as an approved instrument.

   a. Cavity ring-down spectroscopy
   b. Breathalyzer
   c. Coblentz Society
   d. Cold vapour atomic fluorescence spectroscopy

2. _____ is the chemical compound with the formula SO_3. In the gaseous form, this species is a significant pollutant, being the primary agent in acid rain. It is prepared on massive scales as a precursor to sulfuric acid.

   a. hydrogen fluoride
   b. Sulfur trioxide
   c. 1,8-Diaminonaphthalene
   d. Flowers of sulfur

3. . A _____ is a molecule that may bind chemically to other molecules to form a polymer.
Chapter 4. Reactions in Aqueous Solutions

Visit Cram101.com for full Practice Exams

The term 'monomeric protein' may also be used to describe one of the proteins making up a multiprotein complex. The most common natural _____ is glucose, which is linked by glycosidic bonds into polymers such as cellulose and starch, and is over 77% of the mass of all plant matter.

a. 1,2,4-Butanetriol
b. Butene
c. Butyl cyanoacrylate
d. Monomer

4. A _____ is a chemical reaction that results in an equilibrium mixture of reactants and products. For a reaction involving two reactants and two products this can be expressed symbolically as $aA + bB \rightleftharpoons cC + dD$

A and B can react to form C and D or, in the reverse reaction, C and D can react to form A and B. This is distinct from reversible process in thermodynamics.

The concentrations of reactants and products in an equilibrium mixture are determined by the analytical concentrations of the reagents (A and B or C and D) and the equilibrium constant, K. The magnitude of the equilibrium constant depends on the Gibbs free energy change for the reaction.

a. Saturation
b. Reversible reaction
c. Singlet oxygen
d. Smoluchowski factor

5. In chemistry, a _____ is a homogeneous mixture composed of only one phase. In such a mixture, a solute is a substance dissolved in another substance, known as a solvent. The solvent does the dissolving.

a. Sublimation
b. Solution
c. Elementary reaction
d. Extent of reaction

1. b
2. b
3. d
4. b
5. b

You can take the complete Chapter Practice Test

for Chapter 4. Reactions in Aqueous Solutions
on all key terms, persons, places, and concepts.

Online 99 Cents

http://www.epub14.1.20267.4.cram101.com/

Use www.Cram101.com for all your study needs

including Cram101's online interactive problem solving labs in

chemistry, statistics, mathematics, and more.

Chapter 5. Gases

CHAPTER OUTLINE: KEY TERMS, PEOPLE, PLACES, CONCEPTS

Partial pressure

Hydrogen

Hydrogen cyanide

Intermolecular force

Vapor

Arsenic

Cyanide

Newton

Torr

Atmospheric pressure

Robert Boyle

Absolute zero

Celsius

Avogadro

Gas constant

Ideal gas

Density

Mass

Molar mass

Chapter 5. Gases

CHAPTER OUTLINE: KEY TERMS, PEOPLE, PLACES, CONCEPTS

_______________ Stoichiometry

_______________ Chemical reaction

_______________ Mixture

_______________ Concentration

_______________ Mole

_______________ Mole fraction

_______________ Potassium

_______________ Potassium chlorate

_______________ Chlorate

_______________ Vapor pressure

_______________ Water vapor

_______________ Nitrogen

_______________ Joule

_______________ Kinetic energy

_______________ Binding energy

_______________ Nuclear binding energy

_______________ Thermal

_______________ Root-mean-square speed

_______________ Diffusion

Chapter 5. Gases

CHAPTER OUTLINE: KEY TERMS, PEOPLE, PLACES, CONCEPTS

	Helium
	Escape velocity
	Velocity
	Effusion
	Thomas Garnett
	Van der Waals constants
	Van der Waals equation

CHAPTER HIGHLIGHTS & NOTES: KEY TERMS, PEOPLE, PLACES, CONCEPTS

Partial pressure

In a mixture of ideal gases, each gas has a partial pressure which is the pressure which the gas would have if it alone occupied the volume. The total pressure of a gas mixture is the sum of the partial pressures of each individual gas in the mixture.

In chemistry, the partial pressure of a gas in a mixture of gases is defined as above.

Hydrogen

Hydrogen is the chemical element with atomic number 1. It is represented by the symbol H. With an average atomic weight of 1.00794 u (1.007825 u for hydrogen-1), hydrogen is the lightest element and its monatomic form (H_1) is the most abundant chemical substance, constituting roughly 75% of the Universe's baryonic mass. Non-remnant stars are mainly composed of hydrogen in its plasma state.

At standard temperature and pressure, hydrogen is a colorless, odorless, tasteless, non-toxic, nonmetallic, highly combustible diatomic gas with the molecular formula H_2.

Hydrogen cyanide

Hydrogen cyanide is a chemical compound with chemical formula HCN.

Chapter 5. Gases

	It is a colorless, extremely poisonous liquid that boils slightly above room temperature at 26 °C (79 °F). Hydrogen cyanide is a linear molecule, with a triple bond between carbon and nitrogen. A minor tautomer of HCN is HNC, hydrogen isocyanide.
Intermolecular force	Intermolecular forces are forces of attraction or repulsion which act between neighboring particles: atoms, molecules or ions. They are weak compared to the intramolecular forces, the forces which keep a molecule together. For example, the covalent bond present within HCl molecules is much stronger than the forces present between the neighbouring molecules, which exist when the molecules are sufficiently close to each other.
Vapor	A vapor or vapour is a substance in the gas phase at a temperature lower than its critical point. This means that the vapor can be condensed to a liquid or to a solid by increasing its pressure without reducing the temperature. For example, water has a critical temperature of 374 °C (647 K), which is the highest temperature at which liquid water can exist.
Arsenic	Arsenic is a chemical element with the symbol As, atomic number 33 and relative atomic mass 74.92. Arsenic occurs in many minerals, usually in conjunction with sulfur and metals, and also as a pure elemental crystal. It was first documented by Albertus Magnus in 1250. Arsenic is a metalloid. It can exist in various allotropes, although only the grey form has important use in industry.
Cyanide	A cyanide is a chemical compound that contains the cyano group, -C≡N, which consists of a carbon atom triple-bonded to a nitrogen atom. Cyanides most commonly refer to salts of the anion CN^-, which is isoelectronic with carbon monoxide and with molecular nitrogen. Most cyanides are highly toxic.
Newton	The newton (symbol: N) is the SI derived unit of force. It is named after Isaac Newton in recognition of his work on classical mechanics, specifically Newton's second law of motion. The newton is the SI unit for force; it is equal to the amount of net force required to accelerate a mass of one kilogram at a rate of one metre per second squared.
Torr	The torr is a non-SI unit of pressure with the ratio of 760 to 1 standard atmosphere, chosen to be roughly equal to the fluid pressure exerted by a millimetre of mercury, i.e., a pressure of 1 Torr is approximately equal to 1 mmHg. Note that the symbol is spelled exactly the same as the unit, but the symbol is capitalized, as is customary in metric units derived from names.

Chapter 5. Gases

Atmospheric pressure	Atmospheric pressure is the force per unit area exerted into a surface by the weight of air above that surface in the atmosphere of Earth . In most circumstances atmospheric pressure is closely approximated by the hydrostatic pressure caused by the mass of air above the measurement point. Low-pressure areas have less atmospheric mass above their location, whereas high-pressure areas have more atmospheric mass above their location.
Robert Boyle	Robert Boyle, FRS, (25 January 1627 - 31 December 1691) was a 17th-century natural philosopher, chemist, physicist, and inventor, also noted for his writings in theology. He has been variously described as Irish, English and Anglo-Irish, his father having come to Ireland from England during the time of the Plantations. Although his research clearly has its roots in the alchemical tradition, Boyle is largely regarded today as the first modern chemist, and therefore one of the founders of modern chemistry, and one of the pioneers of modern experimental scientific method.
Absolute zero	Absolute zero is the theoretical temperature at which entropy reaches its minimum value. The laws of thermodynamics state that absolute zero cannot be reached using only thermodynamic means. A system at absolute zero still possesses quantum mechanical zero-point energy, the energy of its ground state.
Celsius	Celsius is a scale and unit of measurement for temperature. It is named after the Swedish astronomer Anders Celsius who developed a similar temperature scale two years before his death. The degree Celsius can refer to a specific temperature on the Celsius scale as well as a unit to indicate a temperature interval, a difference between two temperatures or an uncertainty.
Avogadro	Avogadro (software) is a molecular editor designed for cross-platform use in computational chemistry, molecular modeling, bioinformatics, materials science, and related areas. It is extensible through a plugin architecture. •Molecular builder/editor for Windows, Linux, and Mac OS X.•All source code is available under the GNU GPL.•Translations into Chinese, French, German, Italian, Russian, and Spanish.•Supports multi-threaded rendering and computation.•Plugin architecture for developers, including rendering, interactive tools, commands, and Python scripts.•OpenBabel import of files, input generation for multiple computational chemistry packages, crystallography, and biomolecules..
Gas constant	The gas constant is a physical constant which is featured in many fundamental equations in the physical sciences, such as the ideal gas law and the Nernst equation. It is equivalent to the Boltzmann constant, but expressed in units of energy (i.e. the pressure-volume product) per temperature increment per mole (rather than energy per temperature increment per particle). The constant is also a combination of the constants from Boyle's Law, Charles' Law, Avogadro's Law, and Gay-Lussac's Law.

Chapter 5. Gases

Ideal gas	Property database An ideal gas is a theoretical gas composed of a set of randomly-moving, non-interacting point particles. The ideal gas concept is useful because it obeys the ideal gas law, a simplified equation of state, and is amenable to analysis under statistical mechanics. At normal conditions such as standard temperature and pressure, most real gases behave qualitatively like an ideal gas.
Density	The mass density is defined as its mass per unit volume. The symbol most often used for density is ρ . In some cases (for instance, in the United States oil and gas industry), density is also defined as its weight per unit volume; although, this quantity is more properly called specific weight.
Mass	The mass recorded by a mass spectrometer can refer to different physical quantities depending on the characteristics of the instrument and the manner in which the mass spectrum is displayed. The accurate mass (more appropriately, the measured accurate mass) is an experimentally determined mass that allows the elemental composition to be determined. For molecules with mass below 200 u, a 5 ppm accuracy is sufficient to uniquely determine the elemental composition.
Molar mass	Molar mass, symbol M, is a physical property of a given substance (chemical element or chemical compound), namely its mass per amount of substance. The base SI unit for mass is the kilogram and that for amount of substance is the mole. Thus, the derived unit for molar mass is kg/mol.
Stoichiometry	Stoichiometry is a branch of chemistry that deals with the relative quantities of reactants and products in chemical reactions. In a balanced chemical reaction, the relations among quantities of reactants and products typically form a ratio of whole numbers. For example, in a reaction that forms ammonia (NH_3), exactly one molecule of nitrogen (N_2) reacts with three molecules of hydrogen (H_2) to produce two molecules of NH_3: $N_2 + 3\,H_2 \rightarrow 2\,NH_3$ Stoichiometry can be used to find quantities such as the amount of products (in mass, moles, volume, etc).
Chemical reaction	A chemical reaction is a process that leads to the transformation of one set of chemical substances to another. Chemical reactions can be either spontaneous, requiring no input of energy, or non-spontaneous, typically following the input of some type of energy, such as heat, light or electricity.

Chapter 5. Gases

Mixture	In chemistry, a mixture is a material system made up by two or more different substances which are mixed but are not combined chemically. Mixture refers to the physical combination of two or more substances the identities of which are retained and are mixed in the form of alloys, solutions, suspensions, and colloids.
	Mixtures are the product of a mechanical blending or mixing of chemical substances like elements and compounds, without chemical bonding or other chemical change, so that each ingredient substance retains its own chemical properties and makeup.
Concentration	In chemistry, concentration is defined as the abundance of a constituent divided by the total volume of a mixture. Furthermore, in chemistry, four types of mathematical description can be distinguished: mass concentration, molar concentration, number concentration, and volume concentration. The term concentration can be applied to any kind of chemical mixture, but most frequently it refers to solutes in solutions.
Mole	The mole is a unit of measurement for the amount of substance or chemical amount. It is one of the base units in the International System of Units, and has the unit symbol mol.
	The name mole is an 1897 translation of the German unit Mol, coined by the chemist Wilhelm Ostwald in 1893, although the related concept of equivalent mass had been in use at least a century earlier.
Mole fraction	In chemistry, the mole fraction x_i is defined as the amount of a constituent n_i divided by the total amount of all constituents in a mixture n_{tot} : $$x_i = \frac{n_i}{n_{tot}}$$ The sum of all the mole fractions is equal to 1: $$\sum_{i=1}^{N} n_i = n_{tot}; \ \sum_{i=1}^{N} x_i = 1$$ The mole fraction is also called the amount fraction. It is identical to the number fraction, which is defined as the number of molecules of a constituent N_i divided by the total number of all molecules N_{tot}. It is one way of expressing the composition of a mixture with a dimensionless quantity (mass fraction is another).
Potassium	Potassium is the chemical element with the symbol K and atomic number 19. Elemental potassium is a soft silvery-white alkali metal that oxidizes rapidly in air and is very reactive with water, generating sufficient heat to ignite the hydrogen emitted in the reaction.

Chapter 5. Gases

Because potassium and sodium are chemically very similar, it took a long time before their salts were differentiated. The existence of multiple elements in their salts was suspected from 1702, and this was proven in 1807 when potassium and sodium were individually isolated from different salts by electrolysis.

Potassium chlorate	Potassium chlorate is a compound containing potassium, chlorine and oxygen atoms, with the molecular formula $KClO_3$. In its pure form, it is a white crystalline substance. It is the most common chlorate in industrial use.
Chlorate	The chlorate anion has the formula ClO-3. In this case, the chlorine atom is in the +5 oxidation state. 'Chlorate' can also refer to chemical compounds containing this anion; chlorates are the salts of chloric acid.
Vapor pressure	Vapor pressure is the pressure exerted by a vapor in thermodynamic equilibrium with its condensed phases (solid or liquid) at a given temperature in a closed system. The equilibrium vapor pressure is an indication of a liquid's evaporation rate. It relates to the tendency of particles to escape from the liquid .
Water vapor	Water vapor, also aqueous vapor, is the gas phase of water. It is one state of water within the hydrosphere. Water vapor can be produced from the evaporation or boiling of liquid water or from the sublimation of ice.
Nitrogen	Nitrogen is a chemical element that has the symbol N, atomic number of 7 and atomic mass 14.00674 u. Elemental nitrogen is a colorless, odorless, tasteless, and mostly inert diatomic gas at standard conditions, constituting 78.09% by volume of Earth's atmosphere. The element nitrogen was discovered as a separable component of air, by Scottish physician Daniel Rutherford, in 1772.
Joule	The joule is a derived unit of energy or work in the International System of Units. It is equal to the energy expended (or work done) in applying a force of one newton through a distance of one metre (1 newton metre or N·m), or in passing an electric current of one ampere through a resistance of one ohm for one second. he English physicist James Prescott Joule.
Kinetic energy	The kinetic energy of an object is the energy which it possesses due to its motion. It is defined as the work needed to accelerate a body of a given mass from rest to its stated velocity. Having gained this energy during its acceleration, the body maintains this kinetic energy unless its speed changes.

Chapter 5. Gases

Binding energy	Binding energy is the mechanical energy required to disassemble a whole into separate parts. A bound system typically has a lower potential energy than its constituent parts; this is what keeps the system together--often this means that energy is released upon the creation of a bound state. The usual convention is that this corresponds to a positive binding energy.
Nuclear binding energy	Nuclear binding energy is the energy required to split a nucleus of an atom into its component parts. The component parts are neutrons and protons, which are collectively called nucleons. The binding energy of nuclei is always a positive number, since all nuclei require net energy to separate them into individual protons and neutrons.
Thermal	A thermal column is a column of rising air in the lower altitudes of the Earth's atmosphere. Thermals are created by the uneven heating of the Earth's surface from solar radiation, and are an example of convection, specifically atmospheric convection. The Sun warms the ground, which in turn warms the air directly above it.
Root-mean-square speed	Root-mean-square speed is the measure of the speed of particles in a gas that is most convenient for problem solving within the kinetic theory of gases. It is defined as the square root of the average velocity-squared of the molecules in a gas. It is given by the formula $$v_{\text{rms}} = \sqrt{\dfrac{3RT}{M_m}}$$ where v_{rms} is the root mean square of the speed, M_m is the molar mass of the gas in kilograms per mole, R is the molar gas constant, and T is the temperature in kelvin.
Diffusion	Diffusion is one of several transport phenomena that occur in nature. A distinguishing feature of diffusion is that it results in mixing or mass transport without requiring bulk motion. Thus, diffusion should not be confused with convection or advection, which are other transport mechanisms that use bulk motion to move particles from one place to another.
Helium	Helium is the chemical element with atomic number 2 and an atomic weight of 4.002602, which is represented by the symbol He. It is a colorless, odorless, tasteless, non-toxic, inert, monatomic gas that heads the noble gas group in the periodic table. Its boiling and melting points are the lowest among the elements and it exists only as a gas except in extreme conditions.
Escape velocity	In physics, escape velocity is the speed at which the kinetic energy plus the gravitational potential energy of an object is zero. It is the speed needed to 'break free' from a gravitational field without further propulsion. For a spherically-symmetric body, escape velocity is calculated by the formula

Visit Cram101.com for full Practice Exams

Chapter 5. Gases

$$v_e = \sqrt{\frac{2GM}{r}},$$

where G is the universal gravitational constant ($G=6.67\times10^{-11}$ m^3 kg^{-1} s^{-2}), M the mass of the planet, star or other body, and r the distance from the center of gravity.

Velocity	In physics, velocity is speed in a given direction. Speed describes only how fast an object is moving, whereas velocity gives both the speed and direction of the object's motion. To have a constant velocity, an object must have a constant speed and motion in a constant direction.
Effusion	In physics, effusion is the process in which individual molecules flow through a hole without collisions between molecules. This occurs if the diameter of the hole is considerably smaller than the mean free path of the molecules. According to Graham's law, the rate at which gases effuse (i.e., how many molecules pass through the hole per second) is dependent on their molecular weight; gases with a lower molecular weight effuse more quickly than gases with a higher molecular weight.
Thomas Garnett	Thomas Garnett (1766-1802) was an English physician and natural philosopher. He was born 21 April 1766 at Casterton in Westmoreland, where his father had a small landed property. After attending Sedbergh School, he was at the age of fifteen articled at his own request to the celebrated John Dawson (surgeon) of Sedbergh, Yorkshire, surgeon and mathematician.
Van der Waals constants	The following table lists the van der Waals constants (from the van der Waals equation) for a number of common gases and volatile liquids. Units:1 J·m^3/mol^2 = 0.1 m^6·Pa/mol^2 = 10 L^2·bar/mol^{2}1 L^{2}atm/mol^2 = 101 325 J·m^3/kmol^2 = 101 325 Pa·m^6/kmol^{2}1 dm^3/mol = 1 L/mol = 1 m^3/kmol (where kmol is kilomoles = 1000 moles) Source: Weast. R. C. (Ed)., Handbook of Chemistry and Physics (53rd Edn)., Cleveland:Chemical Rubber Co., 1972.
Van der Waals equation	The van der Waals equation is an equation of state for a fluid composed of particles that have a non-zero volume and a pairwise attractive inter-particle force (such as the van der Waals force). It was derived by Johannes Diderik van der Waals in 1873, who received the Nobel prize in 1910 for 'his work on the equation of state for gases and liquids'. The equation is based on a modification of the ideal gas law and approximates the behavior of real fluids, taking into account the nonzero size of molecules and the attraction between them.

Chapter 5. Gases

1. _____, also aqueous vapor, is the gas phase of water. It is one state of water within the hydrosphere. _____ can be produced from the evaporation or boiling of liquid water or from the sublimation of ice.

   a. 1,2-Dioxetanedione
   b. Water dimer
   c. Water memory
   d. Water vapor

2. _____, FRS, (25 January 1627 - 31 December 1691) was a 17th-century natural philosopher, chemist, physicist, and inventor, also noted for his writings in theology. He has been variously described as Irish, English and Anglo-Irish, his father having come to Ireland from England during the time of the Plantations.

   Although his research clearly has its roots in the alchemical tradition, Boyle is largely regarded today as the first modern chemist, and therefore one of the founders of modern chemistry, and one of the pioneers of modern experimental scientific method.

   a. C. D. Broad
   b. Robert Boyle
   c. Jeffrey Bub
   d. Gerd Buchdahl

3. The _____ is a non-SI unit of pressure with the ratio of 760 to 1 standard atmosphere, chosen to be roughly equal to the fluid pressure exerted by a millimetre of mercury, i.e., a pressure of 1 _____ is approximately equal to 1 mmHg. Note that the symbol is spelled exactly the same as the unit, but the symbol is capitalized, as is customary in metric units derived from names. It was named after Evangelista Torricelli, an Italian physicist and mathematician who discovered the principle of the barometer in 1644.

   a. 1,2-Dioxetanedione
   b. N-Methylconiine
   c. MPTP
   d. Torr

4. _____ is a chemical compound with chemical formula HCN. It is a colorless, extremely poisonous liquid that boils slightly above room temperature at 26 °C (79 °F). _____ is a linear molecule, with a triple bond between carbon and nitrogen. A minor tautomer of HCN is HNC, hydrogen isocyanide.

   a. Zyklon B
   b. Silicon
   c. Hydrogen cyanide
   d. Phase-change material

5. . In chemistry, a _____ is a material system made up by two or more different substances which are mixed but are not combined chemically. _____ refers to the physical combination of two or more substances the identities of which are retained and are mixed in the form of alloys, solutions, suspensions, and colloids.

_____s are the product of a mechanical blending or mixing of chemical substances like elements and compounds, without chemical bonding or other chemical change, so that each ingredient substance retains its own chemical properties and makeup.

a. Dispersion
b. Mixture
c. Homogeneous
d. Pitch

ANSWER KEY
Chapter 5. Gases

1. d
2. b
3. d
4. c
5. b

You can take the complete Chapter Practice Test

for Chapter 5. Gases
on all key terms, persons, places, and concepts.

Online 99 Cents

http://www.epub14.1.20267.5.cram101.com/

Use www.Cram101.com for all your study needs

including Cram101's online interactive problem solving labs in

chemistry, statistics, mathematics, and more.

Chapter 6. Thermochemistry

CHAPTER OUTLINE: KEY TERMS, PEOPLE, PLACES, CONCEPTS

	Chemical energy
	Kinetic energy
	Potential
	Radiant energy
	Solar energy
	Thermal
	Thermal energy
	Conservation of energy
	Radiation
	Closed system
	Combustion
	Hydrogen
	Isolated system
	Open system
	Thermochemistry
	Molecule
	Endothermic
	Exothermic
	Mercury oxide

Chapter 6. Thermochemistry

CHAPTER OUTLINE: KEY TERMS, PEOPLE, PLACES, CONCEPTS

- Oxide
- First law of thermodynamics
- Thermodynamics
- Chemical reaction
- Thermodynamic state
- Internal energy
- Sulfur
- Methane
- Partial pressure
- Adiabatic process
- Snowmaking
- Enthalpy
- Thermochemical equation
- Calorimetry
- Heat capacity
- Calorimeter
- Calorie
- Carbon
- Graphite

Chapter 6. Thermochemistry

CHAPTER OUTLINE: KEY TERMS, PEOPLE, PLACES, CONCEPTS

_____	Oxygen
_____	Standard state
_____	Oxidation state
_____	Standard enthalpy of reaction
_____	Carbon dioxide
_____	Carbon monoxide
_____	Monoxide
_____	Thermite
_____	Solution
_____	Iodine
_____	Lattice energy
_____	Sulfur trioxide
_____	Trioxide

Chapter 6. Thermochemistry

Chemical energy	In chemistry, Chemical energy is the potential of a chemical substance to undergo a transformation through a chemical reaction or, to transform other chemical substances. Breaking or making of chemical bonds involves energy, which may be either absorbed or evolved from a chemical system. Energy that can be released because of a reaction between a set of chemical substances is equal to the difference between the energy content of the products and the reactants.
Kinetic energy	The kinetic energy of an object is the energy which it possesses due to its motion. It is defined as the work needed to accelerate a body of a given mass from rest to its stated velocity. Having gained this energy during its acceleration, the body maintains this kinetic energy unless its speed changes.
Potential	•In linguistics, the potential mood•The mathematical study of potentials is known as potential theory; it is the study of harmonic functions on manifolds. This mathematical formulation arises from the fact that, in physics, the scalar potential is irrotational, and thus has a vanishing Laplacian -- the very definition of a harmonic function.•In physics, a potential may refer to the scalar potential or to the vector potential. In either case, it is a field defined in space, from which many important physical properties may be derived.
Radiant energy	Radiant energy is the energy of electromagnetic waves. The quantity of radiant energy may be calculated by integrating radiant flux (or power) with respect to time and, like all forms of energy, its SI unit is the joule. The term is used particularly when radiation is emitted by a source into the surrounding environment.
Solar energy	Solar energy, radiant light and heat from the sun, has been harnessed by humans since ancient times using a range of ever-evolving technologies. Solar energy technologies include solar heating, solar photovoltaics, solar thermal electricity and solar architecture, which can make considerable contributions to solving some of the most urgent problems the world now faces. Solar technologies are broadly characterized as either passive solar or active solar depending on the way they capture, convert and distribute solar energy.
Thermal	A thermal column is a column of rising air in the lower altitudes of the Earth's atmosphere. Thermals are created by the uneven heating of the Earth's surface from solar radiation, and are an example of convection, specifically atmospheric convection. The Sun warms the ground, which in turn warms the air directly above it.
Thermal energy	Thermal energy is the part of the total internal energy of a thermodynamic system or sample of matter that results in the system temperature.

The internal energy, also often called the thermodynamic energy, includes other forms of energy in a thermodynamic system in addition to thermal energy, namely forms of potential energy that do not influence temperature, such as the chemical energy stored in its molecular structure and electronic configuration, intermolecular interactions associated with phase changes that do not influence temperature (i.e., latent energy), and the nuclear binding energy that binds the sub-atomic particles of matter.

Microscopically, the thermal energy is partly the kinetic energy of a system's constituent particles, which may be atoms, molecules, electrons, or particles in plasmas.

Conservation of energy	The law of conservation of energy, first formulated in the nineteenth century, is a law of physics. It states that the total amount of energy in an isolated system remains constant over time. The total energy is said to be conserved over time.
Radiation	In physics, radiation is a process in which energetic particles or energetic waves travel through a medium or space. Two types of radiation are commonly differentiated in the way they interact with normal chemical matter: ionizing and non-ionizing radiation. The word radiation is often colloquially used in reference to ionizing radiation but the term radiation may correctly also refer to non-ionizing radiation.
Closed system	The term closed system has different meanings in different contexts. In thermodynamics, a closed system can exchange energy (as heat or work), but not matter, with its surroundings. In contrast, an isolated system cannot exchange any of heat, work, or matter with the surroundings, while an open system can exchange all of heat, work and matter.
Combustion	Combustion or burning is the sequence of exothermic chemical reactions between a fuel and an oxidant accompanied by the production of heat and conversion of chemical species. The release of heat can result in the production of light in the form of either glowing or a flame. Fuels of interest often include organic compounds (especially hydrocarbons) in the gas, liquid or solid phase.
Hydrogen	Hydrogen is the chemical element with atomic number 1. It is represented by the symbol H. With an average atomic weight of 1.00794 u (1.007825 u for hydrogen-1), hydrogen is the lightest element and its monatomic form (H_1) is the most abundant chemical substance, constituting roughly 75% of the Universe's baryonic mass. Non-remnant stars are mainly composed of hydrogen in its plasma state.

Chapter 6. Thermochemistry

Isolated system	In the natural sciences an isolated system is a physical system without any external exchange - neither matter nor energy can enter or exit, but can only move around inside. Truly isolated systems cannot exist in nature, other than possibly the universe itself, and they are thus hypothetical concepts only. It obeys in particular the first of the conservation laws: its total energy - mass stays constant.
Open system	An open system is a system which continuously interacts with its environment. An open system should be contrasted with the concept of an isolated system which exchanges neither energy, matter,nor information with its environment. The concept of an 'open system' was formalized within a framework that enabled one to interrelate the theory of the organism, thermodynamics, and evolutionary theory.
Thermochemistry	Thermochemistry is the study of the energy and heat associated with chemical reactions and/or physical transformations. A reaction may release or absorb energy, and a phase change may do the same, such as in melting and boiling. Thermochemistry focuses on these energy changes, particularly on the system's energy exchange with its surroundings.
Molecule	A molecule is an electrically neutral group of two or more atoms held together by covalent chemical bonds. Molecules are distinguished from ions by their lack of electrical charge. However, in quantum physics, organic chemistry, and biochemistry, the term molecule is often used less strictly, also being applied to polyatomic ions.
Endothermic	In thermodynamics, the word endothermic describes a process or reaction in which the system absorbs energy from the surroundings in the form of heat. It is a modern coinage formed from Greek roots (as is often the case with scientific terminology). The prefix endo- derives from the Greek word 'endon' meaning 'within,' and the latter part of the word comes from the Greek word root 'therm' (θερμ-) meaning 'hot.' Hence it refers to a reaction that needs heat.
Exothermic	In thermodynamics, the term exothermic describes a process or reaction that releases energy from the system, usually in the form of heat, but also in the form of light (e.g. a spark, flame, or explosion), electricity (e.g. a battery), or sound (e.g. burning hydrogen). Its etymology stems from the prefix exo and the Greek word thermasi (meaning 'to heat'). The term exothermic was first coined by Marcellin Berthelot.
Mercury oxide	Mercury oxide, has a formula of HgO. It has a red or orange color. Mercury(II) oxide is a solid at room temperature and pressure. The mineral form montroydite is very rarely found.
Oxide	An oxide is a chemical compound that contains at least one oxygen atom and one other element in its chemical formula. Metal oxides typically contain an anion of oxygen in the oxidation state of -2.

Chapter 6. Thermochemistry

Most of the Earth's crust consists of solid oxides, the result of elements being oxidized by the oxygen in air or in water . Hydrocarbon combustion affords the two principal carbon oxides: carbon monoxide and carbon dioxide.

First law of thermodynamics	The first law of thermodynamics is a version of the law of conservation of energy, specialized for thermodynamical systems. It is usually formulated by stating that the change in the internal energy of a closed system is equal to the amount of heat supplied to the system, minus the amount of work performed by the system on its surroundings. The law of conservation of energy can be stated: The energy of an isolated system is constant.
Thermodynamics	Thermodynamics is the branch of natural science concerned with heat and its relation to other forms of energy and work. It defines macroscopic variables (such as temperature, entropy, and pressure) that describe average properties of material bodies and radiation, and explains how they are related and by what laws they change with time. Thermodynamics does not describe the microscopic constituents of matter, and its laws can be derived from statistical mechanics.
Chemical reaction	A chemical reaction is a process that leads to the transformation of one set of chemical substances to another. Chemical reactions can be either spontaneous, requiring no input of energy, or non-spontaneous, typically following the input of some type of energy, such as heat, light or electricity. Classically, chemical reactions encompass changes that strictly involve the motion of electrons in the forming and breaking of chemical bonds, although the general concept of a chemical reaction, in particular the notion of a chemical equation, is applicable to transformations of elementary particles (such as illustrated by Feynman diagrams), as well as nuclear reactions.
Thermodynamic state	ImgProperty databaseimg

A thermodynamic state is a set of values of properties of a thermodynamic system that must be specified to reproduce the system. The individual parameters are known as state variables, state parameters or thermodynamic variables. Once a sufficient set of thermodynamic variables have been specified, values of all other properties of the system are uniquely determined. |
| Internal energy | In thermodynamics, the internal energy is the total energy contained by a thermodynamic system. It is the energy needed to create the system, but excludes the energy to displace the system's surroundings, any energy associated with a move as a whole, or due to external force fields. Internal energy has two major components, kinetic energy and potential energy. |
| Sulfur | Sulfur or sulphur is the chemical element with atomic number 16. In the periodic table it is represented by the symbol S. It is an abundant, multivalent non-metal. |

Chapter 6. Thermochemistry

Under normal conditions, sulfur atoms form cyclic octatomic molecules with chemical formula S_8. Elemental sulfur is a bright yellow crystalline solid when at room temperature.

Methane	Methane is a chemical compound with the chemical formula CH4. It is the simplest alkane, the main component of natural gas, and probably the most abundant organic compound on earth. The relative abundance of methane makes it an attractive fuel. However, because it is a gas at normal conditions, methane is difficult to transport from its source.
Partial pressure	In a mixture of ideal gases, each gas has a partial pressure which is the pressure which the gas would have if it alone occupied the volume. The total pressure of a gas mixture is the sum of the partial pressures of each individual gas in the mixture.
	In chemistry, the partial pressure of a gas in a mixture of gases is defined as above.
Adiabatic process	Property database
	In thermodynamics, an adiabatic process is a conversion that occurs without input or release of heat within a system. Many rapid chemical and physical processes are described in this way. Such processes are usually followed or preceded by events that do involve heat.
Snowmaking	Snowmaking is the production of snow by forcing water and pressurized air through a 'snow gun' or 'snow cannon', on ski slopes. Snowmaking is mainly used at ski resorts to supplement natural snow. This allows ski resorts to improve the reliability of their snow cover and to extend their ski seasons.
Enthalpy	Enthalpy is a measure of the total energy of a thermodynamic system. It includes the internal energy, which is the energy required to create a system, and the amount of energy required to make room for it by displacing its environment and establishing its volume and pressure.
	Enthalpy is a thermodynamic potential.
Thermochemical equation	A Thermochemical Equation is a balanced stoichiometric chemical equation that includes the enthalpy change, ΔH. In variable form, a thermochemical equation would look like this:A + B → CΔH = (±) #
	Where {A, B, C} are the usual agents of a chemical equation with coefficients and '(±) #' is a positive or negative numerical value, usually with units of kJ.Understanding Aspects of Thermochemical Equations
	Enthalpy (H) is the transfer of energy in a reaction (for chemical reactions it is in the form of heat) and ΔH is the change in enthalpy. ΔH is a state function.

Chapter 6. Thermochemistry

Calorimetry	Calorimetry is the science of measuring the heat of chemical reactions or physical changes. Calorimetry is performed with a calorimeter. The word calorimetry is derived from the Latin word calor, meaning heat.
Heat capacity	Heat capacity or thermal capacity, is the measurable physical quantity that characterizes the amount of heat required to change a substance's temperature by a given amount. In the International System of Units (SI), heat capacity is expressed in units of joule(s) (J) per kelvin (K).
	Derived quantities that specify heat capacity as an intensive property, i.e., independent of the size of a sample, are the molar heat capacity, which is the heat capacity per mole of a pure substance, and the specific heat capacity, often simply called specific heat, which is the heat capacity per unit mass of a material.
Calorimeter	A calorimeter is an object used for calorimetry, or the process of measuring the heat of chemical reactions or physical changes as well as heat capacity. Differential scanning calorimeters, isothermal microcalorimeters, titration calorimeters and accelerated rate calorimeters are among the most common types. A simple calorimeter just consists of a thermometer attached to a metal container full of water suspended above a combustion chamber.
Calorie	The calorie is a pre-SI metric unit of energy. It was first defined by Nicolas Clément in 1824 as a unit of heat, entering French and English dictionaries between 1841 and 1867. In most fields its use is archaic, having been replaced by the SI unit of energy, the joule. However, in many countries it remains in common use as a unit of food energy.
Carbon	Carbon is the chemical element with symbol C and atomic number 6. As a member of group 14 on the periodic table, it is nonmetallic and tetravalent--making four electrons available to form covalent chemical bonds. There are three naturally occurring isotopes, with ^{12}C and ^{13}C being stable, while ^{14}C is radioactive, decaying with a half-life of about 5,730 years. Carbon is one of the few elements known since antiquity.
Graphite	The mineral graphite is an allotrope of carbon. It was named by Abraham Gottlob Werner in 1789 from the Ancient Greek γρ?φω (grapho), 'to draw/write', for its use in pencils, where it is commonly called lead (not to be confused with the metallic element lead). Unlike diamond (another carbon allotrope), graphite is an electrical conductor, a semimetal.
Oxygen	Oxygen is the element with atomic number 8 and represented by the symbol O.

Chapter 6. Thermochemistry

Its name derives from the Greek roots ?ξ?ς (oxys) ('acid', literally 'sharp', referring to the sour taste of acids) and -γεν?ς (-genes) ('producer', literally 'begetter'), because at the time of naming, it was mistakenly thought that all acids required oxygen in their composition. At standard temperature and pressure, two atoms of the element bind to form dioxygen, a very pale blue, odorless, tasteless diatomic gas with the formula O_2.

Oxygen is a member of the chalcogen group on the periodic table and is a highly reactive nonmetallic element that readily forms compounds (notably oxides) with almost all other elements.

Standard state

In chemistry, the standard state of a material (pure substance, mixture or solution) is a reference point used to calculate its properties under different conditions. In principle, the choice of standard state is arbitrary, although the International Union of Pure and Applied Chemistry (IUPAC) recommends a conventional set of standard states for general use. IUPAC recommends using a standard pressure p^0 = 1 bar (100 kilopascals).

Oxidation state

In chemistry, the oxidation state is an indicator of the degree of oxidation of an atom in a chemical compound. The formal oxidation state is the hypothetical charge that an atom would have if all bonds to atoms of different elements were 100% ionic. Oxidation states are typically represented by integers, which can be positive, negative, or zero.

Standard enthalpy of reaction

The standard enthalpy of reaction is the enthalpy change that occurs in a system when one mole of matter is transformed by a chemical reaction under standard conditions.

For a generic chemical reaction $-v_A$ A + $-v_B$ B + ... → v_P P + v_Q Q ...

the standard enthalpy of reaction $\Delta_r H^?$ is related to the standard enthalpy of formation $\Delta_f H^0$ of the reactants and products by the following equation:

$$\Delta_r H^\ominus = \sum_B v_B \Delta_f H^\ominus (B)$$

In this equation, v_B is the stoichiometric coefficient of entity B.

A similar enthalpy change is the standard enthalpy of formation, which has been determined for a vast number of substances. The enthalpy change of any reaction under any conditions can be computed, given the standard enthalpy of formation of the reactants and products.

Carbon dioxide

Carbon dioxide is a naturally occurring chemical compound composed of two oxygen atoms covalently bonded to a single carbon atom. It is a gas at standard temperature and pressure and exists in Earth's atmosphere in this state, as a trace gas at a concentration of 0.039% by volume.

As part of the carbon cycle known as photosynthesis, plants, algae, and cyanobacteria absorb carbon dioxide, light, and water to produce carbohydrate energy for themselves and oxygen as a waste product.

| Carbon monoxide | Carbon monoxide also called carbonous oxide, is a colorless, odorless, and tasteless gas which is slightly lighter than air. It is highly toxic to humans and animals in higher quantities, although it is also produced in normal animal metabolism in low quantities, and is thought to have some normal biological functions. |

Carbon monoxide consists of one carbon atom and one oxygen atom, connected by a triple bond which consists of two covalent bonds as well as one dative covalent bond.

| Monoxide | A monoxide is any oxide containing just one atom of oxygen in the molecule. For example, Potassium oxide (K_2O), has only one atom of oxygen, and is thus a monoxide. Water (H_2O) is also a monoxide. |

| Thermite | Thermite is a pyrotechnic composition of a metal powder and a metal oxide that produces an exothermic oxidation-reduction reaction known as a thermite reaction. If aluminium is the reducing agent it is called an aluminothermic reaction. Most varieties are not explosive, but can create bursts of extremely high temperatures focused on a very small area for a short period of time. |

| Solution | In chemistry, a solution is a homogeneous mixture composed of only one phase. In such a mixture, a solute is a substance dissolved in another substance, known as a solvent. The solvent does the dissolving. |

| Iodine | |

Iodine is a chemical element with the symbol I and atomic number 53./ syllable break' style='border-bottom:1px dotted'>.?da?n-o-dyne, 'a?.?d?n-o-d?n, or 'a?.?di?n-o-deen in both American and British English. The name is from Greek ?οειδ?ς ioeides, meaning violet or purple, due to the color of elemental iodine vapor.

Iodine and its compounds are primarily used in nutrition, and industrially in the production of acetic acid and certain polymers.

| Lattice energy | The lattice energy of a ionic solid is a measure of the strength of bonds in that ionic compound. It is usually defined as the enthalpy of formation of the ionic compound from gaseous ions and as such is invariably exothermic. |

Chapter 6. Thermochemistry

Sulfur trioxide	Sulfur trioxide is the chemical compound with the formula SO_3. In the gaseous form, this species is a significant pollutant, being the primary agent in acid rain. It is prepared on massive scales as a precursor to sulfuric acid.
Trioxide	A trioxide is a compound with three oxygen atoms. For metals with the M_2O_3 formula there are several common structures. Al_2O_3, Cr_2O_3, Fe_2O_3, and V_2O_3 adopt the corundum structure.

1. In thermodynamics, the word _____ describes a process or reaction in which the system absorbs energy from the surroundings in the form of heat. It is a modern coinage formed from Greek roots (as is often the case with scientific terminology). The prefix endo- derives from the Greek word 'endon' meaning 'within,' and the latter part of the word comes from the Greek word root 'therm' (θερμ-) meaning 'hot.' Hence it refers to a reaction that needs heat.

   a. Energy accounting
   b. Energy carrier
   c. Energy quality
   d. Endothermic

2. The law of _____, first formulated in the nineteenth century, is a law of physics. It states that the total amount of energy in an isolated system remains constant over time. The total energy is said to be conserved over time.

   a. 1,2-Dioxetanedione
   b. Thermal equilibrium
   c. Thermal expansion
   d. Conservation of energy

3. _____ also called carbonous oxide, is a colorless, odorless, and tasteless gas which is slightly lighter than air. It is highly toxic to humans and animals in higher quantities, although it is also produced in normal animal metabolism in low quantities, and is thought to have some normal biological functions.

   _____ consists of one carbon atom and one oxygen atom, connected by a triple bond which consists of two covalent bonds as well as one dative covalent bond.

   a. Herbicide
   b. Carbon monoxide
   c. 1,2-Dioxetanedione
   d. Chloromethane

4. .

_____ is the chemical element with atomic number 1. It is represented by the symbol H. With an average atomic weight of 1.00794 u (1.007825 u for _____-1), _____ is the lightest element and its monatomic form (H_1) is the most abundant chemical substance, constituting roughly 75% of the Universe's baryonic mass. Non-remnant stars are mainly composed of _____ in its plasma state.

At standard temperature and pressure, _____ is a colorless, odorless, tasteless, non-toxic, nonmetallic, highly combustible diatomic gas with the molecular formula H_2.

a. Potassium
b. Silicon
c. Hydrogen
d. Sulfate crust

5. In chemistry, the _____ is an indicator of the degree of oxidation of an atom in a chemical compound. The formal _____ is the hypothetical charge that an atom would have if all bonds to atoms of different elements were 100% ionic. _____s are typically represented by integers, which can be positive, negative, or zero.

a. Oxidation state
b. Steam digester
c. Supersaturation
d. Sympathetic cooling

1. d
2. d
3. b
4. c
5. a

You can take the complete Chapter Practice Test

for Chapter 6. Thermochemistry
on all key terms, persons, places, and concepts.

Online 99 Cents

http://www.epub14.1.20267.6.cram101.com/

Use www.Cram101.com for all your study needs

including Cram101's online interactive problem solving labs in

chemistry, statistics, mathematics, and more.

Chapter 7. Quantum Theory and the Electronic Structure of Atoms

_____ Amplitude

_____ Frequency

_____ Planck

_____ Quantum

_____ Wavelength

_____ Electromagnetic radiation

_____ Magnetic field

_____ Radiation

_____ Spectrum

_____ Photoelectric effect

_____ Photon

_____ Work function

_____ Bohr model

_____ Hydrogen

_____ Hydrogen atom

_____ Atom

_____ Diffusion

_____ Emission spectrum

_____ Partial pressure

Chapter 7. Quantum Theory and the Electronic Structure of Atoms

CHAPTER OUTLINE: KEY TERMS, PEOPLE, PLACES, CONCEPTS

Transuranium element

Ground state

Principal quantum number

Quantum number

Rydberg constant

Balmer series

Density

Electron

Electron density

Lanthanide

Ruby laser

Laser

Thomson

Electron microscope

Scanning electron microscope

Microscope

Werner Heisenberg

Uncertainty principle

Probability

_____ | Quantum mechanics

_____ | Wave function

_____ | Mechanic

_____ | Atomic orbital

_____ | Angular momentum

_____ | Magnetic quantum number

_____ | Momentum

_____ | Ozone

_____ | Cytosine

_____ | Aufbau principle

_____ | Electron configuration

_____ | Magnetism

_____ | Pauli exclusion principle

_____ | Diamagnetism

_____ | Paramagnetism

_____ | Shielding effect

_____ | Immunodeficiency

_____ | Atomic theory

_____ | Noble gas

	Chromium
	Isomer
	Actinide
	Quantum dot
	Corona
	Helium

CHAPTER HIGHLIGHTS & NOTES: KEY TERMS, PEOPLE, PLACES, CONCEPTS

Amplitude	Amplitude is the magnitude of change in the oscillating variable with each oscillation within an oscillating system. For example, sound waves in air are oscillations in atmospheric pressure and their amplitudes are proportional to the change in pressure during one oscillation. If a variable undergoes regular oscillations, and a graph of the system is drawn with the oscillating variable as the vertical axis and time as the horizontal axis, the amplitude is visually represented by the vertical distance between the extrema of the curve and the equilibrium value.
Frequency	Frequency is the number of occurrences of a repeating event per unit time. It is also referred to as temporal frequency. The period is the duration of one cycle in a repeating event, so the period is the reciprocal of the frequency.
Planck	Planck is a space observatory of the European Space Agency (ESA) and designed to observe the anisotropies of the cosmic microwave background (CMB) over the entire sky, at a high sensitivity and angular resolution. Planck was built in the Cannes Mandelieu Space Center by Thales Alenia Space and created as the third Medium-Sized Mission (M3) of the European Space Agency's Horizon 2000 Scientific Programme. The project, initially called COBRAS/SAMBA, is named in honour of the German physicist Max Planck (1858-1947), who won the Nobel Prize for Physics in 1918.
Quantum	In physics, a quantum is the minimum amount of any physical entity involved in an interaction.

Chapter 7. Quantum Theory and the Electronic Structure of Atoms

	Behind this, one finds the fundamental notion that a physical property may be 'quantized,' referred to as 'the hypothesis of quantization'. This means that the magnitude can take on only certain discrete values.
Wavelength	In physics, the wavelength of a sinusoidal wave is the spatial period of the wave--the distance over which the wave's shape repeats. It is usually determined by considering the distance between consecutive corresponding points of the same phase, such as crests, troughs, or zero crossings, and is a characteristic of both traveling waves and standing waves, as well as other spatial wave patterns. Wavelength is commonly designated by the Greek letter lambda (λ).
Electromagnetic radiation	Electromagnetic radiation is a form of energy emitted and absorbed by charged particles, which exhibits wave-like behavior as it travels through space. EMR has both electric and magnetic field components, which stand in a fixed ratio of intensity to each other, and which oscillate in phase perpendicular to each other and perpendicular to the direction of energy and wave propagation. In vacuum, electromagnetic radiation propagates at a characteristic speed, the speed of light.
Magnetic field	A magnetic field is a mathematical description of the magnetic influence of electric currents and magnetic materials. The magnetic field at any given point is specified by both a direction and a magnitude ; as such it is a vector field. The magnetic field is most commonly defined in terms of the Lorentz force it exerts on moving electric charges.
Radiation	In physics, radiation is a process in which energetic particles or energetic waves travel through a medium or space. Two types of radiation are commonly differentiated in the way they interact with normal chemical matter: ionizing and non-ionizing radiation. The word radiation is often colloquially used in reference to ionizing radiation but the term radiation may correctly also refer to non-ionizing radiation.
Spectrum	A spectrum is a condition that is not limited to a specific set of values but can vary infinitely within a continuum. The word saw its first scientific use within the field of optics to describe the rainbow of colors in visible light when separated using a prism; it has since been applied by analogy to many fields other than optics. Thus, one might talk about the spectrum of political opinion, or the spectrum of activity of a drug, or the autism spectrum.
Photoelectric effect	In the photoelectric effect, electrons are emitted from matter (metals and non-metallic solids, liquids or gases) as a consequence of their absorption of energy from electromagnetic radiation of very short wavelength, such as visible or ultraviolet radiation. Electrons emitted in this manner may be referred to as photoelectrons. First observed by Heinrich Hertz in 1887, the phenomenon is also known as the Hertz effect, although the latter term has fallen out of general use.
Photon	In physics, a photon is an elementary particle, the quantum of light and all other forms of electromagnetic radiation, and the force carrier for the electromagnetic force.

	The effects of this force are easily observable at both the microscopic and macroscopic level, because the photon has no rest mass; this allows for interactions at long distances. Like all elementary particles, photons are currently best explained by quantum mechanics and exhibit wave-particle duality, exhibiting properties of both waves and particles.
Work function	In solid-state physics, the work function is the minimum energy (usually measured in electron volts) needed to remove an electron from a solid to a point immediately outside the solid surface (or energy needed to move an electron from the Fermi level into vacuum). Here 'immediately' means that the final electron position is far from the surface on the atomic scale but still close to the solid on the macroscopic scale. The work function is a characteristic property for any solid phase of a substance with a conduction band (whether empty or partly filled).
Bohr model	In atomic physics, the Bohr model, introduced by Niels Bohr in 1913, depicts the atom as a small, positively charged nucleus surrounded by electrons that travel in circular orbits around the nucleus--similar in structure to the solar system, but with electrostatic forces providing attraction, rather than gravity. This was an improvement on the earlier cubic model (1902), the plum-pudding model (1904), the Saturnian model (1904), and the Rutherford model (1911). Since the Bohr model is a quantum-physics-based modification of the Rutherford model, many sources combine the two, referring to the Rutherford-Bohr model.
Hydrogen	Hydrogen is the chemical element with atomic number 1. It is represented by the symbol H. With an average atomic weight of 1.00794 u (1.007825 u for hydrogen-1), hydrogen is the lightest element and its monatomic form (H_1) is the most abundant chemical substance, constituting roughly 75% of the Universe's baryonic mass. Non-remnant stars are mainly composed of hydrogen in its plasma state. At standard temperature and pressure, hydrogen is a colorless, odorless, tasteless, non-toxic, nonmetallic, highly combustible diatomic gas with the molecular formula H_2.
Hydrogen atom	A hydrogen atom is an atom of the chemical element hydrogen. The electrically neutral atom contains a single positively-charged proton and a single negatively-charged electron bound to the nucleus by the Coulomb force. Atomic hydrogen comprises about 75% of the elemental mass of the universe.
Atom	The atom is a basic unit of matter that consists of a dense central nucleus surrounded by a cloud of negatively charged electrons. The atomic nucleus contains a mix of positively charged protons and electrically neutral neutrons (except in the case of hydrogen-1, which is the only stable nuclide with no neutrons).

Chapter 7. Quantum Theory and the Electronic Structure of Atoms

Diffusion	Diffusion is one of several transport phenomena that occur in nature. A distinguishing feature of diffusion is that it results in mixing or mass transport without requiring bulk motion. Thus, diffusion should not be confused with convection or advection, which are other transport mechanisms that use bulk motion to move particles from one place to another.
Emission spectrum	The emission spectrum of a chemical element or chemical compound is the spectrum of frequencies of electromagnetic radiation emitted by the element's atoms or the compound's molecules when they are returned to a lower energy state. Each element's emission spectrum is unique. Therefore, spectroscopy can be used to identify the elements in matter of unknown composition.
Partial pressure	In a mixture of ideal gases, each gas has a partial pressure which is the pressure which the gas would have if it alone occupied the volume. The total pressure of a gas mixture is the sum of the partial pressures of each individual gas in the mixture. In chemistry, the partial pressure of a gas in a mixture of gases is defined as above.
Transuranium element	In chemistry, transuranium elements (also known as transuranic elements) are the chemical elements with atomic numbers greater than 92 (the atomic number of uranium). None of these elements are stable and each of them decays radioactively into other elements. Of the elements with atomic numbers 1 to 92, all can be found in nature, having stable (such as hydrogen), or very long half-life (such as polonium) isotopes, or are created as common products of the decay of uranium and thorium (such as radon).
Ground state	The ground state of a quantum mechanical system is its lowest-energy state; the energy of the ground state is known as the zero-point energy of the system. An excited state is any state with energy greater than the ground state. The ground state of a quantum field theory is usually called the vacuum state or the vacuum.
Principal quantum number	In the principal quantum number symbolized as n is the first of a set of quantum numbers (which includes: the principal quantum number, the azimuthal quantum number, the magnetic quantum number, and the spin quantum number) of an atomic orbital. The principal quantum number can only have positive integer values. As n increases, the orbital becomes larger and the electron spends more time farther from the nucleus.
Quantum number	Quantum numbers describe values of conserved quantities in the dynamics of the quantum system. Perhaps the most peculiar aspect of quantum mechanics is the quantization of observable quantities, since quantum numbers are discrete sets of integers or half-integers.

Chapter 7. Quantum Theory and the Electronic Structure of Atoms

CHAPTER HIGHLIGHTS & NOTES: KEY TERMS, PEOPLE, PLACES, CONCEPTS

Rydberg constant	The Rydberg constant, symbol R_∞, is a physical constant relating to atomic spectra, in the science of spectroscopy. The constant first arose as an empirical fitting parameter in the Rydberg formula for the hydrogen spectral series, but Niels Bohr later showed that its value could be calculated from more fundamental constants, explaining the relationship via his 'Bohr model'. As of 2010, R_∞ is the most accurately measured fundamental physical constant.
Balmer series	The Balmer series, is the designation of one of a set of six different named series describing the spectral line emissions of the hydrogen atom. The Balmer series is calculated using the Balmer formula, an empirical equation discovered by Johann Balmer in 1885. The visible spectrum of light from hydrogen displays four wavelengths, 410 nm, 434 nm, 486 nm, and 656 nm, that correspond to emissions of photons by electrons in excited states transitioning to the quantum level described by the principal quantum number n equals 2. There are also a number of ultraviolet Balmer lines with wavelengths shorter than 400 nm.
Density	The mass density is defined as its mass per unit volume. The symbol most often used for density is ρ. In some cases (for instance, in the United States oil and gas industry), density is also defined as its weight per unit volume; although, this quantity is more properly called specific weight.
Electron	The electron is a subatomic particle with a negative elementary electric charge. It has no known components or substructure; in other words, it is generally thought to be an elementary particle. An electron has a mass that is approximately 1/1836 that of the proton.
Electron density	Electron density is the measure of the probability of an electron being present at a specific location. In molecules, regions of electron density are usually found around the atom, and its bonds. In delocalized or conjugated systems, such as phenol, benzene and compounds such as hemoglobin and chlorophyll, the electron density covers an entire region, i.e., in benzene they are found above and below the planar ring.
Lanthanide	The lanthanide, from lanthanum through lutetium. These fifteen lanthanide elements, along with the chemically similar elements scandium and yttrium, are often collectively known as the rare earth elements. The informal chemical symbol Ln is used in general discussions of lanthanide chemistry to refer to any lanthanide.
Ruby laser	A ruby laser is a solid-state laser that uses a synthetic ruby crystal as its gain medium.

Chapter 7. Quantum Theory and the Electronic Structure of Atoms

The first working laser was a ruby laser made by Theodore H. 'Ted' Maiman at Hughes Research Laboratories on May 16, 1960.

Ruby lasers produce pulses of visible light at a wavelength of 694.3 nm, which is a deep red color.

Laser

A laser is a device that emits light (electromagnetic radiation) through a process of optical amplification based on the stimulated emission of photons. The term 'laser' originated as an acronym for Light Amplification by Stimulated Emission of Radiation. The emitted laser light is notable for its high degree of spatial and temporal coherence, unattainable using other technologies.

Thomson

The thomson (symbol: Th) is a unit that has appeared infrequently in scientific literature relating to the field of mass spectrometry as a unit of mass-to-charge ratio. The unit was proposed by Cooks and Rockwood naming it in honour of J. J. Thomson who measured the mass-to-charge ratio of electrons and ions.

The thomson is defined as

$$1 \text{ Th} = 1 \, \frac{u}{e} = 1 \, \frac{Da}{e} = 1.036426 \times 10^{-8} \, kg \, C^{-1}$$

where u represents the unified atomic mass unit, Da represents the unit dalton, and e represents the elementary charge which is the electric charge unit in the atomic unit system.

Electron microscope

An electron microscope is a type of microscope that uses a beam of electrons to illuminate the specimen and produce a magnified image. Electron microscopes (EM) have a greater resolving power than a light-powered optical microscope, because electrons have wavelengths about 100,000 times shorter than visible light (photons), and can achieve better than 50 pm resolution and magnifications of up to about 10,000,000x, whereas ordinary, non-confocal light microscopes are limited by diffraction to about 200 nm resolution and useful magnifications below 2000x.

The electron microscope uses electrostatic and electromagnetic 'lenses' to control the electron beam and focus it to form an image.

Scanning electron microscope

A scanning electron microscope is a type of electron microscope that images a sample by scanning it with a beam of electrons in a raster scan pattern. The electrons interact with the atoms that make up the sample producing signals that contain information about the sample's surface topography, composition, and other properties such as electrical conductivity.

Chapter 7. Quantum Theory and the Electronic Structure of Atoms

CHAPTER HIGHLIGHTS & NOTES: KEY TERMS, PEOPLE, PLACES, CONCEPTS

Microscope	A microscope is an instrument used to see objects that are too small for the naked eye. The science of investigating small objects using such an instrument is called microscopy. Microscopic means invisible to the eye unless aided by a microscope.
Werner Heisenberg	Werner Heisenberg was a German theoretical physicist who made foundational contributions to quantum mechanics and is best known for asserting the uncertainty principle of quantum theory. In addition, he made important contributions to nuclear physics, quantum field theory, and particle physics. Heisenberg, along with Max Born and Pascual Jordan, set forth the matrix formulation of quantum mechanics in 1925. Heisenberg was awarded the 1932 Nobel Prize in Physics for his contributions to quantum mechanics, and its application especially to the discovery of the allotropic forms of hydrogen.
Uncertainty principle	In quantum mechanics, the uncertainty principle is any of a variety of mathematical inequalities asserting a fundamental limit on the precision with which certain pairs of physical properties of a particle, such as position x and momentum p, can be simultaneously known. The more precisely the position of some particle is determined, the less precisely its momentum can be known, and vice versa. The original heuristic argument that such a limit should exist was given by Werner Heisenberg in 1927. A more formal inequality relating the standard deviation of position σ_x and the standard deviation of momentum σ_p was derived by Kennard later that year (and independently by Weyl in 1928), $$\sigma_x \sigma_p \geq \frac{\hbar}{2},$$ where h is the reduced Planck constant.
Probability	Probability is ordinarily used to describe an attitude of mind towards some proposition of whose truth is not certain. The proposition of interest is usually of the form 'Will a specific event occur?' The attitude of mind is of the form 'How certain are we that the event will occur?' The certainty we adopt can be described in terms of a numerical measure and this number, between 0 and 1, we call probability. The higher the probability of an event, the more certain we are that the event will occur.
Quantum mechanics	Quantum mechanics is a branch of physics dealing with physical phenomena where the action is on the order of the Planck constant. Quantum mechanics departs from classical mechanics primarily at the quantum realm of atomic and subatomic length scales. QM provides a mathematical description of much of the dual particle-like and wave-like behavior and interactions of energy and matter.

Chapter 7. Quantum Theory and the Electronic Structure of Atoms

Wave function	A wave function is a probability amplitude in quantum mechanics describing the quantum state of a particle and how it behaves. Typically, its values are complex numbers and, for a single particle, it is a function of space and time. The laws of quantum mechanics (the Schrödinger equation) describe how the wave function evolves over time.
Mechanic	A mechanic is a tradesman, craftsman, or technician who uses tools to build or repair machinery. Many mechanics are specialized in a particular field such as auto mechanics, bicycle mechanics, motorcycle mechanics, boiler mechanics, general mechanics, industrial maintenance mechanics (millwrights), air conditioning and refrigeration mechanics, aircraft mechanics, diesel mechanics, and tank mechanics in the armed services. Auto mechanics, for example, have many trades within.
Atomic orbital	An atomic orbital is a mathematical function that describes the wave-like behavior of either one electron or a pair of electrons in an atom. This function can be used to calculate the probability of finding any electron of an atom in any specific region around the atom's nucleus. The term may also refer to the physical region where the electron can be calculated to be, as defined by the particular mathematical form of the orbital.
Angular momentum	In physics, angular momentum, moment of momentum, or rotational momentum is a vector quantity that can be used to describe the overall state of a physical system. The angular momentum L of a particle with respect to some point of origin is $$L = r \times p = r \times mv,$$ where r is the particle's position from the origin, p = mv is its linear momentum, and × denotes the cross product. The angular momentum of a system of particles (e.g. a rigid body) is the sum of angular momenta of the individual particles.
Magnetic quantum number	In atomic physics, the magnetic quantum number is the third of a set of quantum numbers (the principal quantum number, the azimuthal quantum number, the magnetic quantum number, and the spin quantum number) which describe the unique quantum state of an electron and is designated by the letter m. The magnetic quantum number denotes the energy levels available within a subshell. There are a set of quantum numbers associated with the energy states of the atom.
Momentum	In classical mechanics, linear momentum or translational momentum is the product of the mass and velocity of an object: $P \equiv mv$.

Like velocity, linear momentum is a vector quantity, possessing a direction as well as a magnitude. Linear momentum is also a conserved quantity, meaning that if a closed system is not affected by external forces, its total linear momentum cannot change.

Ozone

Ozone or trioxygen, is a triatomic molecule, consisting of three oxygen atoms. It is an allotrope of oxygen that is much less stable than the diatomic allotrope (O_2), breaking down with a half life of about half an hour in the lower atmosphere, to normal dioxygen. Ozone is formed from dioxygen by the action of ultraviolet light and also atmospheric electrical discharges, and is present in low concentrations throughout the Earth's atmosphere.

Cytosine

Cytosine is one of the four main bases found in DNA and RNA, along with adenine, guanine, and thymine (uracil in RNA). It is a pyrimidine derivative, with a heterocyclic aromatic ring and two substituents attached (an amine group at position 4 and a keto group at position 2). The nucleoside of cytosine is cytidine.

Aufbau principle

The Aufbau principle is used to determine the electron configuration of an atom, molecule or ion. The principle postulates a hypothetical process in which an atom is 'built up' by progressively adding electrons. As they are added, they assume their most stable conditions (electron orbitals) with respect to the nucleus and those electrons already there.

Electron configuration

In atomic physics and quantum chemistry, the electron configuration is the distribution of electrons of an atom or molecule in atomic or molecular orbitals. For example, the electron configuration of the neon atom is $1s^2 2s^2 2p^6$.

According to the laws of quantum mechanics, an energy is associated with each electron configuration and, upon certain conditions, electrons are able to move from one orbital to another by emission or absorption of a quantum of energy, in the form of a photon.

Magnetism

Magnetism is a property of materials that respond to an applied magnetic field. Permanent magnets have persistent magnetic fields caused by ferromagnetism. That is the strongest and most familiar type of magnetism.

Pauli exclusion principle

The Pauli exclusion principle is the quantum mechanical principle that no two identical fermions (particles with half-integer spin) may occupy the same quantum state simultaneously. A more rigorous statement is that the total wave function for two identical fermions is anti-symmetric with respect to exchange of the particles. The principle was formulated by Austrian physicist Wolfgang Pauli in 1925.

Diamagnetism

Diamagnetism is the property of an object or material which causes it to create a magnetic field in opposition to an externally applied magnetic field.

Diamagnetism is believed to be due to quantum mechanics (and is understood in terms of Landau levels) and occurs because the external field alters the orbital velocity of electrons around their nuclei, thus changing the magnetic dipole moment. According to Lenz's law, the field of these electrons will oppose the magnetic field changes provided by the applied field.

Paramagnetism

Paramagnetism is a form of magnetism whereby the paramagnetic material is only attracted when in the presence of an externally applied magnetic field. In contrast with this behavior, diamagnetic materials are repelled by magnetic fields. Paramagnetic materials have a relative magnetic permeability greater or equal to unity (i.e., a positive magnetic susceptibility) and hence are attracted to magnetic fields.

Shielding effect

The shielding effect describes the decrease in attraction between an electron and the nucleus in any atom with more than one electron shell. It is also referred to as the screening effect or atomic shielding.

In hydrogen-like atoms (those with only one electron), the net force on the electron is just as large as the electric attraction from the nucleus.

Immunodeficiency

Immunodeficiency is a state in which the immune system's ability to fight infectious disease is compromised or entirely absent. Most cases of immunodeficiency are acquired ('secondary') but some people are born with defects in their immune system, or primary immunodeficiency. Transplant patients take medications to suppress their immune system as an anti-rejection measure, as do some patients suffering from an over-active immune system. A person who has an immunodeficiency of any kind is said to be immunocompromised. An immunocompromised person may be particularly vulnerable to opportunistic infections, in addition to normal infections that could affect everyone.

Atomic theory

In chemistry and physics, atomic theory is a theory of the nature of matter, which states that matter is composed of discrete units called atoms, as opposed to the obsolete notion that matter could be divided into any arbitrarily small quantity. It began as a philosophical concept in ancient Greece (Democritus) and India and entered the scientific mainstream in the early 19th century when discoveries in the field of chemistry showed that matter did indeed behave as if it were made up of particles.

The word 'atom' was applied to the basic particle that constituted a chemical element, because the chemists of the era believed that these were the fundamental particles of matter.

Noble gas

The noble gases are a group of chemical elements with very similar properties: under standard conditions, they are all odorless, colorless, monatomic gases, with very low chemical reactivity.

The six noble gases that occur naturally are helium (He), neon (Ne), argon (Ar), krypton (Kr), xenon (Xe), and the radioactive radon (Rn).

For the first six periods of the periodic table, the noble gases are exactly the members of group 18 of the periodic table.

Chromium

Chromium is a chemical element which has the symbol Cr and atomic number 24. It is the first element in Group 6. It is a steely-gray, lustrous, hard metal that takes a high polish and has a high melting point. It is also odorless, tasteless, and malleable. The name of the element is derived from the Greek word 'chroma' , meaning colour, because many of its compounds are intensely coloured.

Isomer

In chemistry, isomers are compounds with the same molecular formula but different structural formulas. Isomers do not necessarily share similar properties, unless they also have the same functional groups. There are many different classes of isomers, like stereoisomers, enantiomers, geometrical isomers, etc.

Actinide

The actinide, actinium through lawrencium.

The actinide series derives its name from the group 3 element actinium. All but one of the actinides are f-block elements, corresponding to the filling of the 5f electron shell; lawrencium, a d-block element, is also generally considered an actinide.

Quantum dot

Nanotechnology

A quantum dot is a portion of matter (e.g., semiconductor) whose excitons are confined in all three spatial dimensions. Consequently, such materials have electronic properties intermediate between those of bulk semiconductors and those of discrete molecules. They were discovered at the beginning of the 1980s by Alexei Ekimov in a glass matrix and by Louis E. Brus in colloidal solutions.

Corona

A corona is a type of plasma 'atmosphere' of the Sun or other celestial body, extending millions of kilometers into space, most easily seen during a total solar eclipse, but also observable in a coronagraph. The Latin root of the word corona means crown.

The high temperature of the corona gives it unusual spectral features, which led some to suggest, in the 19th century, that it contained a previously unknown element, 'coronium'.

Helium

Chapter 7. Quantum Theory and the Electronic Structure of Atoms

Helium is the chemical element with atomic number 2 and an atomic weight of 4.002602, which is represented by the symbol He. It is a colorless, odorless, tasteless, non-toxic, inert, monatomic gas that heads the noble gas group in the periodic table. Its boiling and melting points are the lowest among the elements and it exists only as a gas except in extreme conditions.

1. A _____ is an atom of the chemical element hydrogen. The electrically neutral atom contains a single positively-charged proton and a single negatively-charged electron bound to the nucleus by the Coulomb force. Atomic hydrogen comprises about 75% of the elemental mass of the universe.

   a. Hydrogen damage
   b. Hydrogen deuteride
   c. Hydrogen embrittlement
   d. Hydrogen atom

2. A _____ is a mathematical description of the magnetic influence of electric currents and magnetic materials. The _____ at any given point is specified by both a direction and a magnitude ; as such it is a vector field. The _____ is most commonly defined in terms of the Lorentz force it exerts on moving electric charges.

   a. Magnetic flux
   b. Magnetic helicity
   c. Magnetic field
   d. Magnetic susceptibility

3. A _____ is a tradesman, craftsman, or technician who uses tools to build or repair machinery. Many _____s are specialized in a particular field such as auto _____s, bicycle _____s, motorcycle _____s, boiler _____s, general _____s, industrial maintenance _____s (millwrights), air conditioning and refrigeration _____s, aircraft _____s, diesel _____s, and tank _____s in the armed services. Auto _____s, for example, have many trades within.

   a. Pharmacy technician
   b. Sonar Technician
   c. Technician Fifth Grade
   d. Mechanic

4. . In solid-state physics, the _____ is the minimum energy (usually measured in electron volts) needed to remove an electron from a solid to a point immediately outside the solid surface (or energy needed to move an electron from the Fermi level into vacuum).

Here 'immediately' means that the final electron position is far from the surface on the atomic scale but still close to the solid on the macroscopic scale. The _____ is a characteristic property for any solid phase of a substance with a conduction band (whether empty or partly filled).

a. Work function
b. Zero mode
c. Zero-point energy
d. 1s Slater-type function

5. In physics, a _____ is the minimum amount of any physical entity involved in an interaction. Behind this, one finds the fundamental notion that a physical property may be 'quantized,' referred to as 'the hypothesis of quantization'. This means that the magnitude can take on only certain discrete values.

a. Quantum 1/f noise
b. Quantum
c. Quantum biology
d. Quantum capacitance

1. d

2. c

3. d

4. a

5. b

You can take the complete Chapter Practice Test

for Chapter 7. Quantum Theory and the Electronic Structure of Atoms
on all key terms, persons, places, and concepts.

Online 99 Cents

http://www.epub14.1.20267.7.cram101.com/

Use www.Cram101.com for all your study needs

including Cram101's online interactive problem solving labs in

chemistry, statistics, mathematics, and more.

Chapter 8. Periodic Relationships Among the Elements

_____ Gallium

_____ Atomic number

_____ Rutherford

_____ Shielding effect

_____ Isomer

_____ Core electron

_____ Electron

_____ Main group element

_____ Valence electron

_____ Group

_____ Aufbau principle

_____ Chemical equation

_____ Electron configuration

_____ Iodine

_____ Effective nuclear charge

_____ Ionic radius

_____ Ionization

_____ Ionization energy

_____ Francium

Chapter 8. Periodic Relationships Among the Elements

CHAPTER OUTLINE: KEY TERMS, PEOPLE, PLACES, CONCEPTS

______ Half-life

______ Melting

______ Melting point

______ Alkali

______ Alkali metal

______ Point

______ Helium

______ Electron affinity

______ Affinity

______ Diagonal

______ Diagonal relationship

______ Hydrogen

______ Lithium

______ Oxygen

______ Potassium

______ Potassium superoxide

______ Sodium

______ Superoxide

______ Hydrocarbon

Chapter 8. Periodic Relationships Among the Elements
CHAPTER OUTLINE: KEY TERMS, PEOPLE, PLACES, CONCEPTS

_____ | Alkaline earth metal

_____ | Barium

_____ | Beryllium

_____ | Calcite

_____ | Sodium peroxide

_____ | Boron

_____ | Strontium

_____ | Oxide

_____ | Carbon

_____ | Nitrogen

_____ | Astatine

_____ | Bromine

_____ | Chlorine

_____ | Fluorine

_____ | Halogen

_____ | Sulfur

_____ | Argon

_____ | Halide

_____ | Neon

Chapter 8. Periodic Relationships Among the Elements

CHAPTER OUTLINE: KEY TERMS, PEOPLE, PLACES, CONCEPTS

_____ | Xenon _____

_____ | Coinage metals _____

_____ | Gold _____

_____ | Gold extraction _____

_____ | Corrosion _____

_____ | Basic oxide _____

_____ | Radon _____

CHAPTER HIGHLIGHTS & NOTES: KEY TERMS, PEOPLE, PLACES, CONCEPTS

Gallium	Gallium is a chemical element that has the symbol Ga and atomic number 31. Elemental gallium does not occur in nature, but as the gallium(III) salt in trace amounts in bauxite and zinc ores. A soft silvery metallic poor metal, elemental gallium is a brittle solid at low temperatures. As it liquefies at temperature slightly above room temperature, it will melt in the hand.
Atomic number	In chemistry and physics, the atomic number is the number of protons found in the nucleus of an atom and therefore identical to the charge number of the nucleus. It is conventionally represented by the symbol Z. The atomic number uniquely identifies a chemical element. In an atom of neutral charge, the atomic number is also equal to the number of electrons.
Rutherford	The rutherford (symbol rd) is an obsolete unit of radioactivity, defined as the activity of a quantity of radioactive material in which one million nuclei decay per second. It is therefore equivalent to one megabecquerel. It was named after Ernest Rutherford.
Shielding effect	The shielding effect describes the decrease in attraction between an electron and the nucleus in any atom with more than one electron shell.

It is also referred to as the screening effect or atomic shielding.

In hydrogen-like atoms (those with only one electron), the net force on the electron is just as large as the electric attraction from the nucleus.

Isomer	In chemistry, isomers are compounds with the same molecular formula but different structural formulas. Isomers do not necessarily share similar properties, unless they also have the same functional groups. There are many different classes of isomers, like stereoisomers, enantiomers, geometrical isomers, etc.
Core electron	Core electrons are the electrons in an atom that are not valence electrons and therefore do not participate in bonding. An example: the carbon atom has a total of 6 electrons, 4 of them being valence electrons. So the remaining 2 electrons must be core electrons.
Electron	The electron is a subatomic particle with a negative elementary electric charge. It has no known components or substructure; in other words, it is generally thought to be an elementary particle. An electron has a mass that is approximately 1/1836 that of the proton.
Main group element	In chemistry and atomic physics, main group elements are elements in groups (periodic columns) whose lightest members are represented by helium, lithium, beryllium, boron, carbon, nitrogen, oxygen, and fluorine as arranged in the periodic table of the elements. Main group elements include elements (except hydrogen) in groups 1 and 2 (s-block), and groups 13 to 18 (p-block). Group 12 elements are usually considered to be transition metals; however, zinc (Zn), cadmium (Cd), and mercury (Hg) share some properties of both groups, and some scientists believe they should be included as main group elements.
Valence electron	In chemistry, valence electrons are the electrons of an atom that can participate in the formation of chemical bonds with other atoms. Valence electrons are their 'own' electrons, present in the free neutral atom, that combine with valence electrons of other atoms to form chemical bonds. In a single covalent bond both atoms contribute one valence electron to form a shared pair.
Group	In chemistry, a group (also known as a family) is a vertical column in the periodic table of the chemical elements. There are 18 groups in the standard periodic table, including the d-block elements, but excluding the f-block elements. The explanation of the pattern of the table is that the elements in a group have similar physical or chemical characteristic of the outermost electron shells of their atoms (i.e. the same core charge), as most chemical properties are dominated by the orbital location of the outermost electron.
Aufbau principle	The Aufbau principle is used to determine the electron configuration of an atom, molecule or ion.

The principle postulates a hypothetical process in which an atom is 'built up' by progressively adding electrons. As they are added, they assume their most stable conditions (electron orbitals) with respect to the nucleus and those electrons already there.

Chemical equation	A chemical equation is the symbolic representation of a chemical reaction where the reactant entities are given on the left hand side and the product entities on the right hand side. The coefficients next to the symbols and formulae of entities are the absolute values of the stoichiometric numbers. The first chemical equation was diagrammed by Jean Beguin in 1615.
Electron configuration	In atomic physics and quantum chemistry, the electron configuration is the distribution of electrons of an atom or molecule in atomic or molecular orbitals. For example, the electron configuration of the neon atom is $1s^2 2s^2 2p^6$. According to the laws of quantum mechanics, an energy is associated with each electron configuration and, upon certain conditions, electrons are able to move from one orbital to another by emission or absorption of a quantum of energy, in the form of a photon.
Iodine	Iodine is a chemical element with the symbol I and atomic number 53./ syllable break' style='border-bottom:1px dotted'>.?da?n-o-dyne, 'a?.?d?n-o-d?n, or 'a?.?di?n-o-deen in both American and British English. The name is from Greek ?οειδ?ς ioeides, meaning violet or purple, due to the color of elemental iodine vapor. Iodine and its compounds are primarily used in nutrition, and industrially in the production of acetic acid and certain polymers.
Effective nuclear charge	The effective nuclear charge is the net positive charge experienced by an electron in a multi-electron atom. The term 'effective' is used because the shielding effect of negatively charged electrons prevents higher orbital electrons from experiencing the full nuclear charge by the repelling effect of inner-layer electrons. The effective nuclear charge experienced by the outer shell electron is also called the core charge.
Ionic radius	Ionic radius, r_{ion}, is the radius of an atom's ion. Although neither atoms nor ions have sharp boundaries, it is important to treat them as if they are hard spheres with radii such that the sum of ionic radii of the cation and anion gives the distance between the ions in a crystal lattice. Ionic radii are typically given in units of either picometers (pm) or Angstroms (Å), with 1 Å = 100 pm.
Ionization	Ionization is the process of converting an atom or molecule into an ion by adding or removing charged particles such as electrons or ions. In the case of ionisation of a gas, ion-pairs are created consisting of a free electron and a +ve ion.

Chapter 8. Periodic Relationships Among the Elements

Ionization energy	The ionization energy of a chemical species, i.e. an atom or molecule, is the energy required to remove electrons from gaseous atoms or ions. The property is alternately still often called the ionization potential, measured in volts. In chemistry it often refers to one mole of a substance (molar ionization energy or enthalpy) and reported in kJ/mol.
Francium	Francium is a chemical element with symbol Fr and atomic number 87. It was formerly known as eka-caesium and actinium K. It is one of the two least electronegative elements, the other being caesium. Francium is a highly radioactive metal that decays into astatine, radium, and radon. As an alkali metal, it has one valence electron.
Half-life	Half-life, abbreviated $t_{1/2}$, is the period of time it takes for the amount of a substance undergoing decay to decrease by half. The name was originally used to describe a characteristic of unstable atoms (radioactive decay), but it may apply to any quantity which follows a set-rate decay. The original term, dating to 1907, was 'half-life period', which was later shortened to 'half-life' in the early 1950s.
Melting	Melting, is a physical process that results in the phase transition of a substance from a solid to a liquid. The internal energy of a substance is increased, typically by the application of heat or pressure, resulting in a rise of its temperature to the melting point, at which the rigid ordering of molecular entities in the solid breaks down to a less-ordered state and the solid liquefies. An object that has melted completely is molten.
Melting point	The melting point of a solid is the temperature at which it changes state from solid to liquid. At the melting point the solid and liquid phase exist in equilibrium. The melting point of a substance depends (usually slightly) on pressure and is usually specified at standard pressure.
Alkali	In chemistry, an alkali is a basic, ionic salt of an alkali metal or alkaline earth metal element. Some authors also define an alkali as a base that dissolves in water. A solution of a soluble base has a pH greater than 7. The adjective alkaline is commonly used in English as a synonym for base, especially for soluble bases.
Alkali metal	The alkali metals are a group of chemical elements in the periodic table with very similar properties: they are all shiny, soft, silvery, highly reactive metals at standard temperature and pressure and readily lose their outermost electron to form cations with charge +1. They can all be cut easily with a knife due to their softness, exposing a shiny surface that tarnishes rapidly in air due to oxidation.

In the modern IUPAC nomenclature, the alkali metals comprise the group 1 elements, excluding hydrogen (H), which is nominally a group 1 element but not normally considered to be an alkali metal as it rarely exhibits behaviour comparable to that of the alkali metals. All the alkali metals react with water, with the heavier alkali metals reacting more vigorously than the lighter ones.

Point

Points, sometimes also called a 'discount point', are a form of pre-paid interest. One point equals one percent of the loan amount. By charging a borrower points, a lender effectively increases the yield on the loan above the amount of the stated interest rate.

Helium

Helium is the chemical element with atomic number 2 and an atomic weight of 4.002602, which is represented by the symbol He. It is a colorless, odorless, tasteless, non-toxic, inert, monatomic gas that heads the noble gas group in the periodic table. Its boiling and melting points are the lowest among the elements and it exists only as a gas except in extreme conditions.

Electron affinity

The electron affinity of an atom or molecule is defined as the amount of energy released when an electron is added to a neutral atom or molecule to form a negative ion. $X + e^- \rightarrow X^-$

This property is measured for atoms and molecules in the gaseous state only, since in the solid or liquid states their energy levels would be changed by contact with other atoms or molecules. A list of the electron affinities was used by Robert S. Mulliken to develop an electronegativity scale for atoms, equal to the average of the electron affinity and ionization potential.

Affinity

Affinity (taxonomy) - mainly in life sciences or natural history - refers to resemblance suggesting a common descent, phylogenetic relationship, or type. The term does, however, have broader application, such as in geology (for example, in descriptive and theoretical works), and similarly in astronomy .

In taxonomy the basis of any particular type of classification is the way in which objects in the domain resemble each other.

Diagonal

A diagonal is a line joining two nonconsecutive vertices of a polygon or polyhedron. Informally, any sloping line is called diagonal. The word 'diagonal' derives from the Greek διαγ?νιος (diagonios), from dia- ('through', 'across') and gonia ('angle', related to gony 'knee'); it was used by both Strabo and Euclid to refer to a line connecting two vertices of a rhombus or cuboid, and later adopted into Latin as diagonus ('slanting line').

Diagonal relationship

A diagonal relationship is said to exist between certain pairs of diagonally adjacent elements in the second and third periods of the periodic table.

These pairs (lithium (Li) and magnesium (Mg), beryllium (Be) and aluminium (Al), boron (B) and silicon (Si) etc). exhibit similar properties; for example, boron and silicon are both semiconductors, forming halides that are hydrolysed in water and have acidic oxides.

Hydrogen

Hydrogen is the chemical element with atomic number 1. It is represented by the symbol H. With an average atomic weight of 1.00794 u (1.007825 u for hydrogen-1), hydrogen is the lightest element and its monatomic form (H_1) is the most abundant chemical substance, constituting roughly 75% of the Universe's baryonic mass. Non-remnant stars are mainly composed of hydrogen in its plasma state.

At standard temperature and pressure, hydrogen is a colorless, odorless, tasteless, non-toxic, nonmetallic, highly combustible diatomic gas with the molecular formula H_2.

Lithium

Lithium is a soft, silver-white metal that belongs to the alkali metal group of chemical elements. It is represented by the symbol Li, and it has the atomic number 3. Under standard conditions it is the lightest metal and the least dense solid element. Like all alkali metals, lithium is highly reactive and flammable.

Oxygen

Oxygen is the element with atomic number 8 and represented by the symbol O. Its name derives from the Greek roots ?ξ?ς (oxys) ('acid', literally 'sharp', referring to the sour taste of acids) and -γεν?ς (-genes) ('producer', literally 'begetter'), because at the time of naming, it was mistakenly thought that all acids required oxygen in their composition. At standard temperature and pressure, two atoms of the element bind to form dioxygen, a very pale blue, odorless, tasteless diatomic gas with the formula O_2.

Oxygen is a member of the chalcogen group on the periodic table and is a highly reactive nonmetallic element that readily forms compounds (notably oxides) with almost all other elements.

Potassium

Potassium is the chemical element with the symbol K and atomic number 19. Elemental potassium is a soft silvery-white alkali metal that oxidizes rapidly in air and is very reactive with water, generating sufficient heat to ignite the hydrogen emitted in the reaction.

	Because potassium and sodium are chemically very similar, it took a long time before their salts were differentiated. The existence of multiple elements in their salts was suspected from 1702, and this was proven in 1807 when potassium and sodium were individually isolated from different salts by electrolysis.
Potassium superoxide	Potassium superoxide is the chemical compound with the formula KO_2. This rare salt of the superoxide ion is produced by burning molten potassium in pure oxygen. Potassium superoxide is used as an oxidizing agent in industrial chemistry, as a CO_2 scrubber, H_2O dehumidifier and O_2 generator in rebreathers, spacecraft, submarines and spacesuit life support systems.
Sodium	Sodium is a chemical element with the symbol Na and atomic number 11. It is a soft, silvery-white, highly reactive metal and is a member of the alkali metals; its only stable isotope is ^{23}Na. The free metal does not occur in nature, but instead must be prepared from its compounds; it was first isolated by Humphry Davy in 1807 by the electrolysis of sodium hydroxide. Sodium is the sixth most abundant element in the Earth's crust, and exists in numerous minerals such as feldspars, sodalite and rock salt.
Superoxide	A superoxide, also known by the obsolete name hyperoxide, is a compound that contains the superoxide anion with the chemical formula O_2^-. The systematic name of the anion is dioxide(1−). Superoxide anion is particularly important as the product of the one-electron reduction of dioxygen O_2, which occurs widely in nature.
Hydrocarbon	In organic chemistry, a hydrocarbon is an organic compound consisting entirely of hydrogen and carbon. Hydrocarbons from which one hydrogen atom has been removed are functional groups, called hydrocarbyls. Aromatic hydrocarbons (arenes), alkanes, alkenes, cycloalkanes and alkyne-based compounds are different types of hydrocarbons.
Alkaline earth metal	The alkaline earth metals are a group of chemical elements in the periodic table with very similar properties: they are all shiny, silvery-white, somewhat reactive metals at standard temperature and pressure and readily lose their two outermost electrons to form cations with charge +2. In the modern IUPAC nomenclature, the alkaline earth metals comprise the group 2 elements.

The alkaline earth metals are beryllium (Be), magnesium (Mg), calcium (Ca), strontium (Sr), barium (Ba), and radium (Ra). This group lies in the s-block of the periodic table as all alkaline earth metals have their outermost electron in an s-orbital. |
| Barium | |

Barium is a chemical element with the symbol Ba and atomic number 56. It is the fifth element in Group 2, a soft silvery metallic alkaline earth metal. Barium is never found in nature in its pure form due to its reactivity with air. Its oxide is historically known as baryta but it reacts with water and carbon dioxide and is not found as a mineral.

Beryllium

Beryllium is the chemical element with the symbol Be and atomic number 4. Because any beryllium synthesized in stars is short-lived, it is a relatively rare element in both the universe and in the crust of the Earth. It is a divalent element which occurs naturally only in combination with other elements in minerals. Notable gemstones which contain beryllium include beryl (aquamarine, emerald) and chrysoberyl.

Calcite

Calcite is a carbonate mineral and the most stable polymorph of calcium carbonate ($CaCO_3$). The other polymorphs are the minerals aragonite and vaterite. Aragonite will change to calcite at 380-470°C, and vaterite is even less stable.

Sodium peroxide

Sodium peroxide is the inorganic compound with the formula Na_2O_2. This solid is the product when sodium is burned with oxygen. It is a strong base and a potent oxidizing agent.

Boron

Boron is the chemical element with atomic number 5 and the chemical symbol B. Because boron is produced entirely by cosmic ray spallation and not by stellar nucleosynthesis, it is a low-abundance element in both the solar system and the Earth's crust. However, boron is concentrated on Earth by the water-solubility of its more common naturally occurring compounds, the borate minerals. These are mined industrially as evaporate ores, such as borax and kernite.

Strontium

Strontium is a chemical element with the symbol Sr and the atomic number 38. An alkaline earth metal, strontium is a soft silver-white or yellowish metallic element that is highly reactive chemically. The metal turns yellow when exposed to air. It occurs naturally in the minerals celestine and strontianite.

Oxide

An oxide is a chemical compound that contains at least one oxygen atom and one other element in its chemical formula. Metal oxides typically contain an anion of oxygen in the oxidation state of −2. Most of the Earth's crust consists of solid oxides, the result of elements being oxidized by the oxygen in air or in water .

Carbon

Carbon is the chemical element with symbol C and atomic number 6. As a member of group 14 on the periodic table, it is nonmetallic and tetravalent--making four electrons available to form covalent chemical bonds. There are three naturally occurring isotopes, with ^{12}C and ^{13}C being stable, while ^{14}C is radioactive, decaying with a half-life of about 5,730 years. Carbon is one of the few elements known since antiquity.

Nitrogen

Nitrogen is a chemical element that has the symbol N, atomic number of 7 and atomic mass 14.00674 u. Elemental nitrogen is a colorless, odorless, tasteless, and mostly inert diatomic gas at standard conditions, constituting 78.09% by volume of Earth's atmosphere. The element nitrogen was discovered as a separable component of air, by Scottish physician Daniel Rutherford, in 1772.

Astatine

Astatine is a radioactive chemical element with the symbol At and atomic number 85. It occurs on Earth only as the result of the radioactive decay of heavier elements. All of its isotopes are short-lived; the most stable is astatine-210, with a half-life of 8.1 hours. Accordingly, much less is known about astatine than most other elements.

Bromine

Bromine ('bro?mi?n-meen or 'bro?m?n-min; from Greek: βρ?μος, brómos, meaning 'stench (of he-goats)') is a chemical element with the symbol Br, an atomic number of 35, and an atomic mass of 79.904. It is in the halogen element group. The element was isolated independently by two chemists, Carl Jacob Löwig and Antoine Jerome Balard, in 1825-1826. Elemental bromine is a fuming red-brown liquid at room temperature, corrosive and toxic, with properties between those of chlorine and iodine. Free bromine does not occur in nature, but occurs as colorless soluble crystalline mineral halide salts, analogous to table salt.

Chlorine

Chlorine is the chemical element with atomic number 17 and symbol Cl. It is the second lightest halogen, with fluorine being the lightest. Chlorine is found in the periodic table in group 17. The element forms diatomic molecules under standard conditions, called dichlorine.

Fluorine

Chapter 8. Periodic Relationships Among the Elements

Fluorine is the chemical element with atomic number 9, represented by the symbol F. It is the lightest element of the halogen column of the periodic table and has a single stable isotope, fluorine-19. At standard pressure and temperature, fluorine is a pale yellow gas composed of diatomic molecules, F_2. In stars, fluorine is rare compared to other light elements. In Earth's crust, fluorine is more common, being the thirteenth most abundant element.

Halogen

The halogens or halogen elements are a series of nonmetal elements from Group 17 IUPAC Style (formerly: VII, VIIA) of the periodic table, comprising fluorine (F), chlorine (Cl), bromine (Br), iodine (I), and astatine (At). The artificially created element 117, provisionally referred to by the systematic name ununseptium, may also be a halogen.

The group of halogens is the only periodic table group which contains elements in all three familiar states of matter at standard temperature and pressure.

Sulfur

Sulfur or sulphur is the chemical element with atomic number 16. In the periodic table it is represented by the symbol S. It is an abundant, multivalent non-metal. Under normal conditions, sulfur atoms form cyclic octatomic molecules with chemical formula S_8. Elemental sulfur is a bright yellow crystalline solid when at room temperature.

Argon

Argon is a chemical element represented by the symbol Ar. Argon has atomic number 18 and is the third element in group 18 of the periodic table (noble gases). Argon is the third most common gas in the Earth's atmosphere, at 0.93% (9,300 ppm), making it approximately 23.8 times more abundant than carbon dioxide (390 ppm).

Halide

A halide is a binary compound, of which one part is a halogen atom and the other part is an element or radical that is less electronegative than the halogen, to make a fluoride, chloride, bromide, iodide, or astatide compound. Many salts are halides. All Group 1 metals form halides which are white solids at room temperature.

Neon

Neon is the chemical element that has the symbol Ne and an atomic number of 10. Although a very common element in the universe, it is rare on Earth. A colorless, inert noble gas under standard conditions, neon gives a distinct reddish-orange glow when used in either low-voltage neon glow lamps or in high-voltage discharge tubes or neon advertising signs.

Xenon	Xenon is a chemical element with the symbol Xe and atomic number 54. A colorless, heavy, odorless noble gas, xenon occurs in the Earth's atmosphere in trace amounts. Although generally unreactive, xenon can undergo a few chemical reactions such as the formation of xenon hexafluoroplatinate, the first noble gas compound to be synthesized. Naturally occurring xenon consists of eight stable isotopes.
Coinage metals	The coinage metals comprise, at minimum, those metallic chemical elements which have historically been used as components in alloys used to mint coins. The term is not perfectly defined, however, since a number of metals have been used to make 'demonstration coins' which have never been used to make monetized coins for any nation-state, but could be. Some of these elements would make excellent coins in theory (for example, zirconium), but their status as coin metals is not clear.
Gold	Gold is a dense, soft, shiny, malleable and ductile metal and is a chemical element with the symbol Au and atomic number 79. Pure gold has a bright yellow color and luster traditionally considered attractive, which it maintains without oxidizing in air or water. Chemically, gold is a transition metal and a group 11 element.
Gold extraction	Gold extraction, mineral processing, hydrometallurgical, and pyrometallurgical processes to be performed on the ore. Gold mining from alluvium ores was once achieved by techniques associated with placer mining such as simple gold panning and sluicing, resulting in direct recovery of small gold nuggets and flakes. Placer mining techniques since the mid to late 20th century have generally only been the practice of artisan miners.
Corrosion	Corrosion is the gradual destruction of material, usually metals, by chemical reaction with its environment. In the most common use of the word, this means electro-chemical oxidation of metals in reaction with an oxidant such as oxygen. Rusting, the formation of iron oxides, is a well-known example of electrochemical corrosion.
Basic oxide	A basic oxide is an oxide that shows basic properties in opposition to acidic oxides and that either•reacts with water to form a base; or•reacts with an acid to form a salt.

Chapter 8. Periodic Relationships Among the Elements

Examples include:•Sodium oxide, which reacts with water to produce sodium hydroxide

Magnesium oxide, which reacts with hydrochloric acid to form magnesium chloride•Copper(II) oxide, which reacts with nitric acid to form copper nitrate

Basic oxides are oxides mostly of metals, especially alkali and alkaline earth metals.

Radon

Radon is a chemical element with the atomic number 86, and is represented by the symbol Rn. It is a radioactive, colorless, odorless, tasteless noble gas, occurring naturally as the decay product of uranium or thorium. Its most stable isotope, ^{222}Rn, has a half-life of 3.8 days.

1. In chemistry, a _____(also known as a family) is a vertical column in the periodic table of the chemical elements. There are 18 groups in the standard periodic table, including the d-block elements, but excluding the f-block elements.

   The explanation of the pattern of the table is that the elements in a group have similar physical or chemical characteristic of the outermost electron shells of their atoms (i.e. the same core charge), as most chemical properties are dominated by the orbital location of the outermost electron.

   a. Boron group
   b. Carbon group
   c. Group
   d. D-block

2.

   _____ is a chemical element with the atomic number 86, and is represented by the symbol Rn. It is a radioactive, colorless, odorless, tasteless noble gas, occurring naturally as the decay product of uranium or thorium. Its most stable isotope, ^{222}Rn, has a half-life of 3.8 days.

   a. Radon
   b. Bismuth silicon oxide
   c. Bismuth strontium calcium copper oxide
   d. Boron monoxide

3. .

Chapter 8. Periodic Relationships Among the Elements

_____ ('bro?mi?n-meen or 'bro?m?n-min; from Greek: βρ?μος, brómos, meaning 'stench (of he-goats)') is a chemical element with the symbol Br, an atomic number of 35, and an atomic mass of 79.904. It is in the halogen element group. The element was isolated independently by two chemists, Carl Jacob Löwig and Antoine Jerome Balard, in 1825-1826. Elemental _____ is a fuming red-brown liquid at room temperature, corrosive and toxic, with properties between those of chlorine and iodine. Free _____ does not occur in nature, but occurs as colorless soluble crystalline mineral halide salts, analogous to table salt.

a. Bromine monochloride
b. Bromine pentafluoride
c. Bromine
d. Bromous acid

4.

_____ is a chemical element that has the symbol Ga and atomic number 31. Elemental _____ does not occur in nature, but as the _____(III) salt in trace amounts in bauxite and zinc ores. A soft silvery metallic poor metal, elemental _____ is a brittle solid at low temperatures. As it liquefies at temperature slightly above room temperature, it will melt in the hand.

a. Germanium
b. Gallium
c. Hafnium
d. Hassium

5.

_____ is a chemical element represented by the symbol Ar. _____ has atomic number 18 and is the third element in group 18 of the periodic table (noble gases). _____ is the third most common gas in the Earth's atmosphere, at 0.93% (9,300 ppm), making it approximately 23.8 times more abundant than carbon dioxide (390 ppm).

a. Ununoctium
b. Disulfur
c. Argon
d. Flowers of sulfur

1. c
2. a
3. c
4. b
5. c

You can take the complete Chapter Practice Test

for Chapter 8. Periodic Relationships Among the Elements
on all key terms, persons, places, and concepts.

Online 99 Cents

http://www.epub14.1.20267.8.cram101.com/

Use www.Cram101.com for all your study needs

including Cram101's online interactive problem solving labs in

chemistry, statistics, mathematics, and more.

Chapter 9. Chemical Bonding I: Basic Concepts

CHAPTER OUTLINE: KEY TERMS, PEOPLE, PLACES, CONCEPTS

Calcium

Calcium oxide

Ionic bond

Hydrogen

Hydrogen bond

Oxide

Coulomb

Enthalpy

Lattice energy

Lithium

Lithium fluoride

Melting

Melting point

Alkali

Alkali metal

Alkali metal halide

Fluoride

Halide

Ionic compound

Chapter 9. Chemical Bonding I: Basic Concepts

CHAPTER OUTLINE: KEY TERMS, PEOPLE, PLACES, CONCEPTS

Metal halides

Point

Chemical formula

Covalent bond

Hydrogen atom

Lewis structure

Atom

Lone pair

Octet rule

Single bond

Electron

Electron pair

Acetone

Bond length

Carbon

Carbon tetrachloride

Double bond

Ethyl acetate

Nitrogen

Triple bond

Acetate

Electronegativity

Hydrogen fluoride

Polar bond

Polarity

Fluorine

Oxidation number

Oxygen

Formal charge

Benzene

Ozone

Beryllium

Beryllium hydride

Boron

Boron trifluoride

Hydride

Trifluoride

Expanded octet

	Molecule
	Radical
	Sulfur
	Sulfur hexafluoride
	Hexafluoride
	Nitric oxide
	Nitroglycerin

CHAPTER HIGHLIGHTS & NOTES: KEY TERMS, PEOPLE, PLACES, CONCEPTS

Calcium	Calcium is the chemical element with the symbol Ca and atomic number 20. It has an atomic mass of 40.078 amu. Calcium is a soft gray alkaline earth metal, and is the fifth-most-abundant element by mass in the Earth's crust. Calcium is also the fifth-most-abundant dissolved ion in seawater by both molarity and mass, after sodium, chloride, magnesium, and sulfate.
Calcium oxide	Calcium oxide commonly known as quicklime or burnt lime, is a widely used chemical compound. It is a white, caustic, alkaline crystalline solid at room temperature. The broadly used term lime connotes calcium-containing inorganic materials, in which carbonates, oxides and hydroxides of calcium, silicon, magnesium, aluminium, and iron predominate, such as limestone.
Ionic bond	An ionic bond is a type of chemical bond formed through an electrostatic attraction between two oppositely charged ions. Ionic bonds are formed between a cation, which is usually a metal, and an anion, which is usually a nonmetal. Pure ionic bonding cannot exist: all ionic compounds have some degree of covalent bonding.

Chapter 9. Chemical Bonding I: Basic Concepts

Hydrogen	Hydrogen is the chemical element with atomic number 1. It is represented by the symbol H. With an average atomic weight of 1.00794 u (1.007825 u for hydrogen-1), hydrogen is the lightest element and its monatomic form (H_1) is the most abundant chemical substance, constituting roughly 75% of the Universe's baryonic mass. Non-remnant stars are mainly composed of hydrogen in its plasma state.

At standard temperature and pressure, hydrogen is a colorless, odorless, tasteless, non-toxic, nonmetallic, highly combustible diatomic gas with the molecular formula H_2. |
| Hydrogen bond | A hydrogen bond is the attractive interaction of a hydrogen atom with an electronegative atom, such as nitrogen, oxygen or fluorine, that comes from another molecule or chemical group. The hydrogen has a polar bonding to another electronegative atom to create the bond. These bonds can occur between molecules (intermolecularly), or within different parts of a single molecule (intramolecularly). |
| Oxide | An oxide is a chemical compound that contains at least one oxygen atom and one other element in its chemical formula. Metal oxides typically contain an anion of oxygen in the oxidation state of −2. Most of the Earth's crust consists of solid oxides, the result of elements being oxidized by the oxygen in air or in water . Hydrocarbon combustion affords the two principal carbon oxides: carbon monoxide and carbon dioxide. |
| Coulomb | The coulomb is the SI derived unit of electric charge. It is defined as the charge transported by a steady current of one ampere in one second: $1\mathrm{C} = 1\mathrm{A} \cdot 1\mathrm{s}$

One coulomb is also the amount of excess charge on the positive side of a capacitance of one farad charged to a potential difference of one volt: $1\mathrm{C} = 1\mathrm{F} \cdot 1\mathrm{V}$

Name and notation

As with every SI unit whose name is derived from the proper name of a person, the first letter of its symbol is upper case (C). When an SI unit is spelled out in English, it should always begin with a lower case letter (coulomb), except where any word would be capitalized, such as at the beginning of a sentence or in capitalized material such as a title. |
| Enthalpy | Enthalpy is a measure of the total energy of a thermodynamic system. It includes the internal energy, which is the energy required to create a system, and the amount of energy required to make room for it by displacing its environment and establishing its volume and pressure. |

Chapter 9. Chemical Bonding I: Basic Concepts

Lattice energy	The lattice energy of a ionic solid is a measure of the strength of bonds in that ionic compound. It is usually defined as the enthalpy of formation of the ionic compound from gaseous ions and as such is invariably exothermic. Lattice energy may also be defined as the energy required to completely separate one mole of a solid ionic compound into gaseous ionic constituents.
Lithium	Lithium is a soft, silver-white metal that belongs to the alkali metal group of chemical elements. It is represented by the symbol Li, and it has the atomic number 3. Under standard conditions it is the lightest metal and the least dense solid element. Like all alkali metals, lithium is highly reactive and flammable.
Lithium fluoride	Lithium fluoride is an inorganic compound with the formula LiF. It is the lithium salt of hydrofluoric acid. This white solid is a simple ionic compound. Its structure is analogous to that of sodium chloride, but it is much less soluble in water.
Melting	Melting, is a physical process that results in the phase transition of a substance from a solid to a liquid. The internal energy of a substance is increased, typically by the application of heat or pressure, resulting in a rise of its temperature to the melting point, at which the rigid ordering of molecular entities in the solid breaks down to a less-ordered state and the solid liquefies. An object that has melted completely is molten.
Melting point	The melting point of a solid is the temperature at which it changes state from solid to liquid. At the melting point the solid and liquid phase exist in equilibrium. The melting point of a substance depends (usually slightly) on pressure and is usually specified at standard pressure.
Alkali	In chemistry, an alkali is a basic, ionic salt of an alkali metal or alkaline earth metal element. Some authors also define an alkali as a base that dissolves in water. A solution of a soluble base has a pH greater than 7. The adjective alkaline is commonly used in English as a synonym for base, especially for soluble bases.
Alkali metal	The alkali metals are a group of chemical elements in the periodic table with very similar properties: they are all shiny, soft, silvery, highly reactive metals at standard temperature and pressure and readily lose their outermost electron to form cations with charge +1. They can all be cut easily with a knife due to their softness, exposing a shiny surface that tarnishes rapidly in air due to oxidation. In the modern IUPAC nomenclature, the alkali metals comprise the group 1 elements, excluding hydrogen (H), which is nominally a group 1 element but not normally considered to be an alkali metal as it rarely exhibits behaviour comparable to that of the alkali metals. All the alkali metals react with water, with the heavier alkali metals reacting more vigorously than the lighter ones.

Chapter 9. Chemical Bonding I: Basic Concepts

Alkali metal halide	Alkali metal halides (also known as alkali halides) are the family of inorganic compounds with the chemical formula MX, where M is an alkali metal and X is a halogen. These compounds are the often commercially significant sources of these metals and halides. The best known of these compounds is sodium chloride, table salt.
Fluoride	Fluoride is the anion F^-, the reduced form of fluorine when as an ion and when bonded to another element. Both organofluorine compounds and inorganic fluorine containing compounds are called fluorides. Fluoride, like other halides, is a monovalent ion (−1 charge).
Halide	A halide is a binary compound, of which one part is a halogen atom and the other part is an element or radical that is less electronegative than the halogen, to make a fluoride, chloride, bromide, iodide, or astatide compound. Many salts are halides. All Group 1 metals form halides which are white solids at room temperature.
Ionic compound	In chemistry, an ionic compound is a chemical compound in which ions are held together in a lattice structure by ionic bonds. Usually, the positively charged portion consists of metal cations and the negatively charged portion is an anion or polyatomic ion. Ions in ionic compounds are held together by the electrostatic forces between oppositely charged bodies.
Metal halides	Metal halides are compounds between metals and halogens. Some, such as sodium chloride are ionic, while others are covalently bonded. Covalently bonded metal halides may be discrete molecules, such as uranium hexafluoride, or they may form polymeric structures, such as palladium chloride.
Point	Points, sometimes also called a 'discount point', are a form of pre-paid interest. One point equals one percent of the loan amount. By charging a borrower points, a lender effectively increases the yield on the loan above the amount of the stated interest rate.
Chemical formula	A chemical formula is a way of expressing information about the atoms that constitute a particular chemical compound. The chemical formula identifies each constituent element by its chemical symbol and indicates the number of atoms of each element found in each discrete molecule of that compound. If a molecule contains more than one atom of a particular element, this quantity is indicated using a subscript after the chemical symbol (although 18th-century books often used superscripts) and also can be combined by more chemical elements.
Covalent bond	A covalent bond is a form of chemical bonding that is characterized by the sharing of pairs of electrons between atoms. The stable balance of attractive and repulsive forces between atoms when they share electrons is known as covalent bonding.

Chapter 9. Chemical Bonding I: Basic Concepts

Hydrogen atom	A hydrogen atom is an atom of the chemical element hydrogen. The electrically neutral atom contains a single positively-charged proton and a single negatively-charged electron bound to the nucleus by the Coulomb force. Atomic hydrogen comprises about 75% of the elemental mass of the universe.
Lewis structure	Lewis structures (also known as Lewis dot diagrams, electron dot diagrams, and electron dot structures) are diagrams that show the bonding between atoms of a molecule and the lone pairs of electrons that may exist in the molecule.
Atom	The atom is a basic unit of matter that consists of a dense central nucleus surrounded by a cloud of negatively charged electrons. The atomic nucleus contains a mix of positively charged protons and electrically neutral neutrons (except in the case of hydrogen-1, which is the only stable nuclide with no neutrons). The electrons of an atom are bound to the nucleus by the electromagnetic force.
Lone pair	In chemistry, a lone pair is a valence electron pair without bonding or sharing with other atoms. They are found in the outermost electron shell of an atom, so lone pairs are a subset of a molecule's valence electrons. They can be identified by examining the outermost energy level of an atom--lone electron pairs consist of paired electrons as opposed to single electrons, which may appear if the atomic orbital is not full.
Octet rule	The octet rule is a chemical rule of thumb that states that atoms of low (<20) atomic number tend to combine in such a way that they each have eight electrons in their valence shells, giving them the same electronic configuration as a noble gas. The rule is applicable to the main-group elements, especially carbon, nitrogen, oxygen, and the halogens, but also to metals such as sodium or magnesium. The valence electrons can be counted using a Lewis electron dot diagram as shown at right for carbon dioxide.
Single bond	A Single bond in chemistry is a chemical bond between two chemical elements involving two bonding electrons. Usually, Single bond is Sigma bond. but diboron is Pi bond.(Molecular orbital diagram#Diboron MO diagram.
Electron	The electron is a subatomic particle with a negative elementary electric charge. It has no known components or substructure; in other words, it is generally thought to be an elementary particle. An electron has a mass that is approximately 1/1836 that of the proton.

Chapter 9. Chemical Bonding I: Basic Concepts

Electron pair	In chemistry, an electron pair consists of two electrons that occupy the same orbital but have opposite spins. Because electrons are fermions, the Pauli exclusion principle forbids these particles from having exactly the same quantum numbers. Therefore the only way to occupy the same orbital, i.e. have the same orbital quantum numbers, is to differ in the spin quantum number.
Acetone	Acetone is the organic compound with the formula $(CH_3)_2CO$, a colorless, mobile, flammable liquid, the simplest example of the ketones. Acetone is miscible with water and serves as an important solvent in its own right, typically as the solvent of choice for cleaning purposes in the laboratory. About 6.7 million tonnes were produced worldwide in 2010, mainly for use as a solvent and production of methyl methacrylate and bisphenol A. It is a common building block in organic chemistry.
Bond length	In molecular geometry, bond length is the average distance between nuclei of two bonded atoms in a molecule. Bond length is related to bond order, when more electrons participate in bond formation the bond will get shorter. Bond length is also inversely related to bond strength and the bond dissociation energy, as (all other things being equal) a stronger bond will be shorter.
Carbon	Carbon is the chemical element with symbol C and atomic number 6. As a member of group 14 on the periodic table, it is nonmetallic and tetravalent--making four electrons available to form covalent chemical bonds. There are three naturally occurring isotopes, with ^{12}C and ^{13}C being stable, while ^{14}C is radioactive, decaying with a half-life of about 5,730 years. Carbon is one of the few elements known since antiquity.
Carbon tetrachloride	Carbon tetrachloride, also known by many other names is the organic compound with the formula CCl_4. It was formerly widely used in fire extinguishers, as a precursor to refrigerants, and as a cleaning agent. It is a colourless liquid with a 'sweet' smell that can be detected at low levels.
Double bond	A double bond in chemistry is a chemical bond between two chemical elements involving four bonding electrons instead of the usual two. The most common double bond, that between two carbon atoms, can be found in alkenes. Many types of double bonds between two different elements exist, for example in a carbonyl group with a carbon atom and an oxygen atom.
Ethyl acetate	Ethyl acetate is the organic compound with the formula $CH_3COOCH_2CH_3$.

This colorless liquid has a characteristic sweet smell (similar to pear drops) and is used in glues, nail polish removers, and cigarettes . Ethyl acetate is the ester of ethanol and acetic acid; it is manufactured on a large scale for use as a solvent.

Nitrogen

Nitrogen is a chemical element that has the symbol N, atomic number of 7 and atomic mass 14.00674 u. Elemental nitrogen is a colorless, odorless, tasteless, and mostly inert diatomic gas at standard conditions, constituting 78.09% by volume of Earth's atmosphere. The element nitrogen was discovered as a separable component of air, by Scottish physician Daniel Rutherford, in 1772.

Triple bond

A triple bond in chemistry is a chemical bond between two chemical elements involving six bonding electrons instead of the usual two in a covalent single bond. The most common triple bond, that between two carbon atoms, can be found in alkynes. Other functional groups containing a triple bond are cyanides and isocyanides.

Acetate

An acetate is a derivative of acetic acid. This term includes salts and esters, as well as the anion found in solution. Most of the approximately 5 billion kilograms of acetic acid produced annually in industry are used in the production of acetates, which usually take the form of polymers.

Electronegativity

Electronegativity, symbol χ, is a chemical property that describes the tendency of an atom or a functional group to attract electrons towards itself. An atom's electronegativity is affected by both its atomic number and the distance that its valence electrons reside from the charged nucleus. The higher the associated electronegativity number, the more an element or compound attracts electrons towards it.

Hydrogen fluoride

Hydrogen fluoride is a chemical compound with the formula HF. This colorless gas is the principal industrial source of fluorine, often in the aqueous form as hydrofluoric acid, and thus is the precursor to many important compounds including pharmaceuticals and polymers (e.g. Teflon). HF is widely used in the petrochemical industry and is a component of many superacids. Hydrogen fluoride boils just below room temperature whereas the other hydrogen halides condense at much lower temperatures.

Polar bond

In chemistry, a polar bond is a type of covalent bond between two atoms or more in which electrons are shared unequally. Because of this, one end of the molecule has a slight, relative negative charge and the other a slight, relative positive charge. An example of atoms bonded by a polar bond is the water molecule, which is made up of two hydrogen atoms and one oxygen atom.

Chapter 9. Chemical Bonding I: Basic Concepts

Polarity	In physics, polarity is a description of an attribute, typically a binary attribute (one with two values), or a vector (a direction). For example:•An electric charge has a polarity of either positive or negative.•A battery contains polarity, with the two + and - terminals. Similar to electric charge, the energy flows from the positive terminal, through the battery, to the negative terminal, and exits the dry cell.•A voltage has a polarity, in that it could be positive or negative (with respect to some other voltage, such as the one at the other end of a battery or electric circuit).•A magnet has a polarity, in that one end is the 'north' and the other is the 'south'.•The spin of an entity in quantum mechanics has a polarity - positive or negative.•Polarized light has waves which all line up in the same direction.
	Chemical polarity is a feature of chemical bonds, where two different atoms in the same molecule have different electronegativity.
Fluorine	Fluorine is the chemical element with atomic number 9, represented by the symbol F. It is the lightest element of the halogen column of the periodic table and has a single stable isotope, fluorine-19. At standard pressure and temperature, fluorine is a pale yellow gas composed of diatomic molecules, F_2. In stars, fluorine is rare compared to other light elements. In Earth's crust, fluorine is more common, being the thirteenth most abundant element.
Oxidation number	In coordination chemistry, the oxidation number of a central atom in a coordination compound is the charge that it would have if all the ligands were removed along with the electron pairs that were shared with the central atom.
	The oxidation number is used in the nomenclature of inorganic compounds. It is represented by a Roman numeral.
Oxygen	Oxygen is the element with atomic number 8 and represented by the symbol O. Its name derives from the Greek roots ?ξ?ς (oxys) ('acid', literally 'sharp', referring to the sour taste of acids) and -γεν?ς (-genes) ('producer', literally 'begetter'), because at the time of naming, it was mistakenly thought that all acids required oxygen in their composition. At standard temperature and pressure, two atoms of the element bind to form dioxygen, a very pale blue, odorless, tasteless diatomic gas with the formula O_2.
	Oxygen is a member of the chalcogen group on the periodic table and is a highly reactive nonmetallic element that readily forms compounds (notably oxides) with almost all other elements.

Formal charge	In chemistry, a formal charge is the charge assigned to an atom in a molecule, assuming that electrons in a chemical bond are shared equally between atoms, regardless of relative electronegativity.
	The formal charge of any atom in a molecule can be calculated by the following equation:
	$$FC = V - N - \frac{B}{2}$$
	Where V is the number of valence electrons of the atom in isolation (atom in ground state); N is the number of non-bonding valence electrons on this atom in the molecule; and B is the total number of electrons shared in covalent bonds with other atoms in the molecule. There are two electrons shared per single covalent bond.
Benzene	Benzene is an organic chemical compound with the molecular formula C_6H_6. Its molecule is composed of 6 carbon atoms joined in a ring, with 1 hydrogen atom attached to each carbon atom. Because its molecules contain only carbon and hydrogen atoms, benzene is classed as a hydrocarbon.
Ozone	Ozone or trioxygen, is a triatomic molecule, consisting of three oxygen atoms. It is an allotrope of oxygen that is much less stable than the diatomic allotrope (O_2), breaking down with a half life of about half an hour in the lower atmosphere, to normal dioxygen. Ozone is formed from dioxygen by the action of ultraviolet light and also atmospheric electrical discharges, and is present in low concentrations throughout the Earth's atmosphere.
Beryllium	Beryllium is the chemical element with the symbol Be and atomic number 4. Because any beryllium synthesized in stars is short-lived, it is a relatively rare element in both the universe and in the crust of the Earth. It is a divalent element which occurs naturally only in combination with other elements in minerals. Notable gemstones which contain beryllium include beryl (aquamarine, emerald) and chrysoberyl.
Beryllium hydride	Beryllium hydride, BeH_2, is a chemical compound of beryllium and hydrogen commonly used in rocket fuel. Unlike the ionically bonded hydrides of the heavier Group 2 elements, beryllium hydride is covalently bonded.
	BeH_2 was first synthesised in 1951 by reacting dimethylberyllium, $Be(CH_3)_2$, with lithium aluminium hydride, $LiAlH_4$.
Boron	

Chapter 9. Chemical Bonding I: Basic Concepts

Boron is the chemical element with atomic number 5 and the chemical symbol B. Because boron is produced entirely by cosmic ray spallation and not by stellar nucleosynthesis, it is a low-abundance element in both the solar system and the Earth's crust. However, boron is concentrated on Earth by the water-solubility of its more common naturally occurring compounds, the borate minerals. These are mined industrially as evaporate ores, such as borax and kernite.

Boron trifluoride	Boron trifluoride is the chemical compound with the formula BF_3. This pungent colourless toxic gas forms white fumes in moist air. It is a useful Lewis acid and a versatile building block for other boron compounds.
Hydride	In chemistry, a hydride is the anion of hydrogen, H^-, or, more commonly, a compound in which one or more hydrogen centres have nucleophilic, reducing, or basic properties. In compounds that are regarded as hydrides, hydrogen is bonded to a more electropositive element or group. Compounds containing metal or metalloid bonds to hydrogen are often referred to as hydrides, even though these hydrogen centres can have a protic character.
Trifluoride	Trifluorides are compounds having three fluorines per formula unit. Many metals form trifluorides, such as iron, the rare earth elements, and the metals in the aluminium and scandium columns of the periodic table. No trifluoride is soluble in water, but several are soluble in other solvents.
Expanded octet	Expanded octet is a colloquial term referring to the phenomenon of hypervalency where a central atom of a molecule bears more than eight valence electrons. Second-period atoms cannot have more than eight valence electrons around the central atom, but atoms in the third (and below) period can. In such a case, the atom is said to have an expanded octet.
Molecule	A molecule is an electrically neutral group of two or more atoms held together by covalent chemical bonds. Molecules are distinguished from ions by their lack of electrical charge. However, in quantum physics, organic chemistry, and biochemistry, the term molecule is often used less strictly, also being applied to polyatomic ions.
Radical	Radicals (often referred to as free radicals) are atoms, molecules, or ions with unpaired electrons on an open shell configuration. Free radicals may have positive, negative or zero charge. Even though they have unpaired electrons, by convention, metals and their ions or complexes with unpaired electrons are not radicals.
Sulfur	Sulfur or sulphur is the chemical element with atomic number 16.

	In the periodic table it is represented by the symbol S. It is an abundant, multivalent non-metal. Under normal conditions, sulfur atoms form cyclic octatomic molecules with chemical formula S_8. Elemental sulfur is a bright yellow crystalline solid when at room temperature.
Sulfur hexafluoride	Sulfur hexafluoride is an inorganic, colorless, odorless, and non-flammable greenhouse gas. SF_6 has an octahedral geometry, consisting of six fluorine atoms attached to a central sulfur atom. It is a hypervalent molecule.
Hexafluoride	A hexafluoride is a chemical compound with the general formula XF_6. Sixteen elements are known to form stable hexafluorides. Nine of these elements are transition metals, three are actinides, and four are nonmetals or metalloids.
Nitric oxide	Nitric oxide, is a molecule with chemical formula NO. It is a free radical and is an important intermediate in the chemical industry. Nitric oxide is a by-product of combustion of substances in the air, as in automobile engines, fossil fuel power plants, and is produced naturally during the electrical discharges of lightning in thunderstorms. In mammals including humans, NO is an important cellular signaling molecule involved in many physiological and pathological processes.
Nitroglycerin	Nitroglycerin also known as nitroglycerine, trinitroglycerin, trinitroglycerine, 1,2,3-trinitroxypropane and glyceryl trinitrate, is a heavy, colorless, oily, explosive liquid produced by nitrating glycerol. Chemically, the substance is an organic nitrate compound rather than a nitro compound, but the traditional name is often retained. Since the 1860s, nitroglycerin has been used as an active ingredient in the manufacture of explosives, mostly dynamite, and as such it is employed in the construction, demolition, and mining industries.

Chapter 9. Chemical Bonding I: Basic Concepts

CHAPTER QUIZ: KEY TERMS, PEOPLE, PLACES, CONCEPTS

1. A _____ is a binary compound, of which one part is a halogen atom and the other part is an element or radical that is less electronegative than the halogen, to make a fluoride, chloride, bromide, iodide, or astatide compound. Many salts are _____ s. All Group 1 metals form _____ s which are white solids at room temperature.

    a. Halotolerance
    b. Halide
    c. Meisenheimer complex
    d. Methoxide

2. _____ is the organic compound with the formula $CH_3COOCH_2CH_3$. This colorless liquid has a characteristic sweet smell (similar to pear drops) and is used in glues, nail polish removers, and cigarettes . _____ is the ester of ethanol and acetic acid; it is manufactured on a large scale for use as a solvent.

    a. Ethyl acetate
    b. Ethyl butyrate
    c. Ethyl lactate
    d. Ethylene carbonate

3. A _____ in chemistry is a chemical bond between two chemical elements involving two bonding electrons.

    Usually, _____ is Sigma bond. but diboron is Pi bond.(Molecular orbital diagram#Diboron MO diagram.

    a. Stacking
    b. Starch gelatinization
    c. Single bond
    d. Symmetric hydrogen bond

4. _____ is an inorganic compound with the formula LiF. It is the lithium salt of hydrofluoric acid. This white solid is a simple ionic compound. Its structure is analogous to that of sodium chloride, but it is much less soluble in water.

    a. Lithium fluoride
    b. Magnesium bromide
    c. Magnesium chloride
    d. Magnesium fluoride

5. _____, symbol χ, is a chemical property that describes the tendency of an atom or a functional group to attract electrons towards itself. An atom's _____ is affected by both its atomic number and the distance that its valence electrons reside from the charged nucleus. The higher the associated _____ number, the more an element or compound attracts electrons towards it.

    a. Energy level
    b. Inert
    c. Ionization energy
    d. Electronegativity

Visit Cram101.com for full Practice Exams

1. b
2. a
3. c
4. a
5. d

You can take the complete Chapter Practice Test

for Chapter 9. Chemical Bonding I: Basic Concepts
on all key terms, persons, places, and concepts.

Online 99 Cents

http://www.epub14.1.20267.9.cram101.com/

Use www.Cram101.com for all your study needs

including Cram101's online interactive problem solving labs in

chemistry, statistics, mathematics, and more.

Chapter 10. Chemical Bonding II: Molecular Geometry and Hybridization of

CHAPTER OUTLINE: KEY TERMS, PEOPLE, PLACES, CONCEPTS

	Molecular geometry
	Atom
	Geometry
	Lone pair
	Molecule
	Triple bond
	Beryllium
	Beryllium chloride
	Chloride
	Methane
	Lewis structure
	Ozone
	Sulfur
	Sulfur hexafluoride
	Hexafluoride
	Amino acid
	Methanol
	Dipole
	Hydrogen

_____ | Hydrogen fluoride

_____ | Fluoride

_____ | Moment

_____ | Carbon

_____ | Carbon dioxide

_____ | Debye

_____ | Hydrogen halide

_____ | Halide

_____ | Microwave oven

_____ | Hydrogen atom

_____ | Atomic orbital

_____ | Potential

_____ | Potential energy

_____ | Boron

_____ | Boron trifluoride

_____ | Trifluoride

_____ | Cytosine

_____ | Double bond

_____ | Ethyl acetate

	Pi bond
	Sigma bond
	Acetate
	Acetone
	Formaldehyde
	Molecular orbital
	Antibonding
	Magnetism
	Oxygen
	Paramagnetism
	Density
	Electron
	Electron density
	Pauli exclusion principle
	Energy level
	Bond order
	Order
	Diatomic molecule
	Nitrogen

	Benzene
	Graphene

CHAPTER HIGHLIGHTS & NOTES: KEY TERMS, PEOPLE, PLACES, CONCEPTS

Molecular geometry	Molecular geometry is the three-dimensional arrangement of the atoms that constitute a molecule. It determines several properties of a substance including its reactivity, polarity, phase of matter, color, magnetism, and biological activity. The molecular geometry can be determined by various spectroscopic methods and diffraction methods.
Atom	The atom is a basic unit of matter that consists of a dense central nucleus surrounded by a cloud of negatively charged electrons. The atomic nucleus contains a mix of positively charged protons and electrically neutral neutrons (except in the case of hydrogen-1, which is the only stable nuclide with no neutrons). The electrons of an atom are bound to the nucleus by the electromagnetic force.
Geometry	Geometry is a branch of mathematics concerned with questions of shape, size, relative position of figures, and the properties of space. A mathematician who works in the field of geometry is called a geometer. Geometry arose independently in a number of early cultures as a body of practical knowledge concerning lengths, areas, and volumes, with elements of a formal mathematical science emerging in the West as early as Thales (6th Century BC).
Lone pair	In chemistry, a lone pair is a valence electron pair without bonding or sharing with other atoms. They are found in the outermost electron shell of an atom, so lone pairs are a subset of a molecule's valence electrons. They can be identified by examining the outermost energy level of an atom--lone electron pairs consist of paired electrons as opposed to single electrons, which may appear if the atomic orbital is not full.
Molecule	A molecule is an electrically neutral group of two or more atoms held together by covalent chemical bonds. Molecules are distinguished from ions by their lack of electrical charge.

Triple bond	A triple bond in chemistry is a chemical bond between two chemical elements involving six bonding electrons instead of the usual two in a covalent single bond. The most common triple bond, that between two carbon atoms, can be found in alkynes. Other functional groups containing a triple bond are cyanides and isocyanides.
Beryllium	Beryllium is the chemical element with the symbol Be and atomic number 4. Because any beryllium synthesized in stars is short-lived, it is a relatively rare element in both the universe and in the crust of the Earth. It is a divalent element which occurs naturally only in combination with other elements in minerals. Notable gemstones which contain beryllium include beryl (aquamarine, emerald) and chrysoberyl.
Beryllium chloride	Beryllium chloride is an inorganic compound with the formula $BeCl_2$. It is a colourless, hygroscopic solid that dissolves well in many polar solvents. Its properties are similar to those of aluminium trichloride.
Chloride	The chloride ion is formed when the element chlorine, a halogen, gains an electron to form an anion (negatively-charged ion) Cl^-. The salts of hydrochloric acid contain chloride ions and can also be called chlorides. The chloride ion, and its salts such as sodium chloride, are very soluble in water.
Methane	Methane is a chemical compound with the chemical formula CH4. It is the simplest alkane, the main component of natural gas, and probably the most abundant organic compound on earth. The relative abundance of methane makes it an attractive fuel. However, because it is a gas at normal conditions, methane is difficult to transport from its source.
Lewis structure	Lewis structures (also known as Lewis dot diagrams, electron dot diagrams, and electron dot structures) are diagrams that show the bonding between atoms of a molecule and the lone pairs of electrons that may exist in the molecule.
Ozone	Ozone or trioxygen, is a triatomic molecule, consisting of three oxygen atoms. It is an allotrope of oxygen that is much less stable than the diatomic allotrope (O_2), breaking down with a half life of about half an hour in the lower atmosphere, to normal dioxygen. Ozone is formed from dioxygen by the action of ultraviolet light and also atmospheric electrical discharges, and is present in low concentrations throughout the Earth's atmosphere.
Sulfur	Sulfur or sulphur is the chemical element with atomic number 16. In the periodic table it is represented by the symbol S. It is an abundant, multivalent non-metal.

	Under normal conditions, sulfur atoms form cyclic octatomic molecules with chemical formula S_8. Elemental sulfur is a bright yellow crystalline solid when at room temperature.
Sulfur hexafluoride	Sulfur hexafluoride is an inorganic, colorless, odorless, and non-flammable greenhouse gas. SF_6 has an octahedral geometry, consisting of six fluorine atoms attached to a central sulfur atom. It is a hypervalent molecule.
Hexafluoride	A hexafluoride is a chemical compound with the general formula XF_6. Sixteen elements are known to form stable hexafluorides. Nine of these elements are transition metals, three are actinides, and four are nonmetals or metalloids.
Amino acid	Amino acids are molecules containing an amine group, a carboxylic acid group, and a side-chain that is specific to each amino acid. The key elements of an amino acid are carbon, hydrogen, oxygen, and nitrogen. They are particularly important in biochemistry, where the term usually refers to alpha-amino acids.
Methanol	Methanol, wood alcohol, wood naphtha or wood spirits, is a chemical with the formula CH_3OH . It is the simplest alcohol, and is a light, volatile, colorless, flammable liquid with a distinctive odor very similar to, but slightly sweeter than, ethanol (drinking alcohol). At room temperature, it is a polar liquid, and is used as an antifreeze, solvent, fuel, and as a denaturant for ethanol.
Dipole	In physics, there are several kinds of dipoles:•An electric dipole is a separation of positive and negative charges. The simplest example of this is a pair of electric charges of equal magnitude but opposite sign, separated by some (usually small) distance. A permanent electric dipole is called an electret.•A magnetic dipole is a closed circulation of electric current.
Hydrogen	Hydrogen is the chemical element with atomic number 1. It is represented by the symbol H. With an average atomic weight of 1.00794 u (1.007825 u for hydrogen-1), hydrogen is the lightest element and its monatomic form (H_1) is the most abundant chemical substance, constituting roughly 75% of the Universe's baryonic mass. Non-remnant stars are mainly composed of hydrogen in its plasma state. At standard temperature and pressure, hydrogen is a colorless, odorless, tasteless, non-toxic, nonmetallic, highly combustible diatomic gas with the molecular formula H_2.
Hydrogen fluoride	Hydrogen fluoride is a chemical compound with the formula HF. This colorless gas is the principal industrial source of fluorine, often in the aqueous form as hydrofluoric acid, and thus is the precursor to many important compounds including pharmaceuticals and polymers (e.g. Teflon).

HF is widely used in the petrochemical industry and is a component of many superacids. Hydrogen fluoride boils just below room temperature whereas the other hydrogen halides condense at much lower temperatures.

| Fluoride | Fluoride is the anion F⁻, the reduced form of fluorine when as an ion and when bonded to another element. Both organofluorine compounds and inorganic fluorine containing compounds are called fluorides. Fluoride, like other halides, is a monovalent ion (−1 charge). |

Moment

A moment is a medieval unit of time equal to 1.5 minutes or .025 of an hour. In modern English it usually refers to 'a short period of time', the exact length remaining ambiguous.

In the Hebrew calendar, a moment (rega) is 1/76 of a part (chelek), or 5/114 of a second in standard units.

Carbon

Carbon is the chemical element with symbol C and atomic number 6. As a member of group 14 on the periodic table, it is nonmetallic and tetravalent--making four electrons available to form covalent chemical bonds. There are three naturally occurring isotopes, with ^{12}C and ^{13}C being stable, while ^{14}C is radioactive, decaying with a half-life of about 5,730 years. Carbon is one of the few elements known since antiquity.

Carbon dioxide

Carbon dioxide is a naturally occurring chemical compound composed of two oxygen atoms covalently bonded to a single carbon atom. It is a gas at standard temperature and pressure and exists in Earth's atmosphere in this state, as a trace gas at a concentration of 0.039% by volume.

As part of the carbon cycle known as photosynthesis, plants, algae, and cyanobacteria absorb carbon dioxide, light, and water to produce carbohydrate energy for themselves and oxygen as a waste product.

Debye

The debye is a CGS unit (a non-SI metric unit) of electric dipole moment named in honor of the physicist Peter J. W. Debye. It is defined as 1×10^{-18} statcoulomb-centimeter. Historically the debye was defined as the dipole moment resulting from two charges of opposite sign but an equal magnitude of 10^{-10} statcoulomb (generally called e.s.u.

Hydrogen halide

Hydrogen halides (or hydrohalic acids) are inorganic compounds with the formula HX where X is one of the halogens: fluorine, chlorine, bromine, iodine, and astatine. Hydrogen halides are gases that dissolve in water to give acids.

Halide	A halide is a binary compound, of which one part is a halogen atom and the other part is an element or radical that is less electronegative than the halogen, to make a fluoride, chloride, bromide, iodide, or astatide compound. Many salts are halides. All Group 1 metals form halides which are white solids at room temperature.
Microwave oven	A microwave oven is a kitchen appliance that heats food by dielectric heating accomplished with radiation used to heat polarized molecules in food. Microwave ovens heat foods quickly and efficiently, because excitation is fairly uniform in the outer 1 inch (25 mm) to 1.5 inches (38 mm) of a dense (high water content) food item; food is more evenly heated throughout (except in thick, dense objects) than generally occurs in other cooking techniques. Dr. Percy Spencer invented the first microwave oven after World War II from radar technology developed during the war.
Hydrogen atom	A hydrogen atom is an atom of the chemical element hydrogen. The electrically neutral atom contains a single positively-charged proton and a single negatively-charged electron bound to the nucleus by the Coulomb force. Atomic hydrogen comprises about 75% of the elemental mass of the universe.
Atomic orbital	An atomic orbital is a mathematical function that describes the wave-like behavior of either one electron or a pair of electrons in an atom. This function can be used to calculate the probability of finding any electron of an atom in any specific region around the atom's nucleus. The term may also refer to the physical region where the electron can be calculated to be, as defined by the particular mathematical form of the orbital.
Potential	•In linguistics, the potential mood•The mathematical study of potentials is known as potential theory; it is the study of harmonic functions on manifolds. This mathematical formulation arises from the fact that, in physics, the scalar potential is irrotational, and thus has a vanishing Laplacian -- the very definition of a harmonic function.•In physics, a potential may refer to the scalar potential or to the vector potential. In either case, it is a field defined in space, from which many important physical properties may be derived.
Potential energy	In physics, potential energy is the energy of a body or a system due to the position of the body or the arrangement of the particles of the system. The SI unit for measuring work and energy is the Joule (symbol J). The term 'potential energy' was coined by the 19th century Scottish engineer and physicist William Rankine.
Boron	

Boron is the chemical element with atomic number 5 and the chemical symbol B. Because boron is produced entirely by cosmic ray spallation and not by stellar nucleosynthesis, it is a low-abundance element in both the solar system and the Earth's crust. However, boron is concentrated on Earth by the water-solubility of its more common naturally occurring compounds, the borate minerals. These are mined industrially as evaporate ores, such as borax and kernite.

Boron trifluoride

Boron trifluoride is the chemical compound with the formula BF_3. This pungent colourless toxic gas forms white fumes in moist air. It is a useful Lewis acid and a versatile building block for other boron compounds.

Trifluoride

Trifluorides are compounds having three fluorines per formula unit. Many metals form trifluorides, such as iron, the rare earth elements, and the metals in the aluminium and scandium columns of the periodic table. No trifluoride is soluble in water, but several are soluble in other solvents.

Cytosine

Cytosine is one of the four main bases found in DNA and RNA, along with adenine, guanine, and thymine (uracil in RNA). It is a pyrimidine derivative, with a heterocyclic aromatic ring and two substituents attached (an amine group at position 4 and a keto group at position 2). The nucleoside of cytosine is cytidine.

Double bond

A double bond in chemistry is a chemical bond between two chemical elements involving four bonding electrons instead of the usual two. The most common double bond, that between two carbon atoms, can be found in alkenes. Many types of double bonds between two different elements exist, for example in a carbonyl group with a carbon atom and an oxygen atom.

Ethyl acetate

Ethyl acetate is the organic compound with the formula $CH_3COOCH_2CH_3$. This colorless liquid has a characteristic sweet smell (similar to pear drops) and is used in glues, nail polish removers, and cigarettes . Ethyl acetate is the ester of ethanol and acetic acid; it is manufactured on a large scale for use as a solvent.

Pi bond

In chemistry, pi bonds (π bonds) are covalent chemical bonds where two lobes of one involved atomic orbital overlap two lobes of the other involved atomic orbital. These orbitals share a nodal plane which passes through both of the involved nuclei.

The Greek letter π in their name refers to p orbitals, since the orbital symmetry of the pi bond is the same as that of the p orbital when seen down the bond axis.

Sigma bond

In chemistry, sigma bonds (σ bonds) are the strongest type of covalent chemical bond. They are formed by head-on overlapping between atomic orbitals.

Acetate	An acetate is a derivative of acetic acid. This term includes salts and esters, as well as the anion found in solution. Most of the approximately 5 billion kilograms of acetic acid produced annually in industry are used in the production of acetates, which usually take the form of polymers.
Acetone	Acetone is the organic compound with the formula $(CH_3)_2CO$, a colorless, mobile, flammable liquid, the simplest example of the ketones.
	Acetone is miscible with water and serves as an important solvent in its own right, typically as the solvent of choice for cleaning purposes in the laboratory. About 6.7 million tonnes were produced worldwide in 2010, mainly for use as a solvent and production of methyl methacrylate and bisphenol A. It is a common building block in organic chemistry.
Formaldehyde	Formaldehyde is an organic compound with the formula CH_2O. It is the simplest form of aldehyde, hence its systematic name methanal.
	A gas at room temperature, formaldehyde is colorless and has a characteristic pungent, irritating odor. It is an important precursor to many other chemical compounds, especially for polymers.
Molecular orbital	In chemistry, a molecular orbital is a mathematical function describing the wave-like behavior of an electron in a molecule. This function can be used to calculate chemical and physical properties such as the probability of finding an electron in any specific region. The term 'orbital' was first used in English by Robert S. Mulliken as the English translation of Schrödinger's 'Eigenfunktion'.
Antibonding	Antibonding is a type of chemical bonding. An antibonding orbital is a form of molecular orbital (MO) that is located outside the region of two distinct nuclei. The overlap of the constituent atomic orbitals is said to be out of phase, and as such the electrons present in each antibonding orbital are repulsive and act to destabilize the molecule as a whole.
Magnetism	Magnetism is a property of materials that respond to an applied magnetic field. Permanent magnets have persistent magnetic fields caused by ferromagnetism. That is the strongest and most familiar type of magnetism.
Oxygen	
	Oxygen is the element with atomic number 8 and represented by the symbol O. Its name derives from the Greek roots ?ξ?ς (oxys) ('acid', literally 'sharp', referring to the sour taste of acids) and -γεν?ς (-genes) ('producer', literally 'begetter'), because at the time of naming, it was mistakenly thought that all acids required oxygen in their composition.

At standard temperature and pressure, two atoms of the element bind to form dioxygen, a very pale blue, odorless, tasteless diatomic gas with the formula O_2.

Oxygen is a member of the chalcogen group on the periodic table and is a highly reactive nonmetallic element that readily forms compounds (notably oxides) with almost all other elements.

Paramagnetism	Paramagnetism is a form of magnetism whereby the paramagnetic material is only attracted when in the presence of an externally applied magnetic field. In contrast with this behavior, diamagnetic materials are repelled by magnetic fields. Paramagnetic materials have a relative magnetic permeability greater or equal to unity (i.e., a positive magnetic susceptibility) and hence are attracted to magnetic fields.
Density	The mass density is defined as its mass per unit volume. The symbol most often used for density is ρ . In some cases (for instance, in the United States oil and gas industry), density is also defined as its weight per unit volume; although, this quantity is more properly called specific weight.
Electron	The electron is a subatomic particle with a negative elementary electric charge. It has no known components or substructure; in other words, it is generally thought to be an elementary particle. An electron has a mass that is approximately 1/1836 that of the proton.
Electron density	Electron density is the measure of the probability of an electron being present at a specific location. In molecules, regions of electron density are usually found around the atom, and its bonds. In de-localized or conjugated systems, such as phenol, benzene and compounds such as hemoglobin and chlorophyll, the electron density covers an entire region, i.e., in benzene they are found above and below the planar ring.
Pauli exclusion principle	The Pauli exclusion principle is the quantum mechanical principle that no two identical fermions (particles with half-integer spin) may occupy the same quantum state simultaneously. A more rigorous statement is that the total wave function for two identical fermions is anti-symmetric with respect to exchange of the particles. The principle was formulated by Austrian physicist Wolfgang Pauli in 1925.
Energy level	A quantum mechanical system or particle that is bound -- that is, confined spatially--can only take on certain discrete values of energy. This contrasts with classical particles, which can have any energy. These discrete values are called energy levels.
Bond order	Bond order is the number of chemical bonds between a pair of atoms.

For example, in diatomic nitrogen N≡N the bond order is 3, while in acetylene H−C≡C−H the bond order between the two carbon atoms is also 3, and the C−H bond order is 1. Bond order gives an indication to the stability of a bond. In a more advanced context, bond order does not need to be an integer.

| Order | Order (subtitled 'A Journal on the Theory of Ordered Sets and its Applications') is a quarterly peer-reviewed academic journal on order theory and its applications, published by Springer Science+Business Media. It was founded in 1984 by University of Calgary mathematics professor Ivan Rival; as of 2010, its editor in chief is Dwight Duffus, the Goodrich C. White Professor of Mathematics & Computer Science at Emory University and a former student of Rival's.

According to the Journal Citation Reports, the 2009 impact factor of Order is 0.408, placing it in the fourth quartile of ranked mathematics journals. |

| Diatomic molecule | Diatomic molecules are molecules composed only of two atoms, of either the same or different chemical elements. The prefix di- is of Greek origin, meaning 2. Common diatomic molecules are hydrogen (H_2), nitrogen (N_2), oxygen (O_2), and carbon monoxide (CO). Seven elements exist as homonuclear diatomic molecules at room temperature: H_2, N_2, O_2, F_2, Cl_2, Br_2, and I_2. |

| Nitrogen | Nitrogen is a chemical element that has the symbol N, atomic number of 7 and atomic mass 14.00674 u. Elemental nitrogen is a colorless, odorless, tasteless, and mostly inert diatomic gas at standard conditions, constituting 78.09% by volume of Earth's atmosphere. The element nitrogen was discovered as a separable component of air, by Scottish physician Daniel Rutherford, in 1772. |

| Benzene | Benzene is an organic chemical compound with the molecular formula C_6H_6. Its molecule is composed of 6 carbon atoms joined in a ring, with 1 hydrogen atom attached to each carbon atom. Because its molecules contain only carbon and hydrogen atoms, benzene is classed as a hydrocarbon. |

| Graphene | Graphene is an allotrope of carbon. Its structure is one-atom-thick planar sheets of sp^2-bonded carbon atoms that are densely packed in a honeycomb crystal lattice. The term graphene was coined as a combination of graphite and the suffix -ene by Hanns-Peter Boehm, who described single-layer carbon foils in 1962. Graphene is most easily visualized as an atomic-scale chicken wire made of carbon atoms and their bonds. |

1. The _____ is a CGS unit (a non-SI metric unit) of electric dipole moment named in honor of the physicist Peter J. W. _____. It is defined as 1×10^{-18} statcoulomb-centimeter. Historically the _____ was defined as the dipole moment resulting from two charges of opposite sign but an equal magnitude of 10^{-10} statcoulomb (generally called e.s.u.

   a. 1,2-Dioxetanedione
   b. Debye
   c. Chlorofluorocarbon
   d. Chloromethane

2. _____ is the anion F⁻, the reduced form of fluorine when as an ion and when bonded to another element. Both organofluorine compounds and inorganic fluorine containing compounds are called _____s. Fluoride, like other halides, is a monovalent ion (−1 charge).

   a. Hydride
   b. Hydrogen anion
   c. Hypothiocyanite
   d. Fluoride

3. _____ is an inorganic, colorless, odorless, and non-flammable greenhouse gas. SF_6 has an octahedral geometry, consisting of six fluorine atoms attached to a central sulfur atom. It is a hypervalent molecule.

   a. Tungsten hexacarbonyl
   b. Tungsten hexachloride
   c. Tungsten hexafluoride
   d. Sulfur hexafluoride

4. _____s (also known as Lewis dot diagrams, electron dot diagrams, and electron dot structures) are diagrams that show the bonding between atoms of a molecule and the lone pairs of electrons that may exist in the molecule.

   a. Ligand
   b. Ligand dependent pathway
   c. Lewis structure
   d. Ligand isomerism

5. _____ is a chemical compound with the chemical formula CH4. It is the simplest alkane, the main component of natural gas, and probably the most abundant organic compound on earth. The relative abundance of _____ makes it an attractive fuel. However, because it is a gas at normal conditions, _____ is difficult to transport from its source.

   a. Nitrogen trifluoride
   b. Disulfide
   c. Ferricyanide
   d. Methane

1. b
2. d
3. d
4. c
5. d

You can take the complete Chapter Practice Test

for Chapter 10. Chemical Bonding II: Molecular Geometry and Hybridization of Atomic Orbitals
on all key terms, persons, places, and concepts.

Online 99 Cents

http://www.epub14.1.20267.10.cram101.com/

Use www.Cram101.com for all your study needs

including Cram101's online interactive problem solving labs in

chemistry, statistics, mathematics, and more.

Chapter 11. Intermolecular Forces and Liquids and Solids

CHAPTER OUTLINE: KEY TERMS, PEOPLE, PLACES, CONCEPTS

	Intermolecular force
	Intramolecular force
	Van der Waals force
	Dipole
	Dispersion
	Helium
	Polarizability
	Boiling point
	Point
	Hydrogen
	Hydrogen bond
	Adhesion
	Capillary action
	Cohesion
	Surface tension
	Glycerol
	Viscosity
	Carbon
	Carbon dioxide

Chapter 11. Intermolecular Forces and Liquids and Solids

CHAPTER OUTLINE: KEY TERMS, PEOPLE, PLACES, CONCEPTS

_____ Crystal structure

_____ Density

_____ Coordination number

_____ Efficiency

_____ Diffraction

_____ Ionic crystal

_____ Single bond

_____ Fluorite

_____ Graphite

_____ Melting

_____ Melting point

_____ Quartz

_____ Sulfur

_____ Alkali

_____ Alkali metal

_____ Molecular orbital

_____ Amorphous solid

_____ Gibbs free energy

_____ Pyrex

_____ | Vapor

_____ | Vapor pressure

_____ | Vaporization

_____ | Condensation

_____ | Dynamic equilibrium

_____ | Sulfur hexafluoride

_____ | Hexafluoride

_____ | Heat fusion

_____ | Cooling curve

_____ | Functional group

_____ | Supercooling

_____ | Group

_____ | Iodine

_____ | Phase diagram

_____ | Triple point

_____ | Dry ice

_____ | Ice skating

_____ | Liquid crystal

Intermolecular force	Intermolecular forces are forces of attraction or repulsion which act between neighboring particles: atoms, molecules or ions. They are weak compared to the intramolecular forces, the forces which keep a molecule together. For example, the covalent bond present within HCl molecules is much stronger than the forces present between the neighbouring molecules, which exist when the molecules are sufficiently close to each other.
Intramolecular force	An intramolecular force is any force that holds together the atoms making up a molecule or compound. They contain all types of chemical bond. They are stronger than intermolecular forces, which are present between atoms or molecules that are not actually bonded.
Van der Waals force	In physical chemistry, the van der Waals force , is the sum of the attractive or repulsive forces between molecules other than those due to covalent bonds, the hydrogen bonds, or the electrostatic interaction of ions with one another or with neutral molecules The term includes:•force between two permanent dipoles (Keesom force)•force between a permanent dipole and a corresponding induced dipole (Debye force)•force between two instantaneously induced dipoles (London dispersion force)
	It is also sometimes used loosely as a synonym for the totality of intermolecular forces. Van der Waals forces are relatively weak compared to covalent bonds, but play a fundamental role in fields as diverse as supramolecular chemistry, structural biology, polymer science, nanotechnology, surface science, and condensed matter physics. Van der Waals forces define many properties of organic compounds, including their solubility in polar and non-polar media.
Dipole	In physics, there are several kinds of dipoles:•An electric dipole is a separation of positive and negative charges. The simplest example of this is a pair of electric charges of equal magnitude but opposite sign, separated by some (usually small) distance. A permanent electric dipole is called an electret.•A magnetic dipole is a closed circulation of electric current.
Dispersion	A dispersion is a system in which particles are dispersed in a continuous phase of a different composition . A dispersion is classified in a number of different ways, including how large the particles are in relation to the particles of the continuous phase, whether or not precipitation occurs, and the presence of Brownian motion.
	There are three main types of dispersions:•Coarse dispersion (Suspension)•Colloid•SolutionTypes of dispersions Structure and Properties of Dispersions
	It is still common belief, that dispersions basically do not display any structure, i.e., the particles dispersed in the liquid or solid matrix (the 'dispersion medium') are assumed to be statistically distributed.
Helium	

Helium is the chemical element with atomic number 2 and an atomic weight of 4.002602, which is represented by the symbol He. It is a colorless, odorless, tasteless, non-toxic, inert, monatomic gas that heads the noble gas group in the periodic table. Its boiling and melting points are the lowest among the elements and it exists only as a gas except in extreme conditions.

Polarizability

Polarizability is the measure of the change in a molecule's electron distribution in response to an applied electric field, which can also be induced by electric interactions with solvents or ionic reagents. It is a property of matter. Polarizabilities determine the dynamical response of a bound system to external fields, and provide insight into a molecule's internal structure.

Boiling point

The boiling point of a substance is the temperature at which the vapor pressure of the liquid equals the environmental pressure surrounding the liquid.

A liquid in a vacuum has a lower boiling point than when that liquid is at atmospheric pressure. A liquid at high-pressure has a higher boiling point than when that liquid is at atmospheric pressure.

Point

Points, sometimes also called a 'discount point', are a form of pre-paid interest. One point equals one percent of the loan amount. By charging a borrower points, a lender effectively increases the yield on the loan above the amount of the stated interest rate.

Hydrogen

Hydrogen is the chemical element with atomic number 1. It is represented by the symbol H. With an average atomic weight of 1.00794 u (1.007825 u for hydrogen-1), hydrogen is the lightest element and its monatomic form (H_1) is the most abundant chemical substance, constituting roughly 75% of the Universe's baryonic mass. Non-remnant stars are mainly composed of hydrogen in its plasma state.

At standard temperature and pressure, hydrogen is a colorless, odorless, tasteless, non-toxic, nonmetallic, highly combustible diatomic gas with the molecular formula H_2.

Hydrogen bond

A hydrogen bond is the attractive interaction of a hydrogen atom with an electronegative atom, such as nitrogen, oxygen or fluorine, that comes from another molecule or chemical group. The hydrogen has a polar bonding to another electronegative atom to create the bond. These bonds can occur between molecules (intermolecularly), or within different parts of a single molecule (intramolecularly).

Adhesion	Adhesion is the tendency of dissimilar particles or surfaces to cling to one another (cohesion refers to the tendency of similar or identical particles/surfaces to cling to one another). The forces that cause adhesion and cohesion can be divided into several types. The intermolecular forces responsible for the function of various kinds of stickers and sticky tape fall into the categories of chemical adhesion, dispersive adhesion, and diffusive adhesion.
Capillary action	Capillary action, is the ability of a liquid to flow in narrow spaces without the assistance of, and in opposition to external forces like gravity. The effect can be seen in the drawing up of liquids between the hairs of a paint-brush, in a thin tube, in porous materials such as paper, in some non-porous materials such as liquified carbon fiber, or in a cell. It occurs because of inter-molecular attractive forces between the liquid and solid surrounding surfaces.
Cohesion	Cohesion (n. lat. cohaerere 'stick or stay together') or cohesive attraction or cohesive force is the action or property of like molecules sticking together, being mutually attractive.
Surface tension	Surface tension is a property of the surface of a liquid that allows it to resist an external force. It is revealed, for example, in the floating of some objects on the surface of water, even though they are denser than water, and in the ability of some insects (e.g. water striders) to run on the water surface. This property is caused by cohesion of similar molecules, and is responsible for many of the behaviors of liquids.
Glycerol	Glycerol is a simple polyol compound. It is a colorless, odorless, viscous liquid that is widely used in pharmaceutical formulations. Glycerol has three hydroxyl groups that are responsible for its solubility in water and its hygroscopic nature.
Viscosity	Viscosity is a measure of the resistance of a fluid which is being deformed by either shear stress or tensile stress. In everyday terms (and for fluids only), viscosity is 'thickness' or 'internal friction'. Thus, water is 'thin', having a lower viscosity, while honey is 'thick', having a higher viscosity.
Carbon	Carbon is the chemical element with symbol C and atomic number 6. As a member of group 14 on the periodic table, it is nonmetallic and tetravalent--making four electrons available to form covalent chemical bonds. There are three naturally occurring isotopes, with ^{12}C and ^{13}C being stable, while ^{14}C is radioactive, decaying with a half-life of about 5,730 years. Carbon is one of the few elements known since antiquity.
Carbon dioxide	Carbon dioxide is a naturally occurring chemical compound composed of two oxygen atoms covalently bonded to a single carbon atom. It is a gas at standard temperature and pressure and exists in Earth's atmosphere in this state, as a trace gas at a concentration of 0.039% by volume.

As part of the carbon cycle known as photosynthesis, plants, algae, and cyanobacteria absorb carbon dioxide, light, and water to produce carbohydrate energy for themselves and oxygen as a waste product.

Crystal structure	In mineralogy and crystallography, crystal structure is a unique arrangement of atoms or molecules in a crystalline liquid or solid. A crystal structure is composed of a pattern, a set of atoms arranged in a particular way, and a lattice exhibiting long-range order and symmetry. Patterns are located upon the points of a lattice, which is an array of points repeating periodically in three dimensions.
Density	The mass density is defined as its mass per unit volume. The symbol most often used for density is ρ. In some cases (for instance, in the United States oil and gas industry), density is also defined as its weight per unit volume; although, this quantity is more properly called specific weight.
Coordination number	In chemistry and crystallography, the coordination number of a central atom in a molecule or crystal is the number of its nearest neighbours. This number is determined somewhat differently for molecules and for crystals.
	In chemistry, the emphasis is on bonding structure in molecules or ions and the coordination number of an atom is determined by simply counting the other atoms to which it is bonded (by either single or multiple bonds).
Efficiency	Efficiency in general describes the extent to which time or effort is well used for the intended task or purpose. It is often used with the specific purpose of relaying the capability of a specific application of effort to produce a specific outcome effectively with a minimum amount or quantity of waste, expense, or unnecessary effort. 'Efficiency' has widely varying meanings in different disciplines.
Diffraction	Diffraction refers to various phenomena which occur when a wave encounters an obstacle. Italian scientist Francesco Maria Grimaldi coined the word 'diffraction' and was the first to record accurate observations of the phenomenon in 1665. In classical physics, the diffraction phenomenon is described as the apparent bending of waves around small obstacles and the spreading out of waves past small openings. Similar effects occur when light waves travel through a medium with a varying refractive index or a sound wave through one with varying acoustic impedance.
Ionic crystal	An ionic crystal is a crystal consisting of ions bound together by their electrostatic attraction.

Examples of such crystals are the alkali halides, including potassium fluoride, potassium chloride, potassium bromide, potassium iodide, sodium fluoride, and other combinations of sodium, caesium, rubidium, or lithium ions with fluoride, bromide, chloride or iodide ions. NaCl has a 6:6 co-ordination.

Single bond

A Single bond in chemistry is a chemical bond between two chemical elements involving two bonding electrons.

Usually, Single bond is Sigma bond. but diboron is Pi bond.(Molecular orbital diagram#Diboron MO diagram.

Fluorite

Fluorite is a halide mineral composed of calcium fluoride, CaF_2. It is an isometric mineral with a cubic habit, though octahedral and more complex isometric forms are not uncommon. Crystal twinning is common and adds complexity to the observed crystal habits.

Graphite

The mineral graphite is an allotrope of carbon. It was named by Abraham Gottlob Werner in 1789 from the Ancient Greek γρ?φω (grapho), 'to draw/write', for its use in pencils, where it is commonly called lead (not to be confused with the metallic element lead). Unlike diamond (another carbon allotrope), graphite is an electrical conductor, a semimetal.

Melting

Melting, is a physical process that results in the phase transition of a substance from a solid to a liquid. The internal energy of a substance is increased, typically by the application of heat or pressure, resulting in a rise of its temperature to the melting point, at which the rigid ordering of molecular entities in the solid breaks down to a less-ordered state and the solid liquefies. An object that has melted completely is molten.

Melting point

The melting point of a solid is the temperature at which it changes state from solid to liquid. At the melting point the solid and liquid phase exist in equilibrium. The melting point of a substance depends (usually slightly) on pressure and is usually specified at standard pressure.

Quartz

Quartz is an abundant mineral in the Earth's continental crust. It is made up of a continuous framework of SiO_4 silicon-oxygen tetrahedra, with each oxygen being shared between two tetrahedra, giving an overall formula SiO_2. There are many different varieties of quartz, several of which are semi-precious gemstones.

Sulfur

Sulfur or sulphur is the chemical element with atomic number 16. In the periodic table it is represented by the symbol S. It is an abundant, multivalent non-metal. Under normal conditions, sulfur atoms form cyclic octatomic molecules with chemical formula S_8.

Chapter 11. Intermolecular Forces and Liquids and Solids

Alkali	In chemistry, an alkali is a basic, ionic salt of an alkali metal or alkaline earth metal element. Some authors also define an alkali as a base that dissolves in water. A solution of a soluble base has a pH greater than 7. The adjective alkaline is commonly used in English as a synonym for base, especially for soluble bases.
Alkali metal	The alkali metals are a group of chemical elements in the periodic table with very similar properties: they are all shiny, soft, silvery, highly reactive metals at standard temperature and pressure and readily lose their outermost electron to form cations with charge +1. They can all be cut easily with a knife due to their softness, exposing a shiny surface that tarnishes rapidly in air due to oxidation. In the modern IUPAC nomenclature, the alkali metals comprise the group 1 elements, excluding hydrogen (H), which is nominally a group 1 element but not normally considered to be an alkali metal as it rarely exhibits behaviour comparable to that of the alkali metals. All the alkali metals react with water, with the heavier alkali metals reacting more vigorously than the lighter ones.
Molecular orbital	In chemistry, a molecular orbital is a mathematical function describing the wave-like behavior of an electron in a molecule. This function can be used to calculate chemical and physical properties such as the probability of finding an electron in any specific region. The term 'orbital' was first used in English by Robert S. Mulliken as the English translation of Schrödinger's 'Eigenfunktion'.
Amorphous solid	Unsolved problems in physics

In condensed matter physics, an amorphous or non-crystalline solid is a solid that lacks the long-range order characteristic of a crystal.

In part of the older literature, the term has been used synonymously with glass. Nowadays, 'amorphous solid' is considered to be the overarching concept, and 'glass' the more special case: A glass is an amorphous solid that transforms into a liquid upon heating through the glass transition. |
| Gibbs free energy | In thermodynamics, the Gibbs free energy is a thermodynamic potential that measures the 'useful' or process-initiating work obtainable from a thermodynamic system at a constant temperature and pressure (isothermal, isobaric). Just as in mechanics, where potential energy is defined as capacity to do work, similarly different potentials have different meanings. The Gibbs free energy is the maximum amount of non-expansion work that can be extracted from a closed system; this maximum can be attained only in a completely reversible process. |
| Pyrex | Pyrex is a brand which was introduced by Corning Incorporated in 1915 for a line of clear, low-thermal-expansion borosilicate glass used for laboratory glassware and kitchenware. |

Corning no longer manufactures or markets Pyrex-branded borosilicate glass kitchenware and bakeware in the United States, but Pyrex borosilicate products are still manufactured under license by various companies. World Kitchen, LLC, which was spun off from Corning in 1998, licensed the Pyrex brand for their own line of kitchenware products -- differentiated by their use of clear tempered soda-lime glass instead of borosilicate.

Vapor

A vapor or vapour is a substance in the gas phase at a temperature lower than its critical point. This means that the vapor can be condensed to a liquid or to a solid by increasing its pressure without reducing the temperature.

For example, water has a critical temperature of 374 °C (647 K), which is the highest temperature at which liquid water can exist.

Vapor pressure

Vapor pressure is the pressure exerted by a vapor in thermodynamic equilibrium with its condensed phases (solid or liquid) at a given temperature in a closed system. The equilibrium vapor pressure is an indication of a liquid's evaporation rate. It relates to the tendency of particles to escape from the liquid .

Vaporization

Vaporization of an element or compound is a phase transition from the liquid phase to gas phase. There are two types of vaporization: evaporation and boiling.

Evaporation is a phase transition from the liquid phase to gas phase that occurs at temperatures below the boiling temperature at a given pressure.

Condensation

Condensation is the change of the physical state of matter from gaseous phase into liquid phase, and is the reverse of vaporization. When the transition happens from the gaseous phase into the solid phase directly, the change is called deposition.

Condensation is initiated by the formation of atomic/molecular clusters of that species within its gaseous volume--like rain drop or snow-flake formation within clouds--or at the contact between such gaseous phase and a (solvent) liquid or solid surface.

Dynamic equilibrium

A dynamic equilibrium exists once a reversible reaction ceases to change its ratio of reactants/products, but substances move between the chemicals at an equal rate, meaning there is no net change. It is a particular example of a system in a steady state. In thermodynamics a closed system is in thermodynamic equilibrium when reactions occur at such rates that the composition of the mixture does not change with time.

Sulfur hexafluoride

Sulfur hexafluoride is an inorganic, colorless, odorless, and non-flammable greenhouse gas.

Chapter 11. Intermolecular Forces and Liquids and Solids

SF_6 has an octahedral geometry, consisting of six fluorine atoms attached to a central sulfur atom. It is a hypervalent molecule.

Hexafluoride	A hexafluoride is a chemical compound with the general formula XF_6. Sixteen elements are known to form stable hexafluorides. Nine of these elements are transition metals, three are actinides, and four are nonmetals or metalloids.
Heat fusion	Heat fusion is a welding process used to join two different pieces of a thermoplastic. This process involves heating both pieces simultaneously and pressing them together. The two pieces then cool together and form a permanent bond.
Cooling curve	A cooling curve is a line graph that represents the change of phase of matter, typically from a gas to a solid or a liquid to a solid. The independent variable (X-axis) is time and the dependent variable (Y-axis) is temperature. Below is an example of a cooling curve used in castings.
Functional group	In organic chemistry, functional groups are lexicon specific groups of atoms or bonds within molecules that are responsible for the characteristic chemical reactions of those molecules. The same functional group will undergo the same or similar chemical reaction(s) regardless of the size of the molecule it is a part of. However, its relative reactivity can be modified by nearby functional groups.
Supercooling	Supercooling, is the process of lowering the temperature of a liquid or a gas below its freezing point without it becoming a solid. A liquid below its standard freezing point will crystallize in the presence of a seed crystal or nucleus around which a crystal structure can form. However, lacking any such nucleus, the liquid phase can be maintained all the way down to the temperature at which crystal homogeneous nucleation occurs.
Group	In chemistry, a group (also known as a family) is a vertical column in the periodic table of the chemical elements. There are 18 groups in the standard periodic table, including the d-block elements, but excluding the f-block elements. The explanation of the pattern of the table is that the elements in a group have similar physical or chemical characteristic of the outermost electron shells of their atoms (i.e. the same core charge), as most chemical properties are dominated by the orbital location of the outermost electron.
Iodine	

Iodine is a chemical element with the symbol I and atomic number 53./ syllable break' style='border-bottom:1px dotted'>.?da?n-o-dyne, 'a?.?d?n-o-d?n, or 'a?.?di?n-o-deen in both American and British English. The name is from Greek ?οειδ?ς ioeides, meaning violet or purple, due to the color of elemental iodine vapor.

Iodine and its compounds are primarily used in nutrition, and industrially in the production of acetic acid and certain polymers.

Phase diagram	A phase diagram in physical chemistry, engineering, mineralogy, and materials science is a type of chart used to show conditions at which thermodynamically distinct phases can occur at equilibrium. In mathematics and physics, 'phase diagram' is used with a different meaning: a synonym for a phase space. Common components of a phase diagram are lines of equilibrium or phase boundaries, which refer to lines that mark conditions under which multiple phases can coexist at equilibrium.
Triple point	In thermodynamics, the triple point of a substance is the temperature and pressure at which the three phases (gas, liquid, and solid) of that substance coexist in thermodynamic equilibrium. For example, the triple point of mercury occurs at a temperature of -38.8344 °C and a pressure of 0.2 mPa. In addition to the triple point between solid, liquid, and gas, there can be triple points involving more than one solid phase, for substances with multiple polymorphs.
Dry ice	Dry ice, is the solid form of carbon dioxide. It is used primarily as a cooling agent. Its advantages include lower temperature than that of water ice and not leaving any residue (other than incidental frost from moisture in the atmosphere).
Ice skating	Ice skating is moving on ice by using ice skates. It can be done for a variety of reasons, including health benefits, leisure, traveling, and various sports. Ice skating occurs both on specially prepared indoor and outdoor tracks, as well as on naturally occurring bodies of frozen water, such as lakes and rivers.
Liquid crystal	Liquid crystals (LCs) are a state of matter that have properties between those of a conventional liquid and those of a solid crystal. For instance, an LC may flow like a liquid, but its molecules may be oriented in a crystal-like way. There are many different types of LC phases, which can be distinguished by their different optical properties (such as birefringence).

Chapter 11. Intermolecular Forces and Liquids and Solids

1. In thermodynamics, the _____ of a substance is the temperature and pressure at which the three phases (gas, liquid, and solid) of that substance coexist in thermodynamic equilibrium. For example, the _____ of mercury occurs at a temperature of −38.8344 °C and a pressure of 0.2 mPa.

   In addition to the _____ between solid, liquid, and gas, there can be _____s involving more than one solid phase, for substances with multiple polymorphs.

   a. Triple point
   b. Polyamorphism
   c. Pourbaix diagram
   d. Recrystallization

2. In organic chemistry, _____s are lexicon specific groups of atoms or bonds within molecules that are responsible for the characteristic chemical reactions of those molecules. The same _____ will undergo the same or similar chemical reaction(s) regardless of the size of the molecule it is a part of. However, its relative reactivity can be modified by nearby _____s.

   a. Functional group
   b. Glycopolymer
   c. Glycorandomization
   d. Heteroatom

3. In mineralogy and crystallography, _____ is a unique arrangement of atoms or molecules in a crystalline liquid or solid. A _____ is composed of a pattern, a set of atoms arranged in a particular way, and a lattice exhibiting long-range order and symmetry. Patterns are located upon the points of a lattice, which is an array of points repeating periodically in three dimensions.

   a. Crystal twinning
   b. Diamond anvil cell
   c. Digital image correlation
   d. Crystal structure

4. In physics, there are several kinds of _____s:•An electric _____ is a separation of positive and negative charges. The simplest example of this is a pair of electric charges of equal magnitude but opposite sign, separated by some (usually small) distance. A permanent electric _____ is called an electret.•A magnetic _____ is a closed circulation of electric current.

   a. Fire point
   b. Freezing-point depression
   c. Fusibility
   d. Dipole

5. . _____s are forces of attraction or repulsion which act between neighboring particles: atoms, molecules or ions. They are weak compared to the intramolecular forces, the forces which keep a molecule together.

For example, the covalent bond present within HCl molecules is much stronger than the forces present between the neighbouring molecules, which exist when the molecules are sufficiently close to each other.

a. Intimate ion pair
b. Intermolecular force
c. Ionic bond
d. Isopeptide bond

1. a
2. a
3. d
4. d
5. b

You can take the complete Chapter Practice Test

for Chapter 11. Intermolecular Forces and Liquids and Solids
on all key terms, persons, places, and concepts.

Online 99 Cents

http://www.epub14.1.20267.11.cram101.com/

Use www.Cram101.com for all your study needs

including Cram101's online interactive problem solving labs in

chemistry, statistics, mathematics, and more.

CHAPTER OUTLINE: KEY TERMS, PEOPLE, PLACES, CONCEPTS

	Alkane
	Brass
	Crystallization
	Sodium
	Sodium acetate
	Solution
	Acetate
	Hydrocarbon
	Solvation
	Concentration
	Mass
	Mass concentration
	Molality
	Mole
	Mole fraction
	Solubility
	Oxygen
	Thermal
	Thermal pollution

Chapter 12. Physical Properties of Solutions

_____ Partial pressure

_____ Amino acid

_____ Carbon

_____ Carbon dioxide

_____ Hemoglobin

_____ Arsenic

_____ Colligative properties

_____ Electrolyte

_____ Ideal solution

_____ Toluene

_____ Tyvek

_____ Fractional distillation

_____ Fractionating column

_____ Positive

_____ Distillation

_____ Boiling-point elevation

_____ Freezing-point depression

_____ Sodium carbonate

_____ Melting

Chapter 12. Physical Properties of Solutions

CHAPTER OUTLINE: KEY TERMS, PEOPLE, PLACES, CONCEPTS

	Antifreeze
	Ethylene
	Ethylene glycol
	Osmotic pressure
	Semipermeable membrane
	Membrane
	Hemolysis
	Crenation
	Transpiration
	Carbon cycle
	Molar mass
	Colloid
	Hemodialysis
	Aerosol
	Emulsion
	Tyndall effect
	Sodium stearate
	Stearate
	Thomas Garnett

Chapter 12. Physical Properties of Solutions

	Alcohol

Alkane	Alkanes (also known as paraffins or saturated hydrocarbons) are chemical compounds that consist only of hydrogen and carbon atoms and are bonded exclusively by single bonds (i.e., they are saturated compounds) without any cycles . Alkanes belong to a homologous series of organic compounds in which the members differ by a constant relative molecular mass of 14. They have 2 main commercial sources, crude oil and natural gas. Each carbon atom has 4 bonds (either C-H or C-C bonds), and each hydrogen atom is joined to a carbon atom (H-C bonds).
Brass	Brass is an alloy of copper and zinc; the proportions of zinc and copper can be varied to create a range of brasses with varying properties. In comparison, bronze is principally an alloy of copper and tin. Bronze does not necessarily contain tin, and a variety of alloys of copper, including alloys with arsenic, phosphorus, aluminium, manganese, and silicon, are commonly termed 'bronze'.
Crystallization	Crystallization is the (natural or artificial) process of formation of solid crystals precipitating from a solution, melt or more rarely deposited directly from a gas. Crystallization is also a chemical solid-liquid separation technique, in which mass transfer of a solute from the liquid solution to a pure solid crystalline phase occurs. In chemical engineering crystallization occurs in a crystallizer.
Sodium	Sodium is a chemical element with the symbol Na and atomic number 11. It is a soft, silvery-white, highly reactive metal and is a member of the alkali metals; its only stable isotope is ^{23}Na. The free metal does not occur in nature, but instead must be prepared from its compounds; it was first isolated by Humphry Davy in 1807 by the electrolysis of sodium hydroxide. Sodium is the sixth most abundant element in the Earth's crust, and exists in numerous minerals such as feldspars, sodalite and rock salt.

Chapter 12. Physical Properties of Solutions

Sodium acetate	Sodium acetate, CH_3COONa, also abbreviated NaOAc, also sodium ethanoate, is the sodium salt of acetic acid. This colourless salt has a wide range of uses. Industrial
	Sodium acetate is used in the textile industry to neutralize sulfuric acid waste streams, and as a photoresist while using aniline dyes.
Solution	In chemistry, a solution is a homogeneous mixture composed of only one phase. In such a mixture, a solute is a substance dissolved in another substance, known as a solvent. The solvent does the dissolving.
Acetate	An acetate is a derivative of acetic acid. This term includes salts and esters, as well as the anion found in solution. Most of the approximately 5 billion kilograms of acetic acid produced annually in industry are used in the production of acetates, which usually take the form of polymers.
Hydrocarbon	In organic chemistry, a hydrocarbon is an organic compound consisting entirely of hydrogen and carbon. Hydrocarbons from which one hydrogen atom has been removed are functional groups, called hydrocarbyls. Aromatic hydrocarbons (arenes), alkanes, alkenes, cycloalkanes and alkyne-based compounds are different types of hydrocarbons.
Solvation	Solvation, also sometimes called dissolution, is the process of attraction and association of molecules of a solvent with molecules or ions of a solute. As ions dissolve in a solvent they spread out and become surrounded by solvent molecules.
	By an IUPAC definition, solvation is an interaction of a solute with the solvent, which leads to stabilization of the solute species in the solution.
Concentration	In chemistry, concentration is defined as the abundance of a constituent divided by the total volume of a mixture. Furthermore, in chemistry, four types of mathematical description can be distinguished: mass concentration, molar concentration, number concentration, and volume concentration. The term concentration can be applied to any kind of chemical mixture, but most frequently it refers to solutes in solutions.
Mass	The mass recorded by a mass spectrometer can refer to different physical quantities depending on the characteristics of the instrument and the manner in which the mass spectrum is displayed.
	The accurate mass (more appropriately, the measured accurate mass) is an experimentally determined mass that allows the elemental composition to be determined. For molecules with mass below 200 u, a 5 ppm accuracy is sufficient to uniquely determine the elemental composition.

Chapter 12. Physical Properties of Solutions

Mass concentration	In chemistry, the mass concentration ρ_i is defined as the mass of a constituent m_i divided by the volume of the mixture V : $\rho_i = \dfrac{m_i}{V}$
	For a pure chemical the mass concentration equals its density. Definition and properties
	The volume V in the definition refers to the volume of the solution, not the volume of the solvent. One liter of a solution usually contains either slightly more or slightly less than 1 liter of solvent because the process of dissolution causes volume of liquid to increase or decrease.
Molality	In chemistry, the molality, b , of a solventsolute combination is defined as the amount of solute, n_{solute} , divided by the mass of the solvent, $m_{solvent}$ (not the mass of the solution): $b = \dfrac{n_{solute}}{m_{solvent}}$
	If a mixture contains more than one solute or solvent, each solvent/solute combination in the mixture is defined in this same way. Origin
	The earliest such definition of the intensive property molality and of its adjectival unit, the now-deprecated molal (formerly, a variant of molar, describing a solution of unit molar concentration), appear to have been coined by G. N. Lewis and M. Randall in their 1923 publication of Thermodynamics and the Free Energies of Chemical Substances. Though the two words are subject to being confused with one another, the molality and molarity of a weak aqueous solution happen to be nearly the same, as one kilogram of water (the solvent) occupies 1 liter of volume at room temperature and the small amount of solute would have little effect on the volume.
Mole	The mole is a unit of measurement for the amount of substance or chemical amount. It is one of the base units in the International System of Units, and has the unit symbol mol.
	The name mole is an 1897 translation of the German unit Mol, coined by the chemist Wilhelm Ostwald in 1893, although the related concept of equivalent mass had been in use at least a century earlier.
Mole fraction	In chemistry, the mole fraction x_i is defined as the amount of a constituent n_i divided by the total amount of all constituents in a mixture n_{tot} : $x_i = \dfrac{n_i}{n_{tot}}$
	$$\sum_{i=1}^{N} n_i = n_{tot}; \quad \sum_{i=1}^{N} x_i = 1$$ The sum of all the mole fractions is equal to 1:

The mole fraction is also called the amount fraction. It is identical to the number fraction, which is defined as the number of molecules of a constituent N_i divided by the total number of all molecules N_{tot}. It is one way of expressing the composition of a mixture with a dimensionless quantity (mass fraction is another).

Solubility

Solubility is the property of a solid, liquid, or gaseous chemical substance called solute to dissolve in a solid, liquid, or gaseous solvent to form a homogeneous solution of the solute in the solvent. The solubility of a substance fundamentally depends on the used solvent as well as on temperature and pressure. The extent of the solubility of a substance in a specific solvent is measured as the saturation concentration, where adding more solute does not increase the concentration of the solution.

Oxygen

Oxygen is the element with atomic number 8 and represented by the symbol O. Its name derives from the Greek roots ?ξ?ς (oxys) ('acid', literally 'sharp', referring to the sour taste of acids) and -γεν?ς (-genes) ('producer', literally 'begetter'), because at the time of naming, it was mistakenly thought that all acids required oxygen in their composition. At standard temperature and pressure, two atoms of the element bind to form dioxygen, a very pale blue, odorless, tasteless diatomic gas with the formula O_2.

Oxygen is a member of the chalcogen group on the periodic table and is a highly reactive nonmetallic element that readily forms compounds (notably oxides) with almost all other elements.

Thermal

A thermal column is a column of rising air in the lower altitudes of the Earth's atmosphere. Thermals are created by the uneven heating of the Earth's surface from solar radiation, and are an example of convection, specifically atmospheric convection. The Sun warms the ground, which in turn warms the air directly above it.

Thermal pollution

Thermal pollution is the degradation of water quality by any process that changes ambient water temperature.

A common cause of thermal pollution is the use of water as a coolant by power plants and industrial manufacturers. When water used as a coolant is returned to the natural environment at a higher temperature, the change in temperature decreases oxygen supply, and affects ecosystem composition.

Partial pressure

In a mixture of ideal gases, each gas has a partial pressure which is the pressure which the gas would have if it alone occupied the volume.

Chapter 12. Physical Properties of Solutions

The total pressure of a gas mixture is the sum of the partial pressures of each individual gas in the mixture.

In chemistry, the partial pressure of a gas in a mixture of gases is defined as above.

Amino acid

Amino acids are molecules containing an amine group, a carboxylic acid group, and a side-chain that is specific to each amino acid. The key elements of an amino acid are carbon, hydrogen, oxygen, and nitrogen. They are particularly important in biochemistry, where the term usually refers to alpha-amino acids.

Carbon

Carbon is the chemical element with symbol C and atomic number 6. As a member of group 14 on the periodic table, it is nonmetallic and tetravalent--making four electrons available to form covalent chemical bonds. There are three naturally occurring isotopes, with ^{12}C and ^{13}C being stable, while ^{14}C is radioactive, decaying with a half-life of about 5,730 years. Carbon is one of the few elements known since antiquity.

Carbon dioxide

Carbon dioxide is a naturally occurring chemical compound composed of two oxygen atoms covalently bonded to a single carbon atom. It is a gas at standard temperature and pressure and exists in Earth's atmosphere in this state, as a trace gas at a concentration of 0.039% by volume.

As part of the carbon cycle known as photosynthesis, plants, algae, and cyanobacteria absorb carbon dioxide, light, and water to produce carbohydrate energy for themselves and oxygen as a waste product.

Hemoglobin

Hemoglobin is the iron-containing oxygen-transport metalloprotein in the red blood cells of all vertebrates (with the exception of the fish family Channichthyidae) as well as the tissues of some invertebrates. Hemoglobin in the blood carries oxygen from the respiratory organs (lungs or gills) to the rest of the body (i.e. the tissues) where it releases the oxygen to burn nutrients to provide energy to power the functions of the organism, and collects the resultant carbon dioxide to bring it back to the respiratory organs to be dispensed from the organism.

In mammals, the protein makes up about 97% of the red blood cells' dry content, and around 35% of the total content (including water).

Arsenic

Arsenic is a chemical element with the symbol As, atomic number 33 and relative atomic mass 74.92.

Arsenic occurs in many minerals, usually in conjunction with sulfur and metals, and also as a pure elemental crystal. It was first documented by Albertus Magnus in 1250. Arsenic is a metalloid. It can exist in various allotropes, although only the grey form has important use in industry.

Colligative properties	In chemistry, colligative properties are properties of solutions that depend upon the ratio of the number of solute particles to the number of solvent molecules in a solution. They are independent of the nature of the solute particles, and are due essentially to the dilution of the solvent by the solute. Colligative properties include: (1) relative lowering of vapor pressure; (2) elevation of boiling point; (3) depression of freezing point and (4) osmotic pressure.
Electrolyte	An electrolyte is any substance containing free ions that make the substance electrically conductive. The most typical electrolyte is an ionic solution, but molten electrolytes and solid electrolytes are also possible. Commonly, electrolytes are solutions of acids, bases or salts.
Ideal solution	In chemistry, an ideal solution is a solution with thermodynamic properties analogous to those of a mixture of ideal gases. The enthalpy of solution is zero as is the volume change on mixing; the closer to zero the enthalpy of solution is, the more 'ideal' the behavior of the solution becomes. The vapour pressure of the solution obeys Raoult's law, and the activity coefficients (which measure deviation from ideality) are equal to one.
Toluene	Toluene, formerly known as toluol, is a clear, water-insoluble liquid with the typical smell of paint thinners. It is a mono-substituted benzene derivative, i.e., one in which a single hydrogen atom from the benzene molecule has been replaced by a univalent group, in this case CH_3. It is an aromatic hydrocarbon that is widely used as an industrial feedstock and as a solvent.
Tyvek	Tyvek is a brand of flashspun high-density polyethylene fibers, a synthetic material; the name is a registered trademark of DuPont. The material is very strong; it is difficult to tear but can easily be cut with scissors or a knife. Water vapor can pass through Tyvek but not liquid water, so the material lends itself to a variety of applications: envelopes, car covers, air and water intrusion barriers (housewrap) under house siding, labels, wristbands, mycology, and graphics.
Fractional distillation	Fractional distillation is the separation of a mixture into its component parts, or fractions, such as in separating chemical compounds by their boiling point by heating them to a temperature at which several fractions of the compound will vaporize. It is a special type of distillation.

Chapter 12. Physical Properties of Solutions

Fractionating column	A fractionating column is an essential item used in the distillation of liquid mixtures so as to separate the mixture into its component parts, or fractions, based on the differences in their volatilities. Fractionating columns are used in small scale laboratory distillations as well as for large-scale industrial distillations.
	A laboratory fractionating column is a piece of glassware used to separate vaporized mixtures of liquid compounds with close volatility.
Positive	A positive is a film or paper record of a scene that represents the color and luminance of objects in that scene with the same colors and luminances (as near as the medium will allow). Color transparencies are an example of positive photography: the range of colors presented in the medium is limited by the tonal range of the original image (dark and light areas correspond). It is opposed to a negative where colors and luminances are reversed: this is due to the chemical or electrical processes involved in recording the scene.
Distillation	Distillation is a method of separating mixtures based on differences in volatilities of components in a boiling liquid mixture. Distillation is a unit operation, or a physical separation process, and not a chemical reaction.
	Commercially, distillation has a number of applications.
Boiling-point elevation	Boiling-point elevation describes the phenomenon that the boiling point of a liquid (a solvent) will be higher when another compound is added, meaning that a solution has a higher boiling point than a pure solvent. This happens whenever a non-volatile solute, such as a salt, is added to a pure solvent, such as water. The boiling point can be measured accurately using an ebullioscope.
Freezing-point depression	Freezing-point depression describes the phenomenon in which the freezing point of a liquid (a solvent) is depressed when another compound is added, meaning that a solution has a lower freezing point than a pure solvent. This happens whenever a non-volatile solute is added to a pure solvent, such as water. The phenomenon may be observed in sea water, which due to its salt content remains liquid at temperatures below 0°C, the freezing point of water.
Sodium carbonate	Sodium carbonate Na_2CO_3 is a sodium salt of carbonic acid. It most commonly occurs as a crystalline heptahydrate, which readily effloresces to form a white powder, the monohydrate. Sodium carbonate is domestically well known for its everyday use as a water softener.
Melting	Melting, is a physical process that results in the phase transition of a substance from a solid to a liquid. The internal energy of a substance is increased, typically by the application of heat or pressure, resulting in a rise of its temperature to the melting point, at which the rigid ordering of molecular entities in the solid breaks down to a less-ordered state and the solid liquefies.

Antifreeze	Antifreeze is a freeze preventive used in internal combustion engines and other heat transfer applications, such as HVAC chillers and solar water heaters. The purpose of antifreeze is to prevent a rigid enclosure from undergoing catastrophic deformation due to expansion when water turns to ice. Antifreezes are chemical compounds added to water to reduce the freezing point of the mixture below the lowest temperature that the system is likely to encounter.
Ethylene	Ethylene is an organic compound, a hydrocarbon with the formula C_2H_4 or $H_2C=CH_2$. It is a colorless flammable gas with a faint 'sweet and musky' odor when pure. It is the simplest alkene (a hydrocarbon with carbon-carbon double bonds), and the simplest unsaturated hydrocarbon after acetylene (C_2H_2).
Ethylene glycol	Ethylene glycol is an organic compound widely used as an automotive antifreeze and a precursor to polymers. In its pure form, it is an odorless, colorless, syrupy, sweet-tasting liquid. Ethylene glycol is toxic, and ingestion can result in death.
Osmotic pressure	Osmotic pressure is the pressure which needs to be applied to a solution to prevent the inward flow of water across a semipermeable membrane. It is also defined as the minimum pressure needed to nullify osmosis. The phenomenon of osmotic pressure arises from the tendency of a pure solvent to move through a semi-permeable membrane and into a solution containing a solute to which the membrane is impermeable.
Semipermeable membrane	A semipermeable membrane, also termed a selectively permeable membrane, a partially permeable membrane or a differentially permeable membrane, is a membrane that will allow certain molecules or ions to pass through it by diffusion and occasionally specialized 'facilitated diffusion'. The rate of passage depends on the pressure, concentration, and temperature of the molecules or solutes on either side, as well as the permeability of the membrane to each solute. Depending on the membrane and the solute, permeability may depend on solute size, solubility, properties, or chemistry.
Membrane	The term membrane most commonly refers to a thin, film-like structure that separates two fluids. It acts as a selective barrier, allowing some particles or chemicals to pass through, but not others. In some cases, especially in anatomy, membrane may refer to a thin film that is primarily a separating structure rather than a selective barrier.
Hemolysis	Hemolysis--from the Greek α?μα (aima, haema, hemo-) meaning 'blood' and λ?σις (lusis, lysis, -lysis) meaning a 'loosing', 'setting free' or 'releasing'--is the rupturing of erythrocytes (red blood cells) and the release of their contents (hemoglobin) into surrounding fluid (e.g., blood plasma).

Chapter 12. Physical Properties of Solutions

Hemolysis may occur in vivo or in vitro (inside or outside the body). In vivo (Inside the body)

In vivo hemolysis can be caused by a large number of medical conditions, including many Gram-positive bacteria (e.g., streptococcus, enterococcus, and staphylococcus), some parasites (e.g., malaria), some autoimmune disorders , and some genetic disorders (e.g., sickle-cell disease or G6PD deficiency).

Crenation

Crenation is the contraction of a cell after exposure to a hypertonic solution, due to the loss of water through osmosis. The word is from the Latin 'crenatus' meaning scalloped or notched, and is named for the scalloped-edged shape the cells take on when crenated.

Crenation occurs because in a hypertonic environment, (that is, the cell has a lower concentration of solutes and, therefore, higher water potential than the surrounding extracellular fluid), osmosis (the diffusion of water) causes a net movement of water out of the cell, causing the cytoplasm to decrease in its volume.

Transpiration

Transpiration is a process similar to evaporation. It is a part of the water cycle, and it is the loss of water vapor from parts of plants (similar to sweating), especially in leaves but also in stems, flowers and roots. Leaf surfaces are dotted with openings which are collectively called stomata, and in most plants they are more numerous on the undersides of the foliage.

Carbon cycle

The carbon cycle is the biogeochemical cycle by which carbon is exchanged among the biosphere, pedosphere, geosphere, hydrosphere, and atmosphere of the Earth. It is one of the most important cycles of the Earth and allows for carbon to be recycled and reused throughout the biosphere and all of its organisms.

The global carbon budget is the balance of the exchanges (incomes and losses) of carbon between the carbon reservoirs or between one specific loop (e.g., atmosphere ↔ biosphere) of the carbon cycle.

Molar mass

Molar mass, symbol M, is a physical property of a given substance (chemical element or chemical compound), namely its mass per amount of substance. The base SI unit for mass is the kilogram and that for amount of substance is the mole. Thus, the derived unit for molar mass is kg/mol.

Colloid

A colloid is a substance microscopically dispersed evenly throughout another substance.

A colloidal system consists of two separate phases: a dispersed phase and a continuous phase in which the colloid is dispersed. A colloidal system may be solid, liquid, or gas.

Hemodialysis	In medicine, hemodialysis is a method for extracorporeal removing waste products such as creatinine and urea, as well as free water from the blood when the kidneys are in renal failure. Hemodialysis is one of three renal replacement therapies (the other two being renal transplant; peritoneal dialysis). An alternate method for extracorporal separation of blood components such as plasma or cells is apheresis.
Aerosol	Technically, an aerosol is a colloid suspension of fine solid particles or liquid droplets in a gas. Examples are clouds, and air pollution such as smog and smoke. In general conversation, aerosol usually refers to an aerosol spray can or the output of such a can.
Emulsion	An emulsion is a mixture of two or more liquids that are normally immiscible (un-blendable). Emulsions are part of a more general class of two-phase systems of matter called colloids. Although the terms colloid and emulsion are sometimes used interchangeably, emulsion is used when both the dispersed and the continuous phase are liquid.
Tyndall effect	The Tyndall effect, is light scattering by particles in a colloid or particles in a fine suspension. he 19th century physicist John Tyndall. It is similar to Rayleigh scattering, in that the intensity of the scattered light depends on the fourth power of the frequency, so blue light is scattered much more strongly than red light.
Sodium stearate	Sodium stearate, is the sodium salt of stearic acid. It is the major component of some types of soap, especially those made from animal fat. It is found in many types of solid deodorants, rubbers, latex paints, and inks.
Stearate	Stearate is the anion form of stearic acid. Formula is $C_{17}H_{35}COO^-$. •Sodium stearate, Na$(C_{17}H_{35}COO)$•Calcium stearate, $Ca(C_{17}H_{35}COO)_2$•Magnesium stearate, $Mg(C_{17}H_{35}COO)_2$.
Thomas Garnett	Thomas Garnett (1766-1802) was an English physician and natural philosopher. He was born 21 April 1766 at Casterton in Westmoreland, where his father had a small landed property. After attending Sedbergh School, he was at the age of fifteen articled at his own request to the celebrated John Dawson (surgeon) of Sedbergh, Yorkshire, surgeon and mathematician.
Alcohol	In chemistry, an alcohol is an organic compound in which the hydroxyl functional group (-OH) is bound to a carbon atom. In particular, this carbon center should be saturated, having single bonds to three other atoms. An important class of alcohols are the simple acyclic alcohols, the general formula for which is $C_nH_{2n+1}OH$. Of those, ethanol (C_2H_5OH) is the type of alcohol found in alcoholic beverages, and in common speech the word alcohol refers specifically to ethanol.

Chapter 12. Physical Properties of Solutions

1. _____ is a freeze preventive used in internal combustion engines and other heat transfer applications, such as HVAC chillers and solar water heaters. The purpose of _____ is to prevent a rigid enclosure from undergoing catastrophic deformation due to expansion when water turns to ice. _____s are chemical compounds added to water to reduce the freezing point of the mixture below the lowest temperature that the system is likely to encounter.

   a. Autoglym
   b. Antifreeze
   c. Mesophase
   d. Mpemba effect

2. In a mixture of ideal gases, each gas has a _____ which is the pressure which the gas would have if it alone occupied the volume. The total pressure of a gas mixture is the sum of the _____s of each individual gas in the mixture.

   In chemistry, the _____ of a gas in a mixture of gases is defined as above.

   a. Partial pressure
   b. Peroxocarbonate
   c. Peroxodicarbonate
   d. Phase-change material

3. In chemistry, the _____ ρ_i is defined as the mass of a constituent m_i divided by the volume of the mixture V :

   $$\rho_i = \frac{m_i}{V}$$

   For a pure chemical the _____ equals its density. Definition and properties

   The volume V in the definition refers to the volume of the solution, not the volume of the solvent. One liter of a solution usually contains either slightly more or slightly less than 1 liter of solvent because the process of dissolution causes volume of liquid to increase or decrease.

   a. Mass concentration
   b. Mass number
   c. Metastability
   d. Miscibility

4. . A _____ is a film or paper record of a scene that represents the color and luminance of objects in that scene with the same colors and luminances (as near as the medium will allow). Color transparencies are an example of _____ photography: the range of colors presented in the medium is limited by the tonal range of the original image (dark and light areas correspond). It is opposed to a negative where colors and luminances are reversed: this is due to the chemical or electrical processes involved in recording the scene.

   a. Sensitivity priority
   b. Positive
   c. Soft box

5. _____ is a brand of flashspun high-density polyethylene fibers, a synthetic material; the name is a registered trademark of DuPont. The material is very strong; it is difficult to tear but can easily be cut with scissors or a knife. Water vapor can pass through _____ but not liquid water, so the material lends itself to a variety of applications: envelopes, car covers, air and water intrusion barriers (housewrap) under house siding, labels, wristbands, mycology, and graphics.

   a. Vectran
   b. WD-40
   c. Tyvek
   d. 1,2-Dioxetanedione

1. b

2. a

3. a

4. b

5. c

You can take the complete Chapter Practice Test

for Chapter 12. Physical Properties of Solutions
on all key terms, persons, places, and concepts.

Online 99 Cents

http://www.epub14.1.20267.12.cram101.com/

Use www.Cram101.com for all your study needs

including Cram101's online interactive problem solving labs in

chemistry, statistics, mathematics, and more.

_____ | Chemical kinetics

_____ | Reaction rate

_____ | Formic acid

_____ | Spectrum

_____ | Lewis structure

_____ | Stoichiometry

_____ | Order

_____ | Dinitrogen pentoxide

_____ | Nitrogen

_____ | Half-life

_____ | Gypsum

_____ | Carbon

_____ | Carbon disulfide

_____ | Radiocarbon dating

_____ | Disulfide

_____ | Collision

_____ | Collision theory

_____ | Activated complex

_____ | Activation

CHAPTER OUTLINE: KEY TERMS, PEOPLE, PLACES, CONCEPTS

_______________ Activation energy

_______________ Arrhenius equation

_______________ Transition state

_______________ Frequency

_______________ Chemical reaction

_______________ Molecular weight

_______________ Molecularity

_______________ Polymer

_______________ Rate-determining step

_______________ Hydrogen

_______________ Hydrogen iodide

_______________ Iodide

_______________ Carbon dioxide

_______________ Catalysis

_______________ Catalyst

_______________ Hydrolysis

_______________ Isotope

_______________ Methyl acetate

_______________ Oxygen

Chapter 13. Chemical Kinetics

CHAPTER OUTLINE: KEY TERMS, PEOPLE, PLACES, CONCEPTS

- Photosynthesis
- Acetate
- Potassium
- Potassium chlorate
- Chlorate
- Amino acid
- Haber process
- Heterogeneous catalysis
- Catalytic converter
- Platinum
- Air pollution
- Carbon monoxide
- Ethyl acetate
- Homogeneous
- Homogeneous catalysis
- Monoxide
- Addition
- Addition reaction
- Enzyme

Chapter 13. Chemical Kinetics

_____ | Enzyme catalysis _____

_____ | Lead chamber process _____

_____ | Active site _____

_____ | Hexokinase _____

_____ | Alcohol _____

_____ | Dehydrogenase _____

CHAPTER HIGHLIGHTS & NOTES: KEY TERMS, PEOPLE, PLACES, CONCEPTS

Chemical kinetics	Chemical kinetics, is the study of rates of chemical processes. Chemical kinetics includes investigations of how different experimental conditions can influence the speed of a chemical reaction and yield information about the reaction's mechanism and transition states, as well as the construction of mathematical models that can describe the characteristics of a chemical reaction. In 1864, Peter Waage and Cato Guldberg pioneered the development of chemical kinetics by formulating the law of mass action, which states that the speed of a chemical reaction is proportional to the quantity of the reacting substances.
Reaction rate	The reaction rate or speed of reaction for a reactant or product in a particular reaction is intuitively defined as how fast or slow a reaction takes place. For example, the oxidation of iron under the atmosphere is a slow reaction that can take many years, but the combustion of butane in a fire is a reaction that takes place in fractions of a second.
	Chemical kinetics is the part of physical chemistry that studies reaction rates.
Formic acid	Formic acid is the simplest carboxylic acid. Its chemical formula is HCOOH or HCO_2H. It was first made chemically in a lab at Roselle Park by scientist Karn Bangs. It is an important intermediate in chemical synthesis and occurs naturally, most notably in the venom of bee and ant stings.

Spectrum	A spectrum is a condition that is not limited to a specific set of values but can vary infinitely within a continuum. The word saw its first scientific use within the field of optics to describe the rainbow of colors in visible light when separated using a prism; it has since been applied by analogy to many fields other than optics. Thus, one might talk about the spectrum of political opinion, or the spectrum of activity of a drug, or the autism spectrum.
Lewis structure	Lewis structures (also known as Lewis dot diagrams, electron dot diagrams, and electron dot structures) are diagrams that show the bonding between atoms of a molecule and the lone pairs of electrons that may exist in the molecule.
Stoichiometry	Stoichiometry is a branch of chemistry that deals with the relative quantities of reactants and products in chemical reactions. In a balanced chemical reaction, the relations among quantities of reactants and products typically form a ratio of whole numbers. For example, in a reaction that forms ammonia (NH_3), exactly one molecule of nitrogen (N_2) reacts with three molecules of hydrogen (H_2) to produce two molecules of NH_3:$N_2 + 3\,H_2 \rightarrow 2\,NH_3$ Stoichiometry can be used to find quantities such as the amount of products (in mass, moles, volume, etc).
Order	Order (subtitled 'A Journal on the Theory of Ordered Sets and its Applications') is a quarterly peer-reviewed academic journal on order theory and its applications, published by Springer Science+Business Media. It was founded in 1984 by University of Calgary mathematics professor Ivan Rival; as of 2010, its editor in chief is Dwight Duffus, the Goodrich C. White Professor of Mathematics & Computer Science at Emory University and a former student of Rival's. According to the Journal Citation Reports, the 2009 impact factor of Order is 0.408, placing it in the fourth quartile of ranked mathematics journals.
Dinitrogen pentoxide	Dinitrogen pentoxide is the chemical compound with the formula N_2O_5. Also known as nitrogen pentoxide, N_2O_5 is one of the binary nitrogen oxides, a family of compounds that only contain nitrogen and oxygen. It is an unstable and potentially dangerous oxidizer that once was used as a reagent when dissolved in chloroform for nitrations but has largely been superseded by NO_2BF_4 (nitronium tetrafluoroborate).
Nitrogen	Nitrogen is a chemical element that has the symbol N, atomic number of 7 and atomic mass 14.00674 u. Elemental nitrogen is a colorless, odorless, tasteless, and mostly inert diatomic gas at standard conditions, constituting 78.09% by volume of Earth's atmosphere.

Chapter 13. Chemical Kinetics

Half-life	Half-life, abbreviated $t_{1/2}$, is the period of time it takes for the amount of a substance undergoing decay to decrease by half. The name was originally used to describe a characteristic of unstable atoms (radioactive decay), but it may apply to any quantity which follows a set-rate decay.

The original term, dating to 1907, was 'half-life period', which was later shortened to 'half-life' in the early 1950s. |
Gypsum	Gypsum is a very soft sulfate mineral composed of calcium sulfate dihydrate, with the chemical formula $CaSO_4 \cdot 2H_2O$. It is found in alabaster, a decorative stone used in Ancient Egypt. It is the second softest mineral on the Mohs scale of mineral hardness. It forms as an evaporite mineral and as a hydration product of anhydrite.
Carbon	Carbon is the chemical element with symbol C and atomic number 6. As a member of group 14 on the periodic table, it is nonmetallic and tetravalent--making four electrons available to form covalent chemical bonds. There are three naturally occurring isotopes, with ^{12}C and ^{13}C being stable, while ^{14}C is radioactive, decaying with a half-life of about 5,730 years. Carbon is one of the few elements known since antiquity.
Carbon disulfide	Carbon disulfide is a colorless volatile liquid with the formula CS_2. The compound is used frequently as a building block in organic chemistry as well as an industrial and chemical non-polar solvent. It has an 'ether-like' odor, but commercial samples are typically contaminated with foul-smelling impurities, such as carbonyl sulfide.
Radiocarbon dating	Radiocarbon dating is a radiometric dating method that uses the naturally occurring radioisotope carbon-14 (^{14}C) to estimate the age of carbon-bearing materials up to about 58,000 to 62,000 years. Raw, i.e., uncalibrated, radiocarbon ages are usually reported in radiocarbon years 'Before Present' (BP), 'Present' being defined as 1950. Such raw ages can be calibrated to give calendar dates. One of the most frequent uses of radiocarbon dating is to estimate the age of organic remains from archaeological sites.
Disulfide	In chemistry, a disulfide usually refers to the structural unit composed of a linked pair of sulfur atoms. Disulfide usually refer to a chemical compound that contains a disulfide bond, such as diphenyl disulfide, $C_6H_5S\text{-}SC_6H_5$.

The disulfide anion is S_2^{2-}, or $^-S\text{-}S^-$. |
| Collision | A collision is an isolated event in which two or more moving bodies (colliding bodies) exert forces on each other for a relatively short time. |

Although the most common colloquial use of the word 'collision' refers to accidents in which two or more objects collide, the scientific use of the word 'collision' implies nothing about the magnitude of the forces.

Some examples of physical interactions that scientists would consider collisions:•An insect touches its antenna to the leaf of a plant.

Collision theory	Collision theory is a theory proposed by William Lewis in 1916 and 1918, that qualitatively explains how chemical reactions occur and why reaction rates differ for different reactions. The collision theory can only occur when the suitable particles of the reactant hit with each other. Only a certain percentage of the sum of the collisions cause any noticeable or significant chemical change; these successful changes are called successful collisions.
Activated complex	In chemistry an activated complex is defined by the International Union of Pure and Applied Chemistry as 'that assembly of atoms which corresponds to an arbitrary infinitesimally small region at or near the col (saddle point) of a potential energy surface'. In other words, it refers to a collection of intermediate structures in a chemical reaction that persist while bonds are breaking and new bonds are forming. It therefore represents not one defined state, but rather a range of transient configurations that a collection of atoms passes through in between clearly defined products and reactants.
Activation	Activation in (bio-)chemical sciences generally refers to the process whereby something is prepared or excited for a subsequent reaction. In chemistry, activation of molecules is where the molecules enter a state that avails for a chemical reaction to occur. The phrase energy of activation refers to the energy the reactants must acquire before they can successfully react with each other to produce the products, that is, to reach the transition state.
Activation energy	In chemistry, activation energy is a term introduced in 1889 by the Swedish scientist Svante Arrhenius that is defined as the energy that must be overcome in order for a chemical reaction to occur. Activation energy may also be defined as the minimum energy required to start a chemical reaction. The activation energy of a reaction is usually denoted by E_a, and given in units of kilojoules per mole.
Arrhenius equation	The Arrhenius equation is a simple, but remarkably accurate, formula for the temperature dependence of the reaction rate constant, and therefore, rate of a chemical reaction. The equation was first proposed by the Dutch chemist J. H. van 't Hoff in 1884; five years later in 1889, the Swedish chemist Svante Arrhenius provided a physical justification and interpretation for it.

Chapter 13. Chemical Kinetics

Transition state	The transition state of a chemical reaction is a particular configuration along the reaction coordinate. It is defined as the state corresponding to the highest energy along this reaction coordinate. At this point, assuming a perfectly irreversible reaction, colliding reactant molecules will always go on to form products.
Frequency	Frequency is the number of occurrences of a repeating event per unit time. It is also referred to as temporal frequency. The period is the duration of one cycle in a repeating event, so the period is the reciprocal of the frequency.
Chemical reaction	A chemical reaction is a process that leads to the transformation of one set of chemical substances to another. Chemical reactions can be either spontaneous, requiring no input of energy, or non-spontaneous, typically following the input of some type of energy, such as heat, light or electricity. Classically, chemical reactions encompass changes that strictly involve the motion of electrons in the forming and breaking of chemical bonds, although the general concept of a chemical reaction, in particular the notion of a chemical equation, is applicable to transformations of elementary particles (such as illustrated by Feynman diagrams), as well as nuclear reactions.
Molecular weight	The molecular mass (m) of a substance is the mass of one molecule of that substance, in unified atomic mass unit(s) u (equal to 1/12 the mass of one atom of the isotope carbon-12). This is numerically equivalent to the relative molecular mass (M_r) of a molecule, frequently referred to by the term molecular weight, which is the ratio of the mass of that molecule to 1/12 of the mass of carbon-12 and is a dimensionless number. Thus, it is incorrect to express relative molecular mass (molecular weight) in daltons (Da).
Molecularity	Molecularity in chemistry is the number of colliding molecular entities that are involved in a single reaction step. While the order of a reaction is derived experimentally, the molecularity is a theoretical concept and can only be applied to elementary reactions. In elementary reactions, the reaction order, the molecularity and the stoichiometric coefficient are the same, although only numerically, because they are different concepts.
Polymer	A polymer is a large molecule (macromolecule) composed of repeating structural units. These sub-units are typically connected by covalent chemical bonds. Although the term polymer is sometimes taken to refer to plastics, it actually encompasses a large class of compounds comprising both natural and synthetic materials with a wide variety of properties.
Rate-determining step	The rate-determining step is a chemistry term for the slowest step in a chemical reaction. The rate-determining step is often compared to the neck of a funnel; the rate at which water flows through the funnel is determined by the width of the neck, not by the speed at which water is poured in. In similar manner, the rate of reaction depends on the rate of the slowest step.

Hydrogen	Hydrogen is the chemical element with atomic number 1. It is represented by the symbol H. With an average atomic weight of 1.00794 u (1.007825 u for hydrogen-1), hydrogen is the lightest element and its monatomic form (H_1) is the most abundant chemical substance, constituting roughly 75% of the Universe's baryonic mass. Non-remnant stars are mainly composed of hydrogen in its plasma state. At standard temperature and pressure, hydrogen is a colorless, odorless, tasteless, non-toxic, nonmetallic, highly combustible diatomic gas with the molecular formula H_2.
Hydrogen iodide	Hydrogen iodide is a diatomic molecule. Aqueous solutions of HI are known as iohydroic acid or hydroiodic acid, a strong acid. Gas and aqueous solution are interconvertible.
Iodide	An iodide ion is the ion I^-. Compounds with iodine in formal oxidation state −1 are called iodides. This page is for the iodide ion and its salts.
Carbon dioxide	Carbon dioxide is a naturally occurring chemical compound composed of two oxygen atoms covalently bonded to a single carbon atom. It is a gas at standard temperature and pressure and exists in Earth's atmosphere in this state, as a trace gas at a concentration of 0.039% by volume. As part of the carbon cycle known as photosynthesis, plants, algae, and cyanobacteria absorb carbon dioxide, light, and water to produce carbohydrate energy for themselves and oxygen as a waste product.
Catalysis	Catalysis is the change in rate of a chemical reaction due to the participation of a substance called a catalyst. Unlike other reagents that participate in the chemical reaction, a catalyst is not consumed by the reaction itself. A catalyst may participate in multiple chemical transformations.
Catalyst	Catalysis is the change in rate of a chemical reaction due to the participation of a substance called a catalyst. Unlike other reagents that participate in the chemical reaction, a catalyst is not consumed by the reaction itself. A catalyst may participate in multiple chemical transformations.
Hydrolysis	Hydrolysis usually means the rupture of chemical bonds by the addition of water. Generally, hydrolysis is a step in the degradation of a substance. In terms of the word's derivation, hydrolysis comes from Greek roots hydro 'water' + lysis 'separation'.
Isotope	Isotopes are variants of a particular chemical element. While all isotopes of a given element share the same number of protons, each isotope differs from the others in its number of neutrons.

Chapter 13. Chemical Kinetics

Methyl acetate	Methyl acetate, acetic acid methyl ester or methyl ethanoate, is a carboxylate ester with the formula CH_3COOCH_3. It is a flammable liquid with a characteristically pleasant smell reminiscent of some glues and nail polish removers. Methyl acetate is occasionally used as a solvent, being weakly polar and lipophilic, but its close relative ethyl acetate is a more common solvent being less toxic and less soluble in water.
Oxygen	Oxygen is the element with atomic number 8 and represented by the symbol O. Its name derives from the Greek roots ?ξ?ς (oxys) ('acid', literally 'sharp', referring to the sour taste of acids) and -γεν?ς (-genes) ('producer', literally 'begetter'), because at the time of naming, it was mistakenly thought that all acids required oxygen in their composition. At standard temperature and pressure, two atoms of the element bind to form dioxygen, a very pale blue, odorless, tasteless diatomic gas with the formula O_2.

Oxygen is a member of the chalcogen group on the periodic table and is a highly reactive nonmetallic element that readily forms compounds (notably oxides) with almost all other elements. |
| Photosynthesis | Photosynthesis is a process used by plants and other organisms to capture the sun's energy to split off water's hydrogen from oxygen. Hydrogen is combined with carbon dioxide (absorbed from air or water) to form glucose and release oxygen. All living cells in turn use fuels derived from glucose and oxidize the hydrogen and carbon to release the sun's energy and reform water and carbon dioxide in the process (cellular respiration). |
| Acetate | An acetate is a derivative of acetic acid. This term includes salts and esters, as well as the anion found in solution. Most of the approximately 5 billion kilograms of acetic acid produced annually in industry are used in the production of acetates, which usually take the form of polymers. |
| Potassium | Potassium is the chemical element with the symbol K and atomic number 19. Elemental potassium is a soft silvery-white alkali metal that oxidizes rapidly in air and is very reactive with water, generating sufficient heat to ignite the hydrogen emitted in the reaction.

Because potassium and sodium are chemically very similar, it took a long time before their salts were differentiated. The existence of multiple elements in their salts was suspected from 1702, and this was proven in 1807 when potassium and sodium were individually isolated from different salts by electrolysis. |

Potassium chlorate	Potassium chlorate is a compound containing potassium, chlorine and oxygen atoms, with the molecular formula $KClO_3$. In its pure form, it is a white crystalline substance. It is the most common chlorate in industrial use.
Chlorate	The chlorate anion has the formula ClO-3. In this case, the chlorine atom is in the +5 oxidation state. 'Chlorate' can also refer to chemical compounds containing this anion; chlorates are the salts of chloric acid.
Amino acid	Amino acids are molecules containing an amine group, a carboxylic acid group, and a side-chain that is specific to each amino acid. The key elements of an amino acid are carbon, hydrogen, oxygen, and nitrogen. They are particularly important in biochemistry, where the term usually refers to alpha-amino acids.
Haber process	The Haber process, is the nitrogen fixation reaction of nitrogen gas and hydrogen gas, over an enriched iron or ruthenium catalyst, which is used to industrially produce ammonia. Despite the fact that 78.1% of the air we breathe is nitrogen, the gas is relatively unavailable because it is so unreactive: nitrogen molecules are held together by strong triple bonds. It was not until the early 20th century that the Haber process was developed to harness the atmospheric abundance of nitrogen to create ammonia, which can then be oxidized to make the nitrates and nitrites essential for the production of nitrate fertilizer and explosives.
Heterogeneous catalysis	In chemistry, heterogeneous catalysis refers to the form of catalysis where the phase of the catalyst differs from that of the reactants. Phase here refers not only to solid, liquid, vs gas, but also immiscible liquids, e.g. oil and water. The great majority of practical heterogeneous catalysts are solids and the great majority of reactants are gases or liquids.
Catalytic converter	A catalytic converter is an exhaust emission control device which converts toxic chemicals in the exhaust of an internal combustion engine into less toxic substances. Inside a catalytic converter, a catalyst stimulates a chemical reaction in which toxic byproducts of combustion are converted to less toxic substances by way of catalysed chemical reactions. The specific reactions vary with the type of catalyst installed.
Platinum	Platinum is a chemical element with the chemical symbol Pt and an atomic number of 78. Its name is derived from the Spanish term platina, which is literally translated into 'little silver'. It is a dense, malleable, ductile, precious, gray-white transition metal.

Chapter 13. Chemical Kinetics

Air pollution	Air pollution is the introduction of chemicals, particulate matter, or biological materials that cause harm or discomfort to humans or other living organisms, or cause damage to the natural environment or built environment, into the atmosphere.
	The atmosphere is a complex dynamic natural gaseous system that is essential to support life on planet Earth. Stratospheric ozone depletion due to air pollution has long been recognized as a threat to human health as well as to the Earth's ecosystems.
Carbon monoxide	Carbon monoxide also called carbonous oxide, is a colorless, odorless, and tasteless gas which is slightly lighter than air. It is highly toxic to humans and animals in higher quantities, although it is also produced in normal animal metabolism in low quantities, and is thought to have some normal biological functions.
	Carbon monoxide consists of one carbon atom and one oxygen atom, connected by a triple bond which consists of two covalent bonds as well as one dative covalent bond.
Ethyl acetate	Ethyl acetate is the organic compound with the formula $CH_3COOCH_2CH_3$. This colorless liquid has a characteristic sweet smell (similar to pear drops) and is used in glues, nail polish removers, and cigarettes . Ethyl acetate is the ester of ethanol and acetic acid; it is manufactured on a large scale for use as a solvent.
Homogeneous	A substance that is uniform in composition is a definition of homogeneous. This is in contrast to a substance that is heterogeneous. The definition of homogeneous strongly depends on the context used.
Homogeneous catalysis	In chemistry, homogeneous catalysis is a sequence of reactions that involve a catalyst in the same phase as the reactants. Most commonly, a homogeneous catalyst is codissolved in a solvent with the reactants. Acid catalysis
	The proton is the most pervasive homogeneous catalyst because water is the most common solvent.
Monoxide	A monoxide is any oxide containing just one atom of oxygen in the molecule. For example, Potassium oxide (K_2O), has only one atom of oxygen, and is thus a monoxide. Water (H_2O) is also a monoxide.
Addition	Addition is a mathematical operation that represents combining collections of objects together into a larger collection. It is signified by the plus sign (+). For example, in the picture on the right, there are 3 + 2 apples--meaning three apples and two other apples--which is the same as five apples.

Addition reaction	An addition reaction, in organic chemistry, is in its simplest terms an organic reaction where two or more molecules combine to form a larger one.
	Addition reactions are limited to chemical compounds that have multiple bonds, such as molecules with carbon-carbon double bonds (alkenes), or with triple bonds (alkynes). Molecules containing carbon--hetero double bonds like carbonyl (C=O) groups, or imine (C=N) groups, can undergo addition as they too have double bond character.
Enzyme	Enzymes ( ) are biological molecules that catalyze (i.e., increase the rates of) chemical reactions. In enzymatic reactions, the molecules at the beginning of the process, called substrates, are converted into different molecules, called products. Almost all chemical reactions in a biological cell need enzymes in order to occur at rates sufficient for life.
Enzyme catalysis	Enzyme catalysis is the catalysis of chemical reactions by specialized proteins known as enzymes. Catalysis of biochemical reactions in the cell is vital due to the very low reaction rates of the uncatalysed reactions.
	The mechanism of enzyme catalysis is similar in principle to other types of chemical catalysis.
Lead chamber process	The lead chamber process was an industrial method used to produce sulfuric acid in large quantities. It has been largely supplanted by the contact process.
	In 1746 in Birmingham, England, John Roebuck began producing sulfuric acid in lead-lined chambers, which were stronger, less expensive, and could be made much larger than the glass containers which had been used previously.
Active site	In biology the active site is part of an enzyme where substrates bind and undergo a chemical reaction. The majority of enzymes are proteins but RNA enzymes called ribozymes also exist. The active site of an enzyme is usually found in a cleft or pocket that is lined by amino acid residues that participate in recognition of the substrate.
Hexokinase	A hexokinase is an enzyme that phosphorylates a six-carbon sugar, a hexose, to a hexose phosphate. In most tissues and organisms, glucose is the most important substrate of hexokinases, and glucose-6-phosphate the most important product.
	Variation across species
	Genes that encode hexokinase have been discovered in each domain of life, ranging from bacteria, yeast, and plants to humans and other vertebrates.

Alcohol	In chemistry, an alcohol is an organic compound in which the hydroxyl functional group (-OH) is bound to a carbon atom. In particular, this carbon center should be saturated, having single bonds to three other atoms.
	An important class of alcohols are the simple acyclic alcohols, the general formula for which is $C_nH_{2n+1}OH$. Of those, ethanol (C_2H_5OH) is the type of alcohol found in alcoholic beverages, and in common speech the word alcohol refers specifically to ethanol.
Dehydrogenase	A dehydrogenase is an enzyme that oxidizes a substrate by transferring one or more hydrides (H^-) to an acceptor, usually $NAD^+/NADP^+$ or a flavin coenzyme such as FAD or FMN.
	Examples•aldehyde dehydrogenase•acetaldehyde dehydrogenase•alcohol dehydrogenase•glutamate dehydrogenase.•lactate dehydrogenase•pyruvate dehydrogenase•glucose-6-phosphate dehydrogenase•glyceraldehyde-3-phosphate dehydrogenase•sorbitol dehydrogenase
	TCA cycle examples:•isocitrate dehydrogenase•alpha-ketoglutarate dehydrogenase•succinate dehydrogenase•malate dehydrogenase.

1. _____ usually means the rupture of chemical bonds by the addition of water. Generally, _____ is a step in the degradation of a substance. In terms of the word's derivation, _____ comes from Greek roots hydro 'water' + lysis 'separation'.

   a. Jacobi coordinates
   b. Hydrolysis
   c. Photoelectrochemical processes
   d. Pyrophorus

2. The _____ anion has the formula ClO-3. In this case, the chlorine atom is in the +5 oxidation state. '_____' can also refer to chemical compounds containing this anion; _____ s are the salts of chloric acid.

   a. Chlorate
   b. Chromite
   c. Copper phosphate
   d. Copper silicide

3. . In chemistry, a _____ usually refers to the structural unit composed of a linked pair of sulfur atoms. _____ usually refer to a chemical compound that contains a _____ bond, such as diphenyl _____, $C_6H_5S-SC_6H_5$. Inorganic vs. organic _____ s

Chapter 13. Chemical Kinetics

The _____ anion is S_2^{2-}, or $^-$S-S$^-$.

a. Ferricyanide
b. Ferrocyanide
c. Fluoride
d. Disulfide

4. _____ is a colorless volatile liquid with the formula CS_2. The compound is used frequently as a building block in organic chemistry as well as an industrial and chemical non-polar solvent. It has an 'ether-like' odor, but commercial samples are typically contaminated with foul-smelling impurities, such as carbonyl sulfide.

a. Charybdotoxin
b. Para-Chloroamphetamine
c. Carbon disulfide
d. Cicutoxin

5. In chemistry an _____ is defined by the International Union of Pure and Applied Chemistry as 'that assembly of atoms which corresponds to an arbitrary infinitesimally small region at or near the col (saddle point) of a potential energy surface'. In other words, it refers to a collection of intermediate structures in a chemical reaction that persist while bonds are breaking and new bonds are forming. It therefore represents not one defined state, but rather a range of transient configurations that a collection of atoms passes through in between clearly defined products and reactants.

a. Activation
b. Activated complex
c. Arrhenius equation
d. Arrhenius plot

1. b

2. a

3. d

4. c

5. b

You can take the complete Chapter Practice Test

for Chapter 13. Chemical Kinetics
on all key terms, persons, places, and concepts.

Online 99 Cents

http://www.epub14.1.20267.13.cram101.com/

Use www.Cram101.com for all your study needs

including Cram101's online interactive problem solving labs in

chemistry, statistics, mathematics, and more.

Chapter 14. Chemical Equilibrium

Chemical equilibrium

Nitrogen

Nitrogen dioxide

Equilibrium constant

Cato Maximilian Guldberg

Mass

Law of mass action

Homogeneous

Activity

Calcium

Calcium carbide

Carbide

Chemical kinetics

Reaction quotient

Concentration

Oxalic acid

Atmospheric pressure

Catalyst

Hemoglobin

	Oxygen
	Amino acid
	Haber process

Chemical equilibrium	In a chemical reaction, chemical equilibrium is the state in which both reactants and products are present at concentrations which have no further tendency to change with time. Usually, this state results when the forward reaction proceeds at the same rate as the reverse reaction. The reaction rates of the forward and reverse reactions are generally not zero but, being equal, there are no net changes in the concentrations of the reactant and product.
Nitrogen	Nitrogen is a chemical element that has the symbol N, atomic number of 7 and atomic mass 14.00674 u. Elemental nitrogen is a colorless, odorless, tasteless, and mostly inert diatomic gas at standard conditions, constituting 78.09% by volume of Earth's atmosphere. The element nitrogen was discovered as a separable component of air, by Scottish physician Daniel Rutherford, in 1772.
Nitrogen dioxide	Nitrogen dioxide is the chemical compound with the formula NO_2. It is one of several nitrogen oxides. NO_2 is an intermediate in the industrial synthesis of nitric acid, millions of tons of which are produced each year.
Equilibrium constant	For a general chemical equilibrium $\alpha A + \beta B... \rightleftharpoons \sigma S + \tau T...$ the equilibrium constant can be defined such that, at equilibrium, $$K = \frac{\{S\}^{\sigma}\{T\}^{\tau}...}{\{A\}^{\alpha}\{B\}^{\beta}...}$$ where {A} is the activity of the chemical species A, etc. (activity is a dimensionless quantity).

Chapter 14. Chemical Equilibrium

Cato Maximilian Guldberg	Cato Maximilian Guldberg was a Norwegian mathematician and chemist. Career Guldberg worked at the Royal Frederick University. Together with his brother-in-law, Peter Waage, he proposed the law of mass action.
Mass	The mass recorded by a mass spectrometer can refer to different physical quantities depending on the characteristics of the instrument and the manner in which the mass spectrum is displayed. The accurate mass (more appropriately, the measured accurate mass) is an experimentally determined mass that allows the elemental composition to be determined. For molecules with mass below 200 u, a 5 ppm accuracy is sufficient to uniquely determine the elemental composition.
Law of mass action	In Chemistry, the law of mass action is a mathematical model that explains and predicts behaviors of solutions in dynamic equilibrium. It can be described with two aspects: 1) the equilibrium aspect, concerning the composition of a reaction mixture at equilibrium and 2) the kinetic aspect concerning the rate equations for elementary reactions. Both aspects stem from the research by Guldberg and Waage (1864-1879) in which equilibrium constants were derived by using kinetic data and the rate equation which they had proposed.
Homogeneous	A substance that is uniform in composition is a definition of homogeneous. This is in contrast to a substance that is heterogeneous. The definition of homogeneous strongly depends on the context used.
Activity	In chemical thermodynamics, activity (symbol a) is a measure of the 'effective concentration' of a species in a mixture, meaning that the species' chemical potential depends on the activity of a real solution in the same way that it would depend on concentration for an ideal solution. By convention, activity is treated as a dimensionless quantity, although its actual value depends on customary choices of standard state for the species. The activity of pure substances in condensed phases (solid or liquids) is normally taken as unity (the number 1).
Calcium	Calcium is the chemical element with the symbol Ca and atomic number 20. It has an atomic mass of 40.078 amu. Calcium is a soft gray alkaline earth metal, and is the fifth-most-abundant element by mass in the Earth's crust.

Calcium carbide	Calcium carbide is a chemical compound with the chemical formula of CaC_2. Its main use industrially is in the production of acetylene and calcium cyanamide.
	The pure material is colorless, however pieces of technical-grade calcium carbide are grey or brown and consist of only 80-85% of CaC_2 (the rest is CaO, Ca_3P_2, CaS, Ca_3N_2, SiC, etc)..
Carbide	In chemistry, a carbide is a compound composed of carbon and a less electronegative element. Carbides can be generally classified by chemical bonding type as follows: (i) salt-like, (ii) covalent compounds, (iii) interstitial compounds, and (iv) 'intermediate' transition metal carbides. Examples include calcium carbide, silicon carbide, tungsten carbide and cementite, each used in key industrial applications.
Chemical kinetics	Chemical kinetics, is the study of rates of chemical processes. Chemical kinetics includes investigations of how different experimental conditions can influence the speed of a chemical reaction and yield information about the reaction's mechanism and transition states, as well as the construction of mathematical models that can describe the characteristics of a chemical reaction. In 1864, Peter Waage and Cato Guldberg pioneered the development of chemical kinetics by formulating the law of mass action, which states that the speed of a chemical reaction is proportional to the quantity of the reacting substances.
Reaction quotient	In chemistry, a reaction quotient: Q_r is a function of the activities or concentrations of the chemical species involved in a chemical reaction. In the special case that the reaction is at equilibrium the reaction quotient is equal to the equilibrium constant.
	A general chemical reaction in which α moles of a reactant A and β moles of a reactant B react to give σ moles of a product S and τ moles of a product T can be written asαA + βB σS + τT
	The reaction is written as an equilibrium even though in many cases it may appear to have gone to completion.
Concentration	In chemistry, concentration is defined as the abundance of a constituent divided by the total volume of a mixture. Furthermore, in chemistry, four types of mathematical description can be distinguished: mass concentration, molar concentration, number concentration, and volume concentration. The term concentration can be applied to any kind of chemical mixture, but most frequently it refers to solutes in solutions.
Oxalic acid	Oxalic acid is an organic compound with the formula $H_2C_2O_4$. This colorless crystalline solid is a dicarboxylic acid. In terms of acid strength, it is about 3,000 times stronger than acetic acid.
Atmospheric pressure	Atmospheric pressure is the force per unit area exerted into a surface by the weight of air above that surface in the atmosphere of Earth .

Chapter 14. Chemical Equilibrium

	In most circumstances atmospheric pressure is closely approximated by the hydrostatic pressure caused by the mass of air above the measurement point. Low-pressure areas have less atmospheric mass above their location, whereas high-pressure areas have more atmospheric mass above their location.
Catalyst	Catalysis is the change in rate of a chemical reaction due to the participation of a substance called a catalyst. Unlike other reagents that participate in the chemical reaction, a catalyst is not consumed by the reaction itself. A catalyst may participate in multiple chemical transformations.
Hemoglobin	Hemoglobin is the iron-containing oxygen-transport metalloprotein in the red blood cells of all vertebrates (with the exception of the fish family Channichthyidae) as well as the tissues of some invertebrates. Hemoglobin in the blood carries oxygen from the respiratory organs (lungs or gills) to the rest of the body (i.e. the tissues) where it releases the oxygen to burn nutrients to provide energy to power the functions of the organism, and collects the resultant carbon dioxide to bring it back to the respiratory organs to be dispensed from the organism. In mammals, the protein makes up about 97% of the red blood cells' dry content, and around 35% of the total content (including water).
Oxygen	Oxygen is the element with atomic number 8 and represented by the symbol O. Its name derives from the Greek roots ?ξ?ς (oxys) ('acid', literally 'sharp', referring to the sour taste of acids) and -γεν?ς (-genes) ('producer', literally 'begetter'), because at the time of naming, it was mistakenly thought that all acids required oxygen in their composition. At standard temperature and pressure, two atoms of the element bind to form dioxygen, a very pale blue, odorless, tasteless diatomic gas with the formula O_2. Oxygen is a member of the chalcogen group on the periodic table and is a highly reactive nonmetallic element that readily forms compounds (notably oxides) with almost all other elements.
Amino acid	Amino acids are molecules containing an amine group, a carboxylic acid group, and a side-chain that is specific to each amino acid. The key elements of an amino acid are carbon, hydrogen, oxygen, and nitrogen. They are particularly important in biochemistry, where the term usually refers to alpha-amino acids.
Haber process	The Haber process, is the nitrogen fixation reaction of nitrogen gas and hydrogen gas, over an enriched iron or ruthenium catalyst, which is used to industrially produce ammonia.

Despite the fact that 78.1% of the air we breathe is nitrogen, the gas is relatively unavailable because it is so unreactive: nitrogen molecules are held together by strong triple bonds. It was not until the early 20th century that the Haber process was developed to harness the atmospheric abundance of nitrogen to create ammonia, which can then be oxidized to make the nitrates and nitrites essential for the production of nitrate fertilizer and explosives.

1. _____ is the chemical compound with the formula NO_2. It is one of several nitrogen oxides. NO_2 is an intermediate in the industrial synthesis of nitric acid, millions of tons of which are produced each year.

   a. Nitrogen oxide
   b. Nitrogen dioxide
   c. Nitryl
   d. Sulfamide

2. _____ was a Norwegian mathematician and chemist.

   Career

   Guldberg worked at the Royal Frederick University. Together with his brother-in-law, Peter Waage, he proposed the law of mass action.

   a. Abul Hasan ibn Musa ibn Arfa Ra'a
   b. Cato Maximilian Guldberg
   c. Ion-association
   d. Isohydric principle

3. . The mass recorded by a _____ spectrometer can refer to different physical quantities depending on the characteristics of the instrument and the manner in which the _____ spectrum is displayed.

   The accurate _____ (more appropriately, the measured accurate mass) is an experimentally determined mass that allows the elemental composition to be determined. For molecules with mass below 200 u, a 5 ppm accuracy is sufficient to uniquely determine the elemental composition.

   a. Mass chromatogram
   b. Mass spectrometry imaging
   c. Mass spectrum

4. In a chemical reaction, _____ is the state in which both reactants and products are present at concentrations which have no further tendency to change with time. Usually, this state results when the forward reaction proceeds at the same rate as the reverse reaction. The reaction rates of the forward and reverse reactions are generally not zero but, being equal, there are no net changes in the concentrations of the reactant and product.

    a. Chemical equilibrium
    b. Chemical stability
    c. Chemisorption
    d. CIDNP

5. _____ is a chemical compound with the chemical formula of CaC_2. Its main use industrially is in the production of acetylene and calcium cyanamide.

The pure material is colorless, however pieces of technical-grade _____ are grey or brown and consist of only 80-85% of CaC_2 (the rest is CaO, Ca_3P_2, CaS, Ca_3N_2, SiC, etc)..

    a. Calcium carbide
    b. Calcium silicide
    c. Copper phosphide
    d. Ferromanganese

ANSWER KEY
Chapter 14. Chemical Equilibrium

1. b
2. b
3. d
4. a
5. a

You can take the complete Chapter Practice Test

for Chapter 14. Chemical Equilibrium
on all key terms, persons, places, and concepts.

Online 99 Cents

http://www.epub14.1.20267.14.cram101.com/

Use www.Cram101.com for all your study needs

including Cram101's online interactive problem solving labs in

chemistry, statistics, mathematics, and more.

Chapter 15. Acids and Bases

CHAPTER OUTLINE: KEY TERMS, PEOPLE, PLACES, CONCEPTS

- Acetic acid
- Conjugate acid
- Hydrogen
- Hydrogen ion
- Hydronium
- Proton
- Autoionization
- Activity
- Petroleum
- Concentration
- PH meter
- Strong acid
- Sulfur
- Sulfur trioxide
- Trioxide
- Alkali
- Alkali metal
- Hydroxide
- Weak acid

Chapter 15. Acids and Bases

CHAPTER OUTLINE: KEY TERMS, PEOPLE, PLACES, CONCEPTS

_______________ Alkaline earth metal

_______________ Metal hydroxide

_______________ Amide

_______________ Nitric acid

_______________ Perchloric acid

_______________ Weak base

_______________ Monomer

_______________ Ascorbic acid

_______________ Formic acid

_______________ Hydrofluoric acid

_______________ Ionization

_______________ Vitamin C

_______________ Quadratic equation

_______________ Amino acid

_______________ Diprotic acid

_______________ Hydrogen sulfide

_______________ Sulfide

_______________ Phosphoric acid

_______________ Molecular structure

Chapter 15. Acids and Bases

CHAPTER OUTLINE: KEY TERMS, PEOPLE, PLACES, CONCEPTS

_____ | Bond strength

_____ | Hydrochloric acid

_____ | Hydrogen halide

_____ | Halide

_____ | Carboxylic acid

_____ | Oxoacid

_____ | Benzoic acid

_____ | Hydrolysis

_____ | Iodine

_____ | Solution

_____ | Ammonium

_____ | Ammonium chloride

_____ | Chloride

_____ | Electron

_____ | Electron configuration

_____ | Acid rain

_____ | Basic oxide

_____ | Oxide

_____ | Carbon

Carbon dioxide

Transition metal

Transition metal oxides

Amphoterism

Boron

Boron trifluoride

Diagonal

Diagonal relationship

Lewis acid

Lewis base

Covalent bond

Trifluoride

Boric acid

Active transport

Cellulose

Electromotive force

Glucose

Titanium

Titanium dioxide

Chapter 15. Acids and Bases

Acetic acid	Acetic acid ?'si?t?k is an organic compound with the chemical formula CH_3CO_2H (also written as CH_3COOH). It is a colourless liquid that when undiluted is also called glacial acetic acid. Acetic acid is the main component of vinegar (apart from water), and has a distinctive sour taste and pungent smell.
Conjugate acid	Within the Brønsted-Lowry acid-base theory (protonic), a conjugate acid is the acid member, HX, of a pair of two compounds that transform into each other by gain or loss of a proton (hydrogen ion). A conjugate acid can also be seen as the chemical substance that releases, or donates, a proton (hydrogen ion) in the forward chemical reaction, hence, the term acid. The base produced, X^-, is called the conjugate base, and it absorbs, or gains, a proton in the backward chemical reaction.
Hydrogen	Hydrogen is the chemical element with atomic number 1. It is represented by the symbol H. With an average atomic weight of 1.00794 u (1.007825 u for hydrogen-1), hydrogen is the lightest element and its monatomic form (H_1) is the most abundant chemical substance, constituting roughly 75% of the Universe's baryonic mass. Non-remnant stars are mainly composed of hydrogen in its plasma state. At standard temperature and pressure, hydrogen is a colorless, odorless, tasteless, non-toxic, nonmetallic, highly combustible diatomic gas with the molecular formula H_2.
Hydrogen ion	Hydrogen ion is recommended by IUPAC as a general term for all ions of hydrogen and its isotopes. Depending on the charge of the ion, two different classes can be distinguished: positively charged ions and negatively charged ions. Under aqueous conditions found in biochemistry, hydrogen ions exist as the hydrated form hydronium, H_3O^+, but these are often still referred to as 'hydrogen ions' or even 'protons' by biochemists.
Hydronium	In chemistry, a hydronium ion is the cation H_3O^+, a type of oxonium ion produced by protonation of water. This cation is often used to represent the nature of the proton in aqueous solution, where the proton is highly solvated (bound to a solvent). The reality is far more complicated, and a proton is bound to several molecules of water, such that other descriptions such as $H_5O_2^+$, $H_7O_3^+$ and $H_9O_4^+$ are increasingly accurate descriptions of the environment of a proton in water.
Proton	The proton is a subatomic particle with the symbol p or p+and a positive electric charge of 1 elementary charge. One or more protons are present in the nucleus of each atom, along with neutrons. The number of protons in each atom is its atomic number.

Chapter 15. Acids and Bases

Autoionization	Autoionization is a process by which atoms or molecules spontaneously emit one of the shell electrons, thus going from a state with charge Z to a state with charge Z?+?1, for example from an electrically neutral state to a singly ionized state.
	Atoms can autoionize when either two or more valence electrons are excited or one or more inner-shell electrons are missing. In the latter case, it is called the Auger effect.
Activity	In chemical thermodynamics, activity (symbol a) is a measure of the 'effective concentration' of a species in a mixture, meaning that the species' chemical potential depends on the activity of a real solution in the same way that it would depend on concentration for an ideal solution.
	By convention, activity is treated as a dimensionless quantity, although its actual value depends on customary choices of standard state for the species. The activity of pure substances in condensed phases (solid or liquids) is normally taken as unity (the number 1).
Petroleum	Petroleum (L. petroleum, from Greek: petra (rock) + Latin: oleum (oil)) or crude oil is a naturally occurring, flammable liquid consisting of a complex mixture of hydrocarbons of various molecular weights and other liquid organic compounds, that are found in geologic formations beneath the Earth's surface. A fossil fuel, it is formed when large quantities of dead organisms, usually zooplankton and algae, are buried underneath sedimentary rock and undergo intense heat and pressure.
	Petroleum is recovered mostly through oil drilling.
Concentration	In chemistry, concentration is defined as the abundance of a constituent divided by the total volume of a mixture. Furthermore, in chemistry, four types of mathematical description can be distinguished: mass concentration, molar concentration, number concentration, and volume concentration. The term concentration can be applied to any kind of chemical mixture, but most frequently it refers to solutes in solutions.
PH meter	A pH meter is an electronic instrument used for measuring the pH (acidity or alkalinity) of a liquid (though special probes are sometimes used to measure the pH of semi-solid substances). A typical pH meter consists of a special measuring probe (a glass electrode) connected to an electronic meter that measures and displays the pH reading.
	The pH probe measures pH as the activity of the hydrogen cations surrounding a thin-walled glass bulb at its tip.
Strong acid	A strong acid is an acid that ionizes completely in an aqueous solution by losing one proton, according to the equation $HA(aq) \rightarrow H^+(aq) + A^-(aq)$

For sulfuric acid which is diprotic, the 'strong acid' designation refers only to dissociation of the first proton $H_2SO_4(aq) \rightarrow H^+(aq) + HSO_4^-(aq)$

More precisely, the acid must be stronger in aqueous solution than hydronium ion, so strong acids are acids with a $pK_a < -1.74$. An example is HCl for which pK_a = -6.3. This generally means that in aqueous solution at standard temperature and pressure, the concentration of hydronium ions is equal to the concentration of strong acid introduced to the solution. While strong acids are generally assumed to be the most corrosive, this is not always true. The carborane superacid H $(CHB_{11}Cl_{11})$, which is one million times stronger than sulfuric acid, is entirely non-corrosive, whereas the weak acid hydrofluoric acid (HF) is extremely corrosive and can dissolve, among other things, glass and all metals except iridium.

Sulfur	Sulfur or sulphur is the chemical element with atomic number 16. In the periodic table it is represented by the symbol S. It is an abundant, multivalent non-metal. Under normal conditions, sulfur atoms form cyclic octatomic molecules with chemical formula S_8. Elemental sulfur is a bright yellow crystalline solid when at room temperature.
Sulfur trioxide	Sulfur trioxide is the chemical compound with the formula SO_3. In the gaseous form, this species is a significant pollutant, being the primary agent in acid rain. It is prepared on massive scales as a precursor to sulfuric acid.
Trioxide	A trioxide is a compound with three oxygen atoms. For metals with the M_2O_3 formula there are several common structures. Al_2O_3, Cr_2O_3, Fe_2O_3, and V_2O_3 adopt the corundum structure.
Alkali	In chemistry, an alkali is a basic, ionic salt of an alkali metal or alkaline earth metal element. Some authors also define an alkali as a base that dissolves in water. A solution of a soluble base has a pH greater than 7. The adjective alkaline is commonly used in English as a synonym for base, especially for soluble bases.
Alkali metal	The alkali metals are a group of chemical elements in the periodic table with very similar properties: they are all shiny, soft, silvery, highly reactive metals at standard temperature and pressure and readily lose their outermost electron to form cations with charge +1. They can all be cut easily with a knife due to their softness, exposing a shiny surface that tarnishes rapidly in air due to oxidation. In the modern IUPAC nomenclature, the alkali metals comprise the group 1 elements, excluding hydrogen (H), which is nominally a group 1 element but not normally considered to be an alkali metal as it rarely exhibits behaviour comparable to that of the alkali metals.

Chapter 15. Acids and Bases

Hydroxide	Hydroxide is a diatomic anion with chemical formula OH^-. It consists of an oxygen and a hydrogen atom held together by a covalent bond, and carrying a negative electric charge. It is an important but usually minor constituent of water.
Weak acid	A weak acid is an acid that dissociates incompletely. It does not release all of its hydrogens in a solution, donating only a partial amount of its protons to the solution. These acids have higher pKa than strong acids, which release all of their hydrogen atoms when dissolved in water.
Alkaline earth metal	The alkaline earth metals are a group of chemical elements in the periodic table with very similar properties: they are all shiny, silvery-white, somewhat reactive metals at standard temperature and pressure and readily lose their two outermost electrons to form cations with charge +2. In the modern IUPAC nomenclature, the alkaline earth metals comprise the group 2 elements.
	The alkaline earth metals are beryllium (Be), magnesium (Mg), calcium (Ca), strontium (Sr), barium (Ba), and radium (Ra). This group lies in the s-block of the periodic table as all alkaline earth metals have their outermost electron in an s-orbital.
Metal hydroxide	Metal hydroxide are hydroxides of metals. •Aluminium hydroxide•Beryllium hydroxide•Cobalt(II) hydroxide•Copper(II) hydroxide•Curium hydroxide•Gold(III) hydroxide•Iron(II) hydroxide•Mercury(II) hydroxide•Nickel(II) hydroxide•Tin(II) hydroxide•Uranyl hydroxide•Zinc hydroxide•Zirconium(IV) hydroxideAlkali metal hydroxides Poor metal hydroxides •Gallium(III) hydroxide•Lead(II) hydroxide•Thallium hydroxideRole in soils
	In soils, it is assumed that larger amounts of natural phenols are released from decomposing plant litter rather than from throughfall in any natural plant community. Decomposition of dead plant material causes complex organic compounds to be slowly oxidized (lignin-like humus) or to break down into simpler forms (sugars and amino sugars, aliphatic and phenolic organic acids), which are further transformed into microbial biomass (microbial humus) or are reorganized, and further oxidized, into humic assemblages (fulvic and humic acids), which bind to clay minerals and metal hydroxides.
Amide	Amide refers to compounds with the functional group $R_nE(O)_xNR'_2$ (R and R' refer to H or organic groups). Most common are 'organic amides' (n = 1, E = C, x = 1), but many other important types of amides are known including phosphor amides (n = 2, E = P, x = 1 and many related formulas) and sulfonamides (E = S, x= 2). The term amide refers both to classes of compounds and to the functional group $(R_nE(O)_xNR'_2)$ within those compounds.
Nitric acid	Nitric acid also known as aqua fortis and spirit of niter, is a highly corrosive and toxic strong mineral acid which is normally colorless but tends to acquire a yellow cast due to the accumulation of oxides of nitrogen if long-stored. Ordinary nitric acid has a concentration of 68%.

Perchloric acid	Perchloric acid is the inorganic compound with the formula $HClO_4$. Usually found as an aqueous solution, this colorless compound is a stronger acid than sulfuric and nitric acids. It is a powerful oxidizer, but its aqueous solutions up to appr. 70% are generally safe, only showing strong acid features and no oxidizing properties.
Weak base	In chemistry, a weak base is a chemical base that does not ionize fully in an aqueous solution. As Brønsted-Lowry bases are proton acceptors, a weak base may also be defined as a chemical base in which protonation is incomplete. This results in a relatively low pH compared to strong bases.
Monomer	A monomer is a molecule that may bind chemically to other molecules to form a polymer. The term 'monomeric protein' may also be used to describe one of the proteins making up a multiprotein complex. The most common natural monomer is glucose, which is linked by glycosidic bonds into polymers such as cellulose and starch, and is over 77% of the mass of all plant matter.
Ascorbic acid	Ascorbic acid is a naturally occurring organic compound with antioxidant properties. It is a white solid, but impure samples can appear yellowish. It dissolves well in water to give mildly acidic solutions.
Formic acid	Formic acid is the simplest carboxylic acid. Its chemical formula is HCOOH or HCO_2H. It was first made chemically in a lab at Roselle Park by scientist Karn Bangs. It is an important intermediate in chemical synthesis and occurs naturally, most notably in the venom of bee and ant stings.
Hydrofluoric acid	Hydrofluoric acid is a solution of hydrogen fluoride in water. It is a valued source of fluorine and is the precursor to numerous pharmaceuticals such as fluoxetine (Prozac) and diverse materials such as PTFE (Teflon).
	Hydrofluoric acid is a highly corrosive acid, capable of dissolving many materials, especially oxides.
Ionization	Ionization is the process of converting an atom or molecule into an ion by adding or removing charged particles such as electrons or ions. In the case of ionisation of a gas, ion-pairs are created consisting of a free electron and a +ve ion.
	The process of ionization works slightly differently depending on whether an ion with a positive or a negative electric charge is being produced.
Vitamin C	Vitamin C is an essential nutrient for humans and certain other animal species. In living organisms ascorbate acts as an antioxidant by protecting the body against oxidative stress.

Chapter 15. Acids and Bases

Quadratic equation	In mathematics, a quadratic equation is a univariate polynomial equation of the second degree. A general quadratic equation can be written in the form $ax^2 + bx + c = 0,$ where x represents a variable or an unknown, and a, b, and c are constants with a ≠ 0. (If a = 0, the equation is a linear equation). The constants a, b, and c are called respectively, the quadratic coefficient, the linear coefficient and the constant term or free term.
Amino acid	Amino acids are molecules containing an amine group, a carboxylic acid group, and a side-chain that is specific to each amino acid. The key elements of an amino acid are carbon, hydrogen, oxygen, and nitrogen. They are particularly important in biochemistry, where the term usually refers to alpha-amino acids.
Diprotic acid	A diprotic acid is an acid such as H_2SO_4 (sulfuric acid) that contains within its molecular structure two hydrogen atoms per molecule capable of dissociating (i.e. ionizable) in water. The complete dissociation of diprotic acids is of the same form as sulfuric acid:$H_2SO_4 \rightarrow H^+(aq) + HSO_4^-(aq)\ K_a = 1 \times 10^3 HSO_4^- \rightarrow H^+(aq) + SO_4^{2-}(aq)\ K_a = 1 \times 10^{-2}$ The dissociation does not happen all at once due to the two stages of dissociation having different K_a values. The first dissociation will, in the case of sulfuric acid, occur completely, but the second one will not.
Hydrogen sulfide	Hydrogen sulfide is the chemical compound with the formula H_2S. It is a colorless, very poisonous, flammable gas with the characteristic foul odor of rotten eggs. It often results from the bacterial breakdown of organic matter in the absence of oxygen, such as in swamps and sewers; this process is commonly known as anaerobic digestion.
Sulfide	A sulfide is an anion of sulfur in its lowest oxidation state of 2-. Sulfide is also a slightly archaic term for thioethers, a common type of organosulfur compound that are well known for their bad odors. The dianion S^{2-} exists only in strongly alkaline aqueous solutions.
Phosphoric acid	Phosphoric acid, is a mineral (inorganic) acid having the chemical formula H_3PO_4. Orthophosphoric acid molecules can combine with themselves to form a variety of compounds which are also referred to as phosphoric acids, but in a more general way. The term phosphoric acid can also refer to a chemical or reagent consisting of phosphoric acids, usually orthophosphoric acid.

| Molecular structure | The molecular structure of a substance is described by the combination of nuclei and electrons that comprise its constitute molecules. This includes the molecular geometry (essentially the arrangement, in space, of the equilibrium positions of the constituent atoms -- in reality, these are in a state of constant vibration, at temperatures above absolute zero), the electronic properties of the bonds, and further molecular properties.

The determination of molecular structure uses a multitude of experimental methods, that include X-ray diffraction, electron diffraction, many kinds of optical spectroscopy, nuclear magnetic resonance, electron spin resonance, and mass spectrometry. |
|---|---|
| Bond strength | In chemistry, bond strength is measured between two atoms joined in a chemical bond. It is the degree to which each atom linked to another atom contributes to the valency of this other atom. Bond strength is intimately linked to bond order. |
| Hydrochloric acid | Hydrochloric acid is a clear, colourless solution of hydrogen chloride (HCl) in water. It is a highly corrosive, strong mineral acid with many industrial uses. Hydrochloric acid is found naturally in gastric acid. |
| Hydrogen halide | Hydrogen halides (or hydrohalic acids) are inorganic compounds with the formula HX where X is one of the halogens: fluorine, chlorine, bromine, iodine, and astatine. Hydrogen halides are gases that dissolve in water to give acids.

The hydrogen halides are diatomic molecules with no tendency to ionize in the gas phase. |
| Halide | A halide is a binary compound, of which one part is a halogen atom and the other part is an element or radical that is less electronegative than the halogen, to make a fluoride, chloride, bromide, iodide, or astatide compound. Many salts are halides. All Group 1 metals form halides which are white solids at room temperature. |
| Carboxylic acid | Carboxylic acids ( ) are organic acids characterized by the presence of at least one carboxyl group. The general formula of a carboxylic acid is R-COOH, where R is some monovalent functional group. A carboxyl group is a functional group consisting of a carbonyl (RR'C=O) and a hydroxyl (R-O-H), which has the formula -C(=O)OH, usually written as -COOH or $-CO_2H$.

Carboxylic acids are Brønsted-Lowry acids because they are proton (H^+) donors. |
| Oxoacid | An oxoacid is an acid that contains oxygen. To be more specific, it is an acid that:•contains oxygen•contains at least one other element•has at least one hydrogen atom bound to oxygen•forms an ion by the loss of one or more protons.

The name oxyacid is sometimes used, although this is not recommended. Description |

Chapter 15. Acids and Bases

Benzoic acid	Benzoic acid, $C_7H_6O_2$ (or C_6H_5COOH), is a colorless crystalline solid and the simplest aromatic carboxylic acid. The name derived from gum benzoin, which was for a long time the only source for benzoic acid. Its salts are used as a food preservative and benzoic acid is an important precursor for the synthesis of many other organic substances.
Hydrolysis	Hydrolysis usually means the rupture of chemical bonds by the addition of water. Generally, hydrolysis is a step in the degradation of a substance. In terms of the word's derivation, hydrolysis comes from Greek roots hydro 'water' + lysis 'separation'.
Iodine	Iodine is a chemical element with the symbol I and atomic number 53./ syllable break' style='border-bottom:1px dotted'>.?da?n-o-dyne, 'a?.?d?n-o-d?n, or 'a?.?di?n-o-deen in both American and British English. The name is from Greek ?οειδ?ς ioeides, meaning violet or purple, due to the color of elemental iodine vapor. Iodine and its compounds are primarily used in nutrition, and industrially in the production of acetic acid and certain polymers.
Solution	In chemistry, a solution is a homogeneous mixture composed of only one phase. In such a mixture, a solute is a substance dissolved in another substance, known as a solvent. The solvent does the dissolving.
Ammonium	The ammonium cation is a positively charged polyatomic cation with the chemical formula NH_4^+. It is formed by the protonation of ammonia (NH_3). Ammonium is also a general name for positively charged or protonated substituted amines and quaternary ammonium cations (NR_4^+), where one or more hydrogen atoms are replaced by organic radical groups (indicated by R).
Ammonium chloride	Ammonium chloride, an inorganic compound with the formula NH_4Cl, is a white crystalline salt, highly soluble in water. Solutions of ammonium chloride are mildly acidic. Sal ammoniac is a name of the natural, mineralogical form of ammonium chloride.
Chloride	The chloride ion is formed when the element chlorine, a halogen, gains an electron to form an anion (negatively-charged ion) Cl^-. The salts of hydrochloric acid contain chloride ions and can also be called chlorides. The chloride ion, and its salts such as sodium chloride, are very soluble in water.
Electron	The electron is a subatomic particle with a negative elementary electric charge. It has no known components or substructure; in other words, it is generally thought to be an elementary particle. An electron has a mass that is approximately 1/1836 that of the proton.

Chapter 15. Acids and Bases

Electron configuration	In atomic physics and quantum chemistry, the electron configuration is the distribution of electrons of an atom or molecule in atomic or molecular orbitals. For example, the electron configuration of the neon atom is $1s^2 2s^2 2p^6$. According to the laws of quantum mechanics, an energy is associated with each electron configuration and, upon certain conditions, electrons are able to move from one orbital to another by emission or absorption of a quantum of energy, in the form of a photon.
Acid rain	Acid rain is a rain or any other form of precipitation that is unusually acidic, meaning that it possesses elevated levels of hydrogen ions (low pH). It can have harmful effects on plants, aquatic animals, and infrastructure. Acid rain is caused by emissions of sulfur dioxide and nitrogen oxides, which react with the water molecules in the atmosphere to produce acids.
Basic oxide	A basic oxide is an oxide that shows basic properties in opposition to acidic oxides and that either•reacts with water to form a base; or•reacts with an acid to form a salt. Examples include:•Sodium oxide, which reacts with water to produce sodium hydroxide Magnesium oxide, which reacts with hydrochloric acid to form magnesium chloride•Copper(II) oxide, which reacts with nitric acid to form copper nitrate Basic oxides are oxides mostly of metals, especially alkali and alkaline earth metals.
Oxide	An oxide is a chemical compound that contains at least one oxygen atom and one other element in its chemical formula. Metal oxides typically contain an anion of oxygen in the oxidation state of −2. Most of the Earth's crust consists of solid oxides, the result of elements being oxidized by the oxygen in air or in water . Hydrocarbon combustion affords the two principal carbon oxides: carbon monoxide and carbon dioxide.
Carbon	Carbon is the chemical element with symbol C and atomic number 6. As a member of group 14 on the periodic table, it is nonmetallic and tetravalent--making four electrons available to form covalent chemical bonds. There are three naturally occurring isotopes, with ^{12}C and ^{13}C being stable, while ^{14}C is radioactive, decaying with a half-life of about 5,730 years. Carbon is one of the few elements known since antiquity.
Carbon dioxide	Carbon dioxide is a naturally occurring chemical compound composed of two oxygen atoms covalently bonded to a single carbon atom. It is a gas at standard temperature and pressure and exists in Earth's atmosphere in this state, as a trace gas at a concentration of 0.039% by volume.

Chapter 15. Acids and Bases

Transition metal	In chemistry, the term transition metal has two possible meanings:•The IUPAC definition states that a transition metal is 'an element whose atom has an incomplete d sub-shell, or which can give rise to cations with an incomplete d sub-shell'.•Most scientists describe a 'transition metal' as any element in the d-block of the periodic table, which includes groups 3 to 12 on the periodic table. All elements in the d-block are metals. In actual practice, the f-block is also included in the form of the lanthanide and actinide series. Jensen has reviewed the history of the terms transition element and d-block.
Transition metal oxides	Transition metal oxides comprise a class of materials that contain transition elements and oxygen. They include insulators as well as (poor) metals. Often the same material may display both types of transport properties, hence a Metal-Insulator transition, obtained by varying either temperature or pressure.
Amphoterism	In chemistry, an amphoteric species is a molecule or ion that can react as an acid as well as a base. Many metals (such as zinc, tin, lead, aluminium, and beryllium) and most metalloids form amphoteric oxides or hydroxides. Amphoterism depends on the oxidation state of the oxide.
Boron	Boron is the chemical element with atomic number 5 and the chemical symbol B. Because boron is produced entirely by cosmic ray spallation and not by stellar nucleosynthesis, it is a low-abundance element in both the solar system and the Earth's crust. However, boron is concentrated on Earth by the water-solubility of its more common naturally occurring compounds, the borate minerals. These are mined industrially as evaporate ores, such as borax and kernite.
Boron trifluoride	Boron trifluoride is the chemical compound with the formula BF_3. This pungent colourless toxic gas forms white fumes in moist air. It is a useful Lewis acid and a versatile building block for other boron compounds.
Diagonal	A diagonal is a line joining two nonconsecutive vertices of a polygon or polyhedron. Informally, any sloping line is called diagonal. The word 'diagonal' derives from the Greek διαγ?νιος (diagonios), from dia- ('through', 'across') and gonia ('angle', related to gony 'knee'); it was used by both Strabo and Euclid to refer to a line connecting two vertices of a rhombus or cuboid, and later adopted into Latin as diagonus ('slanting line').
Diagonal relationship	A diagonal relationship is said to exist between certain pairs of diagonally adjacent elements in the second and third periods of the periodic table. These pairs (lithium (Li) and magnesium (Mg), beryllium (Be) and aluminium (Al), boron (B) and silicon (Si) etc).

Chapter 15. Acids and Bases

Lewis acid	The term Lewis acid refers to a definition of acid published by Gilbert N. Lewis in 1923, specifically: An acid substance is one which can employ an electron lone pair from another molecule in completing the stable group of one of its own atoms. Thus, H^+ is a Lewis acid, since it can accept a lone pair, completing its stable form, which requires two electrons. The modern-day definition of Lewis acid, as given by IUPAC is a molecular entity (and the corresponding chemical species) that is an electron-pair acceptor and therefore able to react with a Lewis base to form a Lewis adduct, by sharing the electron pair furnished by the Lewis base.
Lewis base	A Lewis base is any species that donates a pair of electrons to a Lewis acid to form a Lewis adduct. For example, OH^- and NH_3 are Lewis bases, because they can donate a lone pair of electrons. Some compounds, such as H_2O, are both Lewis acids and Lewis bases, because they can both accept a pair of electrons and donate a pair of electrons, depending upon the reaction. Usually the terms Lewis acid and Lewis base are defined within the context of a specific chemical reaction. For example, in the reaction of Me_3B and NH_3 to give Me_3BNH_3, Me_3B acts as a Lewis acid, and NH_3 acts as a Lewis base. Me_3BNH_3 is the Lewis adduct.
Covalent bond	A covalent bond is a form of chemical bonding that is characterized by the sharing of pairs of electrons between atoms. The stable balance of attractive and repulsive forces between atoms when they share electrons is known as covalent bonding. Covalent bonding includes many kinds of interaction, including σ-bonding, π-bonding, metal-to-metal bonding, agostic interactions, and three-center two-electron bonds.
Trifluoride	Trifluorides are compounds having three fluorines per formula unit. Many metals form trifluorides, such as iron, the rare earth elements, and the metals in the aluminium and scandium columns of the periodic table. No trifluoride is soluble in water, but several are soluble in other solvents.
Boric acid	Boric acid, having chemical formula H_3BO_3 (sometimes written $B(OH)_3$), is a weak acid of boron often used as an antiseptic, insecticide, flame retardant, neutron absorber, or precursor to other chemical compounds. It exists in the form of colorless crystals or a white powder and dissolves in water. When occurring as a mineral, it is called sassolite.
Active transport	Active transport is the movement of a substance against its concentration gradient (from low to high concentration). In all cells, this is usually concerned with accumulating high concentrations of molecules that the cell needs, such as ions, glucose and amino acids.

Chapter 15. Acids and Bases

Cellulose	Cellulose is an organic compound with the formula $(C_6H_{10}O_5)_n$, a polysaccharide consisting of a linear chain of several hundred to over ten thousand β(1→4) linked D-glucose units. Cellulose is the structural component of the primary cell wall of green plants, many forms of algae and the oomycetes. Some species of bacteria secrete it to form biofilms.
Electromotive force	In physics, electromotive force, emf (seldom capitalized), or electromotance (denoted $\mathcal{E}$ and measured in volts) refers to voltage generated by a battery or by the magnetic force according to Faraday's Law, which states that a time varying magnetic field will induce an electric current. Electromotive 'force' is not a force (measured in newtons) but a potential, or energy per unit of charge, measured in volts. Formally, emf is the external work expended per unit of charge to produce an electric potential difference across two open-circuited terminals.
Glucose	Glucose is a simple sugar (monosaccharide) and an important carbohydrate in biology. Cells use it as the primary source of energy and a metabolic intermediate. Glucose is one of the main products of photosynthesis and fuels for cellular respiration.
Titanium	Titanium is a chemical element with the symbol Ti and atomic number 22. It has a low density and is a strong, lustrous, corrosion-resistant (including sea water, aqua regia and chlorine) transition metal with a silver color. Titanium was discovered in Cornwall, Great Britain, by William Gregor in 1791 and named by Martin Heinrich Klaproth for the Titans of Greek mythology. The element occurs within a number of mineral deposits, principally rutile and ilmenite, which are widely distributed in the Earth's crust and lithosphere, and it is found in almost all living things, rocks, water bodies, and soils.
Titanium dioxide	Titanium dioxide, is the naturally occurring oxide of titanium, chemical formula TiO_2. When used as a pigment, it is called titanium white, Pigment White 6, or CI 77891. Generally it comes in two different forms, rutile and anatase. It has a wide range of applications, from paint to sunscreen to food colouring.

Chapter 15. Acids and Bases

CHAPTER QUIZ: KEY TERMS, PEOPLE, PLACES, CONCEPTS

1. The _____ is a subatomic particle with the symbol p or p+and a positive electric charge of 1 elementary charge. One or more _____s are present in the nucleus of each atom, along with neutrons. The number of _____s in each atom is its atomic number.

   a. Proton
   b. Silylium ion
   c. Sulfonium
   d. Tetrafluoroammonium

2. _____, an inorganic compound with the formula NH_4Cl, is a white crystalline salt, highly soluble in water. Solutions of _____ are mildly acidic. Sal ammoniac is a name of the natural, mineralogical form of _____.

   a. Amprolium
   b. Anilinium chloride
   c. Antimony trichloride
   d. Ammonium chloride

3. _____s are compounds having three fluorines per formula unit. Many metals form _____s, such as iron, the rare earth elements, and the metals in the aluminium and scandium columns of the periodic table. No _____ is soluble in water, but several are soluble in other solvents.

   a. Base
   b. Chlorflurazole
   c. Chromophore
   d. Trifluoride

4. _____ is the movement of a substance against its concentration gradient (from low to high concentration). In all cells, this is usually concerned with accumulating high concentrations of molecules that the cell needs, such as ions, glucose and amino acids. If the process uses chemical energy, such as from adenosine triphosphate (ATP), it is termed primary _____.

   a. Active transport
   b. Osmotic pressure
   c. Outer mitochondrial membrane
   d. Calcium hydroxide

5. . In chemistry, a _____ ion is the cation H_3O^+, a type of oxonium ion produced by protonation of water. This cation is often used to represent the nature of the proton in aqueous solution, where the proton is highly solvated (bound to a solvent). The reality is far more complicated, and a proton is bound to several molecules of water, such that other descriptions such as $H_5O_2^+$, $H_7O_3^+$ and $H_9O_4^+$ are increasingly accurate descriptions of the environment of a proton in water.

   a. Kryptonium ion
   b. Lyonium ion
   c. N-Oxoammonium salt

1. a
2. d
3. d
4. a
5. d

You can take the complete Chapter Practice Test

for Chapter 15. Acids and Bases
on all key terms, persons, places, and concepts.

Online 99 Cents

http://www.epub14.1.20267.15.cram101.com/

Use www.Cram101.com for all your study needs

including Cram101's online interactive problem solving labs in

chemistry, statistics, mathematics, and more.

Chapter 16. Acid-Base Equilibria and Solubility Equilibria

CHAPTER OUTLINE: KEY TERMS, PEOPLE, PLACES, CONCEPTS

- Petroleum
- Sodium
- Sodium acetate
- Acetate
- Buffer solution
- Solution
- Phosphate
- Acid-base titration
- Chemical reaction
- Equivalence point
- Hydrochloric acid
- Titration
- PH meter
- Point
- Stoichiometry
- Sodium hydroxide
- Titration curve
- Hydroxide
- Carbonic anhydrase

Chapter 16. Acid-Base Equilibria and Solubility Equilibria

CHAPTER OUTLINE: KEY TERMS, PEOPLE, PLACES, CONCEPTS

__________ Enzyme

__________ Hemoglobin

__________ Oxygen

__________ Acetic acid

__________ Hydrolysis

__________ Weak acid

__________ Weak base

__________ Strong acid

__________ Ionization

__________ Phenolphthalein

__________ Barium

__________ Silver chloride

__________ Solubility

__________ Chloride

__________ Reaction quotient

__________ Molar solubility

__________ Silver bromide

__________ Bromide

__________ Iodine

	Calcium
	Flame test
	Hydrogen
	Hydrogen sulfide
	Sulfide
	Protein
	Iron sulfide

Petroleum

Petroleum (L. petroleum, from Greek: petra (rock) + Latin: oleum (oil)) or crude oil is a naturally occurring, flammable liquid consisting of a complex mixture of hydrocarbons of various molecular weights and other liquid organic compounds, that are found in geologic formations beneath the Earth's surface. A fossil fuel, it is formed when large quantities of dead organisms, usually zooplankton and algae, are buried underneath sedimentary rock and undergo intense heat and pressure.

Petroleum is recovered mostly through oil drilling.

Sodium

Sodium is a chemical element with the symbol Na and atomic number 11. It is a soft, silvery-white, highly reactive metal and is a member of the alkali metals; its only stable isotope is ^{23}Na. The free metal does not occur in nature, but instead must be prepared from its compounds; it was first isolated by Humphry Davy in 1807 by the electrolysis of sodium hydroxide. Sodium is the sixth most abundant element in the Earth's crust, and exists in numerous minerals such as feldspars, sodalite and rock salt.

Chapter 16. Acid-Base Equilibria and Solubility Equilibria

Sodium acetate	Sodium acetate, CH_3COONa, also abbreviated NaOAc, also sodium ethanoate, is the sodium salt of acetic acid. This colourless salt has a wide range of uses. Industrial Sodium acetate is used in the textile industry to neutralize sulfuric acid waste streams, and as a photoresist while using aniline dyes.
Acetate	An acetate is a derivative of acetic acid. This term includes salts and esters, as well as the anion found in solution. Most of the approximately 5 billion kilograms of acetic acid produced annually in industry are used in the production of acetates, which usually take the form of polymers.
Buffer solution	A buffer solution is an aqueous solution consisting of a mixture of a weak acid and its conjugate base or a weak base and its conjugate acid. Its pH changes very little when a small amount of strong acid or base is added to it. Buffer solutions are used as a means of keeping pH at a nearly constant value in a wide variety of chemical applications.
Solution	In chemistry, a solution is a homogeneous mixture composed of only one phase. In such a mixture, a solute is a substance dissolved in another substance, known as a solvent. The solvent does the dissolving.
Phosphate	A phosphate, an inorganic chemical, is a salt of phosphoric acid. In organic chemistry, a phosphate, or organophosphate, is an ester of phosphoric acid. Organic phosphates are important in biochemistry and biogeochemistry or ecology.
Acid-base titration	An acid-base titration is the determination of the concentration of an acid or base by exactly neutralizing the acid/base with an acid or base of known concentration. This allows for quantitative analysis of the concentration of an unknown acid or base solution. It makes use of the neutralization reaction that occurs between acids and bases and the knowledge of how acids and bases will react if their formulas are known.
Chemical reaction	A chemical reaction is a process that leads to the transformation of one set of chemical substances to another. Chemical reactions can be either spontaneous, requiring no input of energy, or non-spontaneous, typically following the input of some type of energy, such as heat, light or electricity. Classically, chemical reactions encompass changes that strictly involve the motion of electrons in the forming and breaking of chemical bonds, although the general concept of a chemical reaction, in particular the notion of a chemical equation, is applicable to transformations of elementary particles (such as illustrated by Feynman diagrams), as well as nuclear reactions.
Equivalence point	The equivalence point, of a chemical reaction is when a titrant is added and is stoichiometrically equal to the amount of moles of substance (known as analyte) present in the sample: the smallest amount of titrant that is sufficient to fully neutralize or react with the analyte.

In some cases there are multiple equivalence points which are multiples of the first equivalent point, such as in the titration of a diprotic acid.

A graph of the titration curve exhibits an inflection point at the equivalence point--where the graph is steepest.

Hydrochloric acid	Hydrochloric acid is a clear, colourless solution of hydrogen chloride (HCl) in water. It is a highly corrosive, strong mineral acid with many industrial uses. Hydrochloric acid is found naturally in gastric acid.
Titration	Titration, is a common laboratory method of quantitative chemical analysis that is used to determine the unknown concentration of an identified analyte. Because volume measurements play a key role in titration, it is also known as volumetric analysis. A reagent, called the titrant or titrator is prepared as a standard solution.
PH meter	A pH meter is an electronic instrument used for measuring the pH (acidity or alkalinity) of a liquid (though special probes are sometimes used to measure the pH of semi-solid substances). A typical pH meter consists of a special measuring probe (a glass electrode) connected to an electronic meter that measures and displays the pH reading. The pH probe measures pH as the activity of the hydrogen cations surrounding a thin-walled glass bulb at its tip.
Point	Points, sometimes also called a 'discount point', are a form of pre-paid interest. One point equals one percent of the loan amount. By charging a borrower points, a lender effectively increases the yield on the loan above the amount of the stated interest rate.
Stoichiometry	Stoichiometry is a branch of chemistry that deals with the relative quantities of reactants and products in chemical reactions. In a balanced chemical reaction, the relations among quantities of reactants and products typically form a ratio of whole numbers. For example, in a reaction that forms ammonia (NH_3), exactly one molecule of nitrogen (N_2) reacts with three molecules of hydrogen (H_2) to produce two molecules of NH_3:$N_2 + 3\,H_2 \rightarrow 2\,NH_3$ Stoichiometry can be used to find quantities such as the amount of products (in mass, moles, volume, etc).
Sodium hydroxide	Sodium hydroxide also known as lye and caustic soda, is a caustic metallic base. It is used in many industries, mostly as a strong chemical base in the manufacture of pulp and paper, textiles, drinking water, soaps and detergents and as a drain cleaner. Worldwide production in 2004 was approximately 60 million tonnes, while demand was 51 million tonnes.

Chapter 16. Acid-Base Equilibria and Solubility Equilibria

Titration curve	Titrations are often recorded on graphs called titration curves, which generally contain the volume of the titrant as the independent variable and the pOH of the solution as the dependent variable (because it changes depending on the composition of the two solutions). The equivalence point on the graph is where all of the starting solution (usually an acid) has been neutralized by the titrant (usually a base). It can be calculated precisely by finding the molarity of the titration curve and computing the points of inflection (where the graph changes concavity); however, in most cases, simple visual inspection of the curve will suffice (in the curve given to the right, both equivalence points are visible, after roughly 15 and 30 mL of NaOH solution has been titrated into the oxalic acid solution.
Hydroxide	Hydroxide is a diatomic anion with chemical formula OH^-. It consists of an oxygen and a hydrogen atom held together by a covalent bond, and carrying a negative electric charge. It is an important but usually minor constituent of water.
Carbonic anhydrase	Eukaryotic-type carbonic anhydrase The carbonic anhydrases form a family of enzymes that catalyze the rapid interconversion of carbon dioxide and water to bicarbonate and protons , a reversible reaction that occurs rather slowly in the absence of a catalyst. The active site of most carbonic anhydrases contains a zinc ion; they are therefore classified as metalloenzymes. One of the functions of the enzyme in animals is to interconvert carbon dioxide and bicarbonate to maintain acid-base balance in blood and other tissues, and to help transport carbon dioxide out of tissues.
Enzyme	Enzymes ( ) are biological molecules that catalyze (i.e., increase the rates of) chemical reactions. In enzymatic reactions, the molecules at the beginning of the process, called substrates, are converted into different molecules, called products. Almost all chemical reactions in a biological cell need enzymes in order to occur at rates sufficient for life.
Hemoglobin	Hemoglobin is the iron-containing oxygen-transport metalloprotein in the red blood cells of all vertebrates (with the exception of the fish family Channichthyidae) as well as the tissues of some invertebrates. Hemoglobin in the blood carries oxygen from the respiratory organs (lungs or gills) to the rest of the body (i.e. the tissues) where it releases the oxygen to burn nutrients to provide energy to power the functions of the organism, and collects the resultant carbon dioxide to bring it back to the respiratory organs to be dispensed from the organism. In mammals, the protein makes up about 97% of the red blood cells' dry content, and around 35% of the total content (including water).

Oxygen	Oxygen is the element with atomic number 8 and represented by the symbol O. Its name derives from the Greek roots ?ξ?ς (oxys) ('acid', literally 'sharp', referring to the sour taste of acids) and -γεν?ς (-genes) ('producer', literally 'begetter'), because at the time of naming, it was mistakenly thought that all acids required oxygen in their composition. At standard temperature and pressure, two atoms of the element bind to form dioxygen, a very pale blue, odorless, tasteless diatomic gas with the formula O_2. Oxygen is a member of the chalcogen group on the periodic table and is a highly reactive nonmetallic element that readily forms compounds (notably oxides) with almost all other elements.
Acetic acid	Acetic acid ?'si?t?k is an organic compound with the chemical formula CH_3CO_2H (also written as CH_3COOH). It is a colourless liquid that when undiluted is also called glacial acetic acid. Acetic acid is the main component of vinegar (apart from water), and has a distinctive sour taste and pungent smell.
Hydrolysis	Hydrolysis usually means the rupture of chemical bonds by the addition of water. Generally, hydrolysis is a step in the degradation of a substance. In terms of the word's derivation, hydrolysis comes from Greek roots hydro 'water' + lysis 'separation'.
Weak acid	A weak acid is an acid that dissociates incompletely. It does not release all of its hydrogens in a solution, donating only a partial amount of its protons to the solution. These acids have higher pKa than strong acids, which release all of their hydrogen atoms when dissolved in water.
Weak base	In chemistry, a weak base is a chemical base that does not ionize fully in an aqueous solution. As Brønsted-Lowry bases are proton acceptors, a weak base may also be defined as a chemical base in which protonation is incomplete. This results in a relatively low pH compared to strong bases.
Strong acid	A strong acid is an acid that ionizes completely in an aqueous solution by losing one proton, according to the equation $HA(aq) \rightarrow H^+(aq) + A^-(aq)$ For sulfuric acid which is diprotic, the 'strong acid' designation refers only to dissociation of the first proton $H_2SO_4(aq) \rightarrow H^+(aq) + HSO_4^-(aq)$ More precisely, the acid must be stronger in aqueous solution than hydronium ion, so strong acids are acids with a $pK_a < -1.74$. An example is HCl for which $pK_a = -6.3$. This generally means that in aqueous solution at standard temperature and pressure, the concentration of hydronium ions is equal to the concentration of strong acid introduced to the solution.

Chapter 16. Acid-Base Equilibria and Solubility Equilibria

While strong acids are generally assumed to be the most corrosive, this is not always true. The carborane superacid $H(CHB_{11}Cl_{11})$, which is one million times stronger than sulfuric acid, is entirely non-corrosive, whereas the weak acid hydrofluoric acid (HF) is extremely corrosive and can dissolve, among other things, glass and all metals except iridium.

Ionization

Ionization is the process of converting an atom or molecule into an ion by adding or removing charged particles such as electrons or ions. In the case of ionisation of a gas, ion-pairs are created consisting of a free electron and a +ve ion.

The process of ionization works slightly differently depending on whether an ion with a positive or a negative electric charge is being produced.

Phenolphthalein

Phenolphthalein is a chemical compound with the formula $C_{20}H_{14}O_4$ and is often written as 'HIn' or 'phph' in shorthand notation. Often used in titrations, it turns colorless in acidic solutions and pink in basic solutions. If the concentration of indicator is particularly strong, it can appear purple.

Barium

Barium is a chemical element with the symbol Ba and atomic number 56. It is the fifth element in Group 2, a soft silvery metallic alkaline earth metal. Barium is never found in nature in its pure form due to its reactivity with air. Its oxide is historically known as baryta but it reacts with water and carbon dioxide and is not found as a mineral.

Silver chloride

Silver chloride is a chemical compound with the chemical formula AgCl. This white crystalline solid is well known for its low solubility in water (this behavior being reminiscent of the chlorides of Tl^+ and Pb^{2+}). Upon illumination or heating, silver chloride converts to silver (and chlorine), which is signalled by greyish or purplish coloration to some samples.

Solubility

Solubility is the property of a solid, liquid, or gaseous chemical substance called solute to dissolve in a solid, liquid, or gaseous solvent to form a homogeneous solution of the solute in the solvent. The solubility of a substance fundamentally depends on the used solvent as well as on temperature and pressure. The extent of the solubility of a substance in a specific solvent is measured as the saturation concentration, where adding more solute does not increase the concentration of the solution.

Chloride

The chloride ion is formed when the element chlorine, a halogen, gains an electron to form an anion (negatively-charged ion) Cl^-. The salts of hydrochloric acid contain chloride ions and can also be called chlorides. The chloride ion, and its salts such as sodium chloride, are very soluble in water.

Chapter 16. Acid-Base Equilibria and Solubility Equilibria

| Reaction quotient | In chemistry, a reaction quotient: Q_r is a function of the activities or concentrations of the chemical species involved in a chemical reaction. In the special case that the reaction is at equilibrium the reaction quotient is equal to the equilibrium constant.

A general chemical reaction in which α moles of a reactant A and β moles of a reactant B react to give σ moles of a product S and τ moles of a product T can be written as αA + βB σS + τT

The reaction is written as an equilibrium even though in many cases it may appear to have gone to completion. |
|---|---|
| Molar solubility | Molar solubility is the number of moles of a substance (the solute) that can be dissolved per liter of solution before the solution becomes saturated. It can be calculated from a substance's Solubility Product constant (K_{sp}) and Stoichiometry. The units are mol/L, sometimes written as M.

Calculation

Given excess of a simple salt A_xB_y in an aqueous solution of no common ions (A or B already present in the solution), the amount of it which enters solution can be calculated as follows:

The Chemical equation for this salt would be: $$A_xB_{y(s)} \Longleftrightarrow xA_{(aq)} + yB_{(aq)}$$ where A, B are ions and x, y are coefficients. |
| Silver bromide | Silver bromide a soft, pale-yellow, water insoluble salt well known (along with other silver halides) for its unusual sensitivity to light. This property has allowed silver halides to become the basis of modern photographic materials. AgBr is widely used in photographic films and is believed by some to have been used for making the Shroud of Turin. |
| Bromide | A bromide is a chemical compound containing a bromide ion, that is a bromine atom with an effective charge of −1. The class name can include ionic compounds such as caesium bromide or covalent compounds such as sulfur dibromide.

Bromide is present in typical seawater (35 PSU) with a concentration of around 65 mg/L, which is around 0.2% of all dissolved salts. Seafoods and deep sea plants generally have high levels of bromide, while foods derived from land have variable amounts. |
| Iodine | |

Iodine is a chemical element with the symbol I and atomic number 53./ syllable break' style='border-bottom:1px dotted'>.?da?n-o-dyne, 'a?.?d?n-o-d?n, or 'a?.?di?n-o-deen in both American and British English. The name is from Greek ?οειδ?ς ioeides, meaning violet or purple, due to the color of elemental iodine vapor.

Iodine and its compounds are primarily used in nutrition, and industrially in the production of acetic acid and certain polymers.

Calcium

Calcium is the chemical element with the symbol Ca and atomic number 20. It has an atomic mass of 40.078 amu. Calcium is a soft gray alkaline earth metal, and is the fifth-most-abundant element by mass in the Earth's crust. Calcium is also the fifth-most-abundant dissolved ion in seawater by both molarity and mass, after sodium, chloride, magnesium, and sulfate.

Flame test

A flame test is a procedure used in chemistry to detect the presence of certain metal ions, based on each element's characteristic emission spectrum. The color of flames in general also depends on temperature.

The test involves introducing a sample of the element or compound to a hot, non-luminous flame, and observing the color that results.

Hydrogen

Hydrogen is the chemical element with atomic number 1. It is represented by the symbol H. With an average atomic weight of 1.00794 u (1.007825 u for hydrogen-1), hydrogen is the lightest element and its monatomic form (H_1) is the most abundant chemical substance, constituting roughly 75% of the Universe's baryonic mass. Non-remnant stars are mainly composed of hydrogen in its plasma state.

At standard temperature and pressure, hydrogen is a colorless, odorless, tasteless, non-toxic, nonmetallic, highly combustible diatomic gas with the molecular formula H_2.

Hydrogen sulfide

Hydrogen sulfide is the chemical compound with the formula H_2S. It is a colorless, very poisonous, flammable gas with the characteristic foul odor of rotten eggs. It often results from the bacterial breakdown of organic matter in the absence of oxygen, such as in swamps and sewers; this process is commonly known as anaerobic digestion.

Sulfide

A sulfide is an anion of sulfur in its lowest oxidation state of 2-.

Sulfide is also a slightly archaic term for thioethers, a common type of organosulfur compound that are well known for their bad odors.

The dianion S^{2-} exists only in strongly alkaline aqueous solutions.

Protein

Proteins are biochemical compounds consisting of one or more polypeptides typically folded into a globular or fibrous form in a biologically functional way. A polypeptide is a single linear polymer chain of amino acids bonded together by peptide bonds between the carboxyl and amino groups of adjacent amino acid residues. The sequence of amino acids in a protein is defined by the sequence of a gene, which is encoded in the genetic code.

Iron sulfide

Iron(II) sulfide or ferrous sulfide (Br.E. sulphide) is a chemical compound with the formula FeS. In practice, iron sulfides are often non-stoichiometric. Powdered iron sulfide is pyrophoric (ignites spontaneously in air).

CHAPTER QUIZ: KEY TERMS, PEOPLE, PLACES, CONCEPTS

1. A _____ is a process that leads to the transformation of one set of chemical substances to another. _____s can be either spontaneous, requiring no input of energy, or non-spontaneous, typically following the input of some type of energy, such as heat, light or electricity. Classically, _____s encompass changes that strictly involve the motion of electrons in the forming and breaking of chemical bonds, although the general concept of a _____, in particular the notion of a chemical equation, is applicable to transformations of elementary particles (such as illustrated by Feynman diagrams), as well as nuclear reactions.

   a. Bradsher cycloaddition
   b. Carbonylation
   c. Chemical reaction
   d. Chemical decomposition

2. An _____ is the determination of the concentration of an acid or base by exactly neutralizing the acid/base with an acid or base of known concentration. This allows for quantitative analysis of the concentration of an unknown acid or base solution. It makes use of the neutralization reaction that occurs between acids and bases and the knowledge of how acids and bases will react if their formulas are known.

   a. Assay
   b. Equivalence point
   c. Iodometry
   d. Acid-base titration

3. . _____, CH_3COONa, also abbreviated NaOAc, also sodium ethanoate, is the sodium salt of acetic acid.

This colourless salt has a wide range of uses. Industrial

_____ is used in the textile industry to neutralize sulfuric acid waste streams, and as a photoresist while using aniline dyes.

a. Sodium diacetate
b. Sodium acetate
c. Triethylammonium acetate
d. White catalyst

4. A _____ is an electronic instrument used for measuring the pH (acidity or alkalinity) of a liquid (though special probes are sometimes used to measure the pH of semi-solid substances). A typical _____ consists of a special measuring probe (a glass electrode) connected to an electronic meter that measures and displays the pH reading.

The pH probe measures pH as the activity of the hydrogen cations surrounding a thin-walled glass bulb at its tip.

a. Photocathode
b. Platinum black
c. PH meter
d. Potentiometric sensor

5.

_____ is the chemical element with the symbol Ca and atomic number 20. It has an atomic mass of 40.078 amu.
_____ is a soft gray alkaline earth metal, and is the fifth-most-abundant element by mass in the Earth's crust.
_____ is also the fifth-most-abundant dissolved ion in seawater by both molarity and mass, after sodium, chloride, magnesium, and sulfate.

a. Carbon
b. Cerium
c. Chromium acetate hydroxide
d. Calcium

ANSWER KEY
Chapter 16. Acid-Base Equilibria and Solubility Equilibria

1. c
2. d
3. b
4. c
5. d

You can take the complete Chapter Practice Test

for Chapter 16. Acid-Base Equilibria and Solubility Equilibria
on all key terms, persons, places, and concepts.

Online 99 Cents

http://www.epub14.1.20267.16.cram101.com/

Use www.Cram101.com for all your study needs

including Cram101's online interactive problem solving labs in

chemistry, statistics, mathematics, and more.

Chapter 17. Entropy, Free Energy, and Equilibrium

CHAPTER OUTLINE: KEY TERMS, PEOPLE, PLACES, CONCEPTS

	Thermodynamics
	Mercury oxide
	Oxide
	Phase transition
	Vaporization
	Graphite
	Molecular vibration
	Rotation
	Carbon
	Vibration
	Second law of thermodynamics
	Third law of thermodynamics
	Standard state
	Oxidation state
	Thermodynamic state
	Efficiency
	Calcium
	Calcium carbide
	Carbide

Chapter 17. Entropy, Free Energy, and Equilibrium

	Melting
	Reaction quotient
	Equilibrium constant
	Living systems
	Metabolism
	Adenosine
	Adenosine diphosphate

CHAPTER HIGHLIGHTS & NOTES: KEY TERMS, PEOPLE, PLACES, CONCEPTS

Thermodynamics	Thermodynamics is the branch of natural science concerned with heat and its relation to other forms of energy and work. It defines macroscopic variables (such as temperature, entropy, and pressure) that describe average properties of material bodies and radiation, and explains how they are related and by what laws they change with time. Thermodynamics does not describe the microscopic constituents of matter, and its laws can be derived from statistical mechanics.
Mercury oxide	Mercury oxide, has a formula of HgO. It has a red or orange color. Mercury(II) oxide is a solid at room temperature and pressure. The mineral form montroydite is very rarely found.
Oxide	An oxide is a chemical compound that contains at least one oxygen atom and one other element in its chemical formula. Metal oxides typically contain an anion of oxygen in the oxidation state of −2. Most of the Earth's crust consists of solid oxides, the result of elements being oxidized by the oxygen in air or in water . Hydrocarbon combustion affords the two principal carbon oxides: carbon monoxide and carbon dioxide.
Phase transition	A phase transition is the transformation of a thermodynamic system from one phase or state of matter to another.

A phase of a thermodynamic system and the states of matter have uniform physical properties.

During a phase transition of a given medium certain properties of the medium change, often discontinuously, as a result of some external condition, such as temperature, pressure, and others.

Vaporization	Vaporization of an element or compound is a phase transition from the liquid phase to gas phase. There are two types of vaporization: evaporation and boiling.

Evaporation is a phase transition from the liquid phase to gas phase that occurs at temperatures below the boiling temperature at a given pressure. |
| Graphite | The mineral graphite is an allotrope of carbon. It was named by Abraham Gottlob Werner in 1789 from the Ancient Greek γρ?φω (grapho), 'to draw/write', for its use in pencils, where it is commonly called lead (not to be confused with the metallic element lead). Unlike diamond (another carbon allotrope), graphite is an electrical conductor, a semimetal. |
| Molecular vibration | A molecular vibration occurs when atoms in a molecule are in periodic motion while the molecule as a whole has constant translational and rotational motion. The frequency of the periodic motion is known as a vibration frequency, and the typical frequencies of molecular vibrations range from less than 10^{12} to approximately 10^{14} Hz.

In general, a molecule with N atoms has 3N - 6 normal modes of vibration, but a linear molecule has 3N - 5 such modes, as rotation about its molecular axis cannot be observed. |
Rotation	A rotation is a circular movement of an object around a center of rotation. A three-dimensional object rotates always around an imaginary line called a rotation axis. If the axis is within the body, and passes through its center of mass the body is said to rotate upon itself, or spin.
Carbon	Carbon is the chemical element with symbol C and atomic number 6. As a member of group 14 on the periodic table, it is nonmetallic and tetravalent--making four electrons available to form covalent chemical bonds. There are three naturally occurring isotopes, with ^{12}C and ^{13}C being stable, while ^{14}C is radioactive, decaying with a half-life of about 5,730 years. Carbon is one of the few elements known since antiquity.
Vibration	Vibration is a mechanical phenomenon whereby oscillations occur about an equilibrium point. The oscillations may be periodic such as the motion of a pendulum or random such as the movement of a tire on a gravel road.

Chapter 17. Entropy, Free Energy, and Equilibrium

Second law of thermodynamics	The second law of thermodynamics is an expression of the tendency that over time, differences in temperature, pressure, and chemical potential equilibrate in an isolated physical system. From the state of thermodynamic equilibrium, the law deduced the principle of the increase of entropy and explains the phenomenon of irreversibility in nature. The second law declares the impossibility of machines that generate usable energy from the abundant internal energy of nature by processes called perpetual motion of the second kind.
Third law of thermodynamics	The third law of thermodynamics is sometimes stated as follows:" At zero kelvin the system must be in a state with the minimum possible energy, and this statement of the third law holds true if the perfect crystal has only one minimum energy state. Entropy is related to the number of possible microstates, and with only one microstate available at zero kelvin, the entropy is exactly zero. A more general form of the third law applies to systems such as glasses that may have more than one minimum energy state:" The constant value (not necessarily zero) is called the residual entropy of the system.
Standard state	In chemistry, the standard state of a material (pure substance, mixture or solution) is a reference point used to calculate its properties under different conditions. In principle, the choice of standard state is arbitrary, although the International Union of Pure and Applied Chemistry (IUPAC) recommends a conventional set of standard states for general use. IUPAC recommends using a standard pressure p^o = 1 bar (100 kilopascals).
Oxidation state	In chemistry, the oxidation state is an indicator of the degree of oxidation of an atom in a chemical compound. The formal oxidation state is the hypothetical charge that an atom would have if all bonds to atoms of different elements were 100% ionic. Oxidation states are typically represented by integers, which can be positive, negative, or zero.
Thermodynamic state	ImgProperty databaseimg A thermodynamic state is a set of values of properties of a thermodynamic system that must be specified to reproduce the system. The individual parameters are known as state variables, state parameters or thermodynamic variables. Once a sufficient set of thermodynamic variables have been specified, values of all other properties of the system are uniquely determined.
Efficiency	Efficiency in general describes the extent to which time or effort is well used for the intended task or purpose. It is often used with the specific purpose of relaying the capability of a specific application of effort to produce a specific outcome effectively with a minimum amount or quantity of waste, expense, or unnecessary effort.

Calcium	Calcium is the chemical element with the symbol Ca and atomic number 20. It has an atomic mass of 40.078 amu. Calcium is a soft gray alkaline earth metal, and is the fifth-most-abundant element by mass in the Earth's crust. Calcium is also the fifth-most-abundant dissolved ion in seawater by both molarity and mass, after sodium, chloride, magnesium, and sulfate.
Calcium carbide	Calcium carbide is a chemical compound with the chemical formula of CaC_2. Its main use industrially is in the production of acetylene and calcium cyanamide.
	The pure material is colorless, however pieces of technical-grade calcium carbide are grey or brown and consist of only 80-85% of CaC_2 (the rest is CaO, Ca_3P_2, CaS, Ca_3N_2, SiC, etc)..
Carbide	In chemistry, a carbide is a compound composed of carbon and a less electronegative element. Carbides can be generally classified by chemical bonding type as follows: (i) salt-like, (ii) covalent compounds, (iii) interstitial compounds, and (iv) 'intermediate' transition metal carbides. Examples include calcium carbide, silicon carbide, tungsten carbide and cementite, each used in key industrial applications.
Melting	Melting, is a physical process that results in the phase transition of a substance from a solid to a liquid. The internal energy of a substance is increased, typically by the application of heat or pressure, resulting in a rise of its temperature to the melting point, at which the rigid ordering of molecular entities in the solid breaks down to a less-ordered state and the solid liquefies. An object that has melted completely is molten.
Reaction quotient	In chemistry, a reaction quotient: Q_r is a function of the activities or concentrations of the chemical species involved in a chemical reaction. In the special case that the reaction is at equilibrium the reaction quotient is equal to the equilibrium constant.
	A general chemical reaction in which α moles of a reactant A and β moles of a reactant B react to give σ moles of a product S and τ moles of a product T can be written asαA + βB σS + τT
	The reaction is written as an equilibrium even though in many cases it may appear to have gone to completion.
Equilibrium constant	For a general chemical equilibrium $\alpha A + \beta B... \rightleftharpoons \sigma S + \tau T...$ the equilibrium constant can be defined such that, at equilibrium, $$K = \frac{\{S\}^{\sigma}\{T\}^{\tau}...}{\{A\}^{\alpha}\{B\}^{\beta}...}$$

Chapter 17. Entropy, Free Energy, and Equilibrium

where {A} is the activity of the chemical species A, etc. (activity is a dimensionless quantity). It is conventional to put the activities of the products in the numerator and those of the reactants in the denominator.

Living systems

Living systems are open self-organizing living things that interact with their environment. These systems are maintained by flows of information, energy and matter.

Some scientists have proposed in the last few decades that a general living systems theory is required to explain the nature of life.

Metabolism

Metabolism is the set of chemical reactions that happen in the cells of living organisms to sustain life. These processes allow organisms to grow and reproduce, maintain their structures, and respond to their environments. The word metabolism can also refer to all chemical reactions that occur in living organisms, including digestion and the transport of substances into and between different cells, in which case the set of reactions within the cells is called intermediary metabolism or intermediate metabolism.

Adenosine

Adenosine is a purine nucleoside comprising a molecule of adenine attached to a ribose sugar molecule (ribofuranose) moiety via a β-N_9-glycosidic bond.

Adenosine plays an important role in biochemical processes, such as energy transfer--as adenosine triphosphate (ATP) and adenosine diphosphate (ADP)--as well as in signal transduction as cyclic adenosine monophosphate, cAMP. It is also an inhibitory neurotransmitter, believed to play a role in promoting sleep and suppressing arousal, with levels increasing with each hour an organism is awake.

Adenosine is often abbreviated Ado.

Adenosine diphosphate

Adenosine diphosphate, abbreviated ADP, is a nucleoside diphosphate. It is an ester of pyrophosphoric acid with the nucleoside adenosine. ADP consists of the pyrophosphate group, the pentose sugar ribose, and the nucleobase adenine.

1. _____ in general describes the extent to which time or effort is well used for the intended task or purpose. It is often used with the specific purpose of relaying the capability of a specific application of effort to produce a specific outcome effectively with a minimum amount or quantity of waste, expense, or unnecessary effort. '_____' has widely varying meanings in different disciplines.

   a. Egain Forecasting
   b. Efficiency
   c. Equivalence of direct radiation
   d. Insulated glazing

2. The _____ is sometimes stated as follows:"

   At zero kelvin the system must be in a state with the minimum possible energy, and this statement of the third law holds true if the perfect crystal has only one minimum energy state. Entropy is related to the number of possible microstates, and with only one microstate available at zero kelvin, the entropy is exactly zero.

   A more general form of the third law applies to systems such as glasses that may have more than one minimum energy state:"

   The constant value (not necessarily zero) is called the residual entropy of the system.

   a. 1,2-Dioxetanedione
   b. Third law of thermodynamics
   c. Scale relativity
   d. Selective adsorption

3. A _____ occurs when atoms in a molecule are in periodic motion while the molecule as a whole has constant translational and rotational motion. The frequency of the periodic motion is known as a vibration frequency, and the typical frequencies of _____ s range from less than 10^{12} to approximately 10^{14} Hz.

   In general, a molecule with N atoms has 3N - 6 normal modes of vibration, but a linear molecule has 3N - 5 such modes, as rotation about its molecular axis cannot be observed.

   a. Molecular vibration
   b. Motional narrowing
   c. Multivariate optical computing
   d. Multivariate optical element

4. . _____ is the branch of natural science concerned with heat and its relation to other forms of energy and work. It defines macroscopic variables (such as temperature, entropy, and pressure) that describe average properties of material bodies and radiation, and explains how they are related and by what laws they change with time. _____ does not describe the microscopic constituents of matter, and its laws can be derived from statistical mechanics.

   a. Biological thermodynamics
   b. Thermodynamics

c. 1,8-Diaminonaphthalene

d. Reflecting telescope

5. _____ is a mechanical phenomenon whereby oscillations occur about an equilibrium point. The oscillations may be periodic such as the motion of a pendulum or random such as the movement of a tire on a gravel road.

_____ is occasionally 'desirable'.

a. Bushing

b. Vibration

c. Conductor gallop

d. Damping

1. b
2. b
3. a
4. b
5. b

You can take the complete Chapter Practice Test

for Chapter 17. Entropy, Free Energy, and Equilibrium
on all key terms, persons, places, and concepts.

Online 99 Cents

http://www.epub14.1.20267.17.cram101.com/

Use www.Cram101.com for all your study needs

including Cram101's online interactive problem solving labs in

chemistry, statistics, mathematics, and more.

CHAPTER OUTLINE: KEY TERMS, PEOPLE, PLACES, CONCEPTS

_____ | Electrochemistry

_____ | Oxidation state

_____ | Redox

_____ | Anode

_____ | Electrode

_____ | Electromotive force

_____ | Galvanic cell

_____ | Half-cell

_____ | Salt bridge

_____ | Cathode

_____ | Potential

_____ | Voltage

_____ | Platinum

_____ | Standard electrode potential

_____ | Catalyst

_____ | Electrocatalyst

_____ | Electrode potential

_____ | Reduction potential

_____ | Diagonal

Chapter 18. Electrochemistry

CHAPTER OUTLINE: KEY TERMS, PEOPLE, PLACES, CONCEPTS

- Coulomb
- Faraday constant
- Michael Faraday
- Concentration
- Nernst equation
- Reaction quotient
- Glass electrode
- Petroleum
- PH meter
- Concentration cell
- Membrane
- Membrane potential
- Zinc
- Sulfur
- Sulfur trioxide
- Trioxide
- Hydrometer
- Lithium
- Fuel cell

Chapter 18. Electrochemistry

CHAPTER OUTLINE: KEY TERMS, PEOPLE, PLACES, CONCEPTS

Thermodynamics

Efficiency

Corrosion

Cathodic protection

Copper carbonate

Passivation

Patina

Downs cell

Electrolytic cell

Sodium

Sodium carbonate

Chloride

Electrolysis

Sodium chloride

Amalgam

Chapter 18. Electrochemistry

Electrochemistry	Electrochemistry is a branch of chemistry that studies chemical reactions which take place in a solution at the interface of an electron conductor (a metal or a semiconductor) and an ionic conductor (the electrolyte), and which involve electron transfer between the electrode and the electrolyte or species in solution.
	If a chemical reaction is driven by an external applied voltage, as in electrolysis, or if a voltage is created by a chemical reaction as in a battery, it is an electrochemical reaction. In contrast, chemical reactions where electrons are transferred between molecules are called oxidation/reduction (redox) reactions.
Oxidation state	In chemistry, the oxidation state is an indicator of the degree of oxidation of an atom in a chemical compound. The formal oxidation state is the hypothetical charge that an atom would have if all bonds to atoms of different elements were 100% ionic. Oxidation states are typically represented by integers, which can be positive, negative, or zero.
Redox	Redox reactions include all chemical reactions in which atoms have their oxidation state changed. This can be either a simple redox process, such as the oxidation of carbon to yield carbon dioxide (CO_2) or the reduction of carbon by hydrogen to yield methane (CH_4), or a complex process such as the oxidation of glucose ($C_6H_{12}O_6$) in the human body through a series of complex electron transfer processes.
	Redox reactions, or oxidation-reduction reactions, have a number of similarities to acid-base reactions.
Anode	An anode is an electrode through which electric current flows into a polarized electrical device. The direction of electric current is, by convention, opposite to the direction of electron flow. In other words, the electrons flow from the anode into, for example, an electrical circuit.
Electrode	An electrode is an electrical conductor used to make contact with a nonmetallic part of a circuit (e.g. a semiconductor, an electrolyte or a vacuum). The word was coined by the scientist Michael Faraday from the Greek words elektron (meaning amber, from which the word electricity is derived) and hodos, a way.
	An electrode in an electrochemical cell is referred to as either an anode or a cathode (words that were also coined by Faraday).
Electromotive force	In physics, electromotive force, emf (seldom capitalized), or electromotance (denoted $\mathcal{E}$ and measured in volts) refers to voltage generated by a battery or by the magnetic force according to Faraday's Law, which states that a time varying magnetic field will induce an electric current.

Electromotive 'force' is not a force (measured in newtons) but a potential, or energy per unit of charge, measured in volts. Formally, emf is the external work expended per unit of charge to produce an electric potential difference across two open-circuited terminals.

Galvanic cell

A Galvanic cell, or Alessandro Volta respectively, is an electrochemical cell that derives electrical energy from spontaneous redox reaction taking place within the cell. It generally consists of two different metals connected by a salt bridge, or individual half-cells separated by a porous membrane.

Volta was the inventor of the voltaic pile, the first electrical battery.

Half-cell

A half-cell is a structure that contains a conductive electrode and a surrounding conductive electrolyte separated by a naturally occurring Helmholtz double layer. Chemical reactions within this layer momentarily pump electric charges between the electrode and the electrolyte, resulting in a potential difference between the electrode and the electrolyte. The typical anode reaction involves a metal atom in the electrode dissolved and transported as a positive ion across the double layer, causing the electrolyte to acquire a net positive charge while the electrode acquires a net negative charge.

Salt bridge

A salt bridge, in chemistry, is a laboratory device used to connect the oxidation and reduction half-cells of a galvanic cell (voltaic cell), a type of electrochemical cell. Salt bridges usually come in two types: glass tube and filter paper.

One type of salt bridge consists of a U-shaped glass tube filled with a relatively inert electrolyte; usually potassium chloride or sodium chloride is used, although the diagram here illustrates the use of a potassium nitrate solution.

Cathode

A cathode is an electrode through which electric current flows out of a polarized electrical device. The direction of electric current is, by convention, opposite to the direction of electron flow. Therefore the electrons flow into the polarized electrical device and out of, for example, the connected electrical circuit.

Potential

•In linguistics, the potential mood•The mathematical study of potentials is known as potential theory; it is the study of harmonic functions on manifolds. This mathematical formulation arises from the fact that, in physics, the scalar potential is irrotational, and thus has a vanishing Laplacian -- the very definition of a harmonic function.•In physics, a potential may refer to the scalar potential or to the vector potential. In either case, it is a field defined in space, from which many important physical properties may be derived.

Chapter 18. Electrochemistry

Voltage	Voltage, otherwise known as electrical potential difference or electric tension (denoted ΔV and measured in volts, or joules per coulomb) is the potential difference between two points -- or the difference in electric potential energy per unit charge between two points. Voltage is equal to the work which would have to be done, per unit charge, against a static electric field to move the charge between two points. A voltage may represent either a source of energy (electromotive force), or it may represent lost or stored energy (potential drop).
Platinum	Platinum is a chemical element with the chemical symbol Pt and an atomic number of 78. Its name is derived from the Spanish term platina, which is literally translated into 'little silver'. It is a dense, malleable, ductile, precious, gray-white transition metal.
Standard electrode potential	In electrochemistry, the standard electrode potential, abbreviated E° or E, is the measure of individual potential of a reversible electrode at standard state, which is with solutes at an effective concentration of 1 mol dm^{-3}, and gases at a pressure of 1 atm. The reduction potential is an intensive property. The values are most often tabulated at 25 °C. The basis for an electrochemical cell such as the galvanic cell is always a redox reaction which can be broken down into two half-reactions: oxidation at anode (loss of electron) and reduction at cathode (gain of electron).
Catalyst	Catalysis is the change in rate of a chemical reaction due to the participation of a substance called a catalyst. Unlike other reagents that participate in the chemical reaction, a catalyst is not consumed by the reaction itself. A catalyst may participate in multiple chemical transformations.
Electrocatalyst	An electrocatalyst is a catalyst that participates in electrochemical reactions. Catalyst materials modify and increase the rate of chemical reactions without being consumed in the process. Electrocatalysts are a specific form of catalysts that function at electrode surfaces or may be the electrode surface itself.
Electrode potential	Electrode potential, E, in electrochemistry, according to an IUPAC definition, is the electromotive force of a cell built of two electrodes:•on the left-hand side is the standard hydrogen electrode, and•on the right-hand side is the electrode the potential of which is being defined. By convention:$E_{Cell} := E_{Cathode} - E_{Anode}$ From the above, for the cell with the standard hydrogen electrode (potential of 0 by convention), one obtains:$E_{Cell} = E_{Right} - 0 = E_{Electrode}$

The left-right convention is consistent with the international agreement that redox potentials be given for reactions written in the form of reduction half-reactions.

Electrode potential is measured in volts (V). Measurement

The measurement is generally conducted using a three-electrode setup :•Working electrode•Counter electrode•Reference electrode (standard hydrogen electrode or an equivalent)

The measured potential of the working electrode may be either that at equilibrium on the working electrode ('reversible potential'), or a potential with a non-zero net reaction on the working electrode but zero net current ('corrosion potential', 'mixed potential'), or a potential with a non-zero net current on the working electrode (like in galvanic corrosion or voltammetry).

Reduction potential	Reduction potential (also known as redox potential, oxidation / reduction potential is a measure of the tendency of a chemical species to acquire electrons and thereby be reduced. Reduction potential is measured in volts (V), or millivolts (mV). Each species has its own intrinsic reduction potential; the more positive the potential, the greater the species' affinity for electrons and tendency to be reduced.
Diagonal	A diagonal is a line joining two nonconsecutive vertices of a polygon or polyhedron. Informally, any sloping line is called diagonal. The word 'diagonal' derives from the Greek διαγ?νιος (diagonios), from dia- ('through', 'across') and gonia ('angle', related to gony 'knee'); it was used by both Strabo and Euclid to refer to a line connecting two vertices of a rhombus or cuboid, and later adopted into Latin as diagonus ('slanting line').
Coulomb	The coulomb is the SI derived unit of electric charge. It is defined as the charge transported by a steady current of one ampere in one second: $1C = 1A \cdot 1s$

One coulomb is also the amount of excess charge on the positive side of a capacitance of one farad charged to a potential difference of one volt: $1C = 1F \cdot 1V$

Name and notation

As with every SI unit whose name is derived from the proper name of a person, the first letter of its symbol is upper case (C). When an SI unit is spelled out in English, it should always begin with a lower case letter (coulomb), except where any word would be capitalized, such as at the beginning of a sentence or in capitalized material such as a title. |

Chapter 18. Electrochemistry

Faraday constant	In physics and chemistry, the Faraday constant is the magnitude of electric charge per mole of electrons. It has the currently accepted value F = 96,485.3365(21) C/mol.
	The constant F has a simple relation to two other physical constants: $F = eN_A$
	where: $e \approx 1.6021766 \times 10^{-19}$ C; $N_A \approx 6.022141 \times 10^{23}$ mol^{-1}.
	N_A is the Avogadro constant (the ratio of the number of particles 'N' to the amount of substance 'n' - a unit mole), and e is the elementary charge or the magnitude of the charge of an electron. This relation is true because the amount of charge of a mole of electrons is equal to the amount of charge in one electron multiplied by the number of electrons in a mole.
Michael Faraday	Michael Faraday, FRS (22 September 1791 - 25 August 1867) was an English chemist and physicist (or natural philosopher, in the terminology of the time) who contributed to the fields of electromagnetism and electrochemistry.
	Michael Faraday studied the magnetic field around a conductor carrying a DC electric current. While conducting these studies, Faraday established the basis for the electromagnetic field concept in physics, subsequently enlarged upon by James Maxwell.
Concentration	In chemistry, concentration is defined as the abundance of a constituent divided by the total volume of a mixture. Furthermore, in chemistry, four types of mathematical description can be distinguished: mass concentration, molar concentration, number concentration, and volume concentration. The term concentration can be applied to any kind of chemical mixture, but most frequently it refers to solutes in solutions.
Nernst equation	In electrochemistry, the Nernst equation is an equation that can be used (in conjunction with other information) to determine the equilibrium reduction potential of a half-cell in an electrochemical cell. It can also be used to determine the total voltage (electromotive force) for a full electrochemical cell. he German physical chemist who first formulated it, Walther Nernst.
Reaction quotient	In chemistry, a reaction quotient: Q_r is a function of the activities or concentrations of the chemical species involved in a chemical reaction. In the special case that the reaction is at equilibrium the reaction quotient is equal to the equilibrium constant.
	A general chemical reaction in which α moles of a reactant A and β moles of a reactant B react to give σ moles of a product S and τ moles of a product T can be written as αA + βB σS + τT
	The reaction is written as an equilibrium even though in many cases it may appear to have gone to completion.

Chapter 18. Electrochemistry

Glass electrode	A glass electrode is a type of ion-selective electrode made of a doped glass membrane that is sensitive to a specific ion. It is an important part of the instrumentation for chemical analysis and physico-chemical studies. In modern practice, widely used membranous ion-selective electrodes (ISE, including glasses) are part of a galvanic cell.
Petroleum	Petroleum (L. petroleum, from Greek: petra (rock) + Latin: oleum (oil)) or crude oil is a naturally occurring, flammable liquid consisting of a complex mixture of hydrocarbons of various molecular weights and other liquid organic compounds, that are found in geologic formations beneath the Earth's surface. A fossil fuel, it is formed when large quantities of dead organisms, usually zooplankton and algae, are buried underneath sedimentary rock and undergo intense heat and pressure. Petroleum is recovered mostly through oil drilling.
PH meter	A pH meter is an electronic instrument used for measuring the pH (acidity or alkalinity) of a liquid (though special probes are sometimes used to measure the pH of semi-solid substances). A typical pH meter consists of a special measuring probe (a glass electrode) connected to an electronic meter that measures and displays the pH reading. The pH probe measures pH as the activity of the hydrogen cations surrounding a thin-walled glass bulb at its tip.
Concentration cell	A Concentration cell is an electrochemical cell that has two equivalent half-cells of the same material differing only in concentrations. One can calculate the potential developed by such a cell using the Nernst Equation. A concentration cell produces a voltage as it attempts to reach equilibrium, which will occur when the concentration in both cells are equal.
Membrane	The term membrane most commonly refers to a thin, film-like structure that separates two fluids. It acts as a selective barrier, allowing some particles or chemicals to pass through, but not others. In some cases, especially in anatomy, membrane may refer to a thin film that is primarily a separating structure rather than a selective barrier.
Membrane potential	Membrane potential (also transmembrane potential is the difference in electrical potential between the interior and the exterior of a biological cell. All animal cells are surrounded by a plasma membrane composed of a lipid bilayer with a variety of types of proteins embedded in it. The membrane potential arises primarily from the interaction between the membrane and the actions of two types of transmembrane proteins embedded in the plasma membrane.
Zinc	Zinc, is a metallic chemical element; it has the symbol Zn and atomic number 30.

Chapter 18. Electrochemistry

It is the first element in group 12 of the periodic table. Zinc is, in some respects, chemically similar to magnesium, because its ion is of similar size and its only common oxidation state is +2. Zinc is the 24th most abundant element in the Earth's crust and has five stable isotopes. The most common zinc ore is sphalerite (zinc blende), a zinc sulfide mineral.

Sulfur

Sulfur or sulphur is the chemical element with atomic number 16. In the periodic table it is represented by the symbol S. It is an abundant, multivalent non-metal. Under normal conditions, sulfur atoms form cyclic octatomic molecules with chemical formula S_8. Elemental sulfur is a bright yellow crystalline solid when at room temperature.

Sulfur trioxide

Sulfur trioxide is the chemical compound with the formula SO_3. In the gaseous form, this species is a significant pollutant, being the primary agent in acid rain. It is prepared on massive scales as a precursor to sulfuric acid.

Trioxide

A trioxide is a compound with three oxygen atoms. For metals with the M_2O_3 formula there are several common structures. Al_2O_3, Cr_2O_3, Fe_2O_3, and V_2O_3 adopt the corundum structure.

Hydrometer

A hydrometer is an instrument used to measure the specific gravity of liquids; that is, the ratio of the density of the liquid to the density of water.

A hydrometer is usually made of glass and consists of a cylindrical stem and a bulb weighted with mercury or lead shot to make it float upright. The liquid to be tested is poured into a tall container, often a graduated cylinder, and the hydrometer is gently lowered into the liquid until it floats freely.

Lithium

Lithium is a soft, silver-white metal that belongs to the alkali metal group of chemical elements. It is represented by the symbol Li, and it has the atomic number 3. Under standard conditions it is the lightest metal and the least dense solid element. Like all alkali metals, lithium is highly reactive and flammable.

Fuel cell

A fuel cell is a device that converts the chemical energy from a fuel into electricity through a chemical reaction with oxygen or another oxidizing agent. Hydrogen is the most common fuel, but hydrocarbons such as natural gas and alcohols like methanol are sometimes used. Fuel cells are different from batteries in that they require a constant source of fuel and oxygen to run, but they can produce electricity continually for as long as these inputs are supplied.

Thermodynamics	Thermodynamics is the branch of natural science concerned with heat and its relation to other forms of energy and work. It defines macroscopic variables (such as temperature, entropy, and pressure) that describe average properties of material bodies and radiation, and explains how they are related and by what laws they change with time. Thermodynamics does not describe the microscopic constituents of matter, and its laws can be derived from statistical mechanics.
Efficiency	Efficiency in general describes the extent to which time or effort is well used for the intended task or purpose. It is often used with the specific purpose of relaying the capability of a specific application of effort to produce a specific outcome effectively with a minimum amount or quantity of waste, expense, or unnecessary effort. 'Efficiency' has widely varying meanings in different disciplines.
Corrosion	Corrosion is the gradual destruction of material, usually metals, by chemical reaction with its environment. In the most common use of the word, this means electro-chemical oxidation of metals in reaction with an oxidant such as oxygen. Rusting, the formation of iron oxides, is a well-known example of electrochemical corrosion.
Cathodic protection	Cathodic protection is a technique used to control the corrosion of a metal surface by making it the cathode of an electrochemical cell. The simplest method to apply CP is by connecting the metal to be protected with another more easily corroded 'sacrificial metal' to act as the anode of the electrochemical cell. For structures where passive galvanic CP is not adequate, including long pipelines, an external power source provides the current.
Copper carbonate	Copper(II) carbonate (often called copper carbonate or cupric carbonate) is a blue-green compound (chemical formula $CuCO_3$) forming part of the verdigris patina that is found on weathered brass, bronze, and copper. The colour can vary from bright blue to green, because there may be a mixture of both copper carbonate and basic copper carbonate in various stages of hydration. It was formerly much used as a pigment, and is still in use for artist's colours.
Passivation	Passivation, in physical chemistry and engineering, is a material becoming 'passive' in relation to being less affected by environmental factors such as air or water. It means a shielding outer layer of corrosion which can be demonstrated with a micro-coating or found occurring spontaneously in nature. Passivation is useful in strengthening, and preserving the appearance of, metallics.
Patina	Patina is a tarnish that forms on the surface of bronze and similar metals (produced by oxidation or other chemical processes); a sheen on wooden furniture produced by age, wear, and polishing; or any such acquired change of a surface through age and exposure. On metal, patina is a coating of various chemical compounds such as oxides or carbonates formed on the surface during exposure to the elements (weathering).

Chapter 18. Electrochemistry

Downs cell	The Downs process is an electrochemical method for the commercial preparation of metallic sodium, in which molten NaCl is electrolyzed in a special apparatus called the Downs cell.
	The Downs cell uses a carbon anode and iron cathode. The electrolyte is sodium chloride that has been fused to a liquid by heating.
Electrolytic cell	An electrolytic cell decomposes chemical compounds by means of electrical energy, in a process called electrolysis; the Greek word lysis means to break up. The result is that the chemical energy is increased. Important examples of electrolysis are the decomposition of water into hydrogen and oxygen, and bauxite into aluminium and other chemicals.
Sodium	Sodium is a chemical element with the symbol Na and atomic number 11. It is a soft, silvery-white, highly reactive metal and is a member of the alkali metals; its only stable isotope is ^{23}Na. The free metal does not occur in nature, but instead must be prepared from its compounds; it was first isolated by Humphry Davy in 1807 by the electrolysis of sodium hydroxide. Sodium is the sixth most abundant element in the Earth's crust, and exists in numerous minerals such as feldspars, sodalite and rock salt.
Sodium carbonate	Sodium carbonate Na_2CO_3 is a sodium salt of carbonic acid. It most commonly occurs as a crystalline heptahydrate, which readily effloresces to form a white powder, the monohydrate. Sodium carbonate is domestically well known for its everyday use as a water softener.
Chloride	The chloride ion is formed when the element chlorine, a halogen, gains an electron to form an anion (negatively-charged ion) Cl^-. The salts of hydrochloric acid contain chloride ions and can also be called chlorides. The chloride ion, and its salts such as sodium chloride, are very soluble in water.
Electrolysis	In chemistry and manufacturing, electrolysis is a method of using a direct electric current (DC) to drive an otherwise non-spontaneous chemical reaction. Electrolysis is commercially highly important as a stage in the separation of elements from naturally occurring sources such as ores using an electrolytic cell.
	The word electrolysis comes from the Greek ?λεκτρον [lýsis] 'dissolution'.
Sodium chloride	Sodium chloride, common salt, table salt or halite, is an ionic compound with the formula NaCl. Sodium chloride is the salt most responsible for the salinity of the ocean and of the extracellular fluid of many multicellular organisms. As the major ingredient in edible salt, it is commonly used as a condiment and food preservative.

Amalgam	Amalgam is an alloy containing mercury. The term is commonly used for the amalgam employed as material for dental fillings, which consists of mercury (50%), silver (~22-32%), tin (~14%), copper (~8%), and other trace metals. In the 1800s, amalgam became the dental restorative material of choice due to its low cost, ease of application, strength, and durability.

1. In chemistry, a _____: Q_r is a function of the activities or concentrations of the chemical species involved in a chemical reaction. In the special case that the reaction is at equilibrium the _____ is equal to the equilibrium constant.

A general chemical reaction in which α moles of a reactant A and β moles of a reactant B react to give σ moles of a product S and τ moles of a product T can be written asαA + βB σS + τT

The reaction is written as an equilibrium even though in many cases it may appear to have gone to completion.

a. Redox indicator
b. Reaction quotient
c. Reversible reaction
d. Saturation

2.

_____, is a metallic chemical element; it has the symbol Zn and atomic number 30. It is the first element in group 12 of the periodic table. _____ is, in some respects, chemically similar to magnesium, because its ion is of similar size and its only common oxidation state is +2. _____ is the 24th most abundant element in the Earth's crust and has five stable isotopes. The most common _____ ore is sphalerite (_____ blende), a _____ sulfide mineral.

a. 1,2-Dioxetanedione
b. Zinc
c. MPTP
d. Myristicin

3. . _____ (also known as redox potential, oxidation / _____ is a measure of the tendency of a chemical species to acquire electrons and thereby be reduced. _____ is measured in volts (V), or millivolts (mV). Each species has its own intrinsic _____; the more positive the potential, the greater the species' affinity for electrons and tendency to be reduced.

a. Reversible charge injection limit
b. Reduction potential

Chapter 18. Electrochemistry

Visit Cram101.com for full Practice Exams

c. Salt bridge

d. Standard electrode potential

4. The term _____ most commonly refers to a thin, film-like structure that separates two fluids. It acts as a selective barrier, allowing some particles or chemicals to pass through, but not others. In some cases, especially in anatomy, _____ may refer to a thin film that is primarily a separating structure rather than a selective barrier.

a. Membrane bioreactor

b. Membrane electrode assembly

c. Membrane

d. Membrane fouling

5. In chemistry, _____ is defined as the abundance of a constituent divided by the total volume of a mixture. Furthermore, in chemistry, four types of mathematical description can be distinguished: mass _____, molar _____, number _____, and volume _____. The term _____ can be applied to any kind of chemical mixture, but most frequently it refers to solutes in solutions.

a. Concentration

b. Crystal structure

c. Dipole

d. Fire point

1. b
2. b
3. b
4. c
5. a

You can take the complete Chapter Practice Test

for Chapter 18. Electrochemistry
on all key terms, persons, places, and concepts.

Online 99 Cents

http://www.epub14.1.20267.18.cram101.com/

Use www.Cram101.com for all your study needs

including Cram101's online interactive problem solving labs in

chemistry, statistics, mathematics, and more.

Chapter 19. Nuclear Chemistry

CHAPTER OUTLINE: KEY TERMS, PEOPLE, PLACES, CONCEPTS

Nuclear chemistry

Elementary particle

Neutron

Nuclear reaction

Nuclear transmutation

Proton

Subatomic particle

Positron

Density

Electron

Electron capture

Nuclear binding energy

Nucleon

Binding energy

Fluorine

Mass

Iodine

Radioactive decay

Helium

Visit Cram101.com for full Practice Exams

Uranium

Uranium oxide

Oxide

Carbon

Carbon disulfide

Radiocarbon dating

Disulfide

Rutherford

Gypsum

Particle accelerator

Tritium

Transuranium element

Nuclear fission

Thermal

Fission products

Chain reaction

Nuclear chain reaction

Atomic mass

Nuclear energy

CHAPTER OUTLINE: KEY TERMS, PEOPLE, PLACES, CONCEPTS

| | Nuclear reactor |

| | Trinitrotoluene |

| | Control rod |

| | Deuterium |

| | Heavy water |

| | Thermal pollution |

| | Neptunium |

| | Functional group |

| | Nuclear fusion |

| | Radioactive waste |

| | Emission spectrum |

| | Group |

| | Radiation |

| | Spectrum |

| | Tokamak |

| | Hydrogen |

| | Lanthanide |

| | Lithium |

| | Isotope |

Thiosulfate

Thyroid

Gland

Curie

Geiger counter

Radium

Chromosome

Genetics

Hydroxyl

Hydroxyl radical

Ionization

Ionization energy

Ionizing radiation

Radical

Amine

Aromatic hydrocarbon

Hydrocarbon

Food irradiation

Irradiation

CHAPTER OUTLINE: KEY TERMS, PEOPLE, PLACES, CONCEPTS

	Boron
	Boron neutron capture therapy
	Neutron capture

CHAPTER HIGHLIGHTS & NOTES: KEY TERMS, PEOPLE, PLACES, CONCEPTS

Nuclear chemistry	Nuclear chemistry is the subfield of chemistry dealing with radioactivity, nuclear processes and nuclear properties. It is the chemistry of radioactive elements such as the actinides, radium and radon together with the chemistry associated with equipment (such as nuclear reactors) which are designed to perform nuclear processes. This includes the corrosion of surfaces and the behavior under conditions of both normal and abnormal operation (such as during an accident).
Elementary particle	In particle physics, an elementary particle is a particle not known to have substructure, thus it is not known to be made up of smaller particles. If an elementary particle truly has no substructure, then it is one of the basic building blocks of the universe from which all other particles are made. In the Standard Model, the elementary particles include the fundamental fermions (including quarks, leptons, and their antiparticles), and the fundamental bosons (including gauge bosons and the Higgs boson).
Neutron	The neutron is a subatomic hadron particle which has the symbol n or n0, no net electric charge and a mass slightly larger than that of a proton. With the exception of hydrogen, nuclei of atoms consist of protons and neutrons, which are therefore collectively referred to as nucleons. The number of protons in a nucleus is the atomic number and defines the type of element the atom forms.
Nuclear reaction	In nuclear physics and nuclear chemistry, a nuclear reaction is semantically considered to be the process in which two nuclei, or else a nucleus of an atom and a subatomic particle (such as a proton, neutron, or high energy electron) from outside the atom, collide to produce products different from the initial particles. In principle, a reaction can involve more than three particles colliding, but because the probability of three or more nuclei to meet at the same time at the same place is much less than for two nuclei, such an event is exceptionally rare.

Chapter 19. Nuclear Chemistry

Nuclear transmutation	Nuclear transmutation is the conversion of one chemical element or isotope into another. In other words, atoms of one element can be changed into atoms of other element by 'transmutation'. This occurs either through nuclear reactions (in which an outside particle reacts with a nucleus), or through radioactive decay (where no outside particle is needed).
Proton	The proton is a subatomic particle with the symbol p or p+and a positive electric charge of 1 elementary charge. One or more protons are present in the nucleus of each atom, along with neutrons. The number of protons in each atom is its atomic number.
Subatomic particle	In physics or chemistry, subatomic particles are the particles, which are smaller than an atom. There are two types of subatomic particles: elementary particles, which are not made of other particles, and composite particles. Particle physics and nuclear physics study these particles and how they interact.
Positron	The positron is the antiparticle or the antimatter counterpart of the electron. The positron has an electric charge of +1e, a spin of 1/2, and has the same mass as an electron. When a low-energy positron collides with a low-energy electron, annihilation occurs, resulting in the production of two or more gamma ray photons .
Density	The mass density is defined as its mass per unit volume. The symbol most often used for density is ρ . In some cases (for instance, in the United States oil and gas industry), density is also defined as its weight per unit volume; although, this quantity is more properly called specific weight.
Electron	The electron is a subatomic particle with a negative elementary electric charge. It has no known components or substructure; in other words, it is generally thought to be an elementary particle. An electron has a mass that is approximately 1/1836 that of the proton.
Electron capture	Electron capture is a process in which a proton-rich nuclide absorbs an inner atomic electron (changing a nuclear proton to a neutron) and simultaneously emits a neutrino. Various photon emissions follow, in order to allow the energy of the atom to fall to the ground state of the new nuclide. Electron capture is the primary decay mode for isotopes with a relative superabundance of protons in the nucleus, but with insufficient energy difference between the isotope and its prospective daughter (with one less positive charge) for the nuclide to decay by emitting a positron.
Nuclear binding energy	Nuclear binding energy is the energy required to split a nucleus of an atom into its component parts. The component parts are neutrons and protons, which are collectively called nucleons.

Chapter 19. Nuclear Chemistry

Nucleon	In chemistry and physics, a nucleon is one of the particles that makes up the atomic nucleus. Each atomic nucleus consists of one or more nucleons, and each atom in turn consists of a cluster of nucleons surrounded by one or more electrons. There are two kinds of nucleon: the neutron and the proton.
Binding energy	Binding energy is the mechanical energy required to disassemble a whole into separate parts. A bound system typically has a lower potential energy than its constituent parts; this is what keeps the system together--often this means that energy is released upon the creation of a bound state. The usual convention is that this corresponds to a positive binding energy.
Fluorine	Fluorine is the chemical element with atomic number 9, represented by the symbol F. It is the lightest element of the halogen column of the periodic table and has a single stable isotope, fluorine-19. At standard pressure and temperature, fluorine is a pale yellow gas composed of diatomic molecules, F_2. In stars, fluorine is rare compared to other light elements. In Earth's crust, fluorine is more common, being the thirteenth most abundant element.
Mass	The mass recorded by a mass spectrometer can refer to different physical quantities depending on the characteristics of the instrument and the manner in which the mass spectrum is displayed. The accurate mass (more appropriately, the measured accurate mass) is an experimentally determined mass that allows the elemental composition to be determined. For molecules with mass below 200 u, a 5 ppm accuracy is sufficient to uniquely determine the elemental composition.
Iodine	Iodine is a chemical element with the symbol I and atomic number 53./ syllable break' style='border-bottom:1px dotted'>.?da?n-o-dyne, 'a?.?d?n-o-d?n, or 'a?.?di?n-o-deen in both American and British English. The name is from Greek ?οειδ?ς ioeides, meaning violet or purple, due to the color of elemental iodine vapor. Iodine and its compounds are primarily used in nutrition, and industrially in the production of acetic acid and certain polymers.

Chapter 19. Nuclear Chemistry

Helium

Helium is the chemical element with atomic number 2 and an atomic weight of 4.002602, which is represented by the symbol He. It is a colorless, odorless, tasteless, non-toxic, inert, monatomic gas that heads the noble gas group in the periodic table. Its boiling and melting points are the lowest among the elements and it exists only as a gas except in extreme conditions.

Uranium

Uranium is a silvery-white metallic chemical element in the actinide series of the periodic table, with atomic number 92. It is assigned the chemical symbol U. A uranium atom has 92 protons and 92 electrons, of which 6 are valence electrons. The uranium nucleus binds between 141 and 146 neutrons, establishing six isotopes (^{233}U through ^{238}U), the most common of which are uranium-238 (146 neutrons) and uranium-235 (143 neutrons). All isotopes are unstable and uranium is weakly radioactive.

Uranium oxide

Uranium oxide is an oxide of the element uranium.

The metal uranium forms several oxides:•Uranium dioxide or uranium(IV) oxide (UO_2, the mineral Uraninite or pitchblende)•Uranium trioxide or uranium(VI) oxide (UO_3)•Triuranium octoxide (U_3O_8, the most stable uranium oxide, yellowcake typically contains 70 to 90 percent triuranium octoxide)•Uranyl peroxide (UO_2O_2 or UO_4)

Uranium dioxide is oxidized in contact with oxygen to form triuranium octoxide. $3\ UO_2 + 4\ O_2 \rightarrow U_3O_8$; at 700 °C (970 K)

Uranium Oxide is one of the few compounds which bonds in Fibonacci numbers of atoms, e.g. 3 Uraniums and 8 Oxygens etc.

Oxide

An oxide is a chemical compound that contains at least one oxygen atom and one other element in its chemical formula. Metal oxides typically contain an anion of oxygen in the oxidation state of −2. Most of the Earth's crust consists of solid oxides, the result of elements being oxidized by the oxygen in air or in water . Hydrocarbon combustion affords the two principal carbon oxides: carbon monoxide and carbon dioxide.

Carbon

Carbon is the chemical element with symbol C and atomic number 6. As a member of group 14 on the periodic table, it is nonmetallic and tetravalent--making four electrons available to form covalent chemical bonds.

There are three naturally occurring isotopes, with ^{12}C and ^{13}C being stable, while ^{14}C is radioactive, decaying with a half-life of about 5,730 years. Carbon is one of the few elements known since antiquity.

Carbon disulfide	Carbon disulfide is a colorless volatile liquid with the formula CS_2. The compound is used frequently as a building block in organic chemistry as well as an industrial and chemical non-polar solvent. It has an 'ether-like' odor, but commercial samples are typically contaminated with foul-smelling impurities, such as carbonyl sulfide.
Radiocarbon dating	Radiocarbon dating is a radiometric dating method that uses the naturally occurring radioisotope carbon-14 (^{14}C) to estimate the age of carbon-bearing materials up to about 58,000 to 62,000 years. Raw, i.e., uncalibrated, radiocarbon ages are usually reported in radiocarbon years 'Before Present' (BP), 'Present' being defined as 1950. Such raw ages can be calibrated to give calendar dates. One of the most frequent uses of radiocarbon dating is to estimate the age of organic remains from archaeological sites.
Disulfide	In chemistry, a disulfide usually refers to the structural unit composed of a linked pair of sulfur atoms. Disulfide usually refer to a chemical compound that contains a disulfide bond, such as diphenyl disulfide, $C_6H_5S\text{-}SC_6H_5$. The disulfide anion is S_2^{2-}, or $^-S\text{-}S^-$.
Rutherford	The rutherford (symbol rd) is an obsolete unit of radioactivity, defined as the activity of a quantity of radioactive material in which one million nuclei decay per second. It is therefore equivalent to one megabecquerel. It was named after Ernest Rutherford.
Gypsum	Gypsum is a very soft sulfate mineral composed of calcium sulfate dihydrate, with the chemical formula $CaSO_4 \cdot 2H_2O$. It is found in alabaster, a decorative stone used in Ancient Egypt. It is the second softest mineral on the Mohs scale of mineral hardness. It forms as an evaporite mineral and as a hydration product of anhydrite.
Particle accelerator	A particle accelerator is a device that uses electromagnetic fields to propel charged particles to high speeds and to contain them in well-defined beams. An ordinary CRT television set is a simple form of accelerator. There are two basic types: electrostatic and oscillating field accelerators.
Tritium	Tritium is a radioactive isotope of hydrogen. The nucleus of tritium contains one proton and two neutrons, whereas the nucleus of protium (by far the most abundant hydrogen isotope) contains one proton and no neutrons. Naturally occurring tritium is extremely rare on Earth, where trace amounts are formed by the interaction of the atmosphere with cosmic rays.

Chapter 19. Nuclear Chemistry

Transuranium element	In chemistry, transuranium elements (also known as transuranic elements) are the chemical elements with atomic numbers greater than 92 (the atomic number of uranium). None of these elements are stable and each of them decays radioactively into other elements. Of the elements with atomic numbers 1 to 92, all can be found in nature, having stable (such as hydrogen), or very long half-life (such as polonium) isotopes, or are created as common products of the decay of uranium and thorium (such as radon).
Nuclear fission	In nuclear physics and nuclear chemistry, nuclear fission refers to either a nuclear reaction or a radioactive decay process in which the nucleus of an atom splits into smaller parts (lighter nuclei), often producing free neutrons and photons (in the form of gamma rays), and releasing a very large amount of energy, even by the energetic standards of radioactive decay. The two nuclei produced are most often of comparable but slightly different sizes, typically with a mass ratio of products of about 3 to 2, for common fissile isotopes. Most fissions are binary fissions (producing two charged fragments), but occasionally (2 to 4 times per 1000 events), three positively charged fragments are produced, in a ternary fission.
Thermal	A thermal column is a column of rising air in the lower altitudes of the Earth's atmosphere. Thermals are created by the uneven heating of the Earth's surface from solar radiation, and are an example of convection, specifically atmospheric convection. The Sun warms the ground, which in turn warms the air directly above it.
Fission products	On this page, a discussion of each of the main elements in the fission product mixture from the nuclear fission of an actinide such as uranium or plutonium is set out by element. Krypton 83-86 Krypton-85 is formed by the fission process with a fission yield of about 0.3%. Only 20% of the fission products of mass 85 become ^{85}Kr itself; the rest passes through a short-lived nuclear isomer and then to stable ^{85}Rb.
Chain reaction	A chain reaction is a sequence of reactions where a reactive product or by-product causes additional reactions to take place. In a chain reaction, positive feedback leads to a self-amplifying chain of events. Chain reactions are one way in which systems which are in thermodynamic non-equilibrium can release energy or increase entropy in order to reach a state of higher entropy.
Nuclear chain reaction	A nuclear chain reaction occurs when one nuclear reaction causes an average of one or more nuclear reactions, thus leading to a self-propagating series of these reactions. The specific nuclear reaction may be the fission of heavy isotopes (e.g.

^{235}U) or the fusion of light isotopes (e.g. ^{2}H and ^{3}H). The nuclear chain reaction releases several million times more energy per reaction than any chemical reaction.

Atomic mass	The atomic mass is the mass of a specific isotope, most often expressed in unified atomic mass units. The atomic mass is the total mass of protons, neutrons and electrons in a single atom. The atomic mass is sometimes incorrectly used as a synonym of relative atomic mass, average atomic mass and atomic weight; these differ subtly from the atomic mass.
Nuclear energy	Nuclear energy usually means the part of the energy of an atomic nucleus, which can be released by fusion or fission or radioactive decay. Nuclear energy also may refer to:•Nuclear binding energy, the energy required to split a nucleus of an atom•Nuclear Energy a bronze sculpture by Henry Moore in the University of Chicago•Nuclear potential energy, the potential energy of the particles inside an atomic nucleus•Nuclear power, the use of sustained nuclear fission to generate heat and electricity•Nuclear technology, applications of nuclear energy including nuclear power, nuclear medicine, and nuclear weapons.
Nuclear reactor	A nuclear reactor is a device to initiate and control a sustained nuclear chain reaction. Most commonly they are used for generating electricity and for the propulsion of ships. Usually heat from nuclear fission is passed to a working fluid (water or gas), which runs through turbines that power either ship's propellers or generators.
Trinitrotoluene	Trinitrotoluene or more specifically, 2,4,6-trinitrotoluene, is a chemical compound with the formula $C_6H_2(NO_2)_3CH_3$. This yellow-colored solid is sometimes used as a reagent in chemical synthesis, but it is best known as a useful explosive material with convenient handling properties. The explosive yield of TNT is considered to be the standard measure of strength of bombs and other explosives.
Control rod	A control rod is a rod made of chemical elements capable of absorbing many neutrons without fissioning themselves. They are used in nuclear reactors to control the rate of fission of uranium and plutonium. Because these elements have different capture cross sections for neutrons of varying energies, the compositions of the control rods must be designed for the neutron spectrum of the reactor it is supposed to control.
Deuterium	Deuterium, is one of two stable isotopes of hydrogen. It has a natural abundance in Earth's oceans of about one atom in 6,420 of hydrogen (~156.25 ppm on an atom basis). Deuterium accounts for approximately 0.0156% of all naturally occurring hydrogen in Earth's oceans, while the most common isotope (hydrogen-1 or protium) accounts for more than 99.98%.
Heavy water	Heavy water, formally called deuterium oxide or

^2H_2O, is a form of water that uses the hydrogen isotope deuterium, rather than the ordinary protium isotope. The colloquial term heavy water is often also used to refer a highly enriched water mixture that contains mostly deuterium oxide but also contains some ordinary water molecules as well; e.g., heavy water used in CANDU reactors is 99.75% enriched by hydrogen atom-fraction (in ordinary water, the deuterium-to-hydrogen ratio is about 156 deuterium atoms per million hydrogen atoms).

Heavy water is not radioactive.

Thermal pollution

Thermal pollution is the degradation of water quality by any process that changes ambient water temperature.

A common cause of thermal pollution is the use of water as a coolant by power plants and industrial manufacturers. When water used as a coolant is returned to the natural environment at a higher temperature, the change in temperature decreases oxygen supply, and affects ecosystem composition.

Neptunium

Neptunium is a chemical element with the symbol Np and atomic number 93. A radioactive metal, neptunium is the first transuranic element, and belongs to the actinide series. Its most stable isotope, ^{237}Np, is a by-product of nuclear reactors and plutonium production, and it can be used as a component in neutron detection equipment. Neptunium is also found in trace amounts in uranium ores due to transmutation reactions.

Functional group

In organic chemistry, functional groups are lexicon specific groups of atoms or bonds within molecules that are responsible for the characteristic chemical reactions of those molecules. The same functional group will undergo the same or similar chemical reaction(s) regardless of the size of the molecule it is a part of. However, its relative reactivity can be modified by nearby functional groups.

Nuclear fusion

Nuclear fusion is the process by which two or more atomic nuclei join together, or 'fuse', to form a single heavier nucleus. This is usually accompanied by the release of large quantities of energy. Fusion is the process that powers active stars, the hydrogen bomb and some experimental devices examining fusion power for electrical generation.

Radioactive waste

Radioactive wastes are wastes that contain radioactive material. Radioactive wastes are usually by-products of nuclear power generation and other applications of nuclear fission or nuclear technology, such as research and medicine.

Emission spectrum	The emission spectrum of a chemical element or chemical compound is the spectrum of frequencies of electromagnetic radiation emitted by the element's atoms or the compound's molecules when they are returned to a lower energy state.
	Each element's emission spectrum is unique. Therefore, spectroscopy can be used to identify the elements in matter of unknown composition.
Group	In chemistry, a group (also known as a family) is a vertical column in the periodic table of the chemical elements. There are 18 groups in the standard periodic table, including the d-block elements, but excluding the f-block elements.
	The explanation of the pattern of the table is that the elements in a group have similar physical or chemical characteristic of the outermost electron shells of their atoms (i.e. the same core charge), as most chemical properties are dominated by the orbital location of the outermost electron.
Radiation	In physics, radiation is a process in which energetic particles or energetic waves travel through a medium or space. Two types of radiation are commonly differentiated in the way they interact with normal chemical matter: ionizing and non-ionizing radiation. The word radiation is often colloquially used in reference to ionizing radiation but the term radiation may correctly also refer to non-ionizing radiation.
Spectrum	A spectrum is a condition that is not limited to a specific set of values but can vary infinitely within a continuum. The word saw its first scientific use within the field of optics to describe the rainbow of colors in visible light when separated using a prism; it has since been applied by analogy to many fields other than optics. Thus, one might talk about the spectrum of political opinion, or the spectrum of activity of a drug, or the autism spectrum.
Tokamak	A tokamak is a device using a magnetic field to confine a plasma in the shape of a torus. Achieving a stable plasma equilibrium requires magnetic field lines that move around the torus in a helical shape. Such a helical field can be generated by adding a toroidal field (traveling around the torus in circles) and a poloidal field (traveling in circles orthogonal to the toroidal field).
Hydrogen	Hydrogen is the chemical element with atomic number 1. It is represented by the symbol H. With an average atomic weight of 1.00794 u (1.007825 u for hydrogen-1), hydrogen is the lightest element and its monatomic form (H_1) is the most abundant chemical substance, constituting roughly 75% of the Universe's baryonic mass. Non-remnant stars are mainly composed of hydrogen in its plasma state.

Chapter 19. Nuclear Chemistry

Lanthanide	The lanthanide, from lanthanum through lutetium. These fifteen lanthanide elements, along with the chemically similar elements scandium and yttrium, are often collectively known as the rare earth elements. The informal chemical symbol Ln is used in general discussions of lanthanide chemistry to refer to any lanthanide.
Lithium	Lithium is a soft, silver-white metal that belongs to the alkali metal group of chemical elements. It is represented by the symbol Li, and it has the atomic number 3. Under standard conditions it is the lightest metal and the least dense solid element. Like all alkali metals, lithium is highly reactive and flammable.
Isotope	Isotopes are variants of a particular chemical element. While all isotopes of a given element share the same number of protons, each isotope differs from the others in its number of neutrons. The term isotope is formed from the Greek roots isos and topos .
Thiosulfate	Thiosulfate is an oxyanion of sulfur. The prefix thio- indicates that thiosulfate ion is a sulfate ion with one oxygen replaced by a sulfur. Thiosulfate occurs naturally and is produced by certain biochemical processes.
Thyroid	The thyroid gland or simply, the thyroid , in vertebrate anatomy, is one of the largest endocrine glands. The thyroid gland is found in the neck, below the thyroid cartilage (which forms the laryngeal prominence, or 'Adam's apple'). The isthmus (the bridge between the two lobes of the thyroid) is located inferior to the cricoid cartilage.
Gland	A gland is an organ in an animal's body that synthesizes a substance for release of substances such as hormones or breast milk, often into the bloodstream (endocrine gland) or into cavities inside the body or its outer surface (exocrine gland). Glands can be divided into 2 groups:•Endocrine glands -- are glands that secrete their products through the basal lamina and lack a duct system.•Exocrine glands -- secrete their products through a duct or directly onto the apical surface, the glands in this group can be divided into three groups: •Apocrine glands -- a portion of the secreting cell's body is lost during secretion.

Curie	The curie is a non-SI unit of radioactivity. It is defined as1 Ci = 3.7×10^{10} decays per second.
	Its continued use is discouraged.
	One Curie is roughly the activity of 1 gram of the radium isotope ^{226}Ra, a substance studied by the Curies.
Geiger counter	A Geiger counter, is a type of particle detector that measures ionizing radiation. They detect the emission of nuclear radiation: alpha particles, beta particles or gamma rays. A Geiger counter detects radiation by ionization produced in a low-pressure gas in a Geiger-Müller tube.
Radium	Radium is a chemical element with atomic number 88, represented by the symbol Ra. Radium is an almost pure-white alkaline earth metal, but it readily oxidizes on exposure to air, becoming black in color. All isotopes of radium are highly radioactive, with the most stable isotope being radium-226, which has a half-life of 1601 years and decays into radon gas.
Chromosome	A chromosome is an organized structure of DNA and protein found in cells. It is a single piece of coiled DNA containing many genes, regulatory elements and other nucleotide sequences. Chromosomes also contain DNA-bound proteins, which serve to package the DNA and control its functions.
Genetics	Genetics, a discipline of biology, is the science of genes, heredity, and variation in living organisms.
	Genetics deals with the molecular structure and function of genes, gene behavior in context of a cell or organism (e.g. dominance and epigenetics), patterns of inheritance from parent to offspring, and gene distribution, variation and change in populations,such as through Genome-Wide Association Studies. Given that genes are universal to living organisms, genetics can be applied to the study of all living systems, from viruses and bacteria, through plants and domestic animals, to humans (as in medical genetics).
Hydroxyl	A hydroxyl is a chemical functional group containing an oxygen atom connected by a covalent bond to a hydrogen atom, a pairing that can be simply understood as a substructure of the water molecule. When it appears, it imparts to chemical structures some of the reactive and interactive properties of the -OH of water (ionizability, hydrogen bonding, etc).. The neutral form of the hydroxyl group is a hydroxyl radical.
Hydroxyl radical	The hydroxyl radical, ˙OH, is the neutral form of the hydroxide ion (OH⁻).

Hydroxyl radicals are highly reactive and consequently short-lived; however, they form an important part of radical chemistry. Most notably hydroxyl radicals are produced from the decomposition of hydroperoxides (ROOH) or, in atmospheric chemistry, by the reaction of excited atomic oxygen with water.

Ionization	Ionization is the process of converting an atom or molecule into an ion by adding or removing charged particles such as electrons or ions. In the case of ionisation of a gas, ion-pairs are created consisting of a free electron and a +ve ion. The process of ionization works slightly differently depending on whether an ion with a positive or a negative electric charge is being produced.
Ionization energy	The ionization energy of a chemical species, i.e. an atom or molecule, is the energy required to remove electrons from gaseous atoms or ions. The property is alternately still often called the ionization potential, measured in volts. In chemistry it often refers to one mole of a substance (molar ionization energy or enthalpy) and reported in kJ/mol.
Ionizing radiation	Ionizing radiation is radiation composed of particles that individually can liberate an electron from an atom or molecule, producing ion-pairs. The ions tend to be especially chemically reactive, and the reactivity produces the high biological damage per unit of energy that is a characteristic of all ionizing radiation. The degree and nature of radiation ionization depends more on the energy and type of the individual radiation particles, and less upon the radiation number.
Radical	Radicals (often referred to as free radicals) are atoms, molecules, or ions with unpaired electrons on an open shell configuration. Free radicals may have positive, negative or zero charge. Even though they have unpaired electrons, by convention, metals and their ions or complexes with unpaired electrons are not radicals.
Amine	Amines are organic compounds and functional groups that contain a basic nitrogen atom with a lone pair. Amines are derivatives of ammonia, wherein one or more hydrogen atoms have been replaced by a substituent such as an alkyl or aryl group. Important amines include amino acids, biogenic amines, trimethylamine, and aniline.
Aromatic hydrocarbon	An aromatic hydrocarbon is a hydrocarbon with alternating double and single bonds between carbon atoms. The term 'aromatic' was assigned before the physical mechanism determining aromaticity was discovered, and was derived from the fact that many of the compounds have a sweet scent. The configuration of six carbon atoms in aromatic compounds is known as a benzene ring, after the simplest possible such hydrocarbon, benzene.

Hydrocarbon	In organic chemistry, a hydrocarbon is an organic compound consisting entirely of hydrogen and carbon. Hydrocarbons from which one hydrogen atom has been removed are functional groups, called hydrocarbyls. Aromatic hydrocarbons (arenes), alkanes, alkenes, cycloalkanes and alkyne-based compounds are different types of hydrocarbons.
Food irradiation	Food irradiation is the process of exposing food to ionizing radiation to destroy microorganisms, bacteria, viruses, or insects that might be present in the food. Further applications include sprout inhibition, delay of ripening, increase of juice yield, and improvement of re-hydration. Irradiated food does not become radioactive, but in some cases there may be subtle chemical changes.
Irradiation	Irradiation is the process by which an object is exposed to radiation. The exposure can originate from various sources, including natural sources. Most frequently the term refers to ionizing radiation, and to a level of radiation that will serve a specific purpose, rather than radiation exposure to normal levels of background radiation.
Boron	Boron is the chemical element with atomic number 5 and the chemical symbol B. Because boron is produced entirely by cosmic ray spallation and not by stellar nucleosynthesis, it is a low-abundance element in both the solar system and the Earth's crust. However, boron is concentrated on Earth by the water-solubility of its more common naturally occurring compounds, the borate minerals. These are mined industrially as evaporate ores, such as borax and kernite.
Boron neutron capture therapy	Boron neutron capture therapy is an experimental form of radiotherapy that uses a neutron beam that interacts with boron injected into a patient. depends on the interaction of slow neutrons with boron-10 to produce alpha particles and lithium nuclei, without producing other types of ionizing radiation. Patients are first given an intravenous injection of a boron-10 containing chemical that preferentially binds to tumor cells.
Neutron capture	Neutron capture is a kind of nuclear reaction in which an atomic nucleus collides with one or more neutrons and they merge to form a heavier nucleus. Since neutrons have no electric charge they can enter a nucleus more easily than positively charged protons, which are repelled electrostatically. Neutron capture plays an important role in the cosmic nucleosynthesis of heavy elements.

Chapter 19. Nuclear Chemistry

1. _____ is the energy required to split a nucleus of an atom into its component parts. The component parts are neutrons and protons, which are collectively called nucleons. The binding energy of nuclei is always a positive number, since all nuclei require net energy to separate them into individual protons and neutrons.

   a. Nuclear fission
   b. Nuclear binding energy
   c. Nuclear fuel
   d. Nuclear fusion

2. _____ or more specifically, 2,4,6-_____, is a chemical compound with the formula $C_6H_2(NO_2)_3CH_3$. This yellow-colored solid is sometimes used as a reagent in chemical synthesis, but it is best known as a useful explosive material with convenient handling properties. The explosive yield of TNT is considered to be the standard measure of strength of bombs and other explosives.

   a. Trinitrotoluene
   b. Photoelectric effect
   c. Photoelectrochemical cell
   d. Photomagnetic effect

3. _____ is an oxyanion of sulfur. The prefix thio- indicates that _____ ion is a sulfate ion with one oxygen replaced by a sulfur. _____ occurs naturally and is produced by certain biochemical processes.

   a. Tribocorrosion
   b. Wet storage stain
   c. Thiosulfate
   d. Red plague

4.

   _____ is the chemical element with atomic number 5 and the chemical symbol B. Because _____ is produced entirely by cosmic ray spallation and not by stellar nucleosynthesis, it is a low-abundance element in both the solar system and the Earth's crust. However, _____ is concentrated on Earth by the water-solubility of its more common naturally occurring compounds, the borate minerals. These are mined industrially as evaporate ores, such as borax and kernite.

   a. Cadmium
   b. Boron
   c. CHON
   d. Chromium

5. .

   _____ is a chemical element with the symbol Np and atomic number 93. A radioactive metal, _____ is the first transuranic element, and belongs to the actinide series. Its most stable isotope, ^{237}Np, is a by-product of nuclear reactors and plutonium production, and it can be used as a component in neutron detection equipment.

_____ is also found in trace amounts in uranium ores due to transmutation reactions.

a. Nobelium

b. Plutonium

c. Promethium

d. Neptunium

1. b

2. a

3. c

4. b

5. d

You can take the complete Chapter Practice Test

for Chapter 19. Nuclear Chemistry
on all key terms, persons, places, and concepts.

Online 99 Cents

http://www.epub14.1.20267.19.cram101.com/

Use www.Cram101.com for all your study needs

including Cram101's online interactive problem solving labs in

chemistry, statistics, mathematics, and more.

Chapter 20. Chemistry in the Atmosphere

CHAPTER OUTLINE: KEY TERMS, PEOPLE, PLACES, CONCEPTS

	Nitrogen
	Nitrogen fixation
	Oxygen
	Photosynthesis
	Denitrification
	Nitrogen cycle
	Oxygen cycle
	Ionosphere
	Mesosphere
	Stratosphere
	Thermosphere
	Ozone
	Photodissociation
	Radiation
	Chlorine
	Chlorine monoxide
	Monoxide
	Aerosol
	Hydroxyl

Hydroxyl radical

Radical

Sulfur

Carbon

Carbon cycle

Carbon dioxide

Greenhouse effect

Emission spectrum

Isotope

Spectrum

Diatomic molecule

Molecular vibration

Molecule

Vibration

Acid rain

Air pollution

Petroleum

Smelting

Sulfur dioxide

CHAPTER OUTLINE: KEY TERMS, PEOPLE, PLACES, CONCEPTS

	Sulfur trioxide
	Carbon monoxide
	Trioxide
	Calcium
	Calcium carbide
	Calcium oxide
	Carbide
	Oxide
	Arsenic
	Nitrogen dioxide
	Peroxyacetyl nitrate
	Methanol
	Platinum
	Radon
	Catalyst
	Carboxyhemoglobin
	Formaldehyde
	Hemoglobin
	Affinity

Chapter 20. Chemistry in the Atmosphere

Nitrogen

Nitrogen is a chemical element that has the symbol N, atomic number of 7 and atomic mass 14.00674 u. Elemental nitrogen is a colorless, odorless, tasteless, and mostly inert diatomic gas at standard conditions, constituting 78.09% by volume of Earth's atmosphere. The element nitrogen was discovered as a separable component of air, by Scottish physician Daniel Rutherford, in 1772.

Nitrogen fixation

Nitrogen fixation is a process by which nitrogen (N_2) in the atmosphere is converted into ammonium (NH_{4+}). Atmospheric nitrogen or elemental nitrogen (N_2) is relatively inert: it does not easily react with other chemicals to form new compounds. Fixation processes free up the nitrogen atoms from their diatomic form (N_2) to be used in other ways.

Oxygen

Oxygen is the element with atomic number 8 and represented by the symbol O. Its name derives from the Greek roots ?ξ?ς (oxys) ('acid', literally 'sharp', referring to the sour taste of acids) and -γεν?ς (-genes) ('producer', literally 'begetter'), because at the time of naming, it was mistakenly thought that all acids required oxygen in their composition. At standard temperature and pressure, two atoms of the element bind to form dioxygen, a very pale blue, odorless, tasteless diatomic gas with the formula O_2.

Oxygen is a member of the chalcogen group on the periodic table and is a highly reactive nonmetallic element that readily forms compounds (notably oxides) with almost all other elements.

Photosynthesis

Photosynthesis is a process used by plants and other organisms to capture the sun's energy to split off water's hydrogen from oxygen. Hydrogen is combined with carbon dioxide (absorbed from air or water) to form glucose and release oxygen. All living cells in turn use fuels derived from glucose and oxidize the hydrogen and carbon to release the sun's energy and reform water and carbon dioxide in the process (cellular respiration).

Denitrification

Denitrification is a microbially facilitated process of nitrate reduction that may ultimately produce molecular nitrogen (N_2) through a series of intermediate gaseous nitrogen oxide products.

This respiratory process reduces oxidized forms of nitrogen in response to the oxidation of an electron donor such as organic matter. The preferred nitrogen electron acceptors in order of most to least thermodynamically favorable include nitrate (NO_3^-), nitrite (NO_2^-), nitric oxide (NO), and nitrous oxide (N_2O)and dinitrigen [N2].

Nitrogen cycle	The nitrogen cycle is the process by which nitrogen is converted between its various chemical forms. This transformation can be carried out to both biological and non-biological processes. Important processes in the nitrogen cycle include fixation, mineralization, nitrification, and denitrification.
Oxygen cycle	The Oxygen cycle is the biogeochemical cycle that describes the movement of oxygen within its three main reservoirs: the atmosphere (air), the total content of biological matter within the biosphere (the global sum of all ecosystems), and the lithosphere (Earth's crust). Failures in the oxygen cycle within the hydrosphere (the combined mass of water found on, under, and over the surface of a planet) can result in the development of hypoxic zones. The main driving factor of the oxygen cycle is photosynthesis, which is responsible for the modern Earth's atmosphere and life as we know it .
Ionosphere	The ionosphere is a part of the upper atmosphere, from about 85 km to 600 km altitude, comprising portions of the mesosphere, thermosphere and exosphere, distinguished because it is ionized by solar radiation. It plays an important part in atmospheric electricity and forms the inner edge of the magnetosphere. It has practical importance because, among other functions, it influences radio propagation to distant places on the Earth.
Mesosphere	The mesosphere is the layer of the Earth's atmosphere that is directly above the stratosphere and directly below the thermosphere. In the mesosphere temperature decreases with increasing height. The upper boundary of the mesosphere is the mesopause, which can be the coldest naturally occurring place on Earth with temperatures below 130 K. The exact upper and lower boundaries of the mesosphere vary with latitude and with season, but the lower boundary of the mesosphere is usually located at heights of about 50 km above the Earth's surface and the mesopause is usually at heights near 100 km, except at middle and high latitudes in summer where it descends to heights of about 85 km.
Stratosphere	The stratosphere is the second major layer of Earth's atmosphere, just above the troposphere, and below the mesosphere. It is stratified in temperature, with warmer layers higher up and cooler layers farther down. This is in contrast to the troposphere near the Earth's surface, which is cooler higher up and warmer farther down.
Thermosphere	The thermosphere is the layer of the Earth's atmosphere directly above the mesosphere and directly below the exosphere. Within this layer, ultraviolet radiation causes ionization. The International Space Station has a stable orbit within the middle of the thermosphere, between 320 and 380 kilometres (200 and 240 mi).
Ozone	Ozone or trioxygen, is a triatomic molecule, consisting of three oxygen atoms. It is an allotrope of oxygen that is much less stable than the diatomic allotrope (O_2), breaking down with a half life of about half an hour in the lower atmosphere, to normal dioxygen.

Chapter 20. Chemistry in the Atmosphere

Photodissociation	Photodissociation, photolysis, or photodecomposition is a chemical reaction in which a chemical compound is broken down by photons. It is defined as the interaction of one or more photons with one target molecule. Photodissociation is not limited to visible light.
Radiation	In physics, radiation is a process in which energetic particles or energetic waves travel through a medium or space. Two types of radiation are commonly differentiated in the way they interact with normal chemical matter: ionizing and non-ionizing radiation. The word radiation is often colloquially used in reference to ionizing radiation but the term radiation may correctly also refer to non-ionizing radiation.
Chlorine	Chlorine is the chemical element with atomic number 17 and symbol Cl. It is the second lightest halogen, with fluorine being the lightest. Chlorine is found in the periodic table in group 17. The element forms diatomic molecules under standard conditions, called dichlorine.
Chlorine monoxide	Chlorine monoxide is a chemical radical with the formula ClO. It plays an important role in the process of ozone depletion. In the stratosphere, chlorine atoms react with ozone molecules to form chlorine monoxide and oxygen. $Cl\cdot + O_3 \rightarrow ClO\cdot + O_2$ This reaction causes the depletion of the ozone layer.
Monoxide	A monoxide is any oxide containing just one atom of oxygen in the molecule. For example, Potassium oxide (K_2O), has only one atom of oxygen, and is thus a monoxide. Water (H_2O) is also a monoxide.
Aerosol	Technically, an aerosol is a colloid suspension of fine solid particles or liquid droplets in a gas. Examples are clouds, and air pollution such as smog and smoke. In general conversation, aerosol usually refers to an aerosol spray can or the output of such a can.
Hydroxyl	A hydroxyl is a chemical functional group containing an oxygen atom connected by a covalent bond to a hydrogen atom, a pairing that can be simply understood as a substructure of the water molecule. When it appears, it imparts to chemical structures some of the reactive and interactive properties of the -OH of water (ionizability, hydrogen bonding, etc).. The neutral form of the hydroxyl group is a hydroxyl radical.
Hydroxyl radical	The hydroxyl radical, $^\bullet OH$, is the neutral form of the hydroxide ion (OH^-). Hydroxyl radicals are highly reactive and consequently short-lived; however, they form an important part of radical chemistry.

Radical	Radicals (often referred to as free radicals) are atoms, molecules, or ions with unpaired electrons on an open shell configuration. Free radicals may have positive, negative or zero charge. Even though they have unpaired electrons, by convention, metals and their ions or complexes with unpaired electrons are not radicals.
Sulfur	Sulfur or sulphur is the chemical element with atomic number 16. In the periodic table it is represented by the symbol S. It is an abundant, multivalent non-metal. Under normal conditions, sulfur atoms form cyclic octatomic molecules with chemical formula S_8. Elemental sulfur is a bright yellow crystalline solid when at room temperature.
Carbon	Carbon is the chemical element with symbol C and atomic number 6. As a member of group 14 on the periodic table, it is nonmetallic and tetravalent--making four electrons available to form covalent chemical bonds. There are three naturally occurring isotopes, with ^{12}C and ^{13}C being stable, while ^{14}C is radioactive, decaying with a half-life of about 5,730 years. Carbon is one of the few elements known since antiquity.
Carbon cycle	The carbon cycle is the biogeochemical cycle by which carbon is exchanged among the biosphere, pedosphere, geosphere, hydrosphere, and atmosphere of the Earth. It is one of the most important cycles of the Earth and allows for carbon to be recycled and reused throughout the biosphere and all of its organisms.
	The global carbon budget is the balance of the exchanges (incomes and losses) of carbon between the carbon reservoirs or between one specific loop (e.g., atmosphere ↔ biosphere) of the carbon cycle.
Carbon dioxide	Carbon dioxide is a naturally occurring chemical compound composed of two oxygen atoms covalently bonded to a single carbon atom. It is a gas at standard temperature and pressure and exists in Earth's atmosphere in this state, as a trace gas at a concentration of 0.039% by volume.
	As part of the carbon cycle known as photosynthesis, plants, algae, and cyanobacteria absorb carbon dioxide, light, and water to produce carbohydrate energy for themselves and oxygen as a waste product.
Greenhouse effect	The greenhouse effect is a process by which thermal radiation from a planetary surface is absorbed by atmospheric greenhouse gases, and is re-radiated in all directions.

Chapter 20. Chemistry in the Atmosphere

Since part of this re-radiation is back towards the surface and the lower atmosphere, it results in an elevation of the average surface temperature above what it would be in the absence of the gases.

Solar radiation at the frequencies of visible light largely passes through the atmosphere to warm the planetary surface, which then emits this energy at the lower frequencies of infrared thermal radiation.

Emission spectrum	The emission spectrum of a chemical element or chemical compound is the spectrum of frequencies of electromagnetic radiation emitted by the element's atoms or the compound's molecules when they are returned to a lower energy state.

Each element's emission spectrum is unique. Therefore, spectroscopy can be used to identify the elements in matter of unknown composition. |
Isotope	Isotopes are variants of a particular chemical element. While all isotopes of a given element share the same number of protons, each isotope differs from the others in its number of neutrons. The term isotope is formed from the Greek roots isos and topos .
Spectrum	A spectrum is a condition that is not limited to a specific set of values but can vary infinitely within a continuum. The word saw its first scientific use within the field of optics to describe the rainbow of colors in visible light when separated using a prism; it has since been applied by analogy to many fields other than optics. Thus, one might talk about the spectrum of political opinion, or the spectrum of activity of a drug, or the autism spectrum.
Diatomic molecule	Diatomic molecules are molecules composed only of two atoms, of either the same or different chemical elements. The prefix di- is of Greek origin, meaning 2. Common diatomic molecules are hydrogen (H_2), nitrogen (N_2), oxygen (O_2), and carbon monoxide (CO). Seven elements exist as homonuclear diatomic molecules at room temperature: H_2, N_2, O_2, F_2, Cl_2, Br_2, and I_2.
Molecular vibration	A molecular vibration occurs when atoms in a molecule are in periodic motion while the molecule as a whole has constant translational and rotational motion. The frequency of the periodic motion is known as a vibration frequency, and the typical frequencies of molecular vibrations range from less than 10^{12} to approximately 10^{14} Hz.

In general, a molecule with N atoms has 3N - 6 normal modes of vibration, but a linear molecule has 3N - 5 such modes, as rotation about its molecular axis cannot be observed. |
| Molecule | A molecule is an electrically neutral group of two or more atoms held together by covalent chemical bonds. Molecules are distinguished from ions by their lack of electrical charge. |

Vibration	Vibration is a mechanical phenomenon whereby oscillations occur about an equilibrium point. The oscillations may be periodic such as the motion of a pendulum or random such as the movement of a tire on a gravel road.
	Vibration is occasionally 'desirable'.
Acid rain	Acid rain is a rain or any other form of precipitation that is unusually acidic, meaning that it possesses elevated levels of hydrogen ions (low pH). It can have harmful effects on plants, aquatic animals, and infrastructure. Acid rain is caused by emissions of sulfur dioxide and nitrogen oxides, which react with the water molecules in the atmosphere to produce acids.
Air pollution	Air pollution is the introduction of chemicals, particulate matter, or biological materials that cause harm or discomfort to humans or other living organisms, or cause damage to the natural environment or built environment, into the atmosphere.
	The atmosphere is a complex dynamic natural gaseous system that is essential to support life on planet Earth. Stratospheric ozone depletion due to air pollution has long been recognized as a threat to human health as well as to the Earth's ecosystems.
Petroleum	Petroleum (L. petroleum, from Greek: petra (rock) + Latin: oleum (oil)) or crude oil is a naturally occurring, flammable liquid consisting of a complex mixture of hydrocarbons of various molecular weights and other liquid organic compounds, that are found in geologic formations beneath the Earth's surface. A fossil fuel, it is formed when large quantities of dead organisms, usually zooplankton and algae, are buried underneath sedimentary rock and undergo intense heat and pressure.
	Petroleum is recovered mostly through oil drilling.
Smelting	Smelting is a form of extractive metallurgy; its main use is to produce a metal from its ore. This includes production of silver, iron, copper and other base metals from their ores. Smelting uses heat and a chemical reducing agent to decompose the ore, driving off other elements as gasses or slag and leaving just the metal behind.
Sulfur dioxide	Sulfur dioxide is the chemical compound with the formula SO_2. It is a poisonous gas with a pungent, irritating smell, that is released by volcanoes and in various industrial processes. Since coal and petroleum often contain sulfur compounds, their combustion generates sulfur dioxide unless the sulfur compounds are removed before burning the fuel.
Sulfur trioxide	Sulfur trioxide is the chemical compound with the formula SO_3. In the gaseous form, this species is a significant pollutant, being the primary agent in acid rain.

Chapter 20. Chemistry in the Atmosphere

Carbon monoxide	Carbon monoxide also called carbonous oxide, is a colorless, odorless, and tasteless gas which is slightly lighter than air. It is highly toxic to humans and animals in higher quantities, although it is also produced in normal animal metabolism in low quantities, and is thought to have some normal biological functions. Carbon monoxide consists of one carbon atom and one oxygen atom, connected by a triple bond which consists of two covalent bonds as well as one dative covalent bond.
Trioxide	A trioxide is a compound with three oxygen atoms. For metals with the M_2O_3 formula there are several common structures. Al_2O_3, Cr_2O_3, Fe_2O_3, and V_2O_3 adopt the corundum structure.
Calcium	Calcium is the chemical element with the symbol Ca and atomic number 20. It has an atomic mass of 40.078 amu. Calcium is a soft gray alkaline earth metal, and is the fifth-most-abundant element by mass in the Earth's crust. Calcium is also the fifth-most-abundant dissolved ion in seawater by both molarity and mass, after sodium, chloride, magnesium, and sulfate.
Calcium carbide	Calcium carbide is a chemical compound with the chemical formula of CaC_2. Its main use industrially is in the production of acetylene and calcium cyanamide. The pure material is colorless, however pieces of technical-grade calcium carbide are grey or brown and consist of only 80-85% of CaC_2 (the rest is CaO, Ca_3P_2, CaS, Ca_3N_2, SiC, etc)..
Calcium oxide	Calcium oxide commonly known as quicklime or burnt lime, is a widely used chemical compound. It is a white, caustic, alkaline crystalline solid at room temperature. The broadly used term lime connotes calcium-containing inorganic materials, in which carbonates, oxides and hydroxides of calcium, silicon, magnesium, aluminium, and iron predominate, such as limestone.
Carbide	In chemistry, a carbide is a compound composed of carbon and a less electronegative element. Carbides can be generally classified by chemical bonding type as follows: (i) salt-like, (ii) covalent compounds, (iii) interstitial compounds, and (iv) 'intermediate' transition metal carbides. Examples include calcium carbide, silicon carbide, tungsten carbide and cementite, each used in key industrial applications.
Oxide	An oxide is a chemical compound that contains at least one oxygen atom and one other element in its chemical formula. Metal oxides typically contain an anion of oxygen in the oxidation state of −2. Most of the Earth's crust consists of solid oxides, the result of elements being oxidized by the oxygen in air or in water .

Arsenic	Arsenic is a chemical element with the symbol As, atomic number 33 and relative atomic mass 74.92. Arsenic occurs in many minerals, usually in conjunction with sulfur and metals, and also as a pure elemental crystal. It was first documented by Albertus Magnus in 1250. Arsenic is a metalloid. It can exist in various allotropes, although only the grey form has important use in industry.
Nitrogen dioxide	Nitrogen dioxide is the chemical compound with the formula NO_2. It is one of several nitrogen oxides. NO_2 is an intermediate in the industrial synthesis of nitric acid, millions of tons of which are produced each year.
Peroxyacetyl nitrate	Peroxyacetyl nitrate is a peroxyacyl nitrate. It is a secondary pollutant present in photochemical smog. It is thermally unstable and decomposes into peroxyethanoyl radicals and nitrogen dioxide gas.
Methanol	Methanol, wood alcohol, wood naphtha or wood spirits, is a chemical with the formula CH_3OH. It is the simplest alcohol, and is a light, volatile, colorless, flammable liquid with a distinctive odor very similar to, but slightly sweeter than, ethanol (drinking alcohol). At room temperature, it is a polar liquid, and is used as an antifreeze, solvent, fuel, and as a denaturant for ethanol.
Platinum	Platinum is a chemical element with the chemical symbol Pt and an atomic number of 78. Its name is derived from the Spanish term platina, which is literally translated into 'little silver'. It is a dense, malleable, ductile, precious, gray-white transition metal.
Radon	Radon is a chemical element with the atomic number 86, and is represented by the symbol Rn. It is a radioactive, colorless, odorless, tasteless noble gas, occurring naturally as the decay product of uranium or thorium. Its most stable isotope, ^{222}Rn, has a half-life of 3.8 days.
Catalyst	Catalysis is the change in rate of a chemical reaction due to the participation of a substance called a catalyst. Unlike other reagents that participate in the chemical reaction, a catalyst is not consumed by the reaction itself. A catalyst may participate in multiple chemical transformations.
Carboxyhemoglobin	Carboxyhemoglobin is a stable complex of carbon monoxide and hemoglobin that forms in red blood cells when carbon monoxide is inhaled or produced in normal metabolism. Large quantities of it hinder delivery of oxygen to the body.

Chapter 20. Chemistry in the Atmosphere

Formaldehyde	Formaldehyde is an organic compound with the formula CH_2O. It is the simplest form of aldehyde, hence its systematic name methanal. A gas at room temperature, formaldehyde is colorless and has a characteristic pungent, irritating odor. It is an important precursor to many other chemical compounds, especially for polymers.
Hemoglobin	Hemoglobin is the iron-containing oxygen-transport metalloprotein in the red blood cells of all vertebrates (with the exception of the fish family Channichthyidae) as well as the tissues of some invertebrates. Hemoglobin in the blood carries oxygen from the respiratory organs (lungs or gills) to the rest of the body (i.e. the tissues) where it releases the oxygen to burn nutrients to provide energy to power the functions of the organism, and collects the resultant carbon dioxide to bring it back to the respiratory organs to be dispensed from the organism. In mammals, the protein makes up about 97% of the red blood cells' dry content, and around 35% of the total content (including water).
Affinity	Affinity (taxonomy) - mainly in life sciences or natural history - refers to resemblance suggesting a common descent, phylogenetic relationship, or type. The term does, however, have broader application, such as in geology (for example, in descriptive and theoretical works), and similarly in astronomy . In taxonomy the basis of any particular type of classification is the way in which objects in the domain resemble each other.

1. _____ is a naturally occurring chemical compound composed of two oxygen atoms covalently bonded to a single carbon atom. It is a gas at standard temperature and pressure and exists in Earth's atmosphere in this state, as a trace gas at a concentration of 0.039% by volume.

   As part of the carbon cycle known as photosynthesis, plants, algae, and cyanobacteria absorb _____, light, and water to produce carbohydrate energy for themselves and oxygen as a waste product.

   a. Carbon dioxide
   b. Carbon tetrachloride
   c. Chlorofluorocarbon
   d. Chloromethane

2. The _____ is the layer of the Earth's atmosphere directly above the mesosphere and directly below the exosphere. Within this layer, ultraviolet radiation causes ionization. The International Space Station has a stable orbit within the middle of the _____, between 320 and 380 kilometres (200 and 240 mi).

   a. Total electron content
   b. Tropopause
   c. Thermosphere
   d. Turbopause

3. _____ is a chemical compound with the chemical formula of CaC_2. Its main use industrially is in the production of acetylene and calcium cyanamide.

   The pure material is colorless, however pieces of technical-grade _____ are grey or brown and consist of only 80-85% of CaC_2 (the rest is CaO, Ca_3P_2, CaS, Ca_3N_2, SiC, etc)..

   a. Calcium carbide
   b. Calcium silicide
   c. Copper phosphide
   d. Ferromanganese

4. A _____ is a chemical functional group containing an oxygen atom connected by a covalent bond to a hydrogen atom, a pairing that can be simply understood as a substructure of the water molecule. When it appears, it imparts to chemical structures some of the reactive and interactive properties of the -OH of water (ionizability, hydrogen bonding, etc).. The neutral form of the _____ group is a _____ radical.

   a. Hydroxyl radical
   b. Hydroxylamine
   c. Hydroxyl
   d. Lime water

5. . A _____ occurs when atoms in a molecule are in periodic motion while the molecule as a whole has constant translational and rotational motion. The frequency of the periodic motion is known as a vibration frequency, and the typical frequencies of _____s range from less than 10^{12} to approximately 10^{14} Hz.

In general, a molecule with N atoms has 3N - 6 normal modes of vibration, but a linear molecule has 3N - 5 such modes, as rotation about its molecular axis cannot be observed.

a. Monochromator
b. Molecular vibration
c. Multivariate optical computing
d. Multivariate optical element

1. a

2. c

3. a

4. c

5. b

You can take the complete Chapter Practice Test

for Chapter 20. Chemistry in the Atmosphere
on all key terms, persons, places, and concepts.

Online 99 Cents

http://www.epub14.1.20267.20.cram101.com/

Use www.Cram101.com for all your study needs

including Cram101's online interactive problem solving labs in

chemistry, statistics, mathematics, and more.

Chapter 21. Metallurgy and the Chemistry of Metals

CHAPTER OUTLINE: KEY TERMS, PEOPLE, PLACES, CONCEPTS

Crown ether

Ether

Mineral

Amalgam

Gangue

Magnetism

Manganese

Metallurgy

Ferromagnetism

Fossil fuel

Pyrometallurgy

Reduction potential

Smelting

Potential

Blast furnace

Calcium

Calcium carbide

Carbide

Furnace

Visit Cram101.com for full Practice Exams

CAST

Cast iron

Pig iron

Oxygen

Cementite

Graphite

Atomic mass

Mass

Carbon

Carbon monoxide

Electrode

Electrode potential

Mond process

Refining

Stainless steel

Arsenic

Monoxide

Conduction band

Valence band

CHAPTER OUTLINE: KEY TERMS, PEOPLE, PLACES, CONCEPTS

	Alkali
	Alkali metal
	Molecular orbital
	Semiconductor
	Impurity
	Ozone
	P-type semiconductor
	Electronegativity
	Hydrocarbon
	Ionization
	Ionization energy
	Potassium
	Potassium superoxide
	Sodium
	Superoxide
	Amino acid
	Solvent
	Hydroxide
	Potassium dichromate

_____ Sodium carbonate _____

_____ Sodium hydroxide _____

_____ Sodium nitrate _____

_____ Solvay process _____

_____ Trona _____

_____ Metal hydroxide _____

_____ Beryllium _____

_____ Dolomite _____

_____ Gunpowder _____

_____ Barium _____

_____ Calcite _____

_____ Calcium oxide _____

_____ Fluorite _____

_____ Gypsum _____

_____ Magnesium oxide _____

_____ Oxide _____

_____ Bauxite _____

_____ Corundum _____

_____ Thermite _____

CHAPTER OUTLINE: KEY TERMS, PEOPLE, PLACES, CONCEPTS

	Chloride
	Hydride

CHAPTER HIGHLIGHTS & NOTES: KEY TERMS, PEOPLE, PLACES, CONCEPTS

Crown ether	Crown ethers are cyclic chemical compounds that consist of a ring containing several ether groups. The most common crown ethers are oligomers of ethylene oxide, the repeating unit being ethyleneoxy, i.e., $-CH_2CH_2O-$. Important members of this series are the tetramer (n = 4), the pentamer (n = 5), and the hexamer (n = 6).
Ether	Wikimedia.org/wikipedia/commons/thumb/5/51/Ether-%28general%29.png/150px-Ether-%28general%29.png' width='150' height='75' /> Ethers ( ) are a class of organic compounds that contain an ether group -- an oxygen atom connected to two alkyl or aryl groups -- of general formula R-O-R'. A typical example is the solvent and anesthetic diethyl ether, commonly referred to simply as 'ether' ($CH_3-CH_2-O-CH_2-CH_3$). Ethers are common in organic chemistry and pervasive in biochemistry, as they are common linkages in carbohydrates and lignin.
Mineral	A mineral is a naturally occurring solid chemical substance formed through biogeochemical processes, having characteristic chemical composition, highly ordered atomic structure, and specific physical properties. By comparison, a rock is an aggregate of minerals and/or mineraloids and does not have a specific chemical composition. Minerals range in composition from pure elements and simple salts to very complex silicates with thousands of known forms.
Amalgam	Amalgam is an alloy containing mercury. The term is commonly used for the amalgam employed as material for dental fillings, which consists of mercury (50%), silver (~22-32%), tin (~14%), copper (~8%), and other trace metals. In the 1800s, amalgam became the dental restorative material of choice due to its low cost, ease of application, strength, and durability.
Gangue	In mining, gangue is the commercially worthless material that surrounds, or is closely mixed with, a wanted mineral in an ore deposit. The separation of mineral from gangue is known as mineral processing, mineral dressing or ore dressing and it is a necessary and often significant aspect of mining.

Chapter 21. Metallurgy and the Chemistry of Metals

Magnetism	Magnetism is a property of materials that respond to an applied magnetic field. Permanent magnets have persistent magnetic fields caused by ferromagnetism. That is the strongest and most familiar type of magnetism.
Manganese	Manganese is a chemical element, designated by the symbol Mn. It has the atomic number 25. It is found as a free element in nature (often in combination with iron), and in many minerals. Manganese is a metal with important industrial metal alloy uses, particularly in stainless steels.
Metallurgy	Metallurgy is a domain of materials science that studies the physical and chemical behavior of metallic elements, their intermetallic compounds, and their mixtures, which are called alloys. It is also the technology of metals: the way in which science is applied to their practical use. Metallurgy is distinguished from the craft of metalworking.
Ferromagnetism	Ferromagnetism is the basic mechanism by which certain materials (such as iron) form permanent magnets, or are attracted to magnets. In physics, several different types of magnetism are distinguished. Ferromagnetism is the strongest type; it is the only type that creates forces strong enough to be felt, and is responsible for the common phenomena of magnetism encountered in everyday life.
Fossil fuel	Fossil fuels are fuels formed by natural resources such as anaerobic decomposition of buried dead organisms. The age of the organisms and their resulting fossil fuels is typically millions of years, and sometimes exceeds 650 million years. The fossil fuels, which contain high percentages of carbon, include coal, petroleum, and natural gas.
Pyrometallurgy	Pyrometallurgy is a branch of extractive metallurgy. It consists of the thermal treatment of minerals and metallurgical ores and concentrates to bring about physical and chemical transformations in the materials to enable recovery of valuable metals. Pyrometallurgical treatment may produce saleable products such as pure metals, or intermediate compounds or alloys, suitable as feed for further processing.
Reduction potential	Reduction potential (also known as redox potential, oxidation / reduction potential is a measure of the tendency of a chemical species to acquire electrons and thereby be reduced. Reduction potential is measured in volts (V), or millivolts (mV). Each species has its own intrinsic reduction potential; the more positive the potential, the greater the species' affinity for electrons and tendency to be reduced.
Smelting	Smelting is a form of extractive metallurgy; its main use is to produce a metal from its ore. This includes production of silver, iron, copper and other base metals from their ores.

Potential	•In linguistics, the potential mood•The mathematical study of potentials is known as potential theory; it is the study of harmonic functions on manifolds. This mathematical formulation arises from the fact that, in physics, the scalar potential is irrotational, and thus has a vanishing Laplacian -- the very definition of a harmonic function.•In physics, a potential may refer to the scalar potential or to the vector potential. In either case, it is a field defined in space, from which many important physical properties may be derived.
Blast furnace	A blast furnace is a type of metallurgical furnace used for smelting to produce industrial metals, generally iron.
	In a blast furnace, fuel, ore, and flux (limestone) are continuously supplied through the top of the furnace, while air (sometimes with oxygen enrichment) is blown into the bottom of the chamber, so that the chemical reactions take place throughout the furnace as the material moves downward. The end products are usually molten metal and slag phases tapped from the bottom, and flue gases exiting from the top of the furnace.
Calcium	Calcium is the chemical element with the symbol Ca and atomic number 20. It has an atomic mass of 40.078 amu. Calcium is a soft gray alkaline earth metal, and is the fifth-most-abundant element by mass in the Earth's crust. Calcium is also the fifth-most-abundant dissolved ion in seawater by both molarity and mass, after sodium, chloride, magnesium, and sulfate.
Calcium carbide	Calcium carbide is a chemical compound with the chemical formula of CaC_2. Its main use industrially is in the production of acetylene and calcium cyanamide.
	The pure material is colorless, however pieces of technical-grade calcium carbide are grey or brown and consist of only 80-85% of CaC_2 (the rest is CaO, Ca_3P_2, CaS, Ca_3N_2, SiC, etc)..
Carbide	In chemistry, a carbide is a compound composed of carbon and a less electronegative element. Carbides can be generally classified by chemical bonding type as follows: (i) salt-like, (ii) covalent compounds, (iii) interstitial compounds, and (iv) 'intermediate' transition metal carbides. Examples include calcium carbide, silicon carbide, tungsten carbide and cementite, each used in key industrial applications.
Furnace	A furnace is a device used for heating. The name derives from Latin fornax, oven.
	In American English and Canadian English, the term furnace on its own is generally used to describe household heating systems based on a central furnace, and sometimes as a synonym for kiln, a device used in the production of ceramics.

Chapter 21. Metallurgy and the Chemistry of Metals

CAST	CAST software is an environment which stems from an initial collaboration of Lorenzo Vigentini with the Laboratory for Cognitive Neuroscience and became a more extensive project in collaboration with Drs Brendan McGonigle and Margaret Chalmers (supported by a British Academy Grant) involving the implementation of a new software to support their research programme exploring human cognition and animal cognition.

CAST is acronym for Computer Assisted Seriation Test. It is a software tool implemented to satisfy two major points:•the necessity of implementing a piece of software flexible enough to be accessed by non-programmers (usually psychologists);•the necessity of implementing a package powerful enough to provide a multimedia environment easy to expand.

The name comes with the idea of a metaphorical stage on which the instructor, or one who proposes/run the test, can define a scenario in which the elements can be organised and a set of exercises organised providing a completely flexible structure of the task for the testing. |
| Cast iron | Cast iron is iron or a ferrous alloy which has been heated until it liquifies, and is then poured into a mould to solidify. It is usually made from pig iron. The alloy constituents affect its colour when fractured: white cast iron has carbide impurities which allow cracks to pass straight through. |
| Pig iron | Pig iron is the intermediate product of smelting iron ore with a high-carbon fuel such as coke, usually with limestone as a flux. Charcoal and anthracite have also been used as fuel. Pig iron has a very high carbon content, typically 3.5-4.5%, which makes it very brittle and not useful directly as a material except for limited applications. |
| Oxygen | Oxygen is the element with atomic number 8 and represented by the symbol O. Its name derives from the Greek roots ?ξ?ς (oxys) ('acid', literally 'sharp', referring to the sour taste of acids) and -γεν?ς (-genes) ('producer', literally 'begetter'), because at the time of naming, it was mistakenly thought that all acids required oxygen in their composition. At standard temperature and pressure, two atoms of the element bind to form dioxygen, a very pale blue, odorless, tasteless diatomic gas with the formula O_2.

Oxygen is a member of the chalcogen group on the periodic table and is a highly reactive nonmetallic element that readily forms compounds (notably oxides) with almost all other elements. |
| Cementite | Cementite, is a chemical compound of iron and carbon, with the formula Fe_3C . By weight, it is 6.67% carbon and 93.3% iron. It has an orthorhombic crystal structure. |
| Graphite | The mineral graphite is an allotrope of carbon. |

It was named by Abraham Gottlob Werner in 1789 from the Ancient Greek γρ?φω (grapho), 'to draw/write', for its use in pencils, where it is commonly called lead (not to be confused with the metallic element lead). Unlike diamond (another carbon allotrope), graphite is an electrical conductor, a semimetal.

Atomic mass	The atomic mass is the mass of a specific isotope, most often expressed in unified atomic mass units. The atomic mass is the total mass of protons, neutrons and electrons in a single atom.
	The atomic mass is sometimes incorrectly used as a synonym of relative atomic mass, average atomic mass and atomic weight; these differ subtly from the atomic mass.
Mass	The mass recorded by a mass spectrometer can refer to different physical quantities depending on the characteristics of the instrument and the manner in which the mass spectrum is displayed.
	The accurate mass (more appropriately, the measured accurate mass) is an experimentally determined mass that allows the elemental composition to be determined. For molecules with mass below 200 u, a 5 ppm accuracy is sufficient to uniquely determine the elemental composition.
Carbon	Carbon is the chemical element with symbol C and atomic number 6. As a member of group 14 on the periodic table, it is nonmetallic and tetravalent--making four electrons available to form covalent chemical bonds. There are three naturally occurring isotopes, with ^{12}C and ^{13}C being stable, while ^{14}C is radioactive, decaying with a half-life of about 5,730 years. Carbon is one of the few elements known since antiquity.
Carbon monoxide	Carbon monoxide also called carbonous oxide, is a colorless, odorless, and tasteless gas which is slightly lighter than air. It is highly toxic to humans and animals in higher quantities, although it is also produced in normal animal metabolism in low quantities, and is thought to have some normal biological functions.
	Carbon monoxide consists of one carbon atom and one oxygen atom, connected by a triple bond which consists of two covalent bonds as well as one dative covalent bond.
Electrode	An electrode is an electrical conductor used to make contact with a nonmetallic part of a circuit (e.g. a semiconductor, an electrolyte or a vacuum). The word was coined by the scientist Michael Faraday from the Greek words elektron (meaning amber, from which the word electricity is derived) and hodos, a way.

Chapter 21. Metallurgy and the Chemistry of Metals

Electrode potential	Electrode potential, E, in electrochemistry, according to an IUPAC definition, is the electromotive force of a cell built of two electrodes:•on the left-hand side is the standard hydrogen electrode, and•on the right-hand side is the electrode the potential of which is being defined.
	By convention:$E_{Cell} := E_{Cathode} - E_{Anode}$
	From the above, for the cell with the standard hydrogen electrode (potential of 0 by convention), one obtains:$E_{Cell} = E_{Right} - 0 = E_{Electrode}$
	The left-right convention is consistent with the international agreement that redox potentials be given for reactions written in the form of reduction half-reactions.
	Electrode potential is measured in volts (V). Measurement
	The measurement is generally conducted using a three-electrode setup :•Working electrode•Counter electrode•Reference electrode (standard hydrogen electrode or an equivalent)
	The measured potential of the working electrode may be either that at equilibrium on the working electrode ('reversible potential'), or a potential with a non-zero net reaction on the working electrode but zero net current ('corrosion potential', 'mixed potential'), or a potential with a non-zero net current on the working electrode (like in galvanic corrosion or voltammetry).
Mond process	The Mond process is a technique created by Ludwig Mond in 1890 to extract and purify nickel. The process was used commercially before the end of the 19th century. It is done by converting nickel oxides (nickel combined with oxygen) into pure nickel.
Refining	Refining (as in non-metallurgical uses) consists of purifying an impure material, in this case a metal. It is to be distinguished from other processes such as smelting and calcining in that those two involve a chemical change to the raw material, whereas in refining, the final material is usually identical chemically to the original one, only it is purer. The processes used are of many types, including pyrometallurgical and hydrometallurgical techniques.
Stainless steel	In metallurgy, stainless steel, is defined as a steel alloy with a minimum of 10.5 or 11% chromium content by mass. Stainless steel does not stain, corrode, or rust as easily as ordinary steel, but it is not stain-proof. It is also called corrosion-resistant steel or CRES when the alloy type and grade are not detailed, particularly in the aviation industry.
Arsenic	

Arsenic is a chemical element with the symbol As, atomic number 33 and relative atomic mass 74.92. Arsenic occurs in many minerals, usually in conjunction with sulfur and metals, and also as a pure elemental crystal. It was first documented by Albertus Magnus in 1250. Arsenic is a metalloid. It can exist in various allotropes, although only the grey form has important use in industry.

| Monoxide | A monoxide is any oxide containing just one atom of oxygen in the molecule. For example, Potassium oxide (K_2O), has only one atom of oxygen, and is thus a monoxide. Water (H_2O) is also a monoxide. |

| Conduction band | In the solid-state physics field of semiconductors and insulators, the conduction band is the range of electron energies, higher than that of the valence band, sufficient to free an electron from binding with its individual atom and allow it to move freely within the atomic lattice of the material. Electrons within the conduction band are mobile charge carriers in solids, responsible for conduction of electric currents in metals and other good electrical conductors. |

| Valence band | In solids, the valence band is the highest range of electron energies in which electrons are normally present at absolute zero temperature.

The valence electrons are bound to individual atoms, as opposed to conduction electrons (found in conductors and semiconductors), which can move freely within the atomic lattice of the material. On a graph of the electronic band structure of a material, the valence band is located below the conduction band, separated from it in insulators and semiconductors by a band gap. |

| Alkali | In chemistry, an alkali is a basic, ionic salt of an alkali metal or alkaline earth metal element. Some authors also define an alkali as a base that dissolves in water. A solution of a soluble base has a pH greater than 7. The adjective alkaline is commonly used in English as a synonym for base, especially for soluble bases. |

| Alkali metal | The alkali metals are a group of chemical elements in the periodic table with very similar properties: they are all shiny, soft, silvery, highly reactive metals at standard temperature and pressure and readily lose their outermost electron to form cations with charge +1. They can all be cut easily with a knife due to their softness, exposing a shiny surface that tarnishes rapidly in air due to oxidation. In the modern IUPAC nomenclature, the alkali metals comprise the group 1 elements, excluding hydrogen (H), which is nominally a group 1 element but not normally considered to be an alkali metal as it rarely exhibits behaviour comparable to that of the alkali metals. All the alkali metals react with water, with the heavier alkali metals reacting more vigorously than the lighter ones. |

Chapter 21. Metallurgy and the Chemistry of Metals

Molecular orbital	In chemistry, a molecular orbital is a mathematical function describing the wave-like behavior of an electron in a molecule. This function can be used to calculate chemical and physical properties such as the probability of finding an electron in any specific region. The term 'orbital' was first used in English by Robert S. Mulliken as the English translation of Schrödinger's 'Eigenfunktion'.
Semiconductor	A semiconductor has electrical conductivity intermediate in magnitude between that of a conductor and an insulator. This means a conductivity roughly in the range of 10^{-2} to 10^4 siemens per centimeter. Semiconductor materials are the foundation of modern electronics, including radio, computers, telephones, and many other devices.
Impurity	Impurities are substances inside a confined amount of liquid, gas, or solid, which differ from the chemical composition of the material or compound.
	Impurities are either naturally occurring or added during synthesis of a chemical or commercial product. During production, impurities may be purposely, accidentally, inevitably, or incidentally added into the substance.
	The level of impurities in a material are generally defined in relative terms. Standards have been established by various organizations that attempt to define the permitted levels of various impurities in a manufactured product. Strictly speaking, then, a material's level of purity can only be stated as being more or less pure than some other material. Destructive impurities
	Impurities can be destructive when they obstruct the working nature of the material. Examples include ash and debris in metals and leaf pieces in blank white papers. The removal of impurities is usually done chemically. For example, in the manufacturing of iron, calcium carbonate is added to the blast furnace to remove silicon dioxide from the iron ore. Zone refining is an economically important method for the purification of semiconductors.
	However, some kinds of impurities can be removed by physical means. A mixture of water and salt can be separated by distillation, with water as the distillate and salt as the solid residue. Impurities are usually physically removed from liquids and gases. Removal of sand particles from metal ore is one example with solids.
	No matter what method is used, it is usually impossible to separate an impurity completely from a material.
Ozone	Ozone or trioxygen, is a triatomic molecule, consisting of three oxygen atoms. It is an allotrope of oxygen that is much less stable than the diatomic allotrope (O_2), breaking down with a half life of about half an hour in the lower atmosphere, to normal dioxygen.

P-type semiconductor	A P-type semiconductor is obtained by carrying out a process of doping: that is, adding a certain type of atoms to the semiconductor in order to increase the number of free charge carriers (in this case positive).
	When the doping material is added, it takes away (accepts) weakly bound outer electrons from the semiconductor atoms. This type of doping agent is also known as an acceptor material and the vacancy left behind by the electron is known as a hole.
Electronegativity	Electronegativity, symbol χ, is a chemical property that describes the tendency of an atom or a functional group to attract electrons towards itself. An atom's electronegativity is affected by both its atomic number and the distance that its valence electrons reside from the charged nucleus. The higher the associated electronegativity number, the more an element or compound attracts electrons towards it.
Hydrocarbon	In organic chemistry, a hydrocarbon is an organic compound consisting entirely of hydrogen and carbon. Hydrocarbons from which one hydrogen atom has been removed are functional groups, called hydrocarbyls. Aromatic hydrocarbons (arenes), alkanes, alkenes, cycloalkanes and alkyne-based compounds are different types of hydrocarbons.
Ionization	Ionization is the process of converting an atom or molecule into an ion by adding or removing charged particles such as electrons or ions. In the case of ionisation of a gas, ion-pairs are created consisting of a free electron and a +ve ion.
	The process of ionization works slightly differently depending on whether an ion with a positive or a negative electric charge is being produced.
Ionization energy	The ionization energy of a chemical species, i.e. an atom or molecule, is the energy required to remove electrons from gaseous atoms or ions. The property is alternately still often called the ionization potential, measured in volts. In chemistry it often refers to one mole of a substance (molar ionization energy or enthalpy) and reported in kJ/mol.
Potassium	
	Potassium is the chemical element with the symbol K and atomic number 19. Elemental potassium is a soft silvery-white alkali metal that oxidizes rapidly in air and is very reactive with water, generating sufficient heat to ignite the hydrogen emitted in the reaction.
	Because potassium and sodium are chemically very similar, it took a long time before their salts were differentiated.

Chapter 21. Metallurgy and the Chemistry of Metals

Potassium superoxide	Potassium superoxide is the chemical compound with the formula KO_2. This rare salt of the superoxide ion is produced by burning molten potassium in pure oxygen. Potassium superoxide is used as an oxidizing agent in industrial chemistry, as a CO_2 scrubber, H_2O dehumidifier and O_2 generator in rebreathers, spacecraft, submarines and spacesuit life support systems.
Sodium	Sodium is a chemical element with the symbol Na and atomic number 11. It is a soft, silvery-white, highly reactive metal and is a member of the alkali metals; its only stable isotope is ^{23}Na. The free metal does not occur in nature, but instead must be prepared from its compounds; it was first isolated by Humphry Davy in 1807 by the electrolysis of sodium hydroxide. Sodium is the sixth most abundant element in the Earth's crust, and exists in numerous minerals such as feldspars, sodalite and rock salt.
Superoxide	A superoxide, also known by the obsolete name hyperoxide, is a compound that contains the superoxide anion with the chemical formula O_2^-. The systematic name of the anion is dioxide(1−). Superoxide anion is particularly important as the product of the one-electron reduction of dioxygen O_2, which occurs widely in nature.
Amino acid	Amino acids are molecules containing an amine group, a carboxylic acid group, and a side-chain that is specific to each amino acid. The key elements of an amino acid are carbon, hydrogen, oxygen, and nitrogen. They are particularly important in biochemistry, where the term usually refers to alpha-amino acids.
Solvent	A solvent is a liquid, solid, or gas that dissolves another solid, liquid, or gaseous solute, resulting in a solution that is soluble in a certain volume of solvent at a specified temperature. Common uses for organic solvents are in dry cleaning (e.g., tetrachloroethylene), as paint thinners (e.g., toluene, turpentine), as nail polish removers and glue solvents (acetone, methyl acetate, ethyl acetate), in spot removers (e.g., hexane, petrol ether), in detergents (citrus terpenes), in perfumes (ethanol), nail polish and in chemical synthesis. The use of inorganic solvents (other than water) is typically limited to research chemistry and some technological processes.
Hydroxide	Hydroxide is a diatomic anion with chemical formula OH^-. It consists of an oxygen and a hydrogen atom held together by a covalent bond, and carrying a negative electric charge. It is an important but usually minor constituent of water.
Potassium dichromate	Potassium dichromate, $K_2Cr_2O_7$, is a common inorganic chemical reagent, most commonly used as an oxidising agent in various laboratory and industrial applications. As with all hexavalent chromium compounds, it is potentially harmful to health and must be handled and disposed of appropriately.

Sodium carbonate	Sodium carbonate Na_2CO_3 is a sodium salt of carbonic acid. It most commonly occurs as a crystalline heptahydrate, which readily effloresces to form a white powder, the monohydrate. Sodium carbonate is domestically well known for its everyday use as a water softener.
Sodium hydroxide	Sodium hydroxide also known as lye and caustic soda, is a caustic metallic base. It is used in many industries, mostly as a strong chemical base in the manufacture of pulp and paper, textiles, drinking water, soaps and detergents and as a drain cleaner. Worldwide production in 2004 was approximately 60 million tonnes, while demand was 51 million tonnes.
Sodium nitrate	Sodium nitrate is the chemical compound with the formula $NaNO_3$. This salt, also known as Chile saltpeter or Peru saltpeter (due to the large deposits found in each country) to distinguish it from ordinary saltpeter, potassium nitrate, is a white solid which is very soluble in water. The mineral form is also known as nitratine, nitratite or soda niter.
Solvay process	The Solvay process, also referred to as the ammonia-soda process, is the major industrial process for the production of soda ash (sodium carbonate). The ammonia-soda process was developed into its modern form by Ernest Solvay during the 1860s. The ingredients for this process are readily available and inexpensive: salt brine (from inland sources or from the sea) and limestone (from mines).
Trona	Trona; $Na_3H(CO_3)_2 \cdot 2H_2O$ is an evaporite mineral. It is mined as the primary source of sodium carbonate in the United States, where it has replaced the Solvay process used in most of the rest of the world for sodium carbonate production.
Metal hydroxide	Metal hydroxide are hydroxides of metals. •Aluminium hydroxide•Beryllium hydroxide•Cobalt(II) hydroxide•Copper(II) hydroxide•Curium hydroxide•Gold(III) hydroxide•Iron(II) hydroxide•Mercury(II) hydroxide•Nickel(II) hydroxide•Tin(II) hydroxide•Uranyl hydroxide•Zinc hydroxide•Zirconium(IV) hydroxideAlkali metal hydroxides Poor metal hydroxides •Gallium(III) hydroxide•Lead(II) hydroxide•Thallium hydroxideRole in soils

In soils, it is assumed that larger amounts of natural phenols are released from decomposing plant litter rather than from throughfall in any natural plant community. Decomposition of dead plant material causes complex organic compounds to be slowly oxidized (lignin-like humus) or to break down into simpler forms (sugars and amino sugars, aliphatic and phenolic organic acids), which are further transformed into microbial biomass (microbial humus) or are reorganized, and further oxidized, into humic assemblages (fulvic and humic acids), which bind to clay minerals and metal hydroxides. |
| Beryllium | Beryllium is the chemical element with the symbol Be and atomic number 4. |

Chapter 21. Metallurgy and the Chemistry of Metals

	Because any beryllium synthesized in stars is short-lived, it is a relatively rare element in both the universe and in the crust of the Earth. It is a divalent element which occurs naturally only in combination with other elements in minerals. Notable gemstones which contain beryllium include beryl (aquamarine, emerald) and chrysoberyl.
Dolomite	Dolomite is a carbonate mineral composed of calcium magnesium carbonate $CaMg(CO_3)_2$. The term is also used to describe the sedimentary carbonate rock dolostone. Dolostone (dolomite rock) is composed predominantly of the mineral dolomite with a stoichiometric ratio of 50% or greater content of magnesium replacing calcium, often as a result of diagenesis.
Gunpowder	Gunpowder, also known since the late 19th century as black powder, is a mixture of sulfur, charcoal, and potassium nitrate. Gunpowder can be made just using potassium nitrate and charcoal (or alternatively without charcoal), but without the sulfur (or coal), the powder is not as strong. It burns rapidly, producing a volume of hot gas made up of carbon dioxide, water, and nitrogen, and a solid residue of potassium sulfide.
Barium	Barium is a chemical element with the symbol Ba and atomic number 56. It is the fifth element in Group 2, a soft silvery metallic alkaline earth metal. Barium is never found in nature in its pure form due to its reactivity with air. Its oxide is historically known as baryta but it reacts with water and carbon dioxide and is not found as a mineral.
Calcite	Calcite is a carbonate mineral and the most stable polymorph of calcium carbonate ($CaCO_3$). The other polymorphs are the minerals aragonite and vaterite. Aragonite will change to calcite at 380-470°C, and vaterite is even less stable.
Calcium oxide	Calcium oxide commonly known as quicklime or burnt lime, is a widely used chemical compound. It is a white, caustic, alkaline crystalline solid at room temperature. The broadly used term lime connotes calcium-containing inorganic materials, in which carbonates, oxides and hydroxides of calcium, silicon, magnesium, aluminium, and iron predominate, such as limestone.
Fluorite	Fluorite is a halide mineral composed of calcium fluoride, CaF_2. It is an isometric mineral with a cubic habit, though octahedral and more complex isometric forms are not uncommon. Crystal twinning is common and adds complexity to the observed crystal habits.
Gypsum	Gypsum is a very soft sulfate mineral composed of calcium sulfate dihydrate, with the chemical formula $CaSO_4 \cdot 2H_2O$. It is found in alabaster, a decorative stone used in Ancient Egypt.

It is the second softest mineral on the Mohs scale of mineral hardness. It forms as an evaporite mineral and as a hydration product of anhydrite.

Magnesium oxide	Magnesium oxide or magnesia, is a white hygroscopic solid mineral that occurs naturally as periclase and is a source of magnesium . It has an empirical formula of MgO and consists of a lattice of Mg^{2+} ions and O^{2-} ions held together by ionic bonds. Magnesium hydroxide forms in the presence of water ($MgO + H_2O \rightarrow Mg(OH)_2$), but it can be reversed by heating it to separate moisture.
Oxide	An oxide is a chemical compound that contains at least one oxygen atom and one other element in its chemical formula. Metal oxides typically contain an anion of oxygen in the oxidation state of −2. Most of the Earth's crust consists of solid oxides, the result of elements being oxidized by the oxygen in air or in water . Hydrocarbon combustion affords the two principal carbon oxides: carbon monoxide and carbon dioxide.
Bauxite	Bauxite is an aluminium ore and is the main provider of aluminium. This form of rock consists mostly of the minerals gibbsite $Al(OH)_3$, boehmite γ-AlO(OH), and diaspore α-AlO(OH), in a mixture with the two iron oxides goethite and hematite, the clay mineral kaolinite, and small amounts of anatase TiO_2. he village Les Baux in southern France, where it was first recognised as containing aluminium and named by the French geologist Pierre Berthier in 1821.
Corundum	Corundum is a crystalline form of aluminium oxide (Al_2O_3) with traces of iron, titanium and chromium. It is a rock-forming mineral. It is one of the naturally clear transparent materials, but can have different colors when impurities are present.
Thermite	Thermite is a pyrotechnic composition of a metal powder and a metal oxide that produces an exothermic oxidation-reduction reaction known as a thermite reaction. If aluminium is the reducing agent it is called an aluminothermic reaction. Most varieties are not explosive, but can create bursts of extremely high temperatures focused on a very small area for a short period of time.
Chloride	The chloride ion is formed when the element chlorine, a halogen, gains an electron to form an anion (negatively-charged ion) Cl^-. The salts of hydrochloric acid contain chloride ions and can also be called chlorides. The chloride ion, and its salts such as sodium chloride, are very soluble in water.
Hydride	In chemistry, a hydride is the anion of hydrogen, H^-, or, more commonly, a compound in which one or more hydrogen centres have nucleophilic, reducing, or basic properties. In compounds that are regarded as hydrides, hydrogen is bonded to a more electropositive element or group.

Chapter 21. Metallurgy and the Chemistry of Metals

1. Amalgam is an alloy containing mercury. The term is commonly used for the _____ employed as material for dental fillings, which consists of mercury (50%), silver (~22-32%), tin (~14%), copper (~8%), and other trace metals. In the 1800s, amalgam became the dental restorative material of choice due to its low cost, ease of application, strength, and durability.

    a. Erethism
    b. Amalgam
    c. Black metal
    d. Blue stone

2. In mining, _____ is the commercially worthless material that surrounds, or is closely mixed with, a wanted mineral in an ore deposit. The separation of mineral from _____ is known as mineral processing, mineral dressing or ore dressing and it is a necessary and often significant aspect of mining. It can be a complicated process, depending on the nature of the minerals involved.

    a. Miner
    b. Mining
    c. Gangue
    d. Cave-in

3. _____ is the basic mechanism by which certain materials (such as iron) form permanent magnets, or are attracted to magnets. In physics, several different types of magnetism are distinguished. _____ is the strongest type; it is the only type that creates forces strong enough to be felt, and is responsible for the common phenomena of magnetism encountered in everyday life.

    a. Flash freezing
    b. Fractional crystallization
    c. Freezing-point depression
    d. Ferromagnetism

4. _____ or magnesia, is a white hygroscopic solid mineral that occurs naturally as periclase and is a source of magnesium . It has an empirical formula of MgO and consists of a lattice of Mg^{2+} ions and O^{2-} ions held together by ionic bonds. Magnesium hydroxide forms in the presence of water ($MgO + H_2O \rightarrow Mg(OH)_2$), but it can be reversed by heating it to separate moisture.

    a. Magnesium oxide
    b. Molybdenum disilicide
    c. Paper clay
    d. Pitchers

5. .

    _____ is a chemical element with the symbol Na and atomic number 11. It is a soft, silvery-white, highly reactive metal and is a member of the alkali metals; its only stable isotope is ^{23}Na.

The free metal does not occur in nature, but instead must be prepared from its compounds; it was first isolated by Humphry Davy in 1807 by the electrolysis of _____ hydroxide. _____ is the sixth most abundant element in the Earth's crust, and exists in numerous minerals such as feldspars, sodalite and rock salt.

a. Sulfur
b. Tungsten
c. Sodium
d. Zinc

1. b
2. c
3. d
4. a
5. c

You can take the complete Chapter Practice Test

for Chapter 21. Metallurgy and the Chemistry of Metals
on all key terms, persons, places, and concepts.

Online 99 Cents

http://www.epub14.1.20267.21.cram101.com/

Use www.Cram101.com for all your study needs

including Cram101's online interactive problem solving labs in

chemistry, statistics, mathematics, and more.

Chapter 22. Nonmetallic Elements and Their Compounds

CHAPTER OUTLINE: KEY TERMS, PEOPLE, PLACES, CONCEPTS

- Nonmetal
- Hydride
- Hydrogen
- Beryllium
- Beryllium hydride
- Diagonal
- Diagonal relationship
- Deuterium
- Gypsum
- International Union of Pure and Applied Chemistry
- Isotope
- Tritium
- Union
- Oxide
- Hydrogenation
- Kinetic isotope effect
- Arsenic
- Fossil fuel
- Fuel cell

_____ | Metallic hydrogen

_____ | Radiation

_____ | Carbon

_____ | Graphite

_____ | Phase diagram

_____ | Atomic mass

_____ | Mass

_____ | Synthetic diamond

_____ | Calcium

_____ | Calcium carbide

_____ | Carbide

_____ | Cyanide

_____ | Cytochrome

_____ | Enzyme

_____ | Hydrogen cyanide

_____ | Silicon carbide

_____ | Chloroform

_____ | Oxidase

_____ | Carbon dioxide

Chapter 22. Nonmetallic Elements and Their Compounds

CHAPTER OUTLINE: KEY TERMS, PEOPLE, PLACES, CONCEPTS

- Carbon monoxide
- Gold
- Gold extraction
- Metallurgy
- Corrosion
- Monoxide
- Coal gasification
- Syngas
- Gasification
- Nitrogen
- Amide
- Amino acid
- Hydrazine
- Nitric oxide
- Nitrogen dioxide
- Nitroglycerin
- Aqua regia
- Nitric acid
- Phosphate

_____ Oxidizing agent

_____ Phosphorus

_____ Ozone

_____ Phosphine

_____ Halide

_____ Hydrogen halide

_____ Phosphoric acid

_____ Oxygen

_____ Superoxide

_____ Basic oxide

_____ Lewis structure

_____ Reducing agent

_____ Frasch process

_____ Pyrite

_____ Sulfur

_____ Methanol

_____ Hydrogen sulfide

_____ Sulfide

_____ Sulfur dioxide

CHAPTER OUTLINE: KEY TERMS, PEOPLE, PLACES, CONCEPTS

Sulfur trioxide

Thioacetamide

Diprotic acid

Trioxide

Carbon disulfide

Contact process

Sulfur hexafluoride

Disulfide

Hexafluoride

Bromine

Chlorine

Fluorine

Halogen

Iodine

Electronegativity

Ionization

Ionization energy

Hydrochloric acid

Hydrogen bromide

Hydrogen fluoride

Hydrogen iodide

Oxoacid

Perchloric acid

Bromide

Fluoride

Iodide

Hypochlorous acid

Polytetrafluoroethylene

Sodium

Sodium fluoride

Ethylene

Silver bromide

Silver iodide

Thyroxine

Tincture of iodine

Amine

Chapter 22. Nonmetallic Elements and Their Compounds

Nonmetal	Nonmetal, is a term used in chemistry when classifying the chemical elements. On the basis of their general physical and chemical properties, every element in the periodic table can be termed either a metal or a nonmetal. (A few elements with intermediate properties are referred to as metalloids).
Hydride	In chemistry, a hydride is the anion of hydrogen, H^-, or, more commonly, a compound in which one or more hydrogen centres have nucleophilic, reducing, or basic properties. In compounds that are regarded as hydrides, hydrogen is bonded to a more electropositive element or group. Compounds containing metal or metalloid bonds to hydrogen are often referred to as hydrides, even though these hydrogen centres can have a protic character.
Hydrogen	Hydrogen is the chemical element with atomic number 1. It is represented by the symbol H. With an average atomic weight of 1.00794 u (1.007825 u for hydrogen-1), hydrogen is the lightest element and its monatomic form (H_1) is the most abundant chemical substance, constituting roughly 75% of the Universe's baryonic mass. Non-remnant stars are mainly composed of hydrogen in its plasma state.

At standard temperature and pressure, hydrogen is a colorless, odorless, tasteless, non-toxic, nonmetallic, highly combustible diatomic gas with the molecular formula H_2. |
| Beryllium | Beryllium is the chemical element with the symbol Be and atomic number 4. Because any beryllium synthesized in stars is short-lived, it is a relatively rare element in both the universe and in the crust of the Earth. It is a divalent element which occurs naturally only in combination with other elements in minerals. Notable gemstones which contain beryllium include beryl (aquamarine, emerald) and chrysoberyl. |
| Beryllium hydride | Beryllium hydride, BeH_2, is a chemical compound of beryllium and hydrogen commonly used in rocket fuel. Unlike the ionically bonded hydrides of the heavier Group 2 elements, beryllium hydride is covalently bonded.

BeH_2 was first synthesised in 1951 by reacting dimethylberyllium, $Be(CH_3)_2$, with lithium aluminium hydride, $LiAlH_4$. |
| Diagonal | A diagonal is a line joining two nonconsecutive vertices of a polygon or polyhedron. Informally, any sloping line is called diagonal. |

Chapter 22. Nonmetallic Elements and Their Compounds

Diagonal relationship	A diagonal relationship is said to exist between certain pairs of diagonally adjacent elements in the second and third periods of the periodic table. These pairs (lithium (Li) and magnesium (Mg), beryllium (Be) and aluminium (Al), boron (B) and silicon (Si) etc). exhibit similar properties; for example, boron and silicon are both semiconductors, forming halides that are hydrolysed in water and have acidic oxides.
Deuterium	Deuterium, is one of two stable isotopes of hydrogen. It has a natural abundance in Earth's oceans of about one atom in 6,420 of hydrogen (~156.25 ppm on an atom basis). Deuterium accounts for approximately 0.0156% of all naturally occurring hydrogen in Earth's oceans, while the most common isotope (hydrogen-1 or protium) accounts for more than 99.98%.
Gypsum	Gypsum is a very soft sulfate mineral composed of calcium sulfate dihydrate, with the chemical formula $CaSO_4 \cdot 2H_2O$. It is found in alabaster, a decorative stone used in Ancient Egypt. It is the second softest mineral on the Mohs scale of mineral hardness. It forms as an evaporite mineral and as a hydration product of anhydrite.
International Union of Pure and Applied Chemistry	The International Union of Pure and Applied Chemistry is an international federation of National Adhering Organizations that represents chemists in individual countries. It is a member of the International Council for Science (ICSU). The international headquarters of IUPAC is located in Zürich, Switzerland.
Isotope	Isotopes are variants of a particular chemical element. While all isotopes of a given element share the same number of protons, each isotope differs from the others in its number of neutrons. The term isotope is formed from the Greek roots isos and topos .
Tritium	Tritium is a radioactive isotope of hydrogen. The nucleus of tritium contains one proton and two neutrons, whereas the nucleus of protium (by far the most abundant hydrogen isotope) contains one proton and no neutrons. Naturally occurring tritium is extremely rare on Earth, where trace amounts are formed by the interaction of the atmosphere with cosmic rays.
Union	In set theory, the union (denoted as $\cup$) of a collection of sets is the set of all distinct elements in the collection. The union of a collection of sets $S_1, S_2, S_3, \ldots, S_n$ gives a set $S_1 \cup S_2 \cup S_3 \cup \ldots \cup S_n$. The union of two sets A and B is the collection of points which are in A or in B : $$A \cup B = \{x : x \in A \text{ or } x \in B\}$$ A simple example: $A = \{1, 2, 3, 4\}$ $B = \{5, 6, 7, 8\}$ $A \cup B = \{1, 2, 3, 4, 5, 6, 7, 8\}$

Another typical example: $A = \{1, 2, 3, 4, 5, 6\}$ $B = \{5, 6, 7, 8\}$
$A \cup B = \{1, 2, 3, 4, 5, 6, 7, 8\}$

Other more complex operations can be done including the union, if the set is for example defined by a property rather than a finite or assumed infinite enumeration of elements.

Oxide

An oxide is a chemical compound that contains at least one oxygen atom and one other element in its chemical formula. Metal oxides typically contain an anion of oxygen in the oxidation state of −2. Most of the Earth's crust consists of solid oxides, the result of elements being oxidized by the oxygen in air or in water . Hydrocarbon combustion affords the two principal carbon oxides: carbon monoxide and carbon dioxide.

Hydrogenation

Hydrogenation, to treat with hydrogen, also a form of chemical reduction, is a chemical reaction between molecular hydrogen (H_2) and another compound or element, usually in the presence of a catalyst. The process is commonly employed to reduce or saturate organic compounds. Hydrogenation typically constitutes the addition of pairs of hydrogen atoms to a molecule, generally an alkene.

Kinetic isotope effect

The kinetic isotope effect is the ratio of reaction rates of two different isotopically labeled molecules in a chemical reaction. It is also called 'isotope fractionation,' although this term is somewhat

$$KIE = \frac{k_H}{k_D}$$

broader in meaning. A KIE involving hydrogen and deuterium is represented as:

with k_H and k_D are reaction rate constants.

Arsenic

Arsenic is a chemical element with the symbol As, atomic number 33 and relative atomic mass 74.92. Arsenic occurs in many minerals, usually in conjunction with sulfur and metals, and also as a pure elemental crystal. It was first documented by Albertus Magnus in 1250. Arsenic is a metalloid. It can exist in various allotropes, although only the grey form has important use in industry.

Fossil fuel

Fossil fuels are fuels formed by natural resources such as anaerobic decomposition of buried dead organisms. The age of the organisms and their resulting fossil fuels is typically millions of years, and sometimes exceeds 650 million years. The fossil fuels, which contain high percentages of carbon, include coal, petroleum, and natural gas.

Chapter 22. Nonmetallic Elements and Their Compounds

Fuel cell	A fuel cell is a device that converts the chemical energy from a fuel into electricity through a chemical reaction with oxygen or another oxidizing agent. Hydrogen is the most common fuel, but hydrocarbons such as natural gas and alcohols like methanol are sometimes used. Fuel cells are different from batteries in that they require a constant source of fuel and oxygen to run, but they can produce electricity continually for as long as these inputs are supplied.
Metallic hydrogen	Metallic hydrogen is a state of hydrogen which results when it is sufficiently compressed and undergoes a phase transition; it is an example of degenerate matter. Solid metallic hydrogen is predicted to consist of a crystal lattice of hydrogen nuclei (namely, protons), with a spacing which is significantly smaller than the Bohr radius. Indeed, the spacing is more comparable with the de Broglie wavelength of the electron.
Radiation	In physics, radiation is a process in which energetic particles or energetic waves travel through a medium or space. Two types of radiation are commonly differentiated in the way they interact with normal chemical matter: ionizing and non-ionizing radiation. The word radiation is often colloquially used in reference to ionizing radiation but the term radiation may correctly also refer to non-ionizing radiation.
Carbon	Carbon is the chemical element with symbol C and atomic number 6. As a member of group 14 on the periodic table, it is nonmetallic and tetravalent--making four electrons available to form covalent chemical bonds. There are three naturally occurring isotopes, with ^{12}C and ^{13}C being stable, while ^{14}C is radioactive, decaying with a half-life of about 5,730 years. Carbon is one of the few elements known since antiquity.
Graphite	The mineral graphite is an allotrope of carbon. It was named by Abraham Gottlob Werner in 1789 from the Ancient Greek γρ?φω (grapho), 'to draw/write', for its use in pencils, where it is commonly called lead (not to be confused with the metallic element lead). Unlike diamond (another carbon allotrope), graphite is an electrical conductor, a semimetal.
Phase diagram	A phase diagram in physical chemistry, engineering, mineralogy, and materials science is a type of chart used to show conditions at which thermodynamically distinct phases can occur at equilibrium. In mathematics and physics, 'phase diagram' is used with a different meaning: a synonym for a phase space. Common components of a phase diagram are lines of equilibrium or phase boundaries, which refer to lines that mark conditions under which multiple phases can coexist at equilibrium.
Atomic mass	The atomic mass is the mass of a specific isotope, most often expressed in unified atomic mass units.

	The atomic mass is the total mass of protons, neutrons and electrons in a single atom.
	The atomic mass is sometimes incorrectly used as a synonym of relative atomic mass, average atomic mass and atomic weight; these differ subtly from the atomic mass.
Mass	The mass recorded by a mass spectrometer can refer to different physical quantities depending on the characteristics of the instrument and the manner in which the mass spectrum is displayed.
	The accurate mass (more appropriately, the measured accurate mass) is an experimentally determined mass that allows the elemental composition to be determined. For molecules with mass below 200 u, a 5 ppm accuracy is sufficient to uniquely determine the elemental composition.
Synthetic diamond	Synthetic diamond is diamond produced in a technological process; as opposed to natural diamond, which is created in geological processes. Synthetic diamond is also widely known as HPHT diamond or CVD diamond, denoting the production method, High-Pressure High-Temperature synthesis and Chemical Vapor Deposition, respectively.
Calcium	Calcium is the chemical element with the symbol Ca and atomic number 20. It has an atomic mass of 40.078 amu. Calcium is a soft gray alkaline earth metal, and is the fifth-most-abundant element by mass in the Earth's crust. Calcium is also the fifth-most-abundant dissolved ion in seawater by both molarity and mass, after sodium, chloride, magnesium, and sulfate.
Calcium carbide	Calcium carbide is a chemical compound with the chemical formula of CaC_2. Its main use industrially is in the production of acetylene and calcium cyanamide.
	The pure material is colorless, however pieces of technical-grade calcium carbide are grey or brown and consist of only 80-85% of CaC_2 (the rest is CaO, Ca_3P_2, CaS, Ca_3N_2, SiC, etc)..
Carbide	In chemistry, a carbide is a compound composed of carbon and a less electronegative element. Carbides can be generally classified by chemical bonding type as follows: (i) salt-like, (ii) covalent compounds, (iii) interstitial compounds, and (iv) 'intermediate' transition metal carbides. Examples include calcium carbide, silicon carbide, tungsten carbide and cementite, each used in key industrial applications.
Cyanide	A cyanide is a chemical compound that contains the cyano group, -C≡N, which consists of a carbon atom triple-bonded to a nitrogen atom. Cyanides most commonly refer to salts of the anion CN^-, which is isoelectric with carbon monoxide and with molecular nitrogen.

Visit Cram101.com for full Practice Exams

Chapter 22. Nonmetallic Elements and Their Compounds

Cytochrome	Cytochromes are, in general, membrane-bound hemoproteins that contain heme groups and carry out electron transport. They are found either as monomeric proteins (e.g., cytochrome c) or as subunits of bigger enzymatic complexes that catalyze redox reactions. They are found in the mitochondrial inner membrane and endoplasmic reticulum of eukaryotes, in the chloroplasts of plants, in photosynthetic microorganisms, and in bacteria.
Enzyme	Enzymes ( ) are biological molecules that catalyze (i.e., increase the rates of) chemical reactions. In enzymatic reactions, the molecules at the beginning of the process, called substrates, are converted into different molecules, called products. Almost all chemical reactions in a biological cell need enzymes in order to occur at rates sufficient for life.
Hydrogen cyanide	Hydrogen cyanide is a chemical compound with chemical formula HCN. It is a colorless, extremely poisonous liquid that boils slightly above room temperature at 26 °C (79 °F). Hydrogen cyanide is a linear molecule, with a triple bond between carbon and nitrogen. A minor tautomer of HCN is HNC, hydrogen isocyanide.
Silicon carbide	Silicon carbide also known as carborundum, is a compound of silicon and carbon with chemical formula SiC. It occurs in nature as the extremely rare mineral moissanite. Silicon carbide powder has been mass-produced since 1893 for use as an abrasive. Grains of silicon carbide can be bonded together by sintering to form very hard ceramics which are widely used in applications requiring high endurance, such as car brakes, car clutches and ceramic plates in bulletproof vests.
Chloroform	Chloroform is an organic compound with formula $CHCl_3$. It is one of the four chloromethanes. The colorless, sweet-smelling, dense liquid is a trihalomethane, and is considered somewhat hazardous.
Oxidase	An oxidase is any enzyme that catalyzes an oxidation-reduction reaction involving molecular oxygen (O_2) as the electron acceptor. In these reactions, oxygen is reduced to water (H_2O) or hydrogen peroxide (H_2O_2). The oxidases are a subclass of the oxidoreductases.
Carbon dioxide	Carbon dioxide is a naturally occurring chemical compound composed of two oxygen atoms covalently bonded to a single carbon atom. It is a gas at standard temperature and pressure and exists in Earth's atmosphere in this state, as a trace gas at a concentration of 0.039% by volume.

Carbon monoxide	Carbon monoxide also called carbonous oxide, is a colorless, odorless, and tasteless gas which is slightly lighter than air. It is highly toxic to humans and animals in higher quantities, although it is also produced in normal animal metabolism in low quantities, and is thought to have some normal biological functions.
	Carbon monoxide consists of one carbon atom and one oxygen atom, connected by a triple bond which consists of two covalent bonds as well as one dative covalent bond.
Gold	Gold is a dense, soft, shiny, malleable and ductile metal and is a chemical element with the symbol Au and atomic number 79.
	Pure gold has a bright yellow color and luster traditionally considered attractive, which it maintains without oxidizing in air or water. Chemically, gold is a transition metal and a group 11 element.
Gold extraction	Gold extraction, mineral processing, hydrometallurgical, and pyrometallurgical processes to be performed on the ore.
	Gold mining from alluvium ores was once achieved by techniques associated with placer mining such as simple gold panning and sluicing, resulting in direct recovery of small gold nuggets and flakes. Placer mining techniques since the mid to late 20th century have generally only been the practice of artisan miners.
Metallurgy	Metallurgy is a domain of materials science that studies the physical and chemical behavior of metallic elements, their intermetallic compounds, and their mixtures, which are called alloys. It is also the technology of metals: the way in which science is applied to their practical use. Metallurgy is distinguished from the craft of metalworking.
Corrosion	Corrosion is the gradual destruction of material, usually metals, by chemical reaction with its environment. In the most common use of the word, this means electro-chemical oxidation of metals in reaction with an oxidant such as oxygen. Rusting, the formation of iron oxides, is a well-known example of electrochemical corrosion.
Monoxide	A monoxide is any oxide containing just one atom of oxygen in the molecule. For example, Potassium oxide (K_2O), has only one atom of oxygen, and is thus a monoxide. Water (H_2O) is also a monoxide.
Coal gasification	Coal gasification is the process of producing coal gas, a type of syngas-a mixture of carbon monoxide (CO), hydrogen (H_2), carbon dioxide (CO_2) and water vapour (H_2O)-from coal.

Chapter 22. Nonmetallic Elements and Their Compounds

Coal gas, which is a combustible gas, was traditionally used as a source of energy for municipal lighting and heat before the advent of industrial-scale production of natural gas, while the hydrogen obtained from gasification can be used for various purposes such as making ammonia, powering a hydrogen economy, or upgrading fossil fuels. Alternatively, the coal gas (also known as 'town gas') can be converted into transportation fuels such as gasoline and diesel through additional treatment via the Fischer-Tropsch process.

Syngas	Syngas is the name given to a gas mixture that contains varying amounts of carbon monoxide and hydrogen. Examples of production methods include steam reforming of natural gas or liquid hydrocarbons to produce hydrogen, the gasification of coal, biomass, and in some types of waste-to-energy gasification facilities. The name comes from their use as intermediates in creating synthetic natural gas (SNG) and for producing ammonia or methanol.
Gasification	Gasification is a process that converts organic or fossil based carbonaceous materials into carbon monoxide, hydrogen and carbon dioxide. This is achieved by reacting the material at high temperatures (>700 °C), without combustion, with a controlled amount of oxygen and/or steam. The resulting gas mixture is called syngas (from synthesis gas or synthetic gas) or producer gas and is itself a fuel.
Nitrogen	Nitrogen is a chemical element that has the symbol N, atomic number of 7 and atomic mass 14.00674 u. Elemental nitrogen is a colorless, odorless, tasteless, and mostly inert diatomic gas at standard conditions, constituting 78.09% by volume of Earth's atmosphere. The element nitrogen was discovered as a separable component of air, by Scottish physician Daniel Rutherford, in 1772.
Amide	Amide refers to compounds with the functional group $R_nE(O)_xNR'_2$ (R and R' refer to H or organic groups). Most common are 'organic amides' (n = 1, E = C, x = 1), but many other important types of amides are known including phosphor amides (n = 2, E = P, x = 1 and many related formulas) and sulfonamides (E = S, x= 2). The term amide refers both to classes of compounds and to the functional group ($R_nE(O)_xNR'_2$) within those compounds.
Amino acid	Amino acids are molecules containing an amine group, a carboxylic acid group, and a side-chain that is specific to each amino acid. The key elements of an amino acid are carbon, hydrogen, oxygen, and nitrogen. They are particularly important in biochemistry, where the term usually refers to alpha-amino acids.
Hydrazine	Hydrazine is an inorganic compound with the formula N_2H_4. It is a colourless flammable liquid with an ammonia-like odor.

Nitric oxide	Nitric oxide, is a molecule with chemical formula NO. It is a free radical and is an important intermediate in the chemical industry. Nitric oxide is a by-product of combustion of substances in the air, as in automobile engines, fossil fuel power plants, and is produced naturally during the electrical discharges of lightning in thunderstorms. In mammals including humans, NO is an important cellular signaling molecule involved in many physiological and pathological processes.
Nitrogen dioxide	Nitrogen dioxide is the chemical compound with the formula NO_2. It is one of several nitrogen oxides. NO_2 is an intermediate in the industrial synthesis of nitric acid, millions of tons of which are produced each year.
Nitroglycerin	Nitroglycerin also known as nitroglycerine, trinitroglycerin, trinitroglycerine, 1,2,3-trinitroxypropane and glyceryl trinitrate, is a heavy, colorless, oily, explosive liquid produced by nitrating glycerol. Chemically, the substance is an organic nitrate compound rather than a nitro compound, but the traditional name is often retained. Since the 1860s, nitroglycerin has been used as an active ingredient in the manufacture of explosives, mostly dynamite, and as such it is employed in the construction, demolition, and mining industries.
Aqua regia	Aqua regia aqua regis (lit. 'king's water'), or nitro-hydrochloric acid is a highly-corrosive mixture of acids, a fuming yellow or red solution. The mixture is formed by freshly mixing concentrated nitric acid and hydrochloric acid, usually in a volume ratio of 1:3. It was named so because it can dissolve the so-called royal or noble metals, gold and platinum. However, titanium, iridium, ruthenium, tantalum, osmium, rhodium and a few other metals are capable of withstanding its corrosive properties.
Nitric acid	Nitric acid also known as aqua fortis and spirit of niter, is a highly corrosive and toxic strong mineral acid which is normally colorless but tends to acquire a yellow cast due to the accumulation of oxides of nitrogen if long-stored. Ordinary nitric acid has a concentration of 68%. When the solution contains more than 86% HNO_3, it is referred to as fuming nitric acid.
Phosphate	A phosphate, an inorganic chemical, is a salt of phosphoric acid. In organic chemistry, a phosphate, or organophosphate, is an ester of phosphoric acid. Organic phosphates are important in biochemistry and biogeochemistry or ecology.
Oxidizing agent	An oxidizing agent can be defined as a substance that removes electrons from another reactant in a redox chemical reaction. The oxidizing agent is 'reduced' by taking electrons onto itself and the reactant is 'oxidized' by having its electrons taken away. Oxygen is the prime example of an oxidizing agent, but it is only one among many.
Phosphorus	

Chapter 22. Nonmetallic Elements and Their Compounds

Phosphorus is the chemical element that has the symbol P and atomic number 15. A multivalent nonmetal of the nitrogen group, phosphorus as a mineral is almost always present in its maximally oxidized state, as inorganic phosphate rocks. Elemental phosphorus exists in two major forms-- white phosphorus and red phosphorus--but due to its high reactivity, phosphorus is never found as a free element on Earth.

The first form of elemental phosphorus to be produced (white phosphorus, in 1669) emits a faint glow upon exposure to oxygen - hence its name given from Greek mythology, Φωσφ?ρος meaning 'light-bearer', referring to the 'Morning Star', the planet Venus.

Ozone	Ozone or trioxygen, is a triatomic molecule, consisting of three oxygen atoms. It is an allotrope of oxygen that is much less stable than the diatomic allotrope (O_2), breaking down with a half life of about half an hour in the lower atmosphere, to normal dioxygen. Ozone is formed from dioxygen by the action of ultraviolet light and also atmospheric electrical discharges, and is present in low concentrations throughout the Earth's atmosphere.
Phosphine	Phosphine is the compound with the chemical formula PH_3. It is a colorless, flammable, toxic gas. Pure phosphine is odorless, but technical grade samples have a highly unpleasant odor like garlic or rotting fish, due to the presence of substituted phosphine and diphosphine.
Halide	A halide is a binary compound, of which one part is a halogen atom and the other part is an element or radical that is less electronegative than the halogen, to make a fluoride, chloride, bromide, iodide, or astatide compound. Many salts are halides. All Group 1 metals form halides which are white solids at room temperature.
Hydrogen halide	Hydrogen halides (or hydrohalic acids) are inorganic compounds with the formula HX where X is one of the halogens: fluorine, chlorine, bromine, iodine, and astatine. Hydrogen halides are gases that dissolve in water to give acids. The hydrogen halides are diatomic molecules with no tendency to ionize in the gas phase.
Phosphoric acid	Phosphoric acid, is a mineral (inorganic) acid having the chemical formula H_3PO_4. Orthophosphoric acid molecules can combine with themselves to form a variety of compounds which are also referred to as phosphoric acids, but in a more general way. The term phosphoric acid can also refer to a chemical or reagent consisting of phosphoric acids, usually orthophosphoric acid.
Oxygen	Oxygen is the element with atomic number 8 and represented by the symbol O.

Its name derives from the Greek roots ?ξ?ς (oxys) ('acid', literally 'sharp', referring to the sour taste of acids) and -γεν?ς (-genes) ('producer', literally 'begetter'), because at the time of naming, it was mistakenly thought that all acids required oxygen in their composition. At standard temperature and pressure, two atoms of the element bind to form dioxygen, a very pale blue, odorless, tasteless diatomic gas with the formula O_2.

Oxygen is a member of the chalcogen group on the periodic table and is a highly reactive nonmetallic element that readily forms compounds (notably oxides) with almost all other elements.

Superoxide	A superoxide, also known by the obsolete name hyperoxide, is a compound that contains the superoxide anion with the chemical formula O_2^-. The systematic name of the anion is dioxide(1−). Superoxide anion is particularly important as the product of the one-electron reduction of dioxygen O_2, which occurs widely in nature.
Basic oxide	A basic oxide is an oxide that shows basic properties in opposition to acidic oxides and that either•reacts with water to form a base; or•reacts with an acid to form a salt.

Examples include:•Sodium oxide, which reacts with water to produce sodium hydroxide

Magnesium oxide, which reacts with hydrochloric acid to form magnesium chloride•Copper(II) oxide, which reacts with nitric acid to form copper nitrate

Basic oxides are oxides mostly of metals, especially alkali and alkaline earth metals. |
Lewis structure	Lewis structures (also known as Lewis dot diagrams, electron dot diagrams, and electron dot structures) are diagrams that show the bonding between atoms of a molecule and the lone pairs of electrons that may exist in the molecule.
Reducing agent	A reducing agent is the element or compound in a reduction-oxidation (redox) reaction that donates an electron to another species; however, since the reducer loses an electron we say it is 'oxidized'. This means that there must be an 'oxidizer'; because if any chemical is an electron donor (reducer), another must be an electron recipient (oxidizer). Thus reducers are 'oxidized' and oxidizers are 'reduced'.
Frasch process	The Frasch process is a method to extract sulfur from underground deposits. It is the only economic method of recovering sulfur from elemental deposits. Most of the world's sulfur was obtained this way until the late 20th century, when sulfur recovered from petroleum and gas sources (recovered sulfur) became more commonplace .
Pyrite	The mineral pyrite, is an iron sulfide with the formula FeS_2.

Chapter 22. Nonmetallic Elements and Their Compounds

	This mineral's metallic luster and pale-to-normal, brass-yellow hue have earned it the nickname fool's gold because of its resemblance to gold. The color has also led to the nicknames brass, brazzle and Brazil, primarily used to refer to pyrite found in coal.
Sulfur	Sulfur or sulphur is the chemical element with atomic number 16. In the periodic table it is represented by the symbol S. It is an abundant, multivalent non-metal. Under normal conditions, sulfur atoms form cyclic octatomic molecules with chemical formula S_8. Elemental sulfur is a bright yellow crystalline solid when at room temperature.
Methanol	Methanol, wood alcohol, wood naphtha or wood spirits, is a chemical with the formula CH_3OH . It is the simplest alcohol, and is a light, volatile, colorless, flammable liquid with a distinctive odor very similar to, but slightly sweeter than, ethanol (drinking alcohol). At room temperature, it is a polar liquid, and is used as an antifreeze, solvent, fuel, and as a denaturant for ethanol.
Hydrogen sulfide	Hydrogen sulfide is the chemical compound with the formula H_2S. It is a colorless, very poisonous, flammable gas with the characteristic foul odor of rotten eggs. It often results from the bacterial breakdown of organic matter in the absence of oxygen, such as in swamps and sewers; this process is commonly known as anaerobic digestion.
Sulfide	A sulfide is an anion of sulfur in its lowest oxidation state of 2-. Sulfide is also a slightly archaic term for thioethers, a common type of organosulfur compound that are well known for their bad odors. The dianion S^{2-} exists only in strongly alkaline aqueous solutions.
Sulfur dioxide	Sulfur dioxide is the chemical compound with the formula SO_2. It is a poisonous gas with a pungent, irritating smell, that is released by volcanoes and in various industrial processes. Since coal and petroleum often contain sulfur compounds, their combustion generates sulfur dioxide unless the sulfur compounds are removed before burning the fuel.
Sulfur trioxide	Sulfur trioxide is the chemical compound with the formula SO_3. In the gaseous form, this species is a significant pollutant, being the primary agent in acid rain. It is prepared on massive scales as a precursor to sulfuric acid.
Thioacetamide	Thioacetamide is an organosulfur compound with the formula C_2H_5NS. This white crystalline solid is soluble in water and serves as a source of sulfide ions in the synthesis of organic and inorganic compounds. It is a prototypical thioamide.

Diprotic acid	A diprotic acid is an acid such as H_2SO_4 (sulfuric acid) that contains within its molecular structure two hydrogen atoms per molecule capable of dissociating (i.e. ionizable) in water. The complete dissociation of diprotic acids is of the same form as sulfuric acid:$H_2SO_4 \rightarrow H^+(aq) + HSO_4^-(aq)$ $K_a = 1 \times 10^3$ $HSO_4^- \rightarrow H^+(aq) + SO_4^{2-}(aq)$ $K_a = 1 \times 10^{-2}$
	The dissociation does not happen all at once due to the two stages of dissociation having different K_a values. The first dissociation will, in the case of sulfuric acid, occur completely, but the second one will not.
Trioxide	A trioxide is a compound with three oxygen atoms. For metals with the M_2O_3 formula there are several common structures. Al_2O_3, Cr_2O_3, Fe_2O_3, and V_2O_3 adopt the corundum structure.
Carbon disulfide	Carbon disulfide is a colorless volatile liquid with the formula CS_2. The compound is used frequently as a building block in organic chemistry as well as an industrial and chemical non-polar solvent. It has an 'ether-like' odor, but commercial samples are typically contaminated with foul-smelling impurities, such as carbonyl sulfide.
Contact process	The contact process is the current method of producing sulphuric acid in the high concentrations needed for industrial processes. Platinum was formerly employed as a catalyst for the reaction, but as it is susceptible to poisoning by arsenic impurities in the sulphur feedstock, vanadium(V) oxide (V_2O_5) is now preferred.
	This process was patented in 1831 by the British vinegar merchant Peregrine Phillips.
Sulfur hexafluoride	Sulfur hexafluoride is an inorganic, colorless, odorless, and non-flammable greenhouse gas. SF_6 has an octahedral geometry, consisting of six fluorine atoms attached to a central sulfur atom. It is a hypervalent molecule.
Disulfide	In chemistry, a disulfide usually refers to the structural unit composed of a linked pair of sulfur atoms. Disulfide usually refer to a chemical compound that contains a disulfide bond, such as diphenyl disulfide, $C_6H_5S\text{-}SC_6H_5$.
	The disulfide anion is S_2^{2-}, or $^-S\text{-}S^-$.
Hexafluoride	A hexafluoride is a chemical compound with the general formula XF_6. Sixteen elements are known to form stable hexafluorides. Nine of these elements are transition metals, three are actinides, and four are nonmetals or metalloids.
Bromine	

Chapter 22. Nonmetallic Elements and Their Compounds

Bromine ('bro?mi?n-meen or 'bro?m?n-min; from Greek: βρ?μος, brómos, meaning 'stench (of he-goats)') is a chemical element with the symbol Br, an atomic number of 35, and an atomic mass of 79.904. It is in the halogen element group. The element was isolated independently by two chemists, Carl Jacob Löwig and Antoine Jerome Balard, in 1825-1826. Elemental bromine is a fuming red-brown liquid at room temperature, corrosive and toxic, with properties between those of chlorine and iodine. Free bromine does not occur in nature, but occurs as colorless soluble crystalline mineral halide salts, analogous to table salt.

Chlorine

Chlorine is the chemical element with atomic number 17 and symbol Cl. It is the second lightest halogen, with fluorine being the lightest. Chlorine is found in the periodic table in group 17. The element forms diatomic molecules under standard conditions, called dichlorine.

Fluorine

Fluorine is the chemical element with atomic number 9, represented by the symbol F. It is the lightest element of the halogen column of the periodic table and has a single stable isotope, fluorine-19. At standard pressure and temperature, fluorine is a pale yellow gas composed of diatomic molecules, F_2. In stars, fluorine is rare compared to other light elements. In Earth's crust, fluorine is more common, being the thirteenth most abundant element.

Halogen

The halogens or halogen elements are a series of nonmetal elements from Group 17 IUPAC Style (formerly: VII, VIIA) of the periodic table, comprising fluorine (F), chlorine (Cl), bromine (Br), iodine (I), and astatine (At). The artificially created element 117, provisionally referred to by the systematic name ununseptium, may also be a halogen.

The group of halogens is the only periodic table group which contains elements in all three familiar states of matter at standard temperature and pressure.

Iodine

Iodine is a chemical element with the symbol I and atomic number 53./ syllable break' style='border-bottom:1px dotted'>.?da?n-o-dyne, 'a?.?d?n-o-d?n, or 'a?.?di?n-o-deen in both American and British English. The name is from Greek ?οειδ?ς ioeides, meaning violet or purple, due to the color of elemental iodine vapor.

Iodine and its compounds are primarily used in nutrition, and industrially in the production of acetic acid and certain polymers.

Electronegativity	Electronegativity, symbol χ, is a chemical property that describes the tendency of an atom or a functional group to attract electrons towards itself. An atom's electronegativity is affected by both its atomic number and the distance that its valence electrons reside from the charged nucleus. The higher the associated electronegativity number, the more an element or compound attracts electrons towards it.
Ionization	Ionization is the process of converting an atom or molecule into an ion by adding or removing charged particles such as electrons or ions. In the case of ionisation of a gas, ion-pairs are created consisting of a free electron and a +ve ion. The process of ionization works slightly differently depending on whether an ion with a positive or a negative electric charge is being produced.
Ionization energy	The ionization energy of a chemical species, i.e. an atom or molecule, is the energy required to remove electrons from gaseous atoms or ions. The property is alternately still often called the ionization potential, measured in volts. In chemistry it often refers to one mole of a substance (molar ionization energy or enthalpy) and reported in kJ/mol.
Hydrochloric acid	Hydrochloric acid is a clear, colourless solution of hydrogen chloride (HCl) in water. It is a highly corrosive, strong mineral acid with many industrial uses. Hydrochloric acid is found naturally in gastric acid.
Hydrogen bromide	Hydrogen bromide is the diatomic molecule HBr. HBr is a gas at standard conditions. Hydrobromic acid forms upon dissolving HBr in water.
Hydrogen fluoride	Hydrogen fluoride is a chemical compound with the formula HF. This colorless gas is the principal industrial source of fluorine, often in the aqueous form as hydrofluoric acid, and thus is the precursor to many important compounds including pharmaceuticals and polymers (e.g. Teflon). HF is widely used in the petrochemical industry and is a component of many superacids. Hydrogen fluoride boils just below room temperature whereas the other hydrogen halides condense at much lower temperatures.
Hydrogen iodide	Hydrogen iodide is a diatomic molecule. Aqueous solutions of HI are known as iohydroic acid or hydroiodic acid, a strong acid. Gas and aqueous solution are interconvertible.
Oxoacid	An oxoacid is an acid that contains oxygen. To be more specific, it is an acid that:•contains oxygen•contains at least one other element•has at least one hydrogen atom bound to oxygen•forms an ion by the loss of one or more protons. The name oxyacid is sometimes used, although this is not recommended. Description

Chapter 22. Nonmetallic Elements and Their Compounds

Perchloric acid	Perchloric acid is the inorganic compound with the formula $HClO_4$. Usually found as an aqueous solution, this colorless compound is a stronger acid than sulfuric and nitric acids. It is a powerful oxidizer, but its aqueous solutions up to appr. 70% are generally safe, only showing strong acid features and no oxidizing properties.
Bromide	A bromide is a chemical compound containing a bromide ion, that is a bromine atom with an effective charge of −1. The class name can include ionic compounds such as caesium bromide or covalent compounds such as sulfur dibromide. Bromide is present in typical seawater (35 PSU) with a concentration of around 65 mg/L, which is around 0.2% of all dissolved salts. Seafoods and deep sea plants generally have high levels of bromide, while foods derived from land have variable amounts.
Fluoride	Fluoride is the anion F^-, the reduced form of fluorine when as an ion and when bonded to another element. Both organofluorine compounds and inorganic fluorine containing compounds are called fluorides. Fluoride, like other halides, is a monovalent ion (−1 charge).
Iodide	An iodide ion is the ion I^-. Compounds with iodine in formal oxidation state −1 are called iodides. This page is for the iodide ion and its salts.
Hypochlorous acid	Hypochlorous acid is a weak acid with the chemical formula HClO. It forms when chlorine dissolves in water. It cannot be isolated in pure form due to rapid equilibration with its precursor. HClO is an oxidizer, and as its sodium salt sodium hypochlorite, (NaClO), or its calcium salt calcium hypochlorite, $(Ca(ClO)_2)$ is used as a bleach, a deodorant, and a disinfectant.
Polytetrafluoroethylene	Polytetrafluoroethylene is a synthetic fluoropolymer of tetrafluoroethylene that finds numerous applications. The most well known brand name of PTFE is Teflon by DuPont Co. PTFE is a fluorocarbon solid, as it is a high-molecular-weight compound consisting wholly of carbon and fluorine.
Sodium	Sodium is a chemical element with the symbol Na and atomic number 11. It is a soft, silvery-white, highly reactive metal and is a member of the alkali metals; its only stable isotope is ^{23}Na. The free metal does not occur in nature, but instead must be prepared from its compounds; it was first isolated by Humphry Davy in 1807 by the electrolysis of sodium hydroxide. Sodium is the sixth most abundant element in the Earth's crust, and exists in numerous minerals such as feldspars, sodalite and rock salt.
Sodium fluoride	Sodium fluoride is an inorganic chemical compound with the formula NaF.

	A colorless solid, it is a source of the fluoride ion in diverse applications. Sodium fluoride is less expensive and less hygroscopic than the related salt potassium fluoride.
	Sodium fluoride is an ionic compound, dissolving to give separated Na^+ and F^- ions.
Ethylene	Ethylene is an organic compound, a hydrocarbon with the formula C_2H_4 or $H_2C=CH_2$. It is a colorless flammable gas with a faint 'sweet and musky' odor when pure. It is the simplest alkene (a hydrocarbon with carbon-carbon double bonds), and the simplest unsaturated hydrocarbon after acetylene (C_2H_2).
Silver bromide	Silver bromide a soft, pale-yellow, water insoluble salt well known (along with other silver halides) for its unusual sensitivity to light. This property has allowed silver halides to become the basis of modern photographic materials. AgBr is widely used in photographic films and is believed by some to have been used for making the Shroud of Turin.
Silver iodide	Silver iodide is an inorganic compound with the formula AgI. The compound is a bright yellow solid, but samples almost always contain impurities of metallic silver that give a gray coloration. The silver contamination arises because AgI is highly photosensitive. This property is exploited in silver-based photography.
Thyroxine	Levothyroxine, also L-thyroxine, is a synthetic form of thyroid hormone (or thyroxine), the hormone normally secreted by the follicular cells of the thyroid gland. Levothyroxine is used to treat thyroid hormone deficiency, and occasionally to prevent the recurrence of thyroid cancer. Levothyroxine differs from natural thyroxine in that it is chemically in the chiral L-form.
Tincture of iodine	Tincture of iodine is a disinfectant, it is also called weak iodine solution. Usually 2-7% elemental iodine, along with potassium iodide or sodium iodide, dissolved in a mixture of ethanol and water. As in the case of Lugol's iodine, the role of iodide and water in the solution is to increase the solubility of the elemental iodine, by turning it to the soluble triiodide anion I_3^-.
Amine	Amines are organic compounds and functional groups that contain a basic nitrogen atom with a lone pair. Amines are derivatives of ammonia, wherein one or more hydrogen atoms have been replaced by a substituent such as an alkyl or aryl group. Important amines include amino acids, biogenic amines, trimethylamine, and aniline.

Chapter 22. Nonmetallic Elements and Their Compounds

1.

_____ is the chemical element with the symbol Ca and atomic number 20. It has an atomic mass of 40.078 amu. _____ is a soft gray alkaline earth metal, and is the fifth-most-abundant element by mass in the Earth's crust. _____ is also the fifth-most-abundant dissolved ion in seawater by both molarity and mass, after sodium, chloride, magnesium, and sulfate.

   a. Calcium
   b. Cerium
   c. Chromium acetate hydroxide
   d. Diborane

2. _____ is an inorganic, colorless, odorless, and non-flammable greenhouse gas. SF_6 has an octahedral geometry, consisting of six fluorine atoms attached to a central sulfur atom. It is a hypervalent molecule.

   a. Tungsten hexacarbonyl
   b. Tungsten hexachloride
   c. Sulfur hexafluoride
   d. Crofton formula

3. _____ is an organic compound, a hydrocarbon with the formula C_2H_4 or $H_2C=CH_2$. It is a colorless flammable gas with a faint 'sweet and musky' odor when pure. It is the simplest alkene (a hydrocarbon with carbon-carbon double bonds), and the simplest unsaturated hydrocarbon after acetylene (C_2H_2).

   a. Ethylene oxide
   b. Ethylene
   c. Isophthalic acid
   d. Isoprene

4. _____, symbol χ, is a chemical property that describes the tendency of an atom or a functional group to attract electrons towards itself. An atom's _____ is affected by both its atomic number and the distance that its valence electrons reside from the charged nucleus. The higher the associated _____ number, the more an element or compound attracts electrons towards it.

   a. Energy level
   b. Inert
   c. Electronegativity
   d. Oxidation state

5. . A _____ is any oxide containing just one atom of oxygen in the molecule. For example, Potassium oxide (K_2O), has only one atom of oxygen, and is thus a _____. Water (H_2O) is also a _____.

   a. Nd:YAB
   b. Nickel oxide
   c. Niobium dioxide

1. a
2. c
3. b
4. c
5. d

You can take the complete Chapter Practice Test

for Chapter 22. Nonmetallic Elements and Their Compounds
on all key terms, persons, places, and concepts.

Online 99 Cents

http://www.epub14.1.20267.22.cram101.com/

Use www.Cram101.com for all your study needs

including Cram101's online interactive problem solving labs in

chemistry, statistics, mathematics, and more.

CHAPTER OUTLINE: KEY TERMS, PEOPLE, PLACES, CONCEPTS

	Isomer
	Chromium
	Iodine
	Electron
	Electron configuration
	Transition metal
	Potential
	Reduction potential
	Hematite
	Oxidation number
	Magnetite
	Metallurgy
	Atomic weight
	Coordination number
	Ethylenediamine
	Atom
	Molecular geometry
	Geometry
	Stereoisomers

_____ Alkene

_____ Stereochemistry

_____ Enantiomer

_____ Mixture

_____ Molecule

_____ Polarimeter

_____ Polaroid

_____ Rotation

_____ Racemic mixture

_____ Crystal field theory

_____ Cytosine

_____ Glass transition

_____ Wavelength

_____ Spectrum

_____ Magnetism

_____ Paramagnetism

_____ Pauli exclusion principle

_____ Spectrochemical series

_____ Diamagnetism

Chapter 23. Transition Metals Chemistry and Coordination Compounds

363

CHAPTER OUTLINE: KEY TERMS, PEOPLE, PLACES, CONCEPTS

Activation

Activation energy

Chemical reaction

Inert

Isotope

Condensation

Heme

Hemoglobin

Living systems

Myoglobin

Oxygen

Porphyrin

Group

Chlorophyll

Cytochrome

Cytochrome c

Photosynthesis

Platinum

Catalyst

Visit Cram101.com for full Practice Exams

Chapter 23. Transition Metals Chemistry and Coordination Compounds

_____ | Cisplatin

_____ | Detergent

_____ | Sodium

CHAPTER HIGHLIGHTS & NOTES: KEY TERMS, PEOPLE, PLACES, CONCEPTS

Isomer	In chemistry, isomers are compounds with the same molecular formula but different structural formulas. Isomers do not necessarily share similar properties, unless they also have the same functional groups. There are many different classes of isomers, like stereoisomers, enantiomers, geometrical isomers, etc.
Chromium	Chromium is a chemical element which has the symbol Cr and atomic number 24. It is the first element in Group 6. It is a steely-gray, lustrous, hard metal that takes a high polish and has a high melting point. It is also odorless, tasteless, and malleable. The name of the element is derived from the Greek word 'chroma' , meaning colour, because many of its compounds are intensely coloured.
Iodine	Iodine is a chemical element with the symbol I and atomic number 53./ syllable break' style='border-bottom:1px dotted'>.?da?n-o-dyne, 'a?.?d?n-o-d?n, or 'a?.?di?n-o-deen in both American and British English. The name is from Greek ?οειδ?ς ioeides, meaning violet or purple, due to the color of elemental iodine vapor.

Iodine and its compounds are primarily used in nutrition, and industrially in the production of acetic acid and certain polymers. |
| Electron | The electron is a subatomic particle with a negative elementary electric charge. It has no known components or substructure; in other words, it is generally thought to be an elementary particle. |

Electron configuration	In atomic physics and quantum chemistry, the electron configuration is the distribution of electrons of an atom or molecule in atomic or molecular orbitals. For example, the electron configuration of the neon atom is $1s^2\ 2s^2\ 2p^6$. According to the laws of quantum mechanics, an energy is associated with each electron configuration and, upon certain conditions, electrons are able to move from one orbital to another by emission or absorption of a quantum of energy, in the form of a photon.
Transition metal	In chemistry, the term transition metal has two possible meanings:•The IUPAC definition states that a transition metal is 'an element whose atom has an incomplete d sub-shell, or which can give rise to cations with an incomplete d sub-shell'.•Most scientists describe a 'transition metal' as any element in the d-block of the periodic table, which includes groups 3 to 12 on the periodic table. All elements in the d-block are metals. In actual practice, the f-block is also included in the form of the lanthanide and actinide series. Jensen has reviewed the history of the terms transition element and d-block.
Potential	•In linguistics, the potential mood•The mathematical study of potentials is known as potential theory; it is the study of harmonic functions on manifolds. This mathematical formulation arises from the fact that, in physics, the scalar potential is irrotational, and thus has a vanishing Laplacian -- the very definition of a harmonic function.•In physics, a potential may refer to the scalar potential or to the vector potential. In either case, it is a field defined in space, from which many important physical properties may be derived.
Reduction potential	Reduction potential (also known as redox potential, oxidation / reduction potential is a measure of the tendency of a chemical species to acquire electrons and thereby be reduced. Reduction potential is measured in volts (V), or millivolts (mV). Each species has its own intrinsic reduction potential; the more positive the potential, the greater the species' affinity for electrons and tendency to be reduced.
Hematite	Hematite is the mineral form of iron(III) oxide (Fe_2O_3), one of several iron oxides. Hematite crystallizes in the rhombohedral system, and it has the same crystal structure as ilmenite and corundum. Hematite and ilmenite form a complete solid solution at temperatures above 950 °C. Hematite is a mineral, colored black to steel or silver-gray, brown to reddish brown, or red.
Oxidation number	In coordination chemistry, the oxidation number of a central atom in a coordination compound is the charge that it would have if all the ligands were removed along with the electron pairs that were shared with the central atom. The oxidation number is used in the nomenclature of inorganic compounds.

Chapter 23. Transition Metals Chemistry and Coordination Compounds

Magnetite	Magnetite is a ferrimagnetic mineral with chemical formula Fe_3O_4, one of several iron oxides and a member of the spinel group. The chemical IUPAC name is iron(II,III) oxide and the common chemical name is ferrous-ferric oxide. The formula for magnetite may also be written as $FeO \cdot Fe_2O_3$, which is one part wüstite (FeO) and one part hematite (Fe_2O_3).
Metallurgy	Metallurgy is a domain of materials science that studies the physical and chemical behavior of metallic elements, their intermetallic compounds, and their mixtures, which are called alloys. It is also the technology of metals: the way in which science is applied to their practical use. Metallurgy is distinguished from the craft of metalworking.
Atomic weight	Atomic weight is a dimensionless physical quantity, the ratio of the average mass of atoms of an element (from a given source) to 1/12 of the mass of an atom of carbon-12 (known as the unified atomic mass unit). The term is usually used, without further qualification, to refer to the standard atomic weights published at regular intervals by the International Union of Pure and Applied Chemistry (IUPAC) and which are intended to be applicable to normal laboratory materials.
Coordination number	In chemistry and crystallography, the coordination number of a central atom in a molecule or crystal is the number of its nearest neighbours. This number is determined somewhat differently for molecules and for crystals. In chemistry, the emphasis is on bonding structure in molecules or ions and the coordination number of an atom is determined by simply counting the other atoms to which it is bonded (by either single or multiple bonds).
Ethylenediamine	Ethylenediamine is the organic compound with the formula $C_2H_4(NH_2)_2$. This colorless liquid with an ammonia-like odor is a strongly basic amine. The liquid fumes upon contact with humid air.
Atom	The atom is a basic unit of matter that consists of a dense central nucleus surrounded by a cloud of negatively charged electrons. The atomic nucleus contains a mix of positively charged protons and electrically neutral neutrons (except in the case of hydrogen-1, which is the only stable nuclide with no neutrons). The electrons of an atom are bound to the nucleus by the electromagnetic force.
Molecular geometry	Molecular geometry is the three-dimensional arrangement of the atoms that constitute a molecule. It determines several properties of a substance including its reactivity, polarity, phase of matter, color, magnetism, and biological activity. The molecular geometry can be determined by various spectroscopic methods and diffraction methods.

Geometry	Geometry is a branch of mathematics concerned with questions of shape, size, relative position of figures, and the properties of space. A mathematician who works in the field of geometry is called a geometer. Geometry arose independently in a number of early cultures as a body of practical knowledge concerning lengths, areas, and volumes, with elements of a formal mathematical science emerging in the West as early as Thales (6th Century BC).
Stereoisomers	Stereoisomers are isomeric molecules that have the same molecular formula and sequence of bonded atoms (constitution), but that differ only in the three-dimensional orientations of their atoms in space. This contrasts with structural isomers, which share the same molecular formula, but the bond connections and/or their order differ(s) between different atoms/groups. In stereoisomers, the order and bond connections of the constituent atoms remain the same, but their orientation in space differs.
Alkene	In organic chemistry, an alkene, olefin, or olefine is an unsaturated chemical compound containing at least one carbon-to-carbon double bond. The simplest acyclic alkenes, with only one double bond and no other functional groups, form an homologous series of hydrocarbons with the general formula C_nH_{2n}. The simplest alkene is ethylene (C_2H_4), which has the International Union of Pure and Applied Chemistry (IUPAC) name ethene.
Stereochemistry	Stereochemistry, a subdiscipline of chemistry, involves the study of the relative spatial arrangement of atoms within molecules. An important branch of stereochemistry is the study of chiral molecules. Stereochemistry is also known as 3D chemistry because the prefix 'stereo-' means 'three-dimensionality'.
Enantiomer	In chemistry, an enantiomer is one of two stereoisomers that are mirror images of each other that are non-superposable (not identical), much as one's left and right hands are the same except for opposite orientation. Organic compounds that contain an asymmetric (chiral) Carbon usually have two non-superimposable structures. These two structures are mirror images of each other and are, thus, commonly called enantiomorphs (enantio = opposite ; morph = form) Hence, optical isomerism (which occurs due to these same mirror-image properties) is now commonly referred to as enantiomerism Enantiopure compounds refer to samples having, within the limits of detection, molecules of only one chirality.

Chapter 23. Transition Metals Chemistry and Coordination Compounds

Mixture	In chemistry, a mixture is a material system made up by two or more different substances which are mixed but are not combined chemically. Mixture refers to the physical combination of two or more substances the identities of which are retained and are mixed in the form of alloys, solutions, suspensions, and colloids. Mixtures are the product of a mechanical blending or mixing of chemical substances like elements and compounds, without chemical bonding or other chemical change, so that each ingredient substance retains its own chemical properties and makeup.
Molecule	A molecule is an electrically neutral group of two or more atoms held together by covalent chemical bonds. Molecules are distinguished from ions by their lack of electrical charge. However, in quantum physics, organic chemistry, and biochemistry, the term molecule is often used less strictly, also being applied to polyatomic ions.
Polarimeter	A polarimeter is a scientific instrument used to measure the angle of rotation caused by passing polarized light through an optically active substance. Some chemical substances are optically active, and polarized (aka unidirectional) light will rotate either to the left (counter-clockwise) or right (clockwise) when passed through these substances. The amount by which the light is rotated is known as the angle of rotation.
Polaroid	Polaroid is the trademark for a type of synthetic plastic sheet which is used to polarize light, made by Polaroid Corporation. Patent The original material, patented in 1929 (U.S. Patent 1,918,848) and further developed in 1932 by Edwin H. Land, consists of many microscopic crystals of iodoquinine sulfate (herapathite) embedded in a transparent nitrocellulose polymer film. The needle-like crystals are aligned during manufacture of the film by stretching or by applying electric or magnetic fields.
Rotation	A rotation is a circular movement of an object around a center of rotation. A three-dimensional object rotates always around an imaginary line called a rotation axis. If the axis is within the body, and passes through its center of mass the body is said to rotate upon itself, or spin.
Racemic mixture	In chemistry, a racemic mixture, is one that has equal amounts of left- and right-handed enantiomers of a chiral molecule. The first known racemic mixture was 'racemic acid', which Louis Pasteur found to be a mixture of the two enantiomeric isomers of tartaric acid. A racemic mixture is denoted by the prefix (±)- or dl- (for sugars the prefix

Crystal field theory	Crystal field theory is a model that describes the breaking of degeneracies of electronic orbital states, usually d or f orbitals, due to a static electric field produced by a surrounding charge distribution (anion neighbors). This theory has been used to describe various spectroscopies of transition metal coordination complexes, in particular optical spectra (colours). CFT successfully accounts for some magnetic properties, colours, hydration enthalpies, and spinel structures of transition metal complexes, but it does not attempt to describe bonding.
Cytosine	Cytosine is one of the four main bases found in DNA and RNA, along with adenine, guanine, and thymine (uracil in RNA). It is a pyrimidine derivative, with a heterocyclic aromatic ring and two substituents attached (an amine group at position 4 and a keto group at position 2). The nucleoside of cytosine is cytidine.
Glass transition	The glass-liquid transition is the reversible transition in amorphous materials from a hard and relatively brittle state into a molten or rubber-like state. An amorphous solid that exhibits a glass transition is called a glass. Supercooling a viscous liquid into the glass state is called vitrification, from the Latin vitreum, 'glass' via French vitrifier.
Wavelength	In physics, the wavelength of a sinusoidal wave is the spatial period of the wave--the distance over which the wave's shape repeats. It is usually determined by considering the distance between consecutive corresponding points of the same phase, such as crests, troughs, or zero crossings, and is a characteristic of both traveling waves and standing waves, as well as other spatial wave patterns. Wavelength is commonly designated by the Greek letter lambda (λ).
Spectrum	A spectrum is a condition that is not limited to a specific set of values but can vary infinitely within a continuum. The word saw its first scientific use within the field of optics to describe the rainbow of colors in visible light when separated using a prism; it has since been applied by analogy to many fields other than optics. Thus, one might talk about the spectrum of political opinion, or the spectrum of activity of a drug, or the autism spectrum.
Magnetism	Magnetism is a property of materials that respond to an applied magnetic field. Permanent magnets have persistent magnetic fields caused by ferromagnetism. That is the strongest and most familiar type of magnetism.
Paramagnetism	Paramagnetism is a form of magnetism whereby the paramagnetic material is only attracted when in the presence of an externally applied magnetic field. In contrast with this behavior, diamagnetic materials are repelled by magnetic fields. Paramagnetic materials have a relative magnetic permeability greater or equal to unity (i.e., a positive magnetic susceptibility) and hence are attracted to magnetic fields.
Pauli exclusion principle	The Pauli exclusion principle is the quantum mechanical principle that no two identical fermions (particles with half-integer spin) may occupy the same quantum state simultaneously.

Chapter 23. Transition Metals Chemistry and Coordination Compounds

A more rigorous statement is that the total wave function for two identical fermions is anti-symmetric with respect to exchange of the particles. The principle was formulated by Austrian physicist Wolfgang Pauli in 1925.

Spectrochemical series	A spectrochemical series is a list of ligands ordered on ligand strength and a list of metal ions based on oxidation number, group and its identity. In crystal field theory, ligands modify the difference in energy between the d orbitals (Δ) called the ligand-field splitting parameter for ligands or the crystal-field splitting parameter, which is mainly reflected in differences in color of similar metal-ligand complexes.

A partial spectrochemical series listing of ligands from small Δ to large Δ is given below. |
| Diamagnetism | Diamagnetism is the property of an object or material which causes it to create a magnetic field in opposition to an externally applied magnetic field.

Diamagnetism is believed to be due to quantum mechanics (and is understood in terms of Landau levels) and occurs because the external field alters the orbital velocity of electrons around their nuclei, thus changing the magnetic dipole moment. According to Lenz's law, the field of these electrons will oppose the magnetic field changes provided by the applied field. |
| Activation | Activation in (bio-)chemical sciences generally refers to the process whereby something is prepared or excited for a subsequent reaction.

In chemistry, activation of molecules is where the molecules enter a state that avails for a chemical reaction to occur. The phrase energy of activation refers to the energy the reactants must acquire before they can successfully react with each other to produce the products, that is, to reach the transition state. |
| Activation energy | In chemistry, activation energy is a term introduced in 1889 by the Swedish scientist Svante Arrhenius that is defined as the energy that must be overcome in order for a chemical reaction to occur. Activation energy may also be defined as the minimum energy required to start a chemical reaction. The activation energy of a reaction is usually denoted by E_a, and given in units of kilojoules per mole. |
| Chemical reaction | A chemical reaction is a process that leads to the transformation of one set of chemical substances to another. Chemical reactions can be either spontaneous, requiring no input of energy, or non-spontaneous, typically following the input of some type of energy, such as heat, light or electricity. |

Inert	In English, to be inert is to be in a state of doing little or nothing. In chemistry, the term inert is used to describe a substance that is not chemically reactive. The noble gases were previously known as inert gases because of their perceived lack of participation in any chemical reactions.
Isotope	Isotopes are variants of a particular chemical element. While all isotopes of a given element share the same number of protons, each isotope differs from the others in its number of neutrons. The term isotope is formed from the Greek roots isos and topos .
Condensation	Condensation is the change of the physical state of matter from gaseous phase into liquid phase, and is the reverse of vaporization. When the transition happens from the gaseous phase into the solid phase directly, the change is called deposition. Condensation is initiated by the formation of atomic/molecular clusters of that species within its gaseous volume--like rain drop or snow-flake formation within clouds--or at the contact between such gaseous phase and a (solvent) liquid or solid surface.
Heme	A heme is a prosthetic group that consists of an iron atom contained in the center of a large heterocyclic organic ring called a porphyrin. Not all porphyrins contain iron, but a substantial fraction of porphyrin-containing metalloproteins have heme as their prosthetic group; these are known as hemoproteins. Hemes are most commonly recognized in their presence as components of hemoglobin, the red pigment in blood, but they are also components of a number of other hemoproteins.
Hemoglobin	Hemoglobin is the iron-containing oxygen-transport metalloprotein in the red blood cells of all vertebrates (with the exception of the fish family Channichthyidae) as well as the tissues of some invertebrates. Hemoglobin in the blood carries oxygen from the respiratory organs (lungs or gills) to the rest of the body (i.e. the tissues) where it releases the oxygen to burn nutrients to provide energy to power the functions of the organism, and collects the resultant carbon dioxide to bring it back to the respiratory organs to be dispensed from the organism. In mammals, the protein makes up about 97% of the red blood cells' dry content, and around 35% of the total content (including water).
Living systems	Living systems are open self-organizing living things that interact with their environment. These systems are maintained by flows of information, energy and matter.

Chapter 23. Transition Metals Chemistry and Coordination Compounds

Myoglobin	Myoglobin is an iron- and oxygen-binding protein found in the muscle tissue of vertebrates in general and in almost all mammals. It is related to hemoglobin, which is the iron- and oxygen-binding protein in blood, specifically in the red blood cells. The only time myoglobin is found in the bloodstream is when it is released following muscle injury.
Oxygen	Oxygen is the element with atomic number 8 and represented by the symbol O. Its name derives from the Greek roots ?ξ?ς (oxys) ('acid', literally 'sharp', referring to the sour taste of acids) and -γεν?ς (-genes) ('producer', literally 'begetter'), because at the time of naming, it was mistakenly thought that all acids required oxygen in their composition. At standard temperature and pressure, two atoms of the element bind to form dioxygen, a very pale blue, odorless, tasteless diatomic gas with the formula O_2.
	Oxygen is a member of the chalcogen group on the periodic table and is a highly reactive nonmetallic element that readily forms compounds (notably oxides) with almost all other elements.
Porphyrin	Porphyrins are a group of organic compounds, many naturally occurring. One of the best-known porphyrins is heme, the pigment in red blood cells; heme is a cofactor of the protein hemoglobin. Porphyrins are heterocyclic macrocycles composed of four modified pyrrole subunits interconnected at their α carbon atoms via methine bridges (=CH-).
Group	In chemistry, a group (also known as a family) is a vertical column in the periodic table of the chemical elements. There are 18 groups in the standard periodic table, including the d-block elements, but excluding the f-block elements.
	The explanation of the pattern of the table is that the elements in a group have similar physical or chemical characteristic of the outermost electron shells of their atoms (i.e. the same core charge), as most chemical properties are dominated by the orbital location of the outermost electron.
Chlorophyll	Chlorophyll is a green pigment found in almost all plants, algae, and cyanobacteria. Its name is derived from the Greek words χλωρος, chloros ('green') and φ?λλον, phyllon ('leaf'). Chlorophyll is an extremely important biomolecule, critical in photosynthesis, which allows plants to absorb energy from light.
Cytochrome	Cytochromes are, in general, membrane-bound hemoproteins that contain heme groups and carry out electron transport.

They are found either as monomeric proteins (e.g., cytochrome c) or as subunits of bigger enzymatic complexes that catalyze redox reactions. They are found in the mitochondrial inner membrane and endoplasmic reticulum of eukaryotes, in the chloroplasts of plants, in photosynthetic microorganisms, and in bacteria.

| Cytochrome c | The Cytochrome complex, or cyt c is a small heme protein found loosely associated with the inner membrane of the mitochondrion. It belongs to the cytochrome c family of proteins. Cytochrome c is a highly soluble protein, unlike other cytochromes, with a solubility of about 100 g/L and is an essential component of the electron transport chain, where it carries one electron. |

| Photosynthesis | Photosynthesis is a process used by plants and other organisms to capture the sun's energy to split off water's hydrogen from oxygen. Hydrogen is combined with carbon dioxide (absorbed from air or water) to form glucose and release oxygen. All living cells in turn use fuels derived from glucose and oxidize the hydrogen and carbon to release the sun's energy and reform water and carbon dioxide in the process (cellular respiration). |

| Platinum | Platinum is a chemical element with the chemical symbol Pt and an atomic number of 78.

Its name is derived from the Spanish term platina, which is literally translated into 'little silver'. It is a dense, malleable, ductile, precious, gray-white transition metal. |

| Catalyst | Catalysis is the change in rate of a chemical reaction due to the participation of a substance called a catalyst. Unlike other reagents that participate in the chemical reaction, a catalyst is not consumed by the reaction itself. A catalyst may participate in multiple chemical transformations. |

| Cisplatin | Cisplatin, cisplatinum, or cis-diamminedichloroplatinum(II) (CDDP) is a chemotherapy drug. It is used to treat various types of cancers, including sarcomas, some carcinomas (e.g. small cell lung cancer, and ovarian cancer), lymphomas, and germ cell tumors. It was the first member of a class of platinum-containing anti-cancer drugs, which now also includes carboplatin and oxaliplatin. |

| Detergent | A detergent is a surfactant or a mixture of surfactants with 'cleaning properties in dilute solutions.' In common usage, 'detergent' refers to alkylbenzenesulfonates, a family of compounds that are similar to soap but are more soluble in hard water, because the polar sulfonate (of detergents) is less likely than the polar carboxyl (of soap) to bind to calcium and other ions found in hard water. In most household contexts, the term detergent by itself refers specifically to laundry detergent or dish detergent, as opposed to hand soap or other types of cleaning agents. |

Chapter 23. Transition Metals Chemistry and Coordination Compounds

Sodium

Sodium is a chemical element with the symbol Na and atomic number 11. It is a soft, silvery-white, highly reactive metal and is a member of the alkali metals; its only stable isotope is ^{23}Na. The free metal does not occur in nature, but instead must be prepared from its compounds; it was first isolated by Humphry Davy in 1807 by the electrolysis of sodium hydroxide. Sodium is the sixth most abundant element in the Earth's crust, and exists in numerous minerals such as feldspars, sodalite and rock salt.

1. In physics, the _____ of a sinusoidal wave is the spatial period of the wave--the distance over which the wave's shape repeats. It is usually determined by considering the distance between consecutive corresponding points of the same phase, such as crests, troughs, or zero crossings, and is a characteristic of both traveling waves and standing waves, as well as other spatial wave patterns. _____ is commonly designated by the Greek letter lambda (λ).

    a. Whispering-gallery wave
    b. Higgs mechanism
    c. Jamming
    d. Wavelength

2. The Cytochrome complex, or cyt c is a small heme protein found loosely associated with the inner membrane of the mitochondrion. It belongs to the _____ family of proteins. _____ is a highly soluble protein, unlike other cytochromes, with a solubility of about 100 g/L and is an essential component of the electron transport chain, where it carries one electron.

    a. Cytochrome c oxidase
    b. Facultative anaerobic organism
    c. Cytochrome c
    d. Glycine cleavage system

3. In chemistry, _____s are compounds with the same molecular formula but different structural formulas. _____s do not necessarily share similar properties, unless they also have the same functional groups. There are many different classes of _____s, like stereoisomers, enantiomers, geometrical _____s, etc.

    a. IUPAC nomenclature of organic chemistry
    b. Isomer
    c. Organic compound
    d. Organic matter

4. . Catalysis is the change in rate of a chemical reaction due to the participation of a substance called a _____.

Chapter 23. Transition Metals Chemistry and Coordination Compounds

Unlike other reagents that participate in the chemical reaction, a _____ is not consumed by the reaction itself. A _____ may participate in multiple chemical transformations.

a. Corrosion inhibitor
b. Catalyst
c. Detackifier
d. Dispersant

5. The _____ is the quantum mechanical principle that no two identical fermions (particles with half-integer spin) may occupy the same quantum state simultaneously. A more rigorous statement is that the total wave function for two identical fermions is anti-symmetric with respect to exchange of the particles. The principle was formulated by Austrian physicist Wolfgang Pauli in 1925.

a. Peptide bond
b. Phosphodiester bond
c. Pi bond
d. Pauli exclusion principle

1. d
2. c
3. b
4. b
5. d

You can take the complete Chapter Practice Test

for Chapter 23. Transition Metals Chemistry and Coordination Compounds
on all key terms, persons, places, and concepts.

Online 99 Cents

http://www.epub14.1.20267.23.cram101.com/

Use www.Cram101.com for all your study needs

including Cram101's online interactive problem solving labs in

chemistry, statistics, mathematics, and more.

Chapter 24. Organic Chemistry

CHAPTER OUTLINE: KEY TERMS, PEOPLE, PLACES, CONCEPTS

- Organic chemistry
- Organic compound
- Functional group
- Hydrocarbon
- Urea
- Fertilizer
- Group
- Alkane
- Anaerobic organism
- Ethane
- Isomer
- Methane
- Natural gas
- Propane
- Pentane
- Alkyl
- Methyl group
- Combustion
- Halogenation

Chapter 24. Organic Chemistry

CHAPTER OUTLINE: KEY TERMS, PEOPLE, PLACES, CONCEPTS

_______ Methylene

_______ Acetylene

_______ Chloride

_______ Carbon

_______ Carbon tetrachloride

_______ Chloroform

_______ Halide

_______ Methyl radical

_______ Molecule

_______ Radical

_______ Stereoisomers

_______ Arsenic

_______ Alkene

_______ Cycloalkane

_______ Cyclohexane

_______ Molecular geometry

_______ Geometry

_______ Unsaturated hydrocarbon

_______ Addition

Chapter 24. Organic Chemistry

CHAPTER OUTLINE: KEY TERMS, PEOPLE, PLACES, CONCEPTS

_______________ Addition reaction

_______________ Chemical reaction

_______________ Propene

_______________ Rotation

_______________ Alkyne

_______________ Calcium

_______________ Calcium carbide

_______________ Carbide

_______________ Aromatic hydrocarbon

_______________ Benzene

_______________ Michael Faraday

_______________ Electron

_______________ Micrograph

_______________ Glucose

_______________ Phenyl group

_______________ Substitution reaction

_______________ Polycyclic aromatic hydrocarbon

_______________ Alcohol

_______________ Alcohol oxidation

CHAPTER OUTLINE: KEY TERMS, PEOPLE, PLACES, CONCEPTS

	Enzyme
	Ethanol
	Hydroxyl
	Methanol
	Dehydrogenase
	Acetic acid
	Condensation
	Condensation reaction
	Denatured alcohol
	Diethyl ether
	Ether
	Ethylene
	Ethylene glycol
	Rubbing alcohol
	Acetaldehyde
	Acetone
	Aldehyde
	Carbonyl
	Carboxylic acid

Chapter 24. Organic Chemistry

_____ | Formaldehyde

_____ | Ketone

_____ | Propyl

_____ | Benzoic acid

_____ | Formic acid

_____ | Amine

_____ | Amino acid

_____ | Aniline

_____ | Ethyl acetate

_____ | Hydrolysis

_____ | Saponification

_____ | Sodium

_____ | Sodium hydroxide

_____ | Acetate

_____ | Hydroxide

_____ | Cholesterol

_____ | Crude

_____ | Fractional distillation

_____ | Fractionating column

	Petroleum
	Distillation
	Fossil fuel
	Gasoline
	Octane
	Otto cycle
	Tetraethyllead

CHAPTER HIGHLIGHTS & NOTES: KEY TERMS, PEOPLE, PLACES, CONCEPTS

Organic chemistry	Organic chemistry is a subdiscipline within chemistry involving the scientific study of the structure, properties, composition, reactions, and preparation (by synthesis or by other means) of carbon-based compounds, hydrocarbons, and their derivatives. These compounds may contain any number of other elements, including hydrogen, nitrogen, oxygen, the halogens as well as phosphorus, silicon, and sulfur. Organic compounds are structurally diverse.
Organic compound	An organic compound is any member of a large class of gaseous, liquid, or solid chemical compounds whose molecules contain carbon. For historical reasons discussed below, a few types of carbon-containing compounds such as carbides, carbonates, simple oxides of carbon, and cyanides, as well as the allotropes of carbon such as diamond and graphite, are considered inorganic. The distinction between 'organic' and 'inorganic' carbon compounds, while 'useful in organizing the vast subject of chemistry... is somewhat arbitrary'.
Functional group	In organic chemistry, functional groups are lexicon specific groups of atoms or bonds within molecules that are responsible for the characteristic chemical reactions of those molecules.

Chapter 24. Organic Chemistry

The same functional group will undergo the same or similar chemical reaction(s) regardless of the size of the molecule it is a part of. However, its relative reactivity can be modified by nearby functional groups.

Hydrocarbon	In organic chemistry, a hydrocarbon is an organic compound consisting entirely of hydrogen and carbon. Hydrocarbons from which one hydrogen atom has been removed are functional groups, called hydrocarbyls. Aromatic hydrocarbons (arenes), alkanes, alkenes, cycloalkanes and alkyne-based compounds are different types of hydrocarbons.
Urea	Urea is an organic compound with the chemical formula $CO(NH_2)_2$. The molecule has two --NH_2 groups joined by a carbonyl (C=O) functional group. Urea serves an important role in the metabolism of nitrogen-containing compounds by animals and is the main nitrogen-containing substance in the urine of mammals.
Fertilizer	Fertilizer is any organic or inorganic material of natural or synthetic origin (other than liming materials) that is added to a soil to supply one or more plant nutrients essential to the growth of plants. A recent assessment found that about 40 to 60% of crop yields are attributable to commercial fertilizer use. They are essential for high-yield harvest: European fertilizer market is expected to grow to €15.3 billion by 2018.
Group	In chemistry, a group (also known as a family) is a vertical column in the periodic table of the chemical elements. There are 18 groups in the standard periodic table, including the d-block elements, but excluding the f-block elements. The explanation of the pattern of the table is that the elements in a group have similar physical or chemical characteristic of the outermost electron shells of their atoms (i.e. the same core charge), as most chemical properties are dominated by the orbital location of the outermost electron.
Alkane	Alkanes (also known as paraffins or saturated hydrocarbons) are chemical compounds that consist only of hydrogen and carbon atoms and are bonded exclusively by single bonds (i.e., they are saturated compounds) without any cycles . Alkanes belong to a homologous series of organic compounds in which the members differ by a constant relative molecular mass of 14. They have 2 main commercial sources, crude oil and natural gas. Each carbon atom has 4 bonds (either C-H or C-C bonds), and each hydrogen atom is joined to a carbon atom (H-C bonds).
Anaerobic organism	An anaerobic organism is any organism that does not require oxygen for growth. It could possibly react negatively and may even die if oxygen is present.

There are three types:•obligate anaerobes, which cannot use oxygen for growth and are even harmed by it•aerotolerant organisms, which cannot use oxygen for growth, but tolerate the presence of it•facultative anaerobes, which can grow without oxygen but can utilize oxygen if it is present

In humans beings these organisms are usually found in gastrointestinal tract.

Ethane

Ethane is a chemical compound with chemical formula C_2H_6. It is the only two-carbon alkane that is an aliphatic hydrocarbon. At standard temperature and pressure, ethane is a colorless, odorless gas.

Isomer

In chemistry, isomers are compounds with the same molecular formula but different structural formulas. Isomers do not necessarily share similar properties, unless they also have the same functional groups. There are many different classes of isomers, like stereoisomers, enantiomers, geometrical isomers, etc.

Methane

Methane is a chemical compound with the chemical formula CH4. It is the simplest alkane, the main component of natural gas, and probably the most abundant organic compound on earth. The relative abundance of methane makes it an attractive fuel. However, because it is a gas at normal conditions, methane is difficult to transport from its source.

Natural gas

Natural gas is a naturally occurring hydrocarbon gas mixture consisting primarily of methane, with up to 20 % of other hydrocarbons as well as impurities in varying amounts such as carbon dioxide. Natural gas is widely used as an important energy source in many applications including heating buildings, generating electricity, providing heat and power to industry, as fuel for vehicles and as a chemical feedstock in the manufacture of products such as plastics and other commercially important organic chemicals.

Natural gas is found in deep underground natural rock formations or associated with other hydrocarbon reservoirs, in coal beds, and as methane clathrates.

Propane

Propane is a three-carbon alkane with the molecular formula C_3H_8, normally a gas, but compressible to a transportable liquid. A by-product of natural gas processing and petroleum refining, it is commonly used as a fuel for engines, oxy-gas torches, barbecues, portable stoves, and residential central heating.

A mixture of propane and butane, used mainly as vehicle fuel, is commonly known as liquefied petroleum gas (LPG or LP gas).

Pentane

Pentane is an organic compound with the formula C_5H_{12} -- that is, an alkane with five carbon atoms.

Chapter 24. Organic Chemistry

	The term may refer to any of three structural isomers, or to a mixture of them: in the IUPAC nomenclature, however, pentane means exclusively the n-pentane isomer; the other two being called 'methylbutane' and 'dimethylpropane'. Cyclopentane is not an isomer of pentane.
Alkyl	In chemistry, an alkyl substituent is an alkane missing one hydrogen. An acyclic alkyl has the general formula C_nH_{2n+1}. A cycloalkyl is derived from a cycloalkane by removal of a hydrogen atom from a ring and has the general formula C_nH_{2n-1}.
Methyl group	Methyl group is an alkyl derived from methane, containing one carbon atom bonded to three hydrogen atoms --CH_3. The group is often abbreviated Me. Such hydrocarbon groups occur in many organic compounds.
Combustion	Combustion or burning is the sequence of exothermic chemical reactions between a fuel and an oxidant accompanied by the production of heat and conversion of chemical species. The release of heat can result in the production of light in the form of either glowing or a flame. Fuels of interest often include organic compounds (especially hydrocarbons) in the gas, liquid or solid phase.
Halogenation	Halogenation is a chemical reaction that involves the reaction of a compound, usually an organic compound, with a halogen. Dehalogenation is the reverse, the removal of a halogen from a molecule. The pathway and stoichiometry of halogenation depends on the structural features and functional groups of the organic substrate as well as the halogen.
Methylene	Methylene is a carbene encountered in organic chemistry. Methylene has a non-linear triplet ground state and is thus paramagnetic. It is not stable in the gaseous state, as it is highly reactive towards itself.
Acetylene	Acetylene is the chemical compound with the formula C_2H_2. It is a hydrocarbon and the simplest alkyne. This colorless gas is widely used as a fuel and a chemical building block.
Chloride	The chloride ion is formed when the element chlorine, a halogen, gains an electron to form an anion (negatively-charged ion) Cl^-. The salts of hydrochloric acid contain chloride ions and can also be called chlorides. The chloride ion, and its salts such as sodium chloride, are very soluble in water.
Carbon	Carbon is the chemical element with symbol C and atomic number 6. As a member of group 14 on the periodic table, it is nonmetallic and tetravalent--making four electrons available to form covalent chemical bonds. There are three naturally occurring isotopes, with ^{12}C and ^{13}C being stable, while ^{14}C is radioactive, decaying with a half-life of about 5,730 years.

Carbon tetrachloride	Carbon tetrachloride, also known by many other names is the organic compound with the formula CCl_4. It was formerly widely used in fire extinguishers, as a precursor to refrigerants, and as a cleaning agent. It is a colourless liquid with a 'sweet' smell that can be detected at low levels.
Chloroform	Chloroform is an organic compound with formula $CHCl_3$. It is one of the four chloromethanes. The colorless, sweet-smelling, dense liquid is a trihalomethane, and is considered somewhat hazardous.
Halide	A halide is a binary compound, of which one part is a halogen atom and the other part is an element or radical that is less electronegative than the halogen, to make a fluoride, chloride, bromide, iodide, or astatide compound. Many salts are halides. All Group 1 metals form halides which are white solids at room temperature.
Methyl radical	Methyl radical is a trivalent radical derived from methane, produced by the ultraviolet disassociation of halomethanes. It can also be produced by the reaction of methane with the hydroxyl radical: $OH^{\bullet} + CH_4 \rightarrow CH_3^{\bullet} + H_2O$.
Molecule	A molecule is an electrically neutral group of two or more atoms held together by covalent chemical bonds. Molecules are distinguished from ions by their lack of electrical charge. However, in quantum physics, organic chemistry, and biochemistry, the term molecule is often used less strictly, also being applied to polyatomic ions.
Radical	Radicals (often referred to as free radicals) are atoms, molecules, or ions with unpaired electrons on an open shell configuration. Free radicals may have positive, negative or zero charge. Even though they have unpaired electrons, by convention, metals and their ions or complexes with unpaired electrons are not radicals.
Stereoisomers	Stereoisomers are isomeric molecules that have the same molecular formula and sequence of bonded atoms (constitution), but that differ only in the three-dimensional orientations of their atoms in space. This contrasts with structural isomers, which share the same molecular formula, but the bond connections and/or their order differ(s) between different atoms/groups. In stereoisomers, the order and bond connections of the constituent atoms remain the same, but their orientation in space differs.
Arsenic	Arsenic is a chemical element with the symbol As, atomic number 33 and relative atomic mass 74.92.

Arsenic occurs in many minerals, usually in conjunction with sulfur and metals, and also as a pure elemental crystal. It was first documented by Albertus Magnus in 1250. Arsenic is a metalloid. It can exist in various allotropes, although only the grey form has important use in industry.

Alkene	In organic chemistry, an alkene, olefin, or olefine is an unsaturated chemical compound containing at least one carbon-to-carbon double bond. The simplest acyclic alkenes, with only one double bond and no other functional groups, form an homologous series of hydrocarbons with the general formula C_nH_{2n}. The simplest alkene is ethylene (C_2H_4), which has the International Union of Pure and Applied Chemistry (IUPAC) name ethene.
Cycloalkane	Cycloalkanes (also called naphthenes - not to be confused with naphthalene) are types of alkanes that have one or more rings of carbon atoms in the chemical structure of their molecules. Alkanes are types of organic hydrocarbon compounds that have only single chemical bonds in their chemical structure. Cycloalkanes consist of only carbon (C) and hydrogen (H) atoms and are saturated because there are no multiple C-C bonds to hydrogenate (add more hydrogen to).
Cyclohexane	Cyclohexane is a cycloalkane with the molecular formula C_6H_{12}. Cyclohexane is used as a nonpolar solvent for the chemical industry, and also as a raw material for the industrial production of adipic acid and caprolactam, both of which being intermediates used in the production of nylon. On an industrial scale, cyclohexane is produced by reacting benzene with hydrogen.
Molecular geometry	Molecular geometry is the three-dimensional arrangement of the atoms that constitute a molecule. It determines several properties of a substance including its reactivity, polarity, phase of matter, color, magnetism, and biological activity. The molecular geometry can be determined by various spectroscopic methods and diffraction methods.
Geometry	Geometry is a branch of mathematics concerned with questions of shape, size, relative position of figures, and the properties of space. A mathematician who works in the field of geometry is called a geometer. Geometry arose independently in a number of early cultures as a body of practical knowledge concerning lengths, areas, and volumes, with elements of a formal mathematical science emerging in the West as early as Thales (6th Century BC).
Unsaturated hydrocarbon	Unsaturated hydrocarbons are hydrocarbons that have double or triple covalent bonds between adjacent carbon atoms.

Those with at least one double bond are called alkenes and those with at least one triple bond are called alkynes. Each double bond is represented by a number preceding the name of the base chain, representing on which hydrocarbon in the chain the double or triple bond can be found.

Addition	Addition is a mathematical operation that represents combining collections of objects together into a larger collection. It is signified by the plus sign (+). For example, in the picture on the right, there are 3 + 2 apples--meaning three apples and two other apples--which is the same as five apples.
Addition reaction	An addition reaction, in organic chemistry, is in its simplest terms an organic reaction where two or more molecules combine to form a larger one.
	Addition reactions are limited to chemical compounds that have multiple bonds, such as molecules with carbon-carbon double bonds (alkenes), or with triple bonds (alkynes). Molecules containing carbon--hetero double bonds like carbonyl (C=O) groups, or imine (C=N) groups, can undergo addition as they too have double bond character.
Chemical reaction	A chemical reaction is a process that leads to the transformation of one set of chemical substances to another. Chemical reactions can be either spontaneous, requiring no input of energy, or non-spontaneous, typically following the input of some type of energy, such as heat, light or electricity. Classically, chemical reactions encompass changes that strictly involve the motion of electrons in the forming and breaking of chemical bonds, although the general concept of a chemical reaction, in particular the notion of a chemical equation, is applicable to transformations of elementary particles (such as illustrated by Feynman diagrams), as well as nuclear reactions.
Propene	Propene, is an unsaturated organic compound having the chemical formula C_3H_6. It has one double bond, and is the second simplest member of the alkene class of hydrocarbons, and it is also second in natural abundance.
	At room temperature and atmospheric pressure, propene is a gas, and as with many other alkenes, it is also colourless with a weak but unpleasant smell.
Rotation	A rotation is a circular movement of an object around a center of rotation. A three-dimensional object rotates always around an imaginary line called a rotation axis. If the axis is within the body, and passes through its center of mass the body is said to rotate upon itself, or spin.
Alkyne	Alkynes are hydrocarbons that have a triple bond between two carbon atoms, with the formula C_nH_{2n-2}. Alkynes are traditionally known as acetylenes, although the name acetylene also refers specifically to C_2H_2, known formally as ethyne using IUPAC nomenclature.

Chapter 24. Organic Chemistry

Calcium	Calcium is the chemical element with the symbol Ca and atomic number 20. It has an atomic mass of 40.078 amu. Calcium is a soft gray alkaline earth metal, and is the fifth-most-abundant element by mass in the Earth's crust. Calcium is also the fifth-most-abundant dissolved ion in seawater by both molarity and mass, after sodium, chloride, magnesium, and sulfate.
Calcium carbide	Calcium carbide is a chemical compound with the chemical formula of CaC_2. Its main use industrially is in the production of acetylene and calcium cyanamide. The pure material is colorless, however pieces of technical-grade calcium carbide are grey or brown and consist of only 80-85% of CaC_2 (the rest is CaO, Ca_3P_2, CaS, Ca_3N_2, SiC, etc)..
Carbide	In chemistry, a carbide is a compound composed of carbon and a less electronegative element. Carbides can be generally classified by chemical bonding type as follows: (i) salt-like, (ii) covalent compounds, (iii) interstitial compounds, and (iv) 'intermediate' transition metal carbides. Examples include calcium carbide, silicon carbide, tungsten carbide and cementite, each used in key industrial applications.
Aromatic hydrocarbon	An aromatic hydrocarbon is a hydrocarbon with alternating double and single bonds between carbon atoms. The term 'aromatic' was assigned before the physical mechanism determining aromaticity was discovered, and was derived from the fact that many of the compounds have a sweet scent. The configuration of six carbon atoms in aromatic compounds is known as a benzene ring, after the simplest possible such hydrocarbon, benzene.
Benzene	Benzene is an organic chemical compound with the molecular formula C_6H_6. Its molecule is composed of 6 carbon atoms joined in a ring, with 1 hydrogen atom attached to each carbon atom. Because its molecules contain only carbon and hydrogen atoms, benzene is classed as a hydrocarbon.
Michael Faraday	Michael Faraday, FRS (22 September 1791 - 25 August 1867) was an English chemist and physicist (or natural philosopher, in the terminology of the time) who contributed to the fields of electromagnetism and electrochemistry. Michael Faraday studied the magnetic field around a conductor carrying a DC electric current. While conducting these studies, Faraday established the basis for the electromagnetic field concept in physics, subsequently enlarged upon by James Maxwell.
Electron	The electron is a subatomic particle with a negative elementary electric charge. It has no known components or substructure; in other words, it is generally thought to be an elementary particle.

Chapter 24. Organic Chemistry

Micrograph	A micrograph is a photograph or digital image taken through a microscope or similar device to show a magnified image of an item. Micrographs are widely used in all fields of microscopy. Types Photomicrograph A light micrograph or photomicrograph is a micrograph prepared using a light microscope, a process referred to as photomicroscopy.
Glucose	Glucose is a simple sugar (monosaccharide) and an important carbohydrate in biology. Cells use it as the primary source of energy and a metabolic intermediate. Glucose is one of the main products of photosynthesis and fuels for cellular respiration.
Phenyl group	In organic chemistry, the phenyl group is a cyclic group of atoms with the formula C_6H_5. Phenyl groups are closely related to benzene. Phenyl groups have six carbon atoms bonded together in a hexagonal planar ring, five of which are bonded to individual hydrogen atoms, with the remaining carbon bonded to a substituent.
Substitution reaction	In a substitution reaction, a functional group in a particular chemical compound is replaced by another group. In organic chemistry, the electrophilic and nucleophilic substitution reactions are of prime importance. Organic substitution reactions are classified in several main organic reaction types depending on whether the reagent that brings about the substitution is considered an electrophile or a nucleophile, whether a reactive intermediate involved in the reaction is a carbocation, a carbanion or a free radical or whether the substrate is aliphatic or aromatic.
Polycyclic aromatic hydrocarbon	Polycyclic aromatic hydrocarbons (PAHs), also known as poly-aromatic hydrocarbons or polynuclear aromatic hydrocarbons, are potent atmospheric pollutants that consist of fused aromatic rings and do not contain heteroatoms or carry substituents. Naphthalene is the simplest example of a PAH. PAHs occur in oil, coal, and tar deposits, and are produced as byproducts of fuel burning (whether fossil fuel or biomass). As a pollutant, they are of concern because some compounds have been identified as carcinogenic, mutagenic, and teratogenic.
Alcohol	In chemistry, an alcohol is an organic compound in which the hydroxyl functional group (-OH) is bound to a carbon atom. In particular, this carbon center should be saturated, having single bonds to three other atoms. An important class of alcohols are the simple acyclic alcohols, the general formula for which is $C_nH_{2n+1}OH$. Of those, ethanol (C_2H_5OH) is the type of alcohol found in alcoholic beverages, and in common speech the word alcohol refers specifically to ethanol.
Alcohol oxidation	Alcohol oxidation is an important organic reaction.

Chapter 24. Organic Chemistry

Primary alcohols ($R-CH_2-OH$) can be oxidized either to aldehydes ($R-CHO$) or to carboxylic acids ($R-CO_2H$), while the oxidation of secondary alcohols (R^1R^2CH-OH) normally terminates at the ketone ($R^1R^2C=O$) stage. Tertiary alcohols ($R^1R^2R^3C-OH$) are resistant to oxidation .

Enzyme	Enzymes ( ) are biological molecules that catalyze (i.e., increase the rates of) chemical reactions. In enzymatic reactions, the molecules at the beginning of the process, called substrates, are converted into different molecules, called products. Almost all chemical reactions in a biological cell need enzymes in order to occur at rates sufficient for life.
Ethanol	Ethanol, pure alcohol, grain alcohol, or drinking alcohol, is a volatile, flammable, colorless liquid. It is a psychoactive drug and one of the oldest recreational drugs. Best known as the type of alcohol found in alcoholic beverages, it is also used in thermometers, as a solvent, and as a fuel.
Hydroxyl	A hydroxyl is a chemical functional group containing an oxygen atom connected by a covalent bond to a hydrogen atom, a pairing that can be simply understood as a substructure of the water molecule. When it appears, it imparts to chemical structures some of the reactive and interactive properties of the -OH of water (ionizability, hydrogen bonding, etc).. The neutral form of the hydroxyl group is a hydroxyl radical.
Methanol	Methanol, wood alcohol, wood naphtha or wood spirits, is a chemical with the formula CH_3OH . It is the simplest alcohol, and is a light, volatile, colorless, flammable liquid with a distinctive odor very similar to, but slightly sweeter than, ethanol (drinking alcohol). At room temperature, it is a polar liquid, and is used as an antifreeze, solvent, fuel, and as a denaturant for ethanol.
Dehydrogenase	A dehydrogenase is an enzyme that oxidizes a substrate by transferring one or more hydrides (H^-) to an acceptor, usually $NAD^+/NADP^+$ or a flavin coenzyme such as FAD or FMN. Examples•aldehyde dehydrogenase•acetaldehyde dehydrogenase•alcohol dehydrogenase•glutamate dehydrogenase.•lactate dehydrogenase•pyruvate dehydrogenase•glucose-6-phosphate dehydrogenase•glyceraldehyde-3-phosphate dehydrogenase•sorbitol dehydrogenase TCA cycle examples:•isocitrate dehydrogenase•alpha-ketoglutarate dehydrogenase•succinate dehydrogenase•malate dehydrogenase.
Acetic acid	Acetic acid ?'si?t?k is an organic compound with the chemical formula CH_3CO_2H (also written as CH_3COOH). It is a colourless liquid that when undiluted is also called glacial acetic acid. Acetic acid is the main component of vinegar (apart from water), and has a distinctive sour taste and pungent smell.

Condensation	Condensation is the change of the physical state of matter from gaseous phase into liquid phase, and is the reverse of vaporization. When the transition happens from the gaseous phase into the solid phase directly, the change is called deposition. Condensation is initiated by the formation of atomic/molecular clusters of that species within its gaseous volume--like rain drop or snow-flake formation within clouds--or at the contact between such gaseous phase and a (solvent) liquid or solid surface.
Condensation reaction	A condensation reaction is a chemical reaction in which two molecules or moieties (functional groups) combine to form one single molecule, together with the loss of a small molecule. When this small molecule is water, it is known as a dehydration reaction; other possible small molecules lost are hydrogen chloride, methanol, or acetic acid. The word 'condensation' suggests a process in which two or more things are brought 'together' to form something 'dense', like in condensation from gaseous to liquid state of matter; this does not imply, however, that condensation reaction products have greater density than reactants.
Denatured alcohol	Denatured alcohol is ethanol that has additives to make it inedible (poisonous), to prevent human consumption. In some cases it is also dyed. Denatured alcohol is used as a solvent and as fuel for spirit burners and camping stoves.
Diethyl ether	Diethyl ether, simply ether, or ethoxyethane, is an organic compound in the ether class with the formula $(C_2H_5)_2O$. It is a colorless, highly volatile flammable liquid with a characteristic odor. It is commonly used as a solvent and was once used as a general anesthetic.
Ether	Wikimedia.org/wikipedia/commons/thumb/5/51/Ether-%28general%29.png/150px-Ether-%28general%29.png' width='150' height='75' /> Ethers ( ) are a class of organic compounds that contain an ether group -- an oxygen atom connected to two alkyl or aryl groups -- of general formula R-O-R'. A typical example is the solvent and anesthetic diethyl ether, commonly referred to simply as 'ether' (CH_3-CH_2-O-CH_2-CH_3). Ethers are common in organic chemistry and pervasive in biochemistry, as they are common linkages in carbohydrates and lignin.
Ethylene	Ethylene is an organic compound, a hydrocarbon with the formula C_2H_4 or $H_2C{=}CH_2$. It is a colorless flammable gas with a faint 'sweet and musky' odor when pure. It is the simplest alkene (a hydrocarbon with carbon-carbon double bonds), and the simplest unsaturated hydrocarbon after acetylene (C_2H_2).
Ethylene glycol	Ethylene glycol is an organic compound widely used as an automotive antifreeze and a precursor to polymers. In its pure form, it is an odorless, colorless, syrupy, sweet-tasting liquid.

Chapter 24. Organic Chemistry

Rubbing alcohol	Rubbing alcohol, USP / B.P. is a liquid prepared and used primarily for topical application. It is prepared from a special denatured alcohol solution and contains 97.5-100% by volume of pure, concentrated ethanol (ethyl alcohol) or isopropyl alcohol (isopropanol). Individual manufacturers can use their own 'formulation standards' in which the ethanol content usually ranges from 70-99% v/v. In the UK the equivalent skin preparation is surgical spirit which is always based on an ethyl alcohol-methyl alcohol mixture.
Acetaldehyde	Acetaldehyde is an organic chemical compound with the formula CH_3CHO, sometimes abbreviated by chemists as MeCHO (Me = methyl). It is one of the most important aldehydes, occurring widely in nature and being produced on a large scale industrially. Acetaldehyde occurs naturally in coffee, bread, and ripe fruit, and is produced by plants as part of their normal metabolism.
Acetone	Acetone is the organic compound with the formula $(CH_3)_2CO$, a colorless, mobile, flammable liquid, the simplest example of the ketones. Acetone is miscible with water and serves as an important solvent in its own right, typically as the solvent of choice for cleaning purposes in the laboratory. About 6.7 million tonnes were produced worldwide in 2010, mainly for use as a solvent and production of methyl methacrylate and bisphenol A. It is a common building block in organic chemistry.
Aldehyde	An aldehyde is an organic compound containing a formyl group. This functional group, with the structure R-CHO, consists of a carbonyl center (a carbon double bonded to oxygen) bonded to hydrogen and an R group, which is any generic alkyl or side chain. The group without R is called the aldehyde group or formyl group.
Carbonyl	In organic chemistry, a carbonyl group is a functional group composed of a carbon atom double-bonded to an oxygen atom: C=O. It is common to several classes of organic compounds, as part of many larger functional groups. The term carbonyl can also refer to carbon monoxide as a ligand in an inorganic or organometallic complex (a metal carbonyl, e.g.
Carboxylic acid	Carboxylic acids ( ) are organic acids characterized by the presence of at least one carboxyl group. The general formula of a carboxylic acid is R-COOH, where R is some monovalent functional group. A carboxyl group is a functional group consisting of a carbonyl (RR'C=O) and a hydroxyl (R-O-H), which has the formula -C(=O)OH, usually written as -COOH or $-CO_2H$. Carboxylic acids are Brønsted-Lowry acids because they are proton (H^+) donors.
Formaldehyde	Formaldehyde is an organic compound with the formula CH_2O.

It is the simplest form of aldehyde, hence its systematic name methanal.

A gas at room temperature, formaldehyde is colorless and has a characteristic pungent, irritating odor. It is an important precursor to many other chemical compounds, especially for polymers.

Ketone	In organic chemistry, a ketone is an organic compound with the structure RC(=O)R', where R and R' can be a variety of carbon-containing substituents. It features a carbonyl group (C=O) bonded to two other carbon atoms. The general formula for ketones is $C_nH_{2n}O$. It is the same for Aldehydes; the difference is however in their respective structures- Ketones have two alkyl substituents (Alkyl groups) at each end of their carbonyl group while Aldehydes have one alkyl substituent at one end of their carbonyl group.
Propyl	In organic chemistry, propyl is a linear three-carbon alkyl substituent with chemical formula $-C_3H_7$. It is the substituent form obtained by removing one hydrogen atom attached to the terminal carbon of propane. A propyl substituent is often represented in organic chemistry with the symbol Pr (not to be confused with the element praseodymium).
Benzoic acid	Benzoic acid, $C_7H_6O_2$ (or C_6H_5COOH), is a colorless crystalline solid and the simplest aromatic carboxylic acid. The name derived from gum benzoin, which was for a long time the only source for benzoic acid. Its salts are used as a food preservative and benzoic acid is an important precursor for the synthesis of many other organic substances.
Formic acid	Formic acid is the simplest carboxylic acid. Its chemical formula is $HCOOH$ or HCO_2H. It was first made chemically in a lab at Roselle Park by scientist Karn Bangs. It is an important intermediate in chemical synthesis and occurs naturally, most notably in the venom of bee and ant stings.
Amine	Amines are organic compounds and functional groups that contain a basic nitrogen atom with a lone pair. Amines are derivatives of ammonia, wherein one or more hydrogen atoms have been replaced by a substituent such as an alkyl or aryl group. Important amines include amino acids, biogenic amines, trimethylamine, and aniline.
Amino acid	Amino acids are molecules containing an amine group, a carboxylic acid group, and a side-chain that is specific to each amino acid. The key elements of an amino acid are carbon, hydrogen, oxygen, and nitrogen. They are particularly important in biochemistry, where the term usually refers to alpha-amino acids.
Aniline	Aniline, phenylamine or aminobenzene is an organic compound with the formula $C_6H_5NH_2$. Consisting of a phenyl group attached to an amino group, aniline is the prototypical aromatic amine.

Chapter 24. Organic Chemistry

Ethyl acetate	Ethyl acetate is the organic compound with the formula $CH_3COOCH_2CH_3$. This colorless liquid has a characteristic sweet smell (similar to pear drops) and is used in glues, nail polish removers, and cigarettes . Ethyl acetate is the ester of ethanol and acetic acid; it is manufactured on a large scale for use as a solvent.
Hydrolysis	Hydrolysis usually means the rupture of chemical bonds by the addition of water. Generally, hydrolysis is a step in the degradation of a substance. In terms of the word's derivation, hydrolysis comes from Greek roots hydro 'water' + lysis 'separation'.
Saponification	Saponification is a process that produces soap, usually from fats and lye. In technical terms, saponification involves base (usually caustic soda NaOH) hydrolysis of triglycerides, which are esters of fatty acids, to form the sodium salt of a carboxylate. In addition to soap, such traditional saponification processes produces glycerol.
Sodium	Sodium is a chemical element with the symbol Na and atomic number 11. It is a soft, silvery-white, highly reactive metal and is a member of the alkali metals; its only stable isotope is ^{23}Na. The free metal does not occur in nature, but instead must be prepared from its compounds; it was first isolated by Humphry Davy in 1807 by the electrolysis of sodium hydroxide. Sodium is the sixth most abundant element in the Earth's crust, and exists in numerous minerals such as feldspars, sodalite and rock salt.
Sodium hydroxide	Sodium hydroxide also known as lye and caustic soda, is a caustic metallic base. It is used in many industries, mostly as a strong chemical base in the manufacture of pulp and paper, textiles, drinking water, soaps and detergents and as a drain cleaner. Worldwide production in 2004 was approximately 60 million tonnes, while demand was 51 million tonnes.
Acetate	An acetate is a derivative of acetic acid. This term includes salts and esters, as well as the anion found in solution. Most of the approximately 5 billion kilograms of acetic acid produced annually in industry are used in the production of acetates, which usually take the form of polymers.
Hydroxide	Hydroxide is a diatomic anion with chemical formula OH^-. It consists of an oxygen and a hydrogen atom held together by a covalent bond, and carrying a negative electric charge. It is an important but usually minor constituent of water.
Cholesterol	Cholesterol is an organic chemical substance classified as a waxy steroid of fat. It is an essential structural component of mammalian cell membranes and is required to establish proper membrane permeability and fluidity.

	In addition to its importance within cells, cholesterol is an important component in the hormonal systems of the body for the manufacture of bile acids, steroid hormones, and vitamin D. Cholesterol is the principal sterol synthesized by animals; in vertebrates it is formed predominantly in the liver.
Crude	Crude (2007) is a 90-minute long feature documentary made by Australian filmmaker Richard Smith attempting to explain the links between formation, extraction and refining as well the link between geology and economy. The film features interviews with oil industry professionals and geologists about the future of oil production and exploration. The interviewed include Dr. Jeremy Leggett, a geologist formerly working with oil exploration for BP and Shell; Dr. Colin Campbell, a retired British petroleum geologist who predicted that oil production would peak by 2007; Lord Ronald Oxburgh, former chairman of Shell; Professor Wallace S. Broecker at Columbia University; and journalist Sonia Shah.
Fractional distillation	Fractional distillation is the separation of a mixture into its component parts, or fractions, such as in separating chemical compounds by their boiling point by heating them to a temperature at which several fractions of the compound will vaporize. It is a special type of distillation. Generally the component parts boil at less than 25 °C from each other under a pressure of one atmosphere (atm).
Fractionating column	A fractionating column is an essential item used in the distillation of liquid mixtures so as to separate the mixture into its component parts, or fractions, based on the differences in their volatilities. Fractionating columns are used in small scale laboratory distillations as well as for large-scale industrial distillations. A laboratory fractionating column is a piece of glassware used to separate vaporized mixtures of liquid compounds with close volatility.
Petroleum	Petroleum (L. petroleum, from Greek: petra (rock) + Latin: oleum (oil)) or crude oil is a naturally occurring, flammable liquid consisting of a complex mixture of hydrocarbons of various molecular weights and other liquid organic compounds, that are found in geologic formations beneath the Earth's surface. A fossil fuel, it is formed when large quantities of dead organisms, usually zooplankton and algae, are buried underneath sedimentary rock and undergo intense heat and pressure. Petroleum is recovered mostly through oil drilling.
Distillation	Distillation is a method of separating mixtures based on differences in volatilities of components in a boiling liquid mixture. Distillation is a unit operation, or a physical separation process, and not a chemical reaction.

Visit Cram101.com for full Practice Exams

Chapter 24. Organic Chemistry

Fossil fuel	Fossil fuels are fuels formed by natural resources such as anaerobic decomposition of buried dead organisms. The age of the organisms and their resulting fossil fuels is typically millions of years, and sometimes exceeds 650 million years. The fossil fuels, which contain high percentages of carbon, include coal, petroleum, and natural gas.
Gasoline	Gasoline 'gæs?li?n, or petrol 'p?tr?l, is a transparent petroleum-derived liquid that is primarily used as a fuel in internal combustion engines. It consists mostly of organic compounds obtained by the fractional distillation of petroleum, enhanced with a variety of additives. Some gasolines also contain ethanol as an alternative fuel.
Octane	Octane is a hydrocarbon and an alkane with the chemical formula C_8H_{18}, and the condensed structural formula $CH_3(CH_2)_6CH_3$. Octane has many structural isomers that differ by the amount and location of branching in the carbon chain. One of these isomers, 2,2,4-trimethylpentane (isooctane) is used as one of the standard values in the octane rating scale.
Otto cycle	Property database
	An Otto cycle is an idealized thermodynamic cycle which describes the functioning of a typical spark ignition reciprocating piston engine, the thermodynamic cycle most commonly found in automobile engines.
	The Otto cycle is constructed out of:TOP and BOTTOM of the loop: a pair of quasi-parallel adiabatic processesLEFT and RIGHT sides of the loop: a pair of parallel isochoric processes
	The adiabatic processes are impermeable to heat: heat flows into the loop through the left pressurizing process and some of it flows back out through the right depressurizing process, and the heat which remains does the work.
	The processes are described by:•Process 1-2 is an isentropic compression of the air as the piston moves from bottom dead centre (BDC) to top dead centre (TDC).•Process 2-3 is a constant-volume heat transfer to the air from an external source while the piston is at top dead centre.
Tetraethyllead	Tetraethyllead abbreviated TEL, is an organolead compound with the formula $(CH_3CH_2)_4Pb$. Its mixing with gasoline (petrol) as an inexpensive additive beginning in the 1920s allowed octane ratings and thus engine compression to be boosted significantly, increasing power and fuel economy. TEL was phased out in view of the toxicity of lead and its deleterious effect on catalytic converters.

1. In a _____, a functional group in a particular chemical compound is replaced by another group. In organic chemistry, the electrophilic and nucleophilic _____s are of prime importance. Organic _____s are classified in several main organic reaction types depending on whether the reagent that brings about the substitution is considered an electrophile or a nucleophile, whether a reactive intermediate involved in the reaction is a carbocation, a carbanion or a free radical or whether the substrate is aliphatic or aromatic.

   a. Substitution reaction
   b. Telomerization
   c. Thermal decomposition
   d. Topotactic

2. _____ is a chemical compound with the chemical formula of CaC_2. Its main use industrially is in the production of acetylene and calcium cyanamide.

   The pure material is colorless, however pieces of technical-grade _____ are grey or brown and consist of only 80-85% of CaC_2 (the rest is CaO, Ca_3P_2, CaS, Ca_3N_2, SiC, etc)..

   a. Calcium hexaboride
   b. Calcium silicide
   c. Calcium carbide
   d. Ferromanganese

3. _____, also known by many other names is the organic compound with the formula CCl_4. It was formerly widely used in fire extinguishers, as a precursor to refrigerants, and as a cleaning agent. It is a colourless liquid with a 'sweet' smell that can be detected at low levels.

   a. Chlorofluorocarbon
   b. Chloromethane
   c. Fire suppression agent FS 49 C2
   d. Carbon tetrachloride

4. _____ is a three-carbon alkane with the molecular formula C_3H_8, normally a gas, but compressible to a transportable liquid. A by-product of natural gas processing and petroleum refining, it is commonly used as a fuel for engines, oxy-gas torches, barbecues, portable stoves, and residential central heating.

   A mixture of _____ and butane, used mainly as vehicle fuel, is commonly known as liquefied petroleum gas (LPG or LP gas).

   a. R-406A
   b. R-407A
   c. R-407c
   d. Propane

5. . In organic chemistry, _____s are lexicon specific groups of atoms or bonds within molecules that are responsible for the characteristic chemical reactions of those molecules.

The same _____ will undergo the same or similar chemical reaction(s) regardless of the size of the molecule it is a part of. However, its relative reactivity can be modified by nearby _____s.

a. Glycopeptide
b. Glycopolymer
c. Functional group
d. Heteroatom

1. a
2. c
3. d
4. d
5. c

You can take the complete Chapter Practice Test

for Chapter 24. Organic Chemistry
on all key terms, persons, places, and concepts.

Online 99 Cents

http://www.epub14.1.20267.24.cram101.com/

Use www.Cram101.com for all your study needs

including Cram101's online interactive problem solving labs in

chemistry, statistics, mathematics, and more.

Chapter 25. Synthetic and Natural Organic Polymers

CHAPTER OUTLINE: KEY TERMS, PEOPLE, PLACES, CONCEPTS

- Addition
- Addition reaction
- Chemical reaction
- Ethyl acetate
- Isomer
- Poly
- Polyethylene
- Polytetrafluoroethylene
- Tyvek
- Acetate
- Polymerization
- Polymer
- Stereoisomers
- Natural rubber
- Elastomer
- Neoprene
- Sulfur
- Synthetic rubber
- Vulcanization

_____ | Adipic acid _____

_____ | Condensation _____

_____ | Condensation reaction _____

_____ | Copolymer _____

_____ | Hexamethylenediamine _____

_____ | Nylon _____

_____ | Polyester _____

_____ | Styrene-butadiene _____

_____ | Dipeptide _____

_____ | Glutamic acid _____

_____ | Glycine _____

_____ | Peptide _____

_____ | Peptide bond _____

_____ | Amide _____

_____ | Protein _____

_____ | Group _____

_____ | Alpha helix _____

_____ | Hydrogen _____

_____ | Hydrogen bond _____

Chapter 25. Synthetic and Natural Organic Polymers

CHAPTER OUTLINE: KEY TERMS, PEOPLE, PLACES, CONCEPTS

- ______ Quaternary
- ______ Cooperativity
- ______ Heme
- ______ Hemoglobin
- ______ Oxygen
- ______ Urea
- ______ Fertilizer
- ______ Cytosine
- ______ Guanine
- ______ Nucleic acid
- ______ Base pair
- ______ Nucleotide
- ______ Valine
- ______ Water vapor
- ______ Electron
- ______ Micrograph
- ______ Vapor
- ______ Permanent
- ______ Arsenic

Chapter 25. Synthetic and Natural Organic Polymers

Addition	Addition is a mathematical operation that represents combining collections of objects together into a larger collection. It is signified by the plus sign (+). For example, in the picture on the right, there are 3 + 2 apples--meaning three apples and two other apples--which is the same as five apples.
Addition reaction	An addition reaction, in organic chemistry, is in its simplest terms an organic reaction where two or more molecules combine to form a larger one. Addition reactions are limited to chemical compounds that have multiple bonds, such as molecules with carbon-carbon double bonds (alkenes), or with triple bonds (alkynes). Molecules containing carbon--hetero double bonds like carbonyl (C=O) groups, or imine (C=N) groups, can undergo addition as they too have double bond character.
Chemical reaction	A chemical reaction is a process that leads to the transformation of one set of chemical substances to another. Chemical reactions can be either spontaneous, requiring no input of energy, or non-spontaneous, typically following the input of some type of energy, such as heat, light or electricity. Classically, chemical reactions encompass changes that strictly involve the motion of electrons in the forming and breaking of chemical bonds, although the general concept of a chemical reaction, in particular the notion of a chemical equation, is applicable to transformations of elementary particles (such as illustrated by Feynman diagrams), as well as nuclear reactions.
Ethyl acetate	Ethyl acetate is the organic compound with the formula $CH_3COOCH_2CH_3$. This colorless liquid has a characteristic sweet smell (similar to pear drops) and is used in glues, nail polish removers, and cigarettes . Ethyl acetate is the ester of ethanol and acetic acid; it is manufactured on a large scale for use as a solvent.
Isomer	In chemistry, isomers are compounds with the same molecular formula but different structural formulas. Isomers do not necessarily share similar properties, unless they also have the same functional groups. There are many different classes of isomers, like stereoisomers, enantiomers, geometrical isomers, etc.
Poly	Poly(p-phenylene) (PPP) is the precursor to a conducting polymer of the rigid-rod polymer host family. Oxidation or the use of dopants is used to convert the non-conductive form to a semiconductor. It is made of repeating p-phenylene units.
Polyethylene	Polyethylene or polythene (IUPAC name polyethene or poly(methylene)) is the most common plastic. The annual production is approximately 80 million metric tons. Its primary use is within packaging (plastic bag, plastic films, geomembranes, containers including bottles, etc)..

Polytetrafluoroethylene	Polytetrafluoroethylene is a synthetic fluoropolymer of tetrafluoroethylene that finds numerous applications. The most well known brand name of PTFE is Teflon by DuPont Co. PTFE is a fluorocarbon solid, as it is a high-molecular-weight compound consisting wholly of carbon and fluorine.
Tyvek	Tyvek is a brand of flashspun high-density polyethylene fibers, a synthetic material; the name is a registered trademark of DuPont. The material is very strong; it is difficult to tear but can easily be cut with scissors or a knife. Water vapor can pass through Tyvek but not liquid water, so the material lends itself to a variety of applications: envelopes, car covers, air and water intrusion barriers (housewrap) under house siding, labels, wristbands, mycology, and graphics.
Acetate	An acetate is a derivative of acetic acid. This term includes salts and esters, as well as the anion found in solution. Most of the approximately 5 billion kilograms of acetic acid produced annually in industry are used in the production of acetates, which usually take the form of polymers.
Polymerization	In polymer chemistry, polymerization is a process of reacting monomer molecules together in a chemical reaction to form polymer chains or three-dimensional networks. There are many forms of polymerization and different systems exist to categorize them. In chemical compounds, polymerization occurs via a variety of reaction mechanisms that vary in complexity due to functional groups present in reacting compounds and their inherent steric effects explained by VSEPR Theory.
Polymer	A polymer is a large molecule (macromolecule) composed of repeating structural units. These sub-units are typically connected by covalent chemical bonds. Although the term polymer is sometimes taken to refer to plastics, it actually encompasses a large class of compounds comprising both natural and synthetic materials with a wide variety of properties.
Stereoisomers	Stereoisomers are isomeric molecules that have the same molecular formula and sequence of bonded atoms (constitution), but that differ only in the three-dimensional orientations of their atoms in space. This contrasts with structural isomers, which share the same molecular formula, but the bond connections and/or their order differ(s) between different atoms/groups. In stereoisomers, the order and bond connections of the constituent atoms remain the same, but their orientation in space differs.
Natural rubber	Natural rubber, is an elastomer (an elastic hydrocarbon polymer) that was originally derived from latex, a milky colloid produced by some plants. The plants would be 'tapped', that is, an incision made into the bark of the tree and the sticky, milk colored latex sap collected and refined into a usable rubber.

Chapter 25. Synthetic and Natural Organic Polymers

Elastomer	An elastomer is a polymer with viscoelasticity (colloquially 'elasticity'), generally having low Young's modulus and high yield strain compared with other materials. The term, which is derived from elastic polymer, is often used interchangeably with the term rubber, although the latter is preferred when referring to vulcanisates. Each of the monomers which link to form the polymer is usually made of carbon, hydrogen, oxygen and/or silicon.
Neoprene	Neoprene are produced by polymerization of chloroprene. Neoprene in general has good chemical stability, and maintains flexibility over a wide temperature range. It is used in a wide variety of applications, such as laptop sleeves, orthopedic braces (wrist, knee, etc)., electrical insulation, liquid and sheet applied elastomeric membranes or flashings, and car fan belts.
Sulfur	Sulfur or sulphur is the chemical element with atomic number 16. In the periodic table it is represented by the symbol S. It is an abundant, multivalent non-metal. Under normal conditions, sulfur atoms form cyclic octatomic molecules with chemical formula S_8. Elemental sulfur is a bright yellow crystalline solid when at room temperature.
Synthetic rubber	Synthetic rubber is any type of artificial elastomer, invariably a polymer. An elastomer is a material with the mechanical property that it can undergo much more elastic deformation under stress than most materials and still return to its previous size without permanent deformation. Synthetic rubber serves as a substitute for natural rubber in many cases, especially when improved material properties are required.
Vulcanization	Vulcanization is a chemical process for converting rubber or related polymers into more durable materials via the addition of sulfur or other equivalent 'curatives.' These additives modify the polymer by forming crosslinks (bridges) between individual polymer chains. Vulcanized materials are less sticky and have superior mechanical properties. A vast array of products are made with vulcanized rubber including tires, shoe soles, hoses, and hockey pucks.
Adipic acid	Adipic acid is the organic compound with the formula $(CH_2)_4(COOH)_2$. From the industrial perspective, it is the most important dicarboxylic acid: About 2.5 billion kilograms of this white crystalline powder are produced annually, mainly as a precursor for the production of nylon. Adipic acid otherwise rarely occurs in nature.
Condensation	Condensation is the change of the physical state of matter from gaseous phase into liquid phase, and is the reverse of vaporization. When the transition happens from the gaseous phase into the solid phase directly, the change is called deposition.

Condensation reaction	A condensation reaction is a chemical reaction in which two molecules or moieties (functional groups) combine to form one single molecule, together with the loss of a small molecule. When this small molecule is water, it is known as a dehydration reaction; other possible small molecules lost are hydrogen chloride, methanol, or acetic acid. The word 'condensation' suggests a process in which two or more things are brought 'together' to form something 'dense', like in condensation from gaseous to liquid state of matter; this does not imply, however, that condensation reaction products have greater density than reactants.
Copolymer	A heteropolymer or copolymer is a polymer derived from two monomeric species, as opposed to a homopolymer where only one monomer is used. Copolymerization refers to methods used to chemically synthesize a copolymer.

Commercially relevant copolymers include ABS plastic, SBR, Nitrile rubber, styrene-acrylonitrile, styrene-isoprene-styrene (SIS) and ethylene-vinyl acetate. |
| Hexamethylenediamine | Hexamethylenediamine is the organic compound with the formula $H_2N(CH_2)_6NH_2$. The molecule is a diamine, consisting of a hexamethylene hydrocarbon chain terminated with amine functional groups. The colorless solid (yellowish for some commercial samples) has a strong amine odor, similar to piperidine. |
| Nylon | Nylon is a generic designation for a family of synthetic polymers known generically as polyamides, first produced on February 28, 1935, by Wallace Carothers at DuPont's research facility at the DuPont Experimental Station. Nylon is one of the most commonly used polymers.

Nylon is a thermoplastic, silky material, first used commercially in a nylon-bristled toothbrush (1938), followed more famously by women's stockings ('nylons'; 1940). |
Polyester	Polyester is a category of polymers which contain the ester functional group in their main chain. Although there are many polyesters, the term 'polyester' as a specific material most commonly refers to polyethylene terephthalate (PET). Polyesters include naturally occurring chemicals, such as in the cutin of plant cuticles, as well as synthetics through step-growth polymerization such as polycarbonate and polybutyrate.
Styrene-butadiene	Styrene-butadiene is a synthetic rubber copolymer consisting of styrene and butadiene. It has good abrasion resistance and good aging stability when protected by additives, and is widely used in car tires, where it may be blended with natural rubber. It was originally developed prior to World War II in Germany,.
Dipeptide	A dipeptide is a molecule consisting of two amino acids joined by a single peptide bond.

Chapter 25. Synthetic and Natural Organic Polymers

Dipeptides are produced from polypeptides by the action of the hydrolase enzyme dipeptidyl peptidase. Dietary proteins are digested to dipeptides and amino acids, and the dipeptides are absorbed more rapidly than the amino acids, because their uptake involves a separate mechanism.

Glutamic acid

Glutamic acid is one of the 20-22 proteinogenic amino acids, and its codons are GAA and GAG. It is a non-essential amino acid. The carboxylate anions and salts of glutamic acid are known as glutamates. In neuroscience, glutamate is an important neurotransmitter that plays a key role in long-term potentiation and is important for learning and memory.

Glycine

Glycine is an organic compound with the formula NH_2CH_2COOH. Having a hydrogen substituent as its side-chain, glycine is the smallest of the 20 amino acids commonly found in proteins. Its codons are GGU, GGC, GGA, GGG cf. the genetic code.

Peptide

Peptides are short polymers of amino acid monomers linked by peptide bonds. They are distinguished from proteins on the basis of size, typically containing fewer than 50 monomer units. The shortest peptides are dipeptides, consisting of two amino acids joined by a single peptide bond.

Peptide bond

A peptide bond is a covalent chemical bond formed between two molecules when the carboxyl group of one molecule reacts with the amino group of the other molecule, causing the release of a molecule of water (H_2O), hence the process is a dehydration synthesis reaction (also known as a condensation reaction), and usually occurs between amino acids. The resulting C(O)NH bond is called a peptide bond, and the resulting molecule is an amide. The four-atom functional group -C (=O)NH- is called a peptide link.

Amide

Amide refers to compounds with the functional group $R_nE(O)_xNR'_2$ (R and R' refer to H or organic groups). Most common are 'organic amides' (n = 1, E = C, x = 1), but many other important types of amides are known including phosphor amides (n = 2, E = P, x = 1 and many related formulas) and sulfonamides (E = S, x= 2). The term amide refers both to classes of compounds and to the functional group ($R_nE(O)_xNR'_2$) within those compounds.

Protein

Proteins are biochemical compounds consisting of one or more polypeptides typically folded into a globular or fibrous form in a biologically functional way. A polypeptide is a single linear polymer chain of amino acids bonded together by peptide bonds between the carboxyl and amino groups of adjacent amino acid residues. The sequence of amino acids in a protein is defined by the sequence of a gene, which is encoded in the genetic code.

Group

In chemistry, a group (also known as a family) is a vertical column in the periodic table of the chemical elements.

There are 18 groups in the standard periodic table, including the d-block elements, but excluding the f-block elements.

The explanation of the pattern of the table is that the elements in a group have similar physical or chemical characteristic of the outermost electron shells of their atoms (i.e. the same core charge), as most chemical properties are dominated by the orbital location of the outermost electron.

Alpha helix	A common motif in the secondary structure of proteins, the alpha helix is a right-handed coiled or spiral conformation, in which every backbone N-H group donates a hydrogen bond to the backbone C=O group of the amino acid four residues earlier ($i + 4 \rightarrow i$ hydrogen bonding). Among types of local structure in proteins, the α-helix is the most regular and the most predictable from sequence, as well as the most prevalent.

Historical development

In the early 1930s, William Astbury showed that there were drastic changes in the X-ray fiber diffraction of moist wool or hair fibers upon significant stretching.

Hydrogen	Hydrogen is the chemical element with atomic number 1. It is represented by the symbol H. With an average atomic weight of 1.00794 u (1.007825 u for hydrogen-1), hydrogen is the lightest element and its monatomic form (H_1) is the most abundant chemical substance, constituting roughly 75% of the Universe's baryonic mass. Non-remnant stars are mainly composed of hydrogen in its plasma state.

At standard temperature and pressure, hydrogen is a colorless, odorless, tasteless, non-toxic, nonmetallic, highly combustible diatomic gas with the molecular formula H_2.

Hydrogen bond	A hydrogen bond is the attractive interaction of a hydrogen atom with an electronegative atom, such as nitrogen, oxygen or fluorine, that comes from another molecule or chemical group. The hydrogen has a polar bonding to another electronegative atom to create the bond. These bonds can occur between molecules (intermolecularly), or within different parts of a single molecule (intramolecularly).
Quaternary	The Quaternary Period is the most recent of the three periods of the Cenozoic Era in the geologic time scale of the ICS. It follows the Neogene Period, spanning 2.588 ± 0.005 million years ago to the present. The Quaternary includes two geologic epochs: the Pleistocene and the Holocene.

Chapter 25. Synthetic and Natural Organic Polymers

CHAPTER HIGHLIGHTS & NOTES: KEY TERMS, PEOPLE, PLACES, CONCEPTS

Overview

Research history

The term Quaternary was proposed by Giovanni Arduino in 1759 for alluvial deposits in the Po river valley in northern Italy.

Cooperativity	Cooperativity is a phenomenon displayed by enzymes or receptors that have multiple binding sites where the affinity of the binding sites for a ligand is increased, positive cooperativity, negative cooperativity, upon the binding of a ligand to a binding site. For example the affinity of hemoglobin's four binding sites for oxygen is increased above that of the unbound hemoglobin when the first oxygen molecule binds. This is referred to as cooperative binding.
Heme	A heme is a prosthetic group that consists of an iron atom contained in the center of a large heterocyclic organic ring called a porphyrin. Not all porphyrins contain iron, but a substantial fraction of porphyrin-containing metalloproteins have heme as their prosthetic group; these are known as hemoproteins. Hemes are most commonly recognized in their presence as components of hemoglobin, the red pigment in blood, but they are also components of a number of other hemoproteins.
Hemoglobin	Hemoglobin is the iron-containing oxygen-transport metalloprotein in the red blood cells of all vertebrates (with the exception of the fish family Channichthyidae) as well as the tissues of some invertebrates. Hemoglobin in the blood carries oxygen from the respiratory organs (lungs or gills) to the rest of the body (i.e. the tissues) where it releases the oxygen to burn nutrients to provide energy to power the functions of the organism, and collects the resultant carbon dioxide to bring it back to the respiratory organs to be dispensed from the organism.
	In mammals, the protein makes up about 97% of the red blood cells' dry content, and around 35% of the total content (including water).
Oxygen	Oxygen is the element with atomic number 8 and represented by the symbol O. Its name derives from the Greek roots ?ξ?ς (oxys) ('acid', literally 'sharp', referring to the sour taste of acids) and -γεν?ς (-genes) ('producer', literally 'begetter'), because at the time of naming, it was mistakenly thought that all acids required oxygen in their composition. At standard temperature and pressure, two atoms of the element bind to form dioxygen, a very pale blue, odorless, tasteless diatomic gas with the formula O_2.

Visit Cram101.com for full Practice Exams

Urea	Urea is an organic compound with the chemical formula $CO(NH_2)_2$. The molecule has two --NH_2 groups joined by a carbonyl (C=O) functional group.
	Urea serves an important role in the metabolism of nitrogen-containing compounds by animals and is the main nitrogen-containing substance in the urine of mammals.
Fertilizer	Fertilizer is any organic or inorganic material of natural or synthetic origin (other than liming materials) that is added to a soil to supply one or more plant nutrients essential to the growth of plants. A recent assessment found that about 40 to 60% of crop yields are attributable to commercial fertilizer use. They are essential for high-yield harvest: European fertilizer market is expected to grow to €15.3 billion by 2018.
Cytosine	Cytosine is one of the four main bases found in DNA and RNA, along with adenine, guanine, and thymine (uracil in RNA). It is a pyrimidine derivative, with a heterocyclic aromatic ring and two substituents attached (an amine group at position 4 and a keto group at position 2). The nucleoside of cytosine is cytidine.
Guanine	Guanine is one of the four main nucleobases found in the nucleic acids DNA and RNA, the others being adenine, cytosine, and thymine (uracil in RNA). In DNA, guanine is paired with cytosine. With the formula $C_5H_5N_5O$, guanine is a derivative of purine, consisting of a fused pyrimidine-imidazole ring system with conjugated double bonds.
Nucleic acid	Nucleic acids are biological molecules essential for known forms of life on this planet; they include DNA (deoxyribonucleic acid) and RNA (ribonucleic acid). Together with proteins, nucleic acids are the most important biological macromolecules; each is found in abundance in all living things, where they function in encoding, transmitting and expressing genetic information.
	Nucleic acids were discovered by Friedrich Miescher in 1869. Experimental studies of nucleic acids constitute a major part of modern biological and medical research, and form a foundation for genome and forensic science, as well as the biotechnology and pharmaceutical industries.
Base pair	In molecular biology and genetics, the linking between two nitrogenous bases on opposite complementary DNA or certain types of RNA strands that are connected via hydrogen bonds is called a base pair. In the canonical Watson-Crick DNA base pairing, adenine (A) forms a base pair with thymine (T) and guanine (G) forms a base pair with cytosine (C). In RNA, thymine is replaced by uracil (U).
Nucleotide	Nucleotides are molecules that, when joined, make up the individual structural units of the nucleic acids RNA and DNA. In addition, nucleotides participate in cellular signaling (cGMP and cAMP), and are incorporated into important cofactors of enzymatic reactions (coenzyme A, FAD, FMN, and $NADP^+$).

Chapter 25. Synthetic and Natural Organic Polymers

Nucleotide derivatives such as the nucleoside triphosphates play central roles in metabolism, in which capacity they serve as sources of chemical energy (ATP and GTP). Nucleotide structure

A nucleotide is composed of a nucleobase (nitrogenous base), a five-carbon sugar (either ribose or 2-deoxyribose), and one phosphate group.

Valine	Valine is an α-amino acid with the chemical formula $HO_2CCH(NH_2)CH(CH_3)_2$. L-Valine is one of 20 proteinogenic amino acids. Its codons are GUU, GUC, GUA, and GUG. This essential amino acid is classified as nonpolar.
Water vapor	Water vapor, also aqueous vapor, is the gas phase of water. It is one state of water within the hydrosphere. Water vapor can be produced from the evaporation or boiling of liquid water or from the sublimation of ice.
Electron	The electron is a subatomic particle with a negative elementary electric charge. It has no known components or substructure; in other words, it is generally thought to be an elementary particle. An electron has a mass that is approximately 1/1836 that of the proton.
Micrograph	A micrograph is a photograph or digital image taken through a microscope or similar device to show a magnified image of an item.
	Micrographs are widely used in all fields of microscopy. Types Photomicrograph
	A light micrograph or photomicrograph is a micrograph prepared using a light microscope, a process referred to as photomicroscopy.
Vapor	A vapor or vapour is a substance in the gas phase at a temperature lower than its critical point. This means that the vapor can be condensed to a liquid or to a solid by increasing its pressure without reducing the temperature.
	For example, water has a critical temperature of 374 °C (647 K), which is the highest temperature at which liquid water can exist.
Permanent	The permanent of a square matrix in linear algebra is a function of the matrix similar to the determinant. The permanent, as well as the determinant, is a polynomial in the entries of the matrix. Both permanent and determinant are special cases of a more general function of a matrix called the immanant.
Arsenic	

Arsenic is a chemical element with the symbol As, atomic number 33 and relative atomic mass 74.92. Arsenic occurs in many minerals, usually in conjunction with sulfur and metals, and also as a pure elemental crystal. It was first documented by Albertus Magnus in 1250. Arsenic is a metalloid. It can exist in various allotropes, although only the grey form has important use in industry.

1. A _____ is a covalent chemical bond formed between two molecules when the carboxyl group of one molecule reacts with the amino group of the other molecule, causing the release of a molecule of water (H_2O), hence the process is a dehydration synthesis reaction (also known as a condensation reaction), and usually occurs between amino acids. The resulting C(O)NH bond is called a _____, and the resulting molecule is an amide. The four-atom functional group -C(=O)NH- is called a peptide link.

    a. Phosphodiester bond
    b. Pi bond
    c. Polar bond
    d. Peptide bond

2. _____, is an elastomer (an elastic hydrocarbon polymer) that was originally derived from latex, a milky colloid produced by some plants. The plants would be 'tapped', that is, an incision made into the bark of the tree and the sticky, milk colored latex sap collected and refined into a usable rubber. The purified form of _____ is the chemical polyisoprene, which can also be produced synthetically.

    a. PEDOT-TMA
    b. Natural rubber
    c. Poly-4-vinylphenol
    d. Polyacetylene

3. _____(p-phenylene) (PPP) is the precursor to a conducting polymer of the rigid-rod polymer host family. Oxidation or the use of dopants is used to convert the non-conductive form to a semiconductor. It is made of repeating p-phenylene units.

    a. Polymer chemistry
    b. Polymer degradation
    c. Poly
    d. Reactive center

4. . _____ is a mathematical operation that represents combining collections of objects together into a larger collection. It is signified by the plus sign (+).

Chapter 25. Synthetic and Natural Organic Polymers

For example, in the picture on the right, there are 3 + 2 apples--meaning three apples and two other apples--which is the same as five apples.

a. Alligation
b. Equality
c. Irreducible fraction
d. Addition

5. _____ are produced by polymerization of chloroprene. _____ in general has good chemical stability, and maintains flexibility over a wide temperature range. It is used in a wide variety of applications, such as laptop sleeves, orthopedic braces (wrist, knee, etc)., electrical insulation, liquid and sheet applied elastomeric membranes or flashings, and car fan belts.

a. Nylon
b. Neoprene
c. Poly
d. Polyamide

1. d
2. b
3. c
4. d
5. b

You can take the complete Chapter Practice Test

for Chapter 25. Synthetic and Natural Organic Polymers
on all key terms, persons, places, and concepts.

Online 99 Cents

http://www.epub14.1.20267.25.cram101.com/

Use www.Cram101.com for all your study needs

including Cram101's online interactive problem solving labs in

chemistry, statistics, mathematics, and more.

CPSIA information can be obtained at www.ICGtesting.com
Printed in the USA
LVOW09s0133030913

350703LV00001B/52/P